THE KOREAN ALPHABET

THE KOREAN ALPHABET

ITS HISTORY AND STRUCTURE

Edited by

YOUNG-KEY KIM-RENAUD

UNIVERSITY OF HAWAI'I PRESS
HONOLULU

Printed in the United States of America

97 98 99 00 01 02 5 4 3 2 1

The Korean alphabet : its history and structure / edited by Young-Key Rim-Renaud.
p. cm.
Includes bibliographical references and index.
ISBN 0-8248-1989-6 (alk. paper)
ISBN 0-8248-1723-0 (pbk., : alk. paper)
1. Korean language—Alphabet. 2. Korean language—Alphabet—History. I. Kim-Renaud, Young-Key.
PL918.K67 1997
495.7'11—dc21 96-39136
CIP

Publication of this book has been assisted by a grant from the Korea Research Foundation.

University of Hawai'i Press books are printed on acid-free paper and meet the guidelines for permanence and durability of the Council on Library Resources

Book design by Paula Newcomb

Typeset by Direct Language Communications, San Francisco

TO KI-MOON LEE

CONTENTS

PREFACE

The people of Korea have long contributed to world civilization with creative work in the arts and sciences. Among their accomplishments, however, their alphabet, commonly known as han'gŭl, stands out as "one of the great intellectual achievements of humankind" (Sampson 1985: 144), being the script that is "perhaps the most remarkable in the world" (Ledyard 1966: 370). The world has witnessed nearly continuous technological advancement in all areas. However, most experts agree that it will be a long time before another writing system comes along that will match han'gŭl's simplicity and efficiency and its elegance and intelligence.

The only alphabet completely native to East Asia, han'gŭl distinguishes itself among writing systems of the world with its scientific qualities and its unusual linguistic fit to the Korean language; most strikingly, its theoretical underpinnings, as well as the time and circumstances of its creation, are clearly known and well recorded. However, although this alphabet was invented in the fifteenth century, it was only following the discovery in 1940 of an original copy of the 1446 document called *Hunmin chŏng'ŭm haerye* (Explanations and Examples of the Correct Sounds for the Instruction of the People), which contained explicit explanations and examples of the linguistic principles used in creating different letterforms, that linguists and scholars of writing systems around the world became keen to probe into its foundations and analyze its features. The design features of han'gŭl succinctly expressed in this brief treatise make possible an examination of the system using modern scientific linguistic methodology.

Following this discovery, the most significant turning point in Korean linguistic history since the alphabet's creation, there has been much vibrant research among Korean scholars on the underlying principles and the origins of han'gŭl. Thus, a recent survey article on research findings on han'gŭl by Hyŏn-hui Yi (1990) contains

213 references. Yet, no comprehensive study of this system by any Korean specialist is available in one place for those who cannot read Korean. The situation improved dramatically with a major work by the American historian and philologist Gari Ledyard (1966), one of the contributors to this volume, but Ledyard's important doctoral dissertation remains unpublished to this day. More recently, han'gŭl seems finally to have caught the attention of non-Koreanist students of writing. The British linguist Geoffrey Sampson (1985) devotes an entire chapter of his ten-chapter book to han'gŭl and creates for it the new graphemic designation "featural system." He uses the Korean example to revolutionize the standard conception of what a writing system is and can be, introducing to the world what Koreanists had been discussing for decades, especially the systematic correlates between graphic shapes and sound values. Han'gŭl now occupies a prominent position in serious books on writing such as those by DeFrancis (1989) and Coulmas (1989). However, none of these scholars is a specialist in the Korean language, and their theories of the Korean writing system must depend on what others have observed.

This volume seeks to fill this gap and to meet international needs by presenting a collection of essays on the cultural-historical and theoretical-linguistic background of the Korean alphabet, written by native and foreign experts on Korean phonology and philology. For this purpose a special symposium was organized in conjunction with the Eighth International Conference on Korean Linguistics, held from August 6 through 8, 1992, at George Washington University, Washington, D.C.

In producing this book, I have received invaluable assistance from many sources. First of all, I gratefully acknowledge financial support from the Korean Ministry of Culture and the Korea Research Foundation. I thank His Excellency Hong-Choo Hyun, former ambassador of the Republic of Korea to the United States, for his ardent support of Korean studies and of this conference in particular. I thank my colleagues at George Washington, especially Linda B. Salamon, dean of Columbian College and Graduate School of Arts and Sciences; Maurice East, dean of Elliott School of International Affairs; and Jonathan Chaves, chairman of the Department of East Asian Languages and Literatures, for their support and encouragement.

I should like to thank my other friends and colleagues for their cooperation, advice, and support. The contributors to this volume graciously endured my constant requests for changes in their manuscripts either in content or in form. They have eagerly shared their ideas and opinions, whenever necessary, from the planning stage of the conference up to the publication of this volume. Ki-Moon Lee of Seoul National University was most generous in contributing his time and wisdom during his visiting year at Harvard to help make the conference a success. Sang-Oak Lee of Seoul National University, secretary-treasurer of the International Circle of Korean Linguistics (ICKL), kindly extended his cooperation and assistance in planning and carrying out the business and special projects of the Circle. John Whitman of Cornell University, newsletter editor of the ICKL, has been helpful to me in many different capacities, encouraging me always with his never-failing cheer. Samuel E. Martin of Yale University and S. Robert Ramsey of the University of Maryland kindly offered their help in reviewing manuscripts and in providing general assistance with the volume. In finalizing the manuscript for publication, Gari Ledyard of Columbia University, Chin W. Kim of the University of Illinois, Urbana, and Ross King of the University of British Columbia provided crucial criticisms and suggestions. James D. McCawley of the University of Chicago and William Poser of Stanford University gave their enthusiastic encouragement and support for the symposium, although they could not participate in the meeting because of earlier conflicting commitments. Joung Ran Kim, Joshua Margolis, Suh Y. Yoon, Joon Woo Lee, Kwang-Jun Ryu, and Sandi Inuzuka were efficient assistants in handling various administrative matters. Two anonymous reviewers of the manuscript gave extremely insightful comments and suggestions. Patricia Crosby, editor at the University of Hawai'i Press, and Sally Serafim, managing editor of the Press, whose courteous and most professional qualities never cease to impress me, have become delightful partners in the production of the book. I am grateful to all these individuals. I am also indebted to Wan-su Choe, curator of Kansong Art Museum, who graciously allowed me to photograph pages of the Hunmin chŏng'ŭm for inclusion in this book.

Finally, we, all the contributors, wish to dedicate this volume to Professor Ki-Moon Lee, our most esteemed colleague and teacher, who has enlightened us not only on so many aspects of the Korean language and its history but also on the importance of studying it with love and sincerity.

REFERENCES

Coulmas, Florian. 1989. The writing systems of the world. Oxford: Basil Blackwell Ltd.

DeFrancis, John. 1989. Visible speech: The diverse oneness of writing systems. Honolulu: University of Hawai'i Press.

Ledyard, Gari. 1966. The Korean language reform of 1446: The origin, background, and early history of the Korean alphabet. Ph.D. dissertation, University of California, Berkeley.

Sampson, Geoffrey. 1985. Writing systems. Stanford: Stanford University Press.

Yi, Hyŏn-hi. 1990. Hunmin chŏng'ŭm. In *Kugŏ yŏn'gu ŏdikkaji wanna?* (How far has Korean language research come?), ed. Korean Language Research Society, Seoul National University Graduate School, 615–631. Seoul: Tong'a Publishing Co.

1

INTRODUCTION

Young-Key Kim-Renaud

The invention of the Korean alphabet, originally called *Hunmin chŏng'ŭm* (Correct Sounds for the Instruction of the People), was suddenly announced at the end of the lunar year in late 1443 or January 1444, with no prior indication of its progress. The new script was promulgated in 1446 by King Sejong (r. 1418–1450), the fourth monarch and the revered ruler of the Chosŏn kingdom or Yi dynasty (1392–1910), whose reign was marked by an extraordinary level of cultural and scientific creation (see Kim-Renaud 1992). The alphabet consisted of twenty-eight letters at the time of its invention, of which twenty-four remain today, as sound change in the language has made four letters obsolete. The *Hunmin chŏng'ŭm* was both a promulgation document and a handbook for learning the alphabet. This basic text was accompanied by a much longer scholarly commentary called *Hunmin chŏng'ŭm haerye* (Explanations and Examples of the Correct Sounds for the Instruction of the People), often referred to simply as *Haerye*, which was compiled in 1446 by Chŏng In-ji, Sin Suk-chu, and others. This invaluable document, long missing until a copy was discovered in 1940, gives the linguistic and philosophical principles behind the invention of the alphabet and its usage, enabling scholars to study them systematically.

Before the invention of the alphabet, Koreans had already had a long tradition of transcribing their language. Korean alphabetic writing is now better known as han'gŭl (the Han [Korean/great] script), a new name with a nationalistic tone believed to have been coined in 1910 by Chu Si-gyŏng, a linguist-patriot and a member of the enlightenment movement. Until that time, almost half a millennium after its invention, the Korean alphabet had been pejoratively called *ŏnmun* (vernacular writing), and Chinese writing still enjoyed prestige among all intellectual and societal elites. In fact, even today, many Koreans, particularly older people in South Korea, believe that true literacy is a function of a person's knowledge of the Chinese classics and Chinese writing. In North Korea, only han'gŭl is used, although North Koreans refer to the alphabet by a different name, *Chosŏn'gŭl* ("script of Chosŏn," Chosŏn being the Korean name for the Democratic People's Republic of Korea) or simply *uri kŭlcha* (our characters). Chinese characters are learned as a separate subject in North Korea. In South Korea, newspapers and scholarly journals still incorporate Chinese characters, although their number has been drastically reduced over recent years (see Appendix 3). There continue to be heated debates among South Koreans on whether to include Chinese characters in written Korean, and it is increasingly considered an elitist idea; it may indeed be only a matter of time before the South follows the same course as the North.

In the two thousand years or more since Chinese was introduced to Korea, Koreans have had to develop a variety of ways to make reading Chinese classics as well as writing Korean vernacular easier. It was clumsy, even painful to use Chinese characters to write down Korean, a polysyllabic, agglutinative language with many grammatical suffixes, so unlike Chinese. Various efforts were made to overcome the difficulty, out of which at least three different but related systems, called *hyangch'al* (local letters), *kugyŏl* (oral formulae), and *idu* (clerk readings), emerged (for a succinct description of these systems, see Ledyard 1966: 29–57). In these writings, existing Chinese characters were applied phonetically to represent Korean sounds, particularly in grammatical particles and phrases but also for some lexical items. The methods used, therefore, were analogous to the ones discernible in the early Japanese poems of the Man'yōshū in Japan. This parallel development is not surprising, as Japanese syntactic structures are very similar to those of Korean. As King notes, it is natural that even some genuinely Chinese characters have gone through not only phonological but semantic shifts, given the intimate experience Koreans had with Chinese writing for such a long time (1996:218). According to Sasse, Koreans even invented more than 150 "Chinese" characters, mainly for writing native words including personal and place names (1980, cited in King 1996: 218).

The first and foremost goal of King Sejong was thus to devise something that would be easy for Koreans to learn and to use. He wanted to invent a writing system first of all for Koreans. This intention is manifest in Sejong's preface to the *Hunmin chŏng'ŭm*: "The innunciants of our country's language are different from those of the Middle Kingdom and are not confluent with [the innunciants of] characters. Therefore, among the stupid people, there have been many who, having something to put into words, have in the end been unable to express their feelings. I have been distressed because of this, and have newly designed twenty-eight letters, which I wish to have everyone practice at their ease and make convenient for their daily use" (translated in Ledyard 1966:224).

However, Sejong was also eager and confident that the new system should be made universally applicable. Chŏng In-ji's postface to the *Haerye* includes the following statement: "Though only twenty-eight letters are used, their shifts and changes in function are endless; they are simple and fine, reduced to the minimum yet universally applicable. Therefore, a wise man can acquaint himself with them before the morning is over; a stupid man can learn them in the space of ten days.... There is no usage not provided for, no direction in which they do not extend. Even the sound of the winds, the cry of the crane, the cackle of fowl and the barking of dogs—all may be written" (translated in Ledyard 1966:258–259).

The alphabet and suprasegmental markers were devised to cover Chinese, the language of a country that represented the entire civilized world for Koreans at the time. Some special symbols not necessary for Korean at all were part of the original inventory. With time, however, many of the symbols unnecessary for writing Korean disappeared from texts and were forgotten, and han'gŭl became a writing system for Korean alone.

If an alphabet is defined as "a system of signs expressing single [distinctive] sounds of speech" (Gelb 1952:166), the Korean writing system is an alphabetic system. The Korean alphabet, however, does not consist of symbols that are arbitrarily selected to signify specific sounds, as is the case with nearly all other alphabets, but there is an iconic relationship between the letters and the sounds they represent. The system is also peculiar in that a known creator one day decided to carefully devise a set of letters, to invent what was needed—a feat supremely difficult and rarely achieved in ancient times, and even unthinkable according to some experts on writing systems (e.g., DeFrancis 1989: 215 and Coulmas 1989: 3). Furthermore, these letters reflect various articulatory traits and phonological alternations, and the underlying principles behind the design are explained with articulatory descriptions of sounds represented by letterforms and philosophical reasoning easily understandable to fifteenth-century Koreans. Another characteristic of the Korean alphabet is that it is not written in a linear, sequential fashion as are most alphabetic systems: Rather, the letters are put together into a syllable block. It is for these reasons among others that the Korean writing system is often described as "unique" (e.g., Ledyard 1966; Ramsey 1992).

This book is a collection of essays, followed by a commentary, focusing on a number of topics, including the linguistic, cultural, and philosophical background of the invention of the alphabet, phonological analyses reflected in the system, and varieties of orthographic experimentation with Korean writing. Many of the essays substantiate Sejong's knowledge of traditional Chinese phonological theory and of other writing systems in East Asia, his profound understanding of the phonological structure of the Korean language, and his concern for simplicity, clarity, and beauty in the creation of the new writing system.

Because the Korean alphabet is unique, it is interesting and reasonable to ask where this ingenious system may have come from and who the real inventor was. In fact, until recently most research on the Korean writing system has focused on its origin. Chin W. Kim summarizes the lively debates on the topic, concluding that han'gŭl is "a synthesis of many writing systems in Asia, all of them coexisting in subtle harmony, subtle enough to make its presence not readily recognizable, but each element detectable enough to invite diverse theories of origins" (1988: 732–733).

One of the working assumptions has been that the Korean alphabet was created by King Sejong and his associates of the Chiphyŏnjŏn (Academy of Worthies). The claim that Sejong was the sole inventor has often been considered a reflection of nationalistic thinking (e.g., Chin W. Kim 1988: 730). However, there has been no scholarly inquiry concerning exactly who the inventor was. Ki-Moon Lee's essay provides various pieces of evidence supporting the contention that the invention was a personal accomplishment of Sejong and not the result of a collaborative project with other major scholar-officials. Sejong's personal ability, his theoretical and linguistic knowledge, his social concern, his self-confidence, and several clear textual records all point to this conclusion.

Creativity does not necessarily imply creation ex nihilo. It is likely that the well-educated and studious king made use of his knowledge of and experience with foreign writing systems and linguistic theories in designing the new script. Both Gari Ledyard and Pyong-Hi Ahn point out the influence of Chinese phonology. Ledyard further hypothesizes that the Mongolian 'Phags-pa alphabet and earlier Mongolian linguistic projects adapting Chinese phonological theory—with which King Sejong and one of the most crucial Chiphyŏnjŏn worthies, Sin Suk-chu, were very familiar—must have played a role in the design of the Korean letter shapes. Another, perhaps the most important, force toward the invention of a simple script, according to Ledyard, was the need for a phonetic script that had been felt for many years preceding the invention. Ahn sees more extensive adaptation of Chinese theory of graphic shapes in the invention of the new script. He contends that Koreans had established a clear writing tradition before the invention of the alphabet and claims that there was a continuity between the *kugyŏl* system and the newly invented alphabet. Both Ledyard and Ahn, however, note that the ideas, if they were imported, were used creatively and that the graphic shapes of han'gŭl depicted the speech organs, for which no precedent is known. Ledyard hypothesizes that there existed not only the principle of "addition" but also that of "reduction," which helps explain some exceptional variations in letter shapes. Ki-Moon Lee, S. Robert Ramsey, and Young-Key Kim-Renaud emphasize that phonological research was the most important basis for designing letter shapes. For example, the inventor discovered that a syllable could be divided into three parts—initial, medial, and final—and the initial and the final could be identical, an advance that Chinese phonologists failed to achieve.

Sang-Oak Lee contends that what seems to be the influence of 'Phags-pa on the Korean letter shapes is only a random coincidence, particularly given that some similar letter shapes represent very different sound values in the two writing systems. Reflecting on the origin of the graphic shapes from a different angle, he presents postulates concerning considerations to which Sejong must have paid attention when deciding among various possibilities for representing a given sound. The two most important principles at work would have been aesthetics and convenience. First, there was an express effort to achieve a balanced syllable shape, based on the notion of density and characterized by symmetry and stability. In addition, there was an attempt to design letters that would require minimum effort to write: For example, the most frequent vowels had vertical strokes, a natural direction of the brush in traditional calligraphy.

Thanks to the invention of the phonetic writing system in the fifteenth century, students of Korean historical linguistics are blessed with some precious data on language change. Sinhang Kang's chapter demonstrates a close correlation between the vowel system of *Tongguk chŏng'un* (Correct Rhymes of the Eastern Country) and the actual Sino-Korean pronunciation of Chinese characters of that time. He then presents a convincing piece of evidence that the vowel system of the time was closer to the modern vowel system than generally thought, challenging the hypothesis that a Great Vowel Shift occurred after the invention of the alphabet (e.g., Wanjin Kim 1963). Kang also believes that analysis of the Sino-Korean readings of the time contributed to the invention of a Korean alphabet with a phonemic inventory of twenty-three consonants and eleven vowels. S. Robert Ramsey, who regards the fifteenth century as an unusual transitional stage in the history of Korean, relies on the recorded material for internal reconstruction. He reveals some interesting findings concerning several consonant clusters, aspirated consonants, and complex tonal patterns that were soon lost in the central dialects. Many "reinforced" consonants are explained by hypothesizing their compound origin in combination with vowel syncope.

Chin W. Kim and Young-Key Kim-Renaud explore the phonological units of the Korean writing system. They both note a systematic representation of certain subsegmental phonetic features and comment on the efficiency of processing. However, they take rather different views in their treatment of this systematicity. C. W. Kim concludes that han'gŭl is a "featural system," concurring with Sampson (1985), and then goes even further to say it is a featural system based on the principle of distinctive features in the Jakobsonian sense. He also gives phonetic and phonological motivation for not representing glides with separate letters but only as diacritics, a point that the inventor must have understood. Kim-Renaud, noting the important characteristics of units at levels smaller and bigger than the phonemic level, tries to show how han'gŭl seems to reflect those phonological features that are most psychologically salient for Korean speakers, as its design features are phonetically and semantically motivated. Some cases in point are the concepts of consonantal strength scale, vowel harmony, boundary phenomena, the syllable, and the particular status of glides and /h/.

She presents several reasons why she hesitates to call Korean writing a featural system, at least in the Jakobsonian sense. Nevertheless, there is no doubt that Sejong had a sophisticated understanding of Korean phonology and that he succeeded in creating a script capable of representing various aspects of Korean native speakers' intuition about the sound system of their language in its written medium.

Since the time of its invention, the Korean writing system has undergone several orthographic reforms. The most important principle established by Sejong and his followers was that the new writing should be written syllabically, although the script was a genuine alphabet (Ledyard 1966: 212). *Hunmin chŏng'ŭm haerye* advocated a principle of shallow spelling, assuming that it would be easier for the "simple masses." However, from the earliest period, there was already an effort to write morphophonemically, as this principle was preferred by Sejong (Ki-Moon Lee 1963, 1972: 75). Orthographic standardizations are invariably linked to specific phonological analyses, and the study of their development reveals various possible linguistic analyses of the language concerned and its changes through history. Spelling reforms also put to a test the quality of the writing system itself.

Ho-min Sohn investigates dissonant orthographic practice in North and South Korea. Divergence is thought to come mainly from dialectal differences and from diverse analyses of certain morphosemantic items, which may or may not have been restructured as new unitary lexical items. In some crucial areas, however, the two parts of the country share the same principles, for example, morphophonemic spelling and word-based spacing. While there is a need for scholars from the North and the South (and even from overseas, when discussing the thorny problem of romanization of Korean) to get together in order to discuss and agree on unified orthographic conventions, Sohn notices some spontaneous efforts for one side to move closer to the other, as shown in some changes made in the recent South Korean orthographic reform, for example writing of the post-consonantal deferential verb ending consistently as in 있습니다 <iss-sŭp-ni-ta>, compared to the South's earlier practice of dropping the *s* in *sŭp* when the preceding syllable ends in tense *s* as in 있읍니다 <iss-ŭp-ni-ta>.

Ross King examines two related but different experiments with Korean writing from Russia and the USSR. He maintains these experiments originated from han'gŭl's then chaotic state due to a painful lack of standardization. The experiments strove for systematicity in orthography, adopting a morphophonemic principle, unconsciously in 1913–1914 but later self-consciously in the Soviet han'gŭl orthography. They also stressed dialect features specific to the Korean language situation in the Russian Far East. King contends that, compared to Chu Si-gyŏng's proposals in Korea, the pre-Soviet experiments with "on-line" or linear writing in Siberia were innovative and bold. Some of the Soviet Far East experimental features are reminiscent of the earlier effort in Siberia. King's chapter provides for the first time valuable data on the language history, dialectology, Korean philology, as well as the Korean writing of Koreans living in an area that has been largely inaccessible to outsiders.

The commentary by Samuel E. Martin is based on the papers presented at the symposium on the Korean alphabet. Most of the essays have since been slightly revised for publication, though not to an extent that requires a new assessment. As readers will see, Martin's commentary is not a simple criticism, but provides his own contribution on the points discussed by each author.

All the authors indicate that han'gŭl indeed is an unusual writing system, and studying it has made each author reflect deeply on the Korean language, its history, and the sociocultural factors behind its invention. We have also seen many new research agendas emerging. For example, there have been implicit or explicit claims as to the optimality of writing han'gŭl in syllable blocks versus linearly. We need further systematic research to substantiate whatever position we may take. Another fascinating topic of inquiry would be to seek a more satisfactory place for han'gŭl in the general typology of writing systems. In fact, the Korean alphabet may reveal linguistically significant insights concerning units in the sound system, not only for Korean but for all languages, that we might have hitherto overlooked. We could also do further psycholinguistic research on the learnability of Korean as a foreign language, on the relationship between written and spoken language, and on the criteria we should emphasize in future language planning. Finally, we might consider possible international applications of han'gŭl, in devising writing systems for societies lacking them.

For romanization of Korean, the McCune-Reischauer system is

generally used, sometimes with slight modification. For example, a hyphen is inserted between the—usually two—syllables of given names by some authors, and an apostrophe is used after an intervocalic <ng>, as in *Chŏng'ŭm*, to make the syllable boundary clearer. Some authors have chosen to use Yale romanization for certain purposes, particularly for the representation of linguistic forms. (A chart with the two systems of romanization is provided in Appendix 4.) Proper names are romanized according to personal preference when known. The Pinyin system is used for romanizing Chinese, and the Hepburn for Japanese.

REFERENCES

Coulmas, Florian. 1989. The writing systems of the world. Oxford: Basil Blackwell Ltd.

DeFrancis, John. 1989. Visible speech: The diverse oneness of writing systems. Honolulu: University of Hawai'i Press.

Gelb, I. J. 1952. A study of writing. Chicago: University of Chicago Press.

Kim, Chin-W. 1988. Origin and structure of the Korean script. *Sojourns in language II*, 721–734. Seoul: Tower Press.

Kim, Wanjin. 1963. Moŭm ch'egye-ŭi sin'goch'al (A new inquiry into the vowel system). *Chindan hakpo* 24: 475–511. Reprinted in *Kugŏŭmun ch'egye-ŭi yŏn'gu* (A study of the Korean phonological system). Seoul: Ilchogak, 1971.

Kim-Renaud, Young-Key, ed. 1992. King Sejong the Great: The light of fifteenth-century Korea. Washington, D.C.: International Circle of Korean Linguistics.

King, Ross. 1996. Korean writing. In *The world's writing systems*, ed. Peter T. Daniels and William Bright, New York: Oxford University Press. 218–227.

Ledyard, Gari. 1966. The Korean language reform of 1446: The origin, background, and early history of the Korean alphabet. Ph.D. dissertation, University of California, Berkeley.

Lee, Ki-Moon. 1963. Kugŏ p'yogipŏb-ŭi yŏksajŏk yŏn'gu (A historical study of Korean orthography). Seoul: Han'guk yŏn'guwŏn (Institute of Korean Studies).

———. 1972. Kugŏ ŭmunsa yŏn'gu (A study of Korean historical phonology). Seoul: Han'guk munhwa yŏn'guso (Institute of Korean Culture Studies), Seoul National University.

Ramsey, S. Robert. 1992. The Korean alphabet. In *King Sejong the Great: The light of fifteenth-century Korea*, ed. Young-Key Kim-Renaud, 43–50. Washington, D.C.: International Circle of Korean Linguistics.

Sampson, Geoffrey. 1985. Writing systems. Stanford: Stanford University Press.

Sasse, Werner. 1980. Chinesische Zeichen erfunden in Korea. *Asiatische Studien* 34: 189–205.

2

THE INVENTOR OF THE KOREAN ALPHABET

Ki-Moon Lee

The invention of the Korean alphabet has long attracted scholarly attention. We have been fascinated by the questions of how and why this remarkable writing system was made, and these aspects of the invention have been intensively researched. But, curiously enough, we have not looked very closely at the question of who invented the Korean alphabet. When all is said and done, the topic has never been seriously discussed.

What is said about the inventor is especially remarkable. Even though all the records from the year of the invention speak of the alphabet as the "personal creation" (*ch'inje*) of the king, the contradictory idea emerged later that the king did not invent the alphabet himself, and it is this latter account of the invention that has persisted down to the present day.

The idea that the king did not personally create the alphabet seems to go back to the *Yongjae ch'onghwa* (volume 7) of Sŏng Hyŏn (1439–1504):

> Sejong established the Ŏnmun ch'ŏng ("Vernacular Script Headquarters") and gave orders to Sin Sukchu, Sŏng Sammun, et al., to create the Vernacular Script. The sounds [that occur as] initial or terminal [of the syllable] are eight letters, those that are initial sounds [only] are eight letters, and the medial sounds are twelve letters. The forms of the letters were made relying upon Indian letters.... Even untutored wives and women can easily understand them. The creative wisdom of the Sage is beyond the power of men.

The aspects of this text that have drawn attention are the hypothesis of an Indic script origin, which first appears here, and the classification of the letters that it presents, which is different from that of the *Hunmin chŏng'ŭm* (1446); but this text is also the place where the assertion that the king did not personally create the alphabet first comes to light. Yet, when looked at closely, the narrative of the text is inconsistent. The first part clearly states that the king did not create the alphabet himself, but the last part hints that he did.

In any event, the idea that the king did not devise the alphabet himself continued into the modern period and has come down to the present day solidly established as the accepted view. As one example, the following can be cited from the *Ŏnmun chi* of Yu Hŭi (1773–1837): "Our King Sejong the Great commanded his scholarly retainers to imitate the form of Mongolian writing and to make inquiries of Huang Zan, and thus created the Vernacular Script." This passage seems to rely for evidence on what is said in the *Sŏngho sasŏl* (volume 7) of Yi Ik (1681–1763). Yi Ik had spoken of the 'Phags-pa script originally made during the reign of Khubilai Khan of the Yuan dynasty and had guessed that the questioning of Huang Zan would also have been about these letters.

In the early part of the twentieth century, Chu Sigyŏng said that there had been collaborators in the invention of the alphabet. This thought appears clearly in his *Taehan kugŏ munpŏp* (1906):

> Question: Who made the National Letters?
> Answer: His Majesty King Sejong the Great of our dynasty made them.

In this passage Chu clearly states that the alphabet was the king's personal creation, but, immediately following this exchange, we find the following question and answer:

> Question: How did His Majesty King Sejong the Great make them?
> Answer: His Majesty King Sejong the Great was concerned that although every nation had made letters and recorded the language of that nation, our nation had not recorded its language and had no writing; and so, establishing the Bureau of National Writing in the Court, he commanded Sin Sukchu, Sŏng Sammun, and others and, imitating the Old Seal and Indian writing, personally made the National Letters. Calling them the Correct Sounds for the Instruction of the People, he circulated them at home

> and abroad, and there was no sound in any language that could not be recorded.

Except for calling the Ŏnmun ch'ŏng the "Kungmun ch'ŏng" (Bureau of National Writing) and adding "Old Seal," this passage repeats what was said by Sŏng Hyŏn in the work cited earlier. Having stated that the king gave orders to the two scholars, Chu goes on to say that the king "personally" made the letters. At first, this statement seems to be a contradiction, but, if we look at the following question and answer, the meaning becomes clear:

> Question: Who were the people who then helped him make the National Letters?
>
> Answer: It was Minister Sin Sukchu of Koryŏng, Royal Secretary Sŏng Sammun of Ch'angnyŏng, Minister Chŏng Inji of Hadong, and others.

Summarizing this view, the Korean alphabet is seen as having been created with Sejong at the center and a number of scholars providing support. This thinking by Chu Sigyŏng was passed on intact to most scholars of the Korean language.

All of these accounts have in common the idea that the king did not invent the alphabet himself. Yet, it is important to distinguish between two different versions of that idea. One is that Sejong gave orders to certain scholars to create the alphabet (the command hypothesis); the other is that Sejong devised the alphabet together with those scholars (the cooperation hypothesis). The cooperation hypothesis is the newer of the two, having clearly developed historically out of the command hypothesis.

Today, almost all Korean language scholars accept the command hypothesis as fact and treat the invention of the alphabet as a kind of committee project (cf. Kim Minsu 1964: 36, Hŏ Ung 1974: 57, Sim Chaegi 1985: 97). Even though many new facts were brought to light after Chu Sigyŏng's work of 1906, the cooperation hypothesis has, unaltered, become mainstream thinking in the field, its influence reaching school textbooks and reference works of various kinds.

This cooperation hypothesis can be seen not only in Korea but also in the works of foreign scholars. In Japan, Kōno Rokurō (1989:105) has written:

> The date and the creator of han'gŭl are known quite clearly. These letters were personally devised by Sejong, the fourth king of the Yi Dynasty.... Nevertheless, although King Sejong, as the greatest monarch of the Yi dynasty, had many accomplishments and was a gifted man of ample education, it cannot be imagined that the king of a nation, busy with the affairs of state, could have, from conceptualization to concrete realization, produced these new letters completely by himself. At King Sejong's disposal was an institution called the Chiphyŏnjŏn (Academy of Worthies) where many young scholars had been gathered, among whom were prodigies such as Sin Sukchu, and so it is certain that there were those who helped the king and participated in the great projects concerning the creation of the new letters.

The idea that it would have been difficult for the king to have invented the new letters by himself also appears in the writings of Korean scholars (for example, Sim Chaegi 1985: 97). Perhaps this idea is the basis that underlies the cooperation hypothesis.

This same account of the invention can also be seen in the most recent writings on the subject by Americans. In American scholarly circles, the originality of the Korean alphabet was recognized in the 1960s (Vos 1964; Ledyard 1966; McCawley 1966); after that, the topic of han'gŭl began to appear in chapters on writing in general linguistic works (for example, Bolinger 1968; Fromkin and Rodman 1983). An example of such a work is a recent book containing the following passage:

> In the fifteenth century, King Sejong of Korea appointed a committee to assist him in designing a new script that would be well suited to the country's language, and usable by ordinary people. The committee did its work brilliantly, and produced the script that is known today as Hangul. It is unique among the world's writing systems, in combining aspects of featural, phonemic and syllabic representation. (Burling 1992:404)

AUTHORSHIP

However, in spite of its widespread acceptance, there is no basis at all for the idea that the king did not create the alphabet himself.

The invention of the Korean alphabet was first revealed to the world in 1443, the twenty-fifth year of Sejong's reign. This fact is recorded in the *Sejong sillok* (vol. 102, the end of the twelfth month of the twenty-fifth year), and, since it is also confirmed in Chŏng Inji's postface to the *Hunmin chŏng'ŭm* (1446), there is no room for doubt. Therefore, the invention of the Korean alphabet took place before the end of 1443, and no record from that period can be found anywhere that hints at someone helping Sejong or doing this work at his command. The first record that some of the scholars of the Chiphyŏnjŏn participated in work related to the Korean alphabet concerns the translation of the Chinese lexical work *Yunhui*, which began by royal command in the second month of 1444 (*Sejong sillok*, vol. 103, twenty-sixth year, second month, *pyŏng-sin*). In addition, as we have seen above, Sŏng Hyŏn said that the new letters were created in the Ŏnmun ch'ŏng, and this statement is also without foundation. The *Yunhui* translation project we have just mentioned was to be done in the Ŭisa ch'ŏng (Office for Deliberation), and, judging from the fact that the name "Ŏnmun ch'ŏng" appears later (*Sejong sillok*, vol. 114, twenty-eighth year, eleventh month, *im-sin*), the Ŏnmun ch'ŏng can be viewed as having been established, at the earliest, after the second month of 1444.[1]

The texts from the year of the invention unanimously speak of Sejong's "personal invention." Among them, it is worth noting that the earliest record of the Korean alphabet (*Sejong sillok*, vol. 102) begins as follows: "This month, His Highness personally created the twenty-eight letters of the Vernacular Script (*ŏnmun*)."[2]

It is easy to imagine that it might have been customary at the time to ascribe all accomplishments to the king. But in fact such was not the case. Rather, of all the many accomplishments of Sejong, this is the only instance in which the *Sejong sillok* described the accomplishment as *ch'inje* ("the personal creation of the king"). Considering this fact, it is clear that the phrase *ch'inje* was not a mere figure of speech. In addition, the following passage can be seen in Chŏng Inji's postface to the *Hunmin chŏng'ŭm* (1446):

> In the winter of the year *kye-hae* (1443–1444), Our Monarch originated and designed the twenty-eight letters of the Correct Sounds, and he adduced in outline examples and appropriєties by which to demonstrate them. He named them "The Correct Sounds for the Instruction of the People."...We note reverentially that under our

> Monarch, with his Heaven-loosed wisdom, the codes and measures that have been proclaimed and enacted exceed and excel those of a hundred kings. The making of the correct sounds is not something that has been transmitted by our ancestors; they have been perfected out of nature itself. Now since there is no place where the all-reaching Pattern is not found, this is certainly not a man-made, isolated thing.

A similar passage can be found in the *Hunmin chŏng'ŭm haerye*. The section titled "Explanation of the Designing of the Letters" first gives an explanation of the principles for constructing the letters, then ends with the following passage: "Oh! With the making of the Correct Sounds, the Pattern of the Myriad Things of Heaven and Earth is completely accounted for. The expansive spirit of it! But for Heaven's opening the sagely mind, could we have given our hands to it?"

What is more, even in the anti-alphabet memorial of the faction led by Ch'oe Malli, vice-director (*pujehak*) of the Chiphyŏnjŏn, the following can be found: "We your lieges humbly observe that the creation of the Vernacular Script is most divinely marvelous and that as an example of bringing wisdom to bear on the creation of things, it stands out preeminently among the creations of a thousand elds" (*Sejong sillok*, vol. 103, twenty-sixth year, second month, *kyŏng-ja*). It can readily be surmised from this statement that, however much Ch'oe Malli and the others were opposed to the alphabet, they did not doubt that it was the king's creation.

Sejong himself makes us believe even more strongly that it was his creation. First, in his preface to the *Hunmin chŏng'ŭm* he says, "I have been distressed because of this and have newly designed twenty-eight letters." If he had not personally created the alphabet, he could not possibly have used such a direct expression in describing his own role. And yet, even stronger language appears in Sejong's censure of Ch'oe Malli and the others upon seeing the anti-alphabet memorial:

> (1) Further, what was the main intention in the Clerk Readings (*idu*) if not to ease things for the people? And if they eased things for the people, will not the present Vernacular Script also ease things for the people? How can you men consider Sŏl Ch'ong to have been right, yet consider the doings of your own reigning king to be wrong?

(2) Further, do you men know anything about rime books? How many initial consonants are there among the Four Tones and the Seven Sounds? If I do not correct these rime books, who will correct them?

(3) Further, in the memorial you use the words, "a new oddity." Since I have become old, it is hard to pass away the days, and I have simply made friends with books of all kinds. I certainly did not make this script because I was "fed up with the old and delighted in the new!"

(4) Further, I am old in years and the routine affairs of the nation are in the sole hands of the Hereditary Scion [crown prince]. It is certainly proper that he participate in the decisions regarding even minor matters, so how much more the Vernacular Script!

These passages are striking evidence that Sejong created the alphabet himself and attached great importance to it. Passage (1), by showing that the basic intent of the alphabet was to "ease things for the people," is consistent with his preface to the *Hunmin chŏng'ŭm* (see below); (2), in connection with the debate over the translation of the *Yunhui*, confronts these officials with their ignorance and shows Sejong's strong sense of mission. Passage (3) reveals the foundation of the invention of the alphabet because it hints, in connection with the words "a new oddity," that the invention arose out of Sejong's long-standing familiarity with the scholarship of the field. And, finally, (4) shows clearly that Sejong regarded the alphabet as very important.

I have mentioned that the invention of the alphabet was completely unknown until its announcement in 1443. It can be surmised that it took place in extreme seclusion. If Sejong had not done this work himself, it would have been impossible to keep it secret in this way. If some of the scholars of the Chiphyŏnjŏn had been involved at all before 1443, that fact would have been made known immediately within the Chiphyŏnjŏn. This can be surmised from the fact that as soon as some of the scholars within the Chiphyŏnjŏn became connected by royal order with the alphabet, the other scholars submitted a memorial to the throne. It is interesting that this memorial attacks the secrecy surrounding the invention of the alphabet:

> It might be said that we had no alternative but to create the Vernacular Script. But this would be a major matter of changing and altering our customs and usages. In such a case you should carry the plan to the ministers of state and even down to all the lower officers; then the people of the country would all say, "It will do." You would still have to announce it in advance, item by item, and further add a triple thought about it. There would be nothing wrong in verifying it with the records of past emperors and kings, nor would there be any shame in investigating the matter in China. People are not deluded in waiting one hundred generations for the sage! After all this, then it could be enacted.

It would have been difficult even for Sejong to maintain complete secrecy. Although there is no way to know how long the work on the invention of the alphabet took, it was certainly no mundane task. It can be imagined that it would have been difficult to keep a great project like this, unprecedented in the history of the Korean people, in complete isolation for very long. Sejong would have wanted to tell someone what he was doing. It is easy to imagine that the crown prince and his other sons could have on occasion become his confidants.

After the invention of the alphabet was made public, the translation of the *Yunhui* became the first project, and the crown prince (later King Munjong), Prince Suyang (later King Sejo), and Prince Anp'yŏng were given responsibility for administering the work (*Sejong sillok*, vol. 103, twenty-sixth year, second month, *pyŏngsin*). It may well have been because the princes had knowledge of the alphabet at that time that Sejong gave them this responsibility. As seen in (4) above, Sejong's position in response to the criticisms of the anti-alphabet memorial of Ch'oe Malli and the others was that the crown prince should participate in matters related to the alphabet. Later, in their prefaces to *Hongmu chŏng'un yŏkhun* (1455)[3] and *Chikhae tongjasŭp*,[4] Sin Sukchu and Sŏng Sammun wrote about Munjong as follows, respectively:

> His Majesty King Munjong the Great, when he was the crown prince, assisted the Great Sage and participated in establishing the sounds and rimes. . . .

> Our Sejong and Munjong were troubled by this and so had already made the Correct Sounds for the Instruction of the People. Thus, for the first time, of all the sounds under Heaven there were none that could not be written down.

Although these two passages differ a little in content, they both show that Munjong was not uninvolved in the invention of the alphabet and that he was particularly interested in the phonology of the riming dictionaries. These statements are believable because they are testimonies from the two people who participated most in the projects that followed the invention of the alphabet.

ORTHOGRAPHY

The Korean alphabet is not an ordinary writing system. The history of world writing is in general a story of borrowing the writing system of a neighboring people, changing it a little, then employing this adapted system to record a new language. As a result, there are scholars who say that in a description of the history of writing it is not appropriate to use the word "invention" (DeFrancis 1989: 215). The Korean alphabet, however, is a distinct exception to this generalization. As a completely new creation, it was unquestionably an "invention." This is the meaning implied by the word "inventor" in the title of this essay.

The Korean alphabet is a writing system constructed on a foundation of in-depth scholarly research. A detailed discussion of this matter falls outside the scope of this essay, but it is clear that phonological research in particular was the most important basis for the invention. The phonological theory that is seen in the structure of the Korean alphabet was based on theory brought in from China, then developed independently in Korea. In particular, the Chinese division of the syllable into two parts was changed into a division into three parts, resulting in what were called "medial sounds." The completely new system set up in connection with these medial sounds was the distinguishing characteristic of this new phonological theory.

The great scholar who developed this theory was none other than the inventor of the Korean alphabet. Was, after all, Sejong this scholar? There is enough evidence to make the claim that he was. I believe that this evidence can be adduced in three areas.

The first is the testimony of people of the time. From a young age, Sejong loved scholarship and took great interest in the study of the classics and history. When the Song dynasty texts *Sìshū dàquán*, *Wǔjīng dàquán*, and *Xìnglǐ dàquán* were brought into Korea

(1419), he not only read these texts himself but even had the *Xìnglǐ dàquán* published in Korea.[5] According to Sin Sukchu, who was directly involved in phonological science "Our King Sejong the Great gave his mind over to phonological study and, having studied it in depth, created a few letters called the Correct Sounds for the Instruction of the People" (*Hongmu chŏng'un yŏkhun*, introduction). The importance of this passage, which clearly and directly speaks of "phonological study" (*unhak*), is striking and unmistakable.

Second, and even more important, what Sejong himself had to say gives us glimpses of his scholarship, especially his great erudition in the field of phonological research. In his censure of the memorial submitted by Ch'oe Malli and the others, he scolds these men for their ignorance of phonology, and when he says, "If I do not correct these rime books, who will correct them?" he shows great confidence and sense of mission (see (2) above). Regardless of the fact that these men were his subjects, if his own mastery of phonology had not been impressive, he could not have said something like this.

Third, alongside these two kinds of indirect evidence, there is also more direct evidence revealing aspects of Sejong's scholarship. Since all the records of the time regarding the alphabet are fragmentary and superficial, it is fortunate indeed that this evidence, which gives us glimpses of the personal scholarly world of Sejong, has been preserved.

In the "Explanation of the Terminal Consonants" section of the *Hunmin chŏng'ŭm haerye*, the following important explanation can be seen:

> That is why the six letters ㆁ [ŋ], ㄴ [n], ㅁ [m], ㅇ [ˈ], ㄹ [r], and ㅿ [z] are terminals for the Level, Rising, and Departing tones, while the rest are all terminals for the Entering Tone. Even so, it will suffice to use [only] the eight letters ㄱ [k], ㆁ [ŋ], ㄷ [t], ㄴ [n], ㅂ [p], ㅁ [m], ㅅ [s], and ㄹ [r] for the terminals. [For terminals] like those in ᄇᆡᆺ 곶 (*pʌys koc*) 'pear blossoms' and 여ᇫ 의 갗 (*yaz·ɨy kach*) 'fox's skin', ㅅ [s] may be applied throughout. Therefore only the letter ㅅ [s] is needed.

In the passage above, two kinds of orthographic rules are presented. In one, sounds like *c*, *z*, and *ch* are written as terminals. In the other, only *s* is written. Since the two rules will be explained later, here note only that they are based on different principles:

(1) ᄇᆡᆺ 곶 pʌys koc, ᅇᅧᇫ의 갗 yəz·ɨy kach

(2) ᄇᆡᆺ 곳 pʌys kos, ᅇᅧᆺ의 갓 yəs·ɨy kas

Of these two kinds of orthography, the fact that the examples given in (1) are adduced shows that the *Hunmin chŏng'ŭm haerye* deliberately chose the kind of orthography given in (2). And, in fact, the orthography used in *Haerye* is consistently that of (2). In the section "Examples of the Use of the Letters," the only examples of terminal sounds given are the eight letters ㄱ, ㆁ, ㄷ, ㄴ, ㅂ, ㅁ, ㅅ, ㄹ (k, ŋ, t, n, p, m, s, r). This type of orthography is used in all the later Middle Korean translation (*ŏnhae*) materials.[6]

Although there are no descriptions of it, it can be surmised that at the time of the compilation of *Haerye* there was a confrontation between those who advocated writing using the orthography of (1) and those who advocated the orthography of (2). There may well have been a considerable debate over which of the two should be employed. In the *Haerye*, two contrasting orthographic principles were examined, and one was chosen. Since no other examples of this kind of selection process can be found, we may surmise that at the time this problem was considered very serious. Who advocated (1) and who advocated (2)? What was the theoretical basis of each of these two positions? It is lamentable that no record of the debate has been preserved. There is at most, from the description given in *Haerye*, just the impression that (1) was considered to be theoretical and (2) to be actual usage.

The orthography seen in the *Yongbi ŏch'ŏn ka*, however, is like that of the examples given in (1). In the *Yongbi ŏch'ŏn ka*, examples are found in which terminal sounds are written with ㅿ [z], ㅈ [c], ㅊ [ch], and ㅍ [ph]:

곶 koc 'flower' (2)
깊– kiph- 'to be deep' (34)
ᄀᆞᇫ kʌz 'edge' (68, 125)
높– noph- 'to be high' (34)
닢 niph 'leaf' (84)
빛나– pichna- 'to shine' (80)
아ᇫ ·az 'younger brother' (24, 103)
우ᇫᄫᅳ– ·uzβɨ 'to be laughable' (16)

좇- coch- 'to follow' (36, 55, 78)
처ᇫ chəz 'first' (12)

This unusual orthographic system that we see in the *Yongbi ŏch'ŏn ka* is also found in the *Wŏrin ch'ŏn'gang chi kok*. There, examples also exist of ㅌ (*th*) used as terminal, something not seen in the *Yongbi ŏch'ŏn ka*. The following examples are taken from volume 1 of the first edition (photocopy published by T'ongmun'gwan in 1961):

곶 koc 'flower' (7, 42, 81, 135, 136, 158, 159, 160)
ᄀᆞᇫ kʌz 'edge' (26, 92, 124)
낮 nac 'daytime' (16)
낱 nath 'piece' (40, 62, 91, 92)
높- noph- 'to be high' (99)
ᄂᆞᆾ nʌch 'face' (49)
맞나- macna- 'to meet' (178)
붚 puph 'drum' (40)
비ᇫ- piz- 'to apply makeup' (121)
비ᇫ이- piz·i- 'to have someone apply makeup' (49, 65, 117, 120)
ᄇᆞᇫ아·디- pʌz·ati- 'to be broken' (158)
앒 ·alph 'front' (70)
우ᇫ- ·uz- 'to laugh' (167, 179)
즈ᇫ cɨz 'countenance' (129, 188)
처ᇫ chəz 'first' (114)

It is extremely interesting that these texts published subsequent to the *Haerye* during Sejong's reign did not follow the *Haerye*'s orthographic rules. How could their authors have dared ignore the authority of the *Haerye*? Here, the orthography of still another text published during Sejong's reign, the *Sŏkpo sangjŏl* (1447), is worth noting. This book follows the orthographic rules of *Haerye* to the letter. It is widely known that Sejong composed the *Wŏrin ch'ŏn'gang chi kok* based on the *Sŏkpo sangjŏl*, which was composed by Prince Suyang (later King Sejo).[7] In addition, the *Yongbi ŏch'ŏn ka* is a text that was completed at Sejong's command and was his special concern from the time preparations were started in 1442 until its publication in 1447. When we consider these facts, it becomes clear that the texts with which Sejong is thought to have been directly involved did not follow the *Haerye* orthographic rules.

Accordingly, it can be imagined that perhaps writing as in example (1) was Sejong's personal advocacy. The contrast with *Sŏkpo sangjŏl* especially lends credence to this conjecture.

There is, moreover, evidence directly substantiating this conjecture. The proof of Sejong's advocacy can be found in the first volume of the *Wŏrin ch'ŏn'gang chi kok*. This particular text was printed with movable type, and, if we look at the examples cited above, we can see that the terminal consonants are the results of later emendations.[8]

Who made these emendations and when were they done? I believe that it was Sejong who, immediately after the text was printed, looked at it and ordered these corrections. When he discovered that the text had not been printed according to the original manuscript but had rather been corrected so that the orthography followed the *Haerye* rules, Sejong must have become furious and immediately given strict orders that it be corrected.

The reason I believe this is what happened is because the *Wŏrin ch'ŏn'gang chi kok* text contained in *Wŏrin sŏkpo* (1459—the fifth year of Sejo's reign) faithfully follows these corrections. As Sejo edited the *Wŏrin sŏkpo*, he set his hand to the *Sŏkpo sangjŏl* part of the text that he himself had written, but he did not touch the *Wŏrin ch'ŏn'gang chi kok* part that his father Sejong had written. Instead, he apparently respected the original form by choosing the emended spellings shown above.[9] This fact can be verified by examining the parts of *Wŏrin ch'ŏn'gang chi kok* contained in the extant volumes of *Wŏrin sŏkpo*.[10]

From the discussion so far, I believe it becomes clear that Sejong had a theory of orthography that at the time was very special and idiosyncratic, and that he applied this theory to the works with which he was directly involved, the *Yongbi ŏch'ŏn ka* and the *Wŏrin ch'ŏn'gang chi kok*. The orthographic differences numbered (1) and (2) were brought up in the *Hunmin chŏng'ŭm haerye* as a result of Sejong's advocacy of this system. Because Sejong stuck stubbornly to his position against that of the ministers responsible for editing the *Haerye* (who advocated a method of orthography for the "foolish common people"), he seems to have believed in the legitimacy of his own theory.

Sejong's orthographic theory is basically in accord with modern han'gŭl orthography; as a result, it is familiar to us today. Yet it is a highly theoretical orthography that can only be analyzed by a scholar versed in Korean morphophonemics.

What is now modern han'gŭl orthography first began to develop around the turn of the twentieth century out of the research done by the youthful scholar Chu Sigyŏng. Chu maintained that what should be written were the "basic sounds" (*ponŭm*), explaining that, for example, in 깊다 (*kiphta*) 'be deep' the letter ㅍ (*ph*) was to be written because it represented the "basic sound" (Chu Sigyŏng 1906). This theory of basic sounds can be said to be one of the most important theories developed by a Korean linguist.[11] Sejong must have explained his theory in a similar way.

Finally, I would like to mention one more unusual characteristic of the orthography in the *Wŏrin ch'ŏn'gang chi kok*. In this text, nouns ending in ㄴ, ㄹ, ㅁ, ㅿ (*n*, *r*, *m*, *z*) and verb stems ending in ㄴ, ㅁ (*n*, *m*) are written as a distinct unit separated from a following particle or inflectional ending. Here are a few examples:

눈 에	nun·əy 'at the eye' (2),	손 ᄋᆞ로	son·ʌro 'with the hand' (66)
일 ᄋᆞᆯ	ir·ʌr 'work [ACC]' (9),	ᄃᆞᆯ 이	tʌr·i 'moon [NOM]' (17, 31)
ᄭᅮᆷ 을	skum·ɨr 'dream [ACC]' (8),	ᄂᆞᆷ 이	nʌm·i 'other people [NOM]' (11)
즈ᇫ 을	cɨz·ɨr 'countenance [ACC]' (188)		
안 아	·an·a 'embracing' (57)		
담 아	tam·a 'putting in' (4),	남 아	nam·a 'remaining' (54)

This representation of grammatical distinctions through the use of syllable construction is sporadically found in texts of the fifteenth century and later, but the *Wŏrin ch'ŏn'gang chi kok* was the first and only systematic attempt of this kind before the "Unification of Han'gŭl Orthography" (*Han'gŭl match'umpŏp t'ong'il an*) of 1933. Moreover, in using this method of representation for nouns and verb stems that, in the terminology of the day, ended in sounds that were "not clear and not muddy" (continuants), this attempt was unique.

In the discussion so far, I have established that Sejong carried out broad-based, in-depth research extending from phonology to morphosyntax and that he reflected the results of this research in his construction of the letters and orthography. In addition, I have shown that his scholarship tended to be extremely theoretical. I have offered the conclusion that the scholar who had the ability to create the Korean alphabet could be no one but Sejong.

WRITING FOR THE PEOPLE

Another factor that comes out of the above discussion is that Sejong was stubborn and decisive. He was a man who carried out the things he advocated and brought them to realization, a person who possessed the ability to combine theory and practice. This last ability, I believe, was the driving force that brought success to the work of creating the Korean alphabet.

Considering the political and cultural conditions of Korea at the time, the creation of the Korean alphabet was no small achievement. The ruling classes of Korea had for a long time enjoyed the special privilege of writing—that is, of Chinese characters and Chinese writing. Thus had grown up with the unspoken conceit that a literate life did not exist apart from China. The creation of writing different from Chinese characters at once meant politically the loss of special privilege and culturally the estrangement from China. It is not at all surprising that the memorial submitted by the Ch'oe Malli faction pointed out exactly these two things:

> Although from ancient times customs and local usages have differed within the Nine Isles, there has never been a case of one of them separately making a script based on the local speech. Only types like the Mongolians, Tanguts, Jurchen, Japanese, and Tibetans have their own graphs. But these are matters of the barbarians and not worth talking about. It has traditionally been said, "Change the barbarians using Chinese ways"; we have never heard of changing toward barbarousness. Through the successions of ages, China has always regarded our country as having the bequeathed customs of Kija, but in matters of culture, literary and material, and in ritual and music, we have rather taken after China. To now separately make the Vernacular Script is to discard China and identify ourselves with the barbarians. This is what is called "throwing away the fragrance of storax and choosing the bullet of the preying mantis." This is most certainly a matter of great implication for our civilization!

> If you put the Vernacular Script into practice, then it will be the Vernacular Script that clerks will exclusively study. They will have no regard for learning. The clerks and the officials will diverge from one another and form two classes with respect to writing. If those who are to become clerks can gain positions with the Vernacular Script, then those who advance afterwards will see that it's like this and regard knowledge of the twenty-seven-letter Vernacular Script as enough to establish themselves in the world. Why should they have to strain their minds and labor their thoughts going through the study of "Nature and Pattern" [in Song Learning]! After several decades of this, there certainly won't be very many people who know characters. They might be able to use the Vernacular Script in application to clerkly matters, but if they don't know the writings of the sages and worthies, "they won't study, their faces will be to the wall." They will be blind with respect to right and wrong in the Pattern of things. They will be futilely expert in the Vernacular Script. But what use can be made of that! The Culture of the Right, which our country has amassed and accumulated, will gradually come to be swept from the earth.

These passages express well the great shock that the creation of the alphabet gave to the ruling classes that included the Ch'oe Malli faction. They were afraid it would lead to the collapse of public order and the overturning of their system of values.

Sejong could not have been unaware of these things. He himself was a representative of this ruling class, and so, as he created the alphabet, he must also have known full well the meaning of what he was doing. In a word, he must have been hoping for the very changes Ch'oe Malli and the others feared. I believe that Sejong's invention of the Korean alphabet cannot be satisfactorily explained unless it is looked at in this way. Sejong's scholarship, as we have seen, was interwoven with studies of the classics and history, and through these studies he seems to have been pursuing an ideal theory of governance. The invention of the alphabet was an embodiment of this theory of governance.

Sejong could conceive of a phonemic writing system because of his knowledge of Mongolian, Tibetan, and Indian writing (see the quotes above). These alphabets were far from being purely phonemic systems, but seeing them enabled Sejong to devise a writing system that was. To borrow an expression from the Ch'oe

Malli faction, Sejong did not hesitate to "identify himself with the barbarians."

We have already seen that Sejong censured the memorial submitted by the Ch'oe Malli faction, but in this censure there is nothing said regarding the passages from the memorial cited above. Presumably Sejong deliberately avoided these issues. But what he said in his introduction to the *Hunmin chŏng'ŭm* of 1446 can be considered an indirect rejoinder. When read in this light, the text takes on a new and deeper meaning:

> The sounds of our country's language are different from those of the Middle Kingdom and are not confluent with the sounds of characters. Therefore, among the ignorant people, there have been many who, having something they want to put into words, have in the end been unable to express their feelings. I have been distressed because of this and have newly designed twenty-eight letters, which I wish to have everyone practice at their ease and make convenient for their daily use.

This text can be considered the promulgation document for the new letters, and in it Sejong expresses his personal awareness of the language of the nation and his strong conviction that writing should also be given to the people.

Sejong does not seem to have intended that the alphabet completely replace Chinese writing. But he also did not create the alphabet for the purpose of making colloquial translations and writing down the pronunciations of Chinese characters. When we consider that in the *Yongbi ŏch'ŏn ka* he gave first importance to the Korean poems or that in the *Wŏrin ch'ŏn'gang chi kok* he had the alphabet printed more conspicuously than the Chinese characters (see note 9), we can sense what Sejong must have been thinking. Through these works, in fact, Sejong opened up a new avenue for Korean literature.

At the very least, Sejong seems to have been thinking of substituting the alphabet for *idu*. There appears to have already been some such talk about *idu* in a writing from 1443, the time when the alphabet was first revealed to the public.[12] The Ch'oe Malli memorial compares the alphabet to *idu*, and Chŏng Inji's postface to the *Hunmin chŏng'ŭm* also says something about this; both seem to be referring to this earlier text. Replacing *idu* with the alphabet signified changing writing in the daily lives of the people, beginning with the general affairs of the state, over to the alphabet. What Ch'oe Malli and the others wrote in their memorial shows that they were aware of Sejong's intentions.

According to the *Sejong sillok*, Sejong suffered from chronic diseases (including diabetes, nervous disorders, and eye complaints), and because of his ill health he took recuperative leaves on several occasions (Lee Sung Nyong 1981). Around the time of the announcement of the alphabet as well, Sejong had gone, in March of 1443, to the Onyang hot springs; and, in the following year (1444), he went twice (March to May, July to September) to the cold springs at Ch'osuri in Ch'ŏngju. Ch'oe Malli's anti-alphabet memorial of February 1444 touches on the March visit to Ch'ŏngju as follows:

> Further, in regard to the [forthcoming] trip to the Pepper Water (Ch'osu) in Ch'ŏngju, the only thing you are concerned with is the crop deficiency. In matters of your train and retinue, you follow the simple and easy; compared to the days of yore, you have reduced things by eight or nine tenths. Even petitions, announcements, and public affairs are entrusted to the administrative departments. Now the Vernacular Script is *not* a matter in which the nation has no alternative but to meet a schedule. On your trip are you going to work assiduously at this alone, thereby impinging on the time [you should be using] for convalescence and treatment?

In the vivid description of this passage, we can see Sejong, immersed in his research even after the alphabet had been completed and announced to the public. Even during the period when his health had deteriorated terribly, he did not take time off even for an instant from his work on the alphabet. This account is another strong piece of evidence that Sejong created the alphabet himself.

As the king's procession left for Ch'ŏngju, the royal palanquin must have been filled with the papers on which Sejong had jotted down his notes about the invention of the alphabet and the subsequent alphabetic projects. In writing this essay, as I dug at the traces of what remains today, from time to time I dreamed of what it might be like if I could but see the notes he had with him on that occasion.

NOTES

The writer is deeply grateful to Professor Robert Ramsey for preparing the English version of this paper.

1. Related to this, Kang Hŭimaeng's short biography of Sin Sukchu in the *Pohanjae chip* (volume 11, appendix) and Yi P'a's epitaph both clearly state that Sejong, after having created the twenty-eight letters of the alphabet, "set up an office in the Court," chose some scholars from among his subjects, and gave them work to do.

2. English translations of passages from the *Sillok* and the *Hunmin chŏng'ŭm* are taken from Ledyard 1966.

3. This text is in the library collection of Koryŏ University, but volumes 1 and 2 have been lost. The preface appears in the *Pohanjae chip*.

4. This text is not extant. The date of completion is also not known. The preface appears in the *Tongmun sŏn* and in the *Sŏng Kŭnbo sŏnsaeng chip*.

5. For a general discussion of Sejong's scholarship, see Lee Sung Nyong 1981. On the connection between the *Xìnglǐ dàquán* and the *Hunmin chŏng'ŭm*, see Kang Sinhang 1963.

6. The only exception was ᅀ (*z*). The genitive form of 여ᅀᆞ (*yəzʌ* 'fox'), which was precisely the word given as an example in the *Haerye*, was almost universally 여ᇫ의, 여ᇫᄋᆡ (*yəz·ɨy, yəz·ʌy*). On the reason for this, see Lee Ki-Moon 1972.

7. See the preface to the *Wŏrin sŏkpo* written by King Sejo.

8. The symbol ㅅ (s) was corrected to ᅀ (z), ㅈ (c), and ㅊ (ch) by adding one or two strokes with a brush; ㄷ (t) was similarly corrected to ㅌ (th). Where we find occurrences of ㅍ (ph) and ㄿ (rph), the original letters had apparently been ㅂ (p) and ㄼ (rp); there are clear indications that these more complex emendations were done by erasing the original symbols and printing new ones. See Nam Kwang'u 1961 and Ahn Pyong-hi 1991.

9. The biggest alteration was that, while in the *Wŏrin ch'ŏn'gang chi kok* the alphabetized readings of Chinese characters had been written larger than the Chinese graphs, in this text the priority was reversed and the Chinese characters written larger.

10. There are a number of other interesting facts related to this text, but they are too complex to discuss in this chapter.

11. For a detailed discussion, see Lee Ki-Moon 1981.

12. On the probability of the existence of this text, see Lee Ki-Moon 1974.

REFERENCES

Ahn Pyong-hi. 1991. *Wŏrin ch'ŏn'gang chi kok* sanggwŏn ŭi kyojŏng e taehayŏ (On the revision of volume one of 'Songs of the moon shining on a thousand rivers'). In *Yi Sŭng'uk festschrift,* 169–177. Seoul: Korean Department, Sogang University.

Bolinger, Dwight. 1968. Aspects of language. New York: Harcourt Brace Jovanovich.

Burling, Robbins. 1992. Patterns of language: Structure, variation, change. San Diego: Academic Press.

Chu Sigyŏng. 1906. Taehan kugŏ munpŏp (The Korean grammar). Seoul: private edition.

DeFrancis, John. 1989. Visible speech: The diverse oneness of writing systems. Honolulu: University of Hawai'i Press.

Fromkin, Victoria, and Robert Rodman. 1983. An introduction to language (third edition). New York: Holt Rinehart Winston.

Hŏ Ung. 1974. Han'gŭl kwa minjok munhwa (Han'gŭl and the national culture). Seoul: Sejong taewang, kinyŏm saŏphoe.

Kang, Sinhang. 1963. *Hunmin chŏngŭm haerye iron kwa Xingli daquan* kwa ŭi yŏn'gwansŏng (The relationship between the theory of HCH and Xingli daquan). *Kugŏ kungmun hak* 26.

Kim Minsu. 1964. Sin kugŏhak sa (The new history of Korean). Seoul.

Kōno Rokurō. 1989. Hanguru to sono kigen. (The han'gŭl and its origin). *Nihon gakushiin kiyō* 43, no. 3: 101–121.

Ledyard, Gari K. 1966. The Korean language reform of 1446: The origin, background, and early history of the Korean alphabet. Ph.D. dissertation, University of California, Berkeley. University Microfilms 66–8333.

Lee Ki-Moon. 1972. Kugŏ ŭm'unsa yŏn'gu (The phonological History of Korean). Seoul: Korean Culture Institute, Seoul National University.

———. 1974. *Hunmin chŏng'ŭm* ch'angje wa kwallyŏn toen myŏt munje (Some problems concerning the invention of HC). *Kugŏhak* 2: 1–15.

———. 1981. Han Hin Saem ŭi ŏn'ŏ mit muncha iron (HHS's theory in language and writing). *Ŏhak yŏn'gu* 17, no. 2: 155–165.

Lee Sung Nyong. 1981. Sejong ŭi hangmun kwa sasang. (Sejong's scholarship and ideology). Seoul: Asea munhwasa.

McCawley, James D. 1966. Review of Yamagiwa 1964. *Language* 42: 170–175.

Nam Kwang'u. 1961. Haeje (Bibliographical explanation). Appended to *Wŏrin ch'ŏn'gang chi kok* (yŏng'inbon). Seoul: T'ongmun'gwan.

Sim Chaegi. 1985. Han'guk saram ŭi mal kwa kŭl (The Korean people's language and writing). Seoul: Chihaksa.

Vos, Frits. 1964. Korean Writing: Idu and Han'gŭl. In Yamagiwa 1964, 29–34.

Yamagiwa, Joseph K., ed. 1964. Papers of the CIC Far Eastern Language Institute. Ann Arbor: University of Michigan.

3

THE INTERNATIONAL LINGUISTIC BACKGROUND OF THE CORRECT SOUNDS FOR THE INSTRUCTION OF THE PEOPLE

Gari Ledyard

King Sejong's marvelous invention of the Korean alphabet, which he called "The Correct Sounds for the Instruction of the People" (*Hunmin chŏng'ŭm*), is often and justly described as an act of epochal genius. The superlatives began with Chŏng Inji, who wrote the postface to the official description and explanation of the script, *Hunmin chŏng'ŭm haerye*, which accompanied the proclamation of the Correct Sounds in 1446.

> The profundity of their origin and the precision of their meaning are more subtle than anything that could have been conceived or developed by us. We note reverentially that under our Noble Highness, with his Heaven-loosed wisdom, our governing and cultural institutions have transcended those of all other kings. In the making of the Correct Sounds there has been no ancestor or transmitter; they have been formed from nature itself. Since their all-reaching Pattern pervades everywhere, how could they have been made by just an individual?[1]

In this paeon, resonant with Neo-Confucian naturalism, Sejong was not a mere inventor, but rather the Heaven-appointed agent of natural principle. The significance of such thought in Sejong's Korea, whose leaders were extending the Confucian revolution that had already been reshaping the nation for a half century, should not be underestimated.

Still, in the real world, where the application of these Confucian verities needed a disciplined, well-trained mind and much mental labor, and where by the canonical authority of the *Great Learning* itself the "extension of knowledge" lay in the "investigation of things," Sejong had to study the mysteries of phonology and ponder the nature of writing. He had to organize in his mind what the sounds of Korean were and realize them graphically in a way that would enable and facilitate the practical business of reading and writing. In this work, even a sage had to look into what wise scholars of the past had written and review the experience of others.

The science of writing was by no means the first difficult subject Sejong had wrestled with. He had already reformed the national music, organized the kingdom's ritual and protocol, laid out and equipped an observatory, corrected the calendar, built a great clock, standardized weights and measures, invented a rain gauge, ordered the country mapped, set the guidelines for the compilation and preservation of history, investigated agronomy, medicine, and pharmacy, improved printing, and established directions for the moral instruction of his subjects. Sejong was educated and inspired by the learning and experience of China, which by all accounts he devoured with broad and endless reading. But in every one of his cultural projects he also attended to local circumstance. He studied what China had done, made sure that his own solutions were just as good or better, adapted them to the nation's own conditions, and in the process created a new Korean reality.

In pursuing these projects, Sejong did not work alone. He always found and fostered some bright, young talent to attend to the practical realization of the task at hand. For his alphabetic and phonological projects he relied principally on Sin Sukchu (1417–1475), a young man of twenty-six when the alphabet was invented, who had distinguished himself in the important normalization of relations with Japan in 1443 and who was known to have a talent for languages.

Sejong's work on the alphabet involved a deep understanding of traditional Chinese phonological theory and a knowledge of other writing systems used in East Asian countries, in particular the Mongolian 'Phags-pa (also written h̲P'ags-pa) alphabet. In this essay I will suggest some problems in his earlier cultural projects that may have stimulated him to invent his alphabet, and I will review the evidence for the influence of Chinese phonological theory, and of the 'Phags-pa alphabet and lexical works in which it was used, on his theoretical approach and on the graphics of the Korean alphabet itself.

THE VERNACULAR DIMENSION OF SEJONG'S CULTURAL PROJECTS

It is especially important in connection with the origins of the Korean alphabet to emphasize that in many of Sejong's earlier projects there was a vernacular language dimension, sometimes only implicit but in several important instances explicitly voiced by Sejong. A review of such cases suggests, already a decade or two before the invention of the alphabet was announced in late 1443 or early 1444,[2] that some Koreans had begun to sense the need for a practical way to write the Korean language.

The earliest Chosŏn dynasty awareness of the problems of a literacy defined solely in terms of classical Chinese came in 1395, when the Ming criminal code (*Da Ming lü*) was issued in a Korean *idu* version titled *TaeMyŏngnyul chikhae*. In a *chikhae* ("direct interpretation"), the basic Chinese text was retained, with inserted Chinese characters that stood for Korean-language particles and grammatical forms. Such adjutories were known by a number of terms, nowadays subsumed under the word *idu*. Since the basic text was read in Sino-Korean and the adjutories were Korean-language elements, a *chikhae* could be called a species of Korean translation, but the resulting language was artificial and stilted, and the reader was by no means freed of the necessity to know a lot of Chinese. A means of writing Korean directly would have achieved a better result and would clearly have been desirable. However, no articulation of such a need is known until Sejong, in 1444, cited the advantages for justice of using a more transparent vernacular in legal procedures.[3]

There are other cases that, although we have no record of royal concern for the Korean language, must have evoked some recognition of the usefulness of a national script. Such cases would have included T'aejong's 1415 order to translate the Chinese Yuan dynasty agricultural handbook *Nongsang jiyao* (Essentials of Agriculture and Sericulture, 1269), and Sejong's assembling of a national commission to compile a text on contemporary Korean farming methods, which resulted in the *Nongsa chiksŏl* of 1429.[4] This might have involved a more effective translation in the former case or a means to convey purely Korean names of plants or practices in the latter. And what of the new Korean songs that Sejong ordered composed for court banquets in 1420 (completed in 1425) or the grand project of 1433 to collect folk songs and ballads from every district and locality in the nation?[5] There were methods for writing Korean verse using only Chinese characters, similar to the *hyangch'al*-type practices used in Silla and Koryŏ for recording vernacular poetry. But relatively few people would have been able to read these awkward and cumbersome texts, and the subtleties of regional expression or vernacular wit—the very essence of folk songs—could only have been lost.

The earliest case in which Sejong is known to have confronted directly the problem of vernacular literacy was the compilation of the *Samgang haengsil* (True Stories of the Practice of the Three Bonds), an illustrated primer on the Confucian virtues of filial piety, loyalty, and wifely constancy, which Sejong ordered compiled in 1432. Each story was written on one page, while the opposite page offered a large picture to illustrate the text in Chinese.[6] Here the connection between popular literacy and ethics education moved Sejong to make the following prescient remarks:

> But since the common people generally do not know characters, even if this book is distributed how can they know its meaning and act upon it unless someone shows them how to read it? I have read in the *Zhou li* [The Rites of Zhou] the statement: "The Agent of the Exterior is charged with communicating the written word to the Four Quarters; he causes the Four Quarters to know the characters in books."[7] Now we can follow this model. Let everyone, in the capital and out, exert themselves in the arts of teaching and instruction... let us seek out people of learning and experience, without regard to class status, strongly urging them to gloss and repeat the text, even to women of all ages.... May the hearts of the people profit by morning and advance by evening; let there be none who do not feel an opening of their natural goodness. Then will our sons think of carrying their filiality to the utmost, our subjects think of pursuing loyalty to the utmost, and our husbands and wives carry the way of marriage to the utmost. When people learn righteousness, then are their feelings of self-renewal aroused, and when this transformation extends to their daily habits, goodness will increase and bring about customs of utmost order. You of the Board of Rites, put into effect my heartfelt wishes! Enlighten and instruct, in the capital and out![8]

The focus of this remarkable exhortation is on instruction in morals, but the method applied is to "gloss and repeat" (*hunsŭp*) a text, and the quotation from the *Zhou li* makes it unequivocally clear that Sejong had in mind teaching people to read. Although in 1434 this could only have involved literacy in Chinese, still the emphasis on popular education, without regard to class status and without the exclusion of women, is explicit and unmistakable. No doubt, it was only a transitory triumph of Confucian idealism over the implacable reality of Confucian hierarchical and male-dominated social norms. Without question, Sejong knew that his scheme surely involved more than mere literacy. Still, ten years later, in 1444, when he announced his invention of the Correct Sounds, one of the first projects to receive royal mention was the use of the new alphabet to translate this very same *Samgang haengsil*. Indeed, Sejong on this occasion had harsh words for Ch'oe Malli and other opponents of the alphabet who had argued against such a translation.[9] Yet for whatever reason, it was only in the reign of King Sŏngjong (r. 1469–1494) that a vernacular version of this text, printed in the upper margin over the original version in Chinese, began to circulate.

Perhaps Sejong's translation priorities had moved elsewhere. In 1442, he had launched the major literary and historical undertaking that resulted in 1447 in the *Yongbi ŏch'ŏn ka* (Song of the Dragons in Heavenly Flight), a paeon in both Korean and Chinese verse to his royal ancestors, with special emphasis on the careers of his grandfather, King T'aejo (r. 1392–1398), and his father King T'aejong (r. 1400–1418).[10] The Korean verses were composed between 1445 and 1447, and constituted the first work of Korean literature to be written in the new alphabet. Evidently there was considerable royal pressure to complete this work; its spelling includes practices not found in other early specimens of Korean alphabetic writing and was probably elaborated before the orthography was fully worked out. It is possible that the *Yongbi ŏch'ŏn ka* itself was the final and decisive stimulus to the invention of the alphabet.

CHINESE PHONOLOGICAL THEORY IN SEJONG'S KOREA

Only on relatively few occasions in world history have individuals consciously applied themselves to inventing a script. In the usual case, alphabets and syllabaries have developed along evolutionary lines, spreading from one region and language to another, often in response to movements of imperial conquest, religious proselytization, or commercial expansion. In cases like Sejong's, where a literacy problem has been seen, considered, and then solved with the invention of a revolutionary and ingenious script, we have the opportunity to investigate how this process developed. Fortunately, for the Korean alphabet we have a lengthy document, titled *Hunmin chŏng'ŭm haerye* (Explanations and Examples for the Correct Sounds for the Instruction of the People; hereafter sometimes abbreviated *Haerye*), which explains the thinking behind the alphabet at considerable length. But that document did not come out of thin air. It was formed from a threshold of knowledge about language sounds and writing that had a long history in the scholarly community of China.

Sejong was an undoubted expert in this field, as he did not hesitate to emphasize when he was challenged by Ch'oe Malli and other academic officials who opposed his alphabet.[11] Beyond Sejong, it is immediately obvious from the *Haerye* and some of the early dictionary projects pursued on Sejong's orders that other scholars, but principally Sin Sukchu, also had an extremely sophisticated understanding of Chinese phonological science. A brief review of this branch of learning is necessary for the following discussion.

Contrary to the conventional wisdom, the Chinese writing system is not at all aphonetic. Any Chinese character has one (occasionally more than one) particular pronunciation and can be used strictly as a phonogram in transcribing foreign words or names. Around the fourth century A.D., Chinese commentators, systematizing already venerable school practices, formalized a procedure for "spelling" the sounds of characters by the method of "turn and cut" (*fanqie,* Korean *panjŏl*). To show the pronunciation of an unknown character, one "cut" the initial consonant from a second character and the rime from a third, and combined them to show the reading of the first. To use an English example, one could indicate the pronunciation of the word *sough* by "cutting" *sun* and *now* (= *sow*), or "cut" *sun* and *cuff* (= *suff*) to show the alternate pronunciation. This method was a bit circular in that it required knowledge of the pronunciations of the characters that were "cut," but it proved to be a workable system and lasted well into the twentieth century. In 543, thousands of *fanqie* spellings were collected by Gu Yewang and included in his dictionary *Yupian* (The Jade Compendium, 543), in which characters were classified by graphic elements. But the greatest breakthrough was made in 601, when Lu Fayan and other scholars produced the epochal riming dictionary *Qieyun* (Cuttings and Rimes, or perhaps Initials and Finals). What was for practical purposes the entire Chinese lexicon was classified first according to the four classical tones of Chinese (Level, Rising, Departing, and Entering—not to be confused with the four tones of Mandarin), then, within each of these, by syllabic finals or "rime" (*yun*)—that is, vowel or diphthong plus final consonant, if any, and tone. Both the initial and final of every character were precisely identified with *fanqie* spellings. The *Qieyun* went though a number of re-editions and revisions during the Tang period (618–906), but the oldest version to survive integrally today is the *Guangyun* (Expanded Rimes) of 1008; it is now the foundation source for our knowledge of what is called Middle Chinese.[12]

A further important breakthrough was achieved during the tenth century, when "rime tables" (*dengyun tu*) were invented, in which initial consonants and syllabic finals were systematically classified. Since the initials were the beginning of the syllable, they were dubbed "character mothers," or *zimu*. Thirty-six of these were identified, named, and grouped according to general articulatory phenomena. Rimes, or finals, were recognized by the names that had become conventionalized in the riming dictionaries and classified into broad groups (*she*), within which standard utterable syllables were arranged by tone and graded into four divisions or "steps" (*deng*), according to the vocalization of the final. The rime tables, developed with a large initial debt to Indian practices of phonological analysis, were further elaborated during the eleventh and twelfth centuries. The classical formulation is generally acknowledged to be the *Qieyun zhizhang tu* (The *Qieyun* in the Palm of Your Hand), often attributed to Sima Guang (1019–1086). Sejong, while personally familiar with all of this work,[13] had special concern for two latter-day monuments of the tradition, the *Gujin yunhui* (Collection of Rimes Ancient and Modern), compiled by Huang Gongshao in 1292 and recognized as the most thorough rime book of the Yuan period, and the *Hongwu zhengyun* (Correct Rimes of the Hongwu Period), the standard Ming dynasty riming dictionary, published in 1375.

Insofar as a direct impact on the Correct Sounds is concerned, the most important legacy of Chinese phonological theory was the

Table 1. Traditional Chinese Initial Consonants, with Fifteenth-century Korean Equivalents

Articulation Mode / **Consonant Class**	全清 WHOLLY CLEAR Voiceless Stops and Affricates	次清 PARTLY CLEAR Voiceless Stops and Affricates	全濁 WHOLLY MUDDY Voiced Stops and Affricates	不清不濁 NEITHER CLEAR NOR MUDDY Voiced Nasals	全清 WHOLLY CLEAR Voiceless Sibilants	全濁 WHOLLY MUDDY Voiced Sibilants
牙音 MOLARS Velar Stops & Nasal	見 k ㄱ k	溪 k' ㅋ k'	群 g' ㄲ kk	疑 ng ㆁ ng		
舌頭音 APICAL LINGUALS Dental Stops & Nasal	端 t ㄷ t	透 t' ㅌ t'	定 d' ㄸ tt	泥 n ㄴ n		
舌上音 RAISED LINGUALS Palatal Stops & Nasal	知 t̂	徹 t̂'	澄 d̂	孃 ṇ		
脣重音 LABIALS HEAVY Bilabial Stops & Nasal	幇 p ㅂ p	滂 p' ㅍ p'	竝 b' ㅃ pp	明 m ㅁ m		
脣輕音 LABIALS LIGHT Dentilabial Spirants	非 f ㅸ ph	敷 (f') (ㆄ) (p'h)	奉 (v') ㅹ (pph)	微 β ㅱ mh		
齒頭音 APICAL INCISORS Dental Affricates	精 ts ㅈ c [ᅎ]	清 ts' ㅊ c' [ᅔ]	從 dz' ㅉ cc [ᅏ]		心 s ㅅ s [ᄼ]	邪 z ㅆ ss [ᄽ]
正齒音 UPRIGHT INCISORS Palatals & Retroflexes	照 tś tṣ [ᅐ]	穿 tś' tṣ' [ᅕ]	牀 dź' dẓ' [ᅑ]		審 ś ṣ [ᄾ]	禪 ź ẓ [ᄿ]
喉音 LARYNGEALS Laryngeals	影 · ㆆ ·	曉 χ ㅎ x	匣 γ ㆅ xx	喻 i ㅇ h		
半舌音 SEMILINGUALS Liquid				來 l ㄹ l		
半齒音 SEMI-INCISORS Dental Nasal Sibilant				日 ńź ㅿ z		

Note: This organization of the traditional Chinese initial consonants (*zimu*) is that of the *Qieyun zhizhang tu*, attributed to Sima Guang (1019–1086). The Middle Chinese sound values are those reconstructed by Bernhard Karlgren (1954). The fifteenth-century Korean alphabetic equivalents are transcribed as in Ledyard 1966; in this transcription, [h] is silent. In the northern Chinese dialects of the fifteenth century, the "wholly muddy" (voiced) consonants had been distributed among the "wholly clears" (voiceless unaspirated) and the "partly clears" (voiceless aspirated) depending on tonal conditions, but dictionaries continued to preserve them as a class. Korean in the fifteenth century had no voiced initial consonants, but lexicographers followed the Chinese in maintaining them as a class in Sino-Korean, indicating them with a doubled letter. The use of the doubled letter for the "reinforced" voiceless series (*toen sori*) is an unrelated and modern orthography.

classification of the initial consonants. This system became the bedrock framework for both the phonetic and the graphic definition of the Korean consonantal letters. This seven-class structure is illustrated in Table 1.

By Sejong's day many changes had developed in this system. In China itself the three contrasting stops (or affricates, spirants) per class had broken down into a system of two contrasts, similar to that which obtains at present in the northern Chinese dialects; and some consonants had merged or were merging with others, creating a new and much simpler system. In the Sino-Korean style of pronunciation of Chinese characters, many of the original distinctions had probably been lost already from the time of Korea's systematic borrowings of the Chinese lexicon in centuries long past; other changes had inevitably occurred in accommodation to the very different phonetic environment of Korean.

In spite of all the changes, which were noted and often deplored, these classical thirty-six initials retained authority as an "uncorrupted" sound system and hence a theoretical ideal. Sejong selected according to his Korean needs, but all of the seventeen letters he did invent fit systematically into the table. In addition, he devised special forms of some letters to accommodate the transcription of Chinese sounds that were not present in Korean (bracketed in Table 1). With these supplementary variants, virtually every space in the table was filled with Korean letters. Only the "raised linguals" (the palatal stops and nasal) were obsolete as a class; these had merged both in China and in Korea with the "upright incisors" (palatal affricates and fricatives) and required no graphs of their own. Apart from these, Sejong skipped only the "partly clear light" labial (theoretically **f'*-), since that had merged in China with its "wholly clear" partner and did not exist in Sino-Korean at all.

The influence of the Chinese system did not stop at the systemic level. As is well known, Sejong designed the graphic shapes of his letters in accordance with a particular factor of articulation in each of the respective classes. This idea cannot be stated better than the description in the *Hunmin chŏng'ŭm haerye*:

> For the initial consonants there are seventeen letters in all. The molar sound ㄱ [k] depicts the outline of the root of the tongue blocking the throat.

> The lingual sound ㄴ [n] depicts the outline of the tongue touching the upper palate.
>
> The labial sound ㅁ [m] depicts the outline of the mouth.
>
> The incisor sound ㅅ [s] depicts the outline of the incisor.
>
> The laryngeal sound ㅇ [h][14] depicts the outline of the throat.
>
> The pronunciation of ㅋ [k'] is a little more severe than that of ㄱ[k]; therefore a stroke is added.
>
> ㄴ [n] then ㄷ [t], ㄷ then ㅌ [t'];
> ㅁ [m] then ㅂ [p], ㅂ then ㅍ [p'];
> ㅅ [s] then ㅈ [c], ㅈ then ㅊ [c'];
> ㅇ [h] then ㆆ [·], ㆆ then ㅎ [x].
>
> The principle of adding strokes in accordance with the pronunciation is in all cases the same; only ㆁ [ŋ] constitutes an exception. The semilingual sound ㄹ [l] and the semi-incisor sound ㅿ [z] likewise depict the outline of the tongue and the incisor, only the form is altered; in these cases the principle of adding strokes does not apply.[15]

This ingenious formulation, which has been often and justly praised, is the crown jewel of Sejong's alphabetic theory. The systematic linkage between phonetic function and graphic shape, based on observed articulatory factors, is absolutely unique in the writing systems of the world. This is a good example of how Sejong often took Chinese theories or precedents and developed them in new and original directions. We will have more to say on the consonantal shapes later when we consider the Mongolian 'Phags-pa factors that may be involved.

Although the Chinese elaborated a highly sophisticated theory of the rime, or syllabic final, recognizing and classifying the key distinctions evident in its vowel sounds and final consonants, their discussions were always in the context of the integral rime. At no point in the traditional discourse did they separate the vowel from the final consonant, and at no point did they recognize the phonemic identity of initial and final consonants. Sejong, very likely with the knowledge of 'Phags-pa practices that I will examine presently, did both of these things. As a result, he had an element he called the "middle sound" (*chungsŏng*), which was the vowel or diphthong. His analysis of vowels represented new thinking that again transcended traditional Chinese phonological thought. The Chinese shadow in the picture he developed was a basic criterion of rime analysis known as the "open" (*kai*) and "closed" (*he*) distinction. By "closed" the Chinese meant either a labialized onset in the rime (i.e., the syllabic final) itself, such as in the rimes *-wan* or *-i̯uĕn*, or a labialized quality in its vocalism overall, such as in the rime *-ung*. "Open" rimes could be defined as lacking this quality, as in *-ăi* or *-i̯en* or *-ek*.

Sejong's adaption of the open-closed distinction in vowels is more subtle than his consonantal treatment, but it is clearly deducible from the discussion in *Hunmin chŏng'ŭm haerye*. His three primary vowels, · [ʌ], ㅡ [ə], and ㅣ [i], had been described in cosmological terms as representing the classical Confucian "Three Powers" (*sancai*), that is, Heaven, Earth, and Man; they had been phonetically defined in terms of tongue retraction and whether they were deep or shallow. They had not been discussed in terms of the open-closed distinction. But the remaining vowels fell into two pairs: on the one hand, ㅏ [a] and ㅓ [e], were described as open, or *pyŏk* (Ch. *bi*); in their pronunciation the mouth was lax and in a state of unforced openness (*chang*). On the other hand, the vowels ㅗ [o] and ㅜ [u] were said to be closed, or *hap* (Ch. *he*); in pronouncing them the mouth was contracted (*suk*), that is to say, pursed or rounded. The latter letters were also used to indicate labialized vocalic onset in the new orthography and in themselves had a labial quality due to the pursing of lips. They were involved in the Sino-Korean spellings of all words described classically as "closed." Given these factors, it is probably no accident that these open and closed pairs are distinguished graphically as well, the former being vertical in structure, the latter horizontal. That Sejong did not use the Chinese terms *kai* and *he*, but rather *pyŏk* and *hap*, was probably because the latter terms also had cosmological connotations and jibed better with this scheme of Heaven, Earth, and Man.

Beyond the invention of the alphabet, Sejong had much broader concerns within the field of Chinese phonology. These seem to have crystallized around the problem of Sino-Korean. It appears that he was unhappy in some degree over the state of Sino-Korean. The details of his thought on this are unknown, but one of the earliest publications to use the new alphabet was the "rime book" *Tongguk chŏng'un* (Correct Rimes of the Eastern Country, 1447), which attempted to standardize Sino-Korean. It is widely recognized today as an artificial and theoretical reform that failed to accommodate the actual pronunciations of the time. Sejong himself regarded it as a failure. When he approved it for distribution to schools in 1448, he said, "The people of this country have long been accustomed to their own popular rimes [i.e., pronunciation]. They cannot suddenly be made to change. Do not force instruction [of this book], and let scholars use it at their discretion."[16] No one will disagree with the wise king's verdict. Still, while the pronunciations of individual characters were in many cases artificial, the overall sound system they represented was well within the cadre of the Korean sound system at that time. Moreover, the *Tongguk chŏng'un* represented a radical and theoretically interesting departure from the classical Chinese rime books.

In accordance with his invariable practice of studying Chinese writings on the subject at hand, Sejong paid particular attention to the *Yunhui* and the *Hongwu zhengyun*, both mentioned earlier. Neither of these was held in much regard by Chinese and Korean literary people, who preferred Tang and Song reference works that were more germane to the phonology of the great bulk of classical Chinese poetry and more oriented to budding scholars preparing for the challenges of the examination hall. Their favorite rime book was the *Libu yunlüe* (The Abridged Rimes of the Board of Rites). This had been published in 1252, although its abbreviated rime scheme had already been in existence a few decades earlier.[17] But precisely because this dictionary related so well to the classics, it was deficient as a guide to contemporary pronunciation. This was especially so after the Yuan dynasty, during which many deep changes had occurred in northern Chinese pronunciation. The *Yunhui*, published during Khubilai's reign in 1292, though conservative in certain respects, had accommodated many of these changes and was much more systematically arranged in phonetic terms than most of the earlier rime books. The *Hongwu zhengyun* had been somewhat carelessly compiled and did not enjoy a high reputation. But it was the official dictionary of the Ming dynasty, and that fact could not be ignored in Korea, given the Chosŏn kingdom's tributary relationship to Ming.

We have very little information on how the Sino-Korean pronunciation of Sejong's day might have been seen to be related to the pronunciation of either the *Yunhui* or the *Hongwu zhengyun*. It was no doubt in order to understand that relationship that Sejong had ordered the *Yunhui* systematically studied and "translated" (*yŏk*), by which he seems to have meant a Korean edition of the Chinese text itself, with Korean alphabetic transliteration of the sound glosses.[18] He would seem to have decided first to find out what Chinese pronunciation was supposed to have been, and then to determine to what degree Sino-Korean pronunciation should or should not conform to it. These studies were not yet finished when the *Tongguk chŏng'un* was completed in 1447, but enough had probably been learned to confirm Sejong in his opinion that its phonetic glosses, which were heavily guided by Chinese theory and rime-book tradition, departed too radically from popular Sino-Korean pronunciation to be of any practical use. Sino-Korean had had at least ten or eleven centuries of independent development by Sejong's day, and while it still showed a clear relationship to the *fanqie* spellings of the Chinese rime books (indeed, in some important respects Sino-Korean was closer to Chinese classical readings than northern Chinese pronunciation was), discordant readings were many and varied.

It is of interest to note that Sejong did not depend for his study of Chinese pronunciation only on the studies of his scholars. He himself was personally familiar with the way contemporary northern Chinese speakers pronounced characters through his study of colloquial Chinese. The first sign of this avocation comes from 1421;[19] by 1435 he was practicing Mandarin every other day.[20] His tutor was Yi Pyŏn, director of the Language Academy (Sayŏg'wŏn), who himself was a living legend for his diligence in perfecting his Chinese.[21]

Sin Sukchu, Sejong's principal phonological investigator, was responsible for all three of the known compilations that resulted from the king's interest in rime books. In addition to the *Tongguk chŏng'un*, there was the *Sasŏng t'onggo* (Complete Investigation of the Four Tones, hereafter *T'onggo*), said by Sin to have been "fixed" (that is, authorized) by Sejong, therefore completed before the latter's death in late March of 1450, and the *Hongmu chŏng'un yŏkhun*, a Korean edition, with Korean alphabetic glosses, of the *Hongwu zhengyun*, which was completed in 1455.[22]

THE 'PHAGS-PA ALPHABET AND SEJONG'S CHINESE PHONOLOGICAL STUDIES

Although the *T'onggo* does not survive today, we are reasonably well informed on its contents through Ch'oe Sejin (1478?–1543), who in his own *Sasŏng t'onghae* (Complete Explanation of the Four Tones; hereafter *T'onghae*), published in 1517,[23] followed the outlines of the *T'onggo* and also reprinted its prolegomena (*pŏmnye*). In the latter, Sin Sukchu twice makes reference to a book he calls *Menggu yun* (Mongol Rimes).[24] According to Ch'oe, Sin also made frequent reference to pronunciations from this source throughout the *T'onggo*. He begins the prolegomena to his own *T'onghae* with a note on a book he called the *Menggu yunlüe* (Abridged Mongol Rimes). He says of it:

> The *Menggu yunlüe* is a compilation of the Yuan dynasty. After the barbarian Yuan moved in to rule China, they used their national letters (*guozi*, i.e., the 'Phags-pa alphabet) to transliterate the sounds of Chinese characters and to make this rime book for the instruction of their countrymen. Their reliance on sound to make syllabic graphs (*zi*) is of the utmost precision and clarity. Of the "popular pronunciations" in the *T'onggo*, most seem to be the same as the readings in the *Mongol Rimes*. Therefore, in now compiling the *T'onghae* we must use the *Mongol Rimes* to verify the distinction between the orthodox [*Hongwu zhengyun* readings] and the popular pronunciation.[25]

As promised, Ch'oe makes constant reference to Mongol readings throughout the body of his dictionary.

On the *Menggu yunlüe* itself, it would appear to be the same kind of book, or the same book under a different title, as the *Menggu ziyun* (Mongol Script Rimes), a hand copy of which has survived and is today in the British Library. It was photolithographically reprinted in China in 1959. This hand copy, which appears to have been made sometime around the middle or late eighteenth century, is nearly complete and has two prefaces, both dated 1308.[26] Through this copy, we can get an excellent idea of how the Mongols' 'Phags-pa alphabet—their "national letters"—were used to transliterate Chinese characters and to provide the organizing structure for a riming dictionary.

Thus, we have an existing Mongol rime book, with a supporting bibliographic history in both China and Korea, that enables us to compare its structure and practices with what we know of Sejong's various phonological projects. I give in Table 2 a conspectus of how the Korean Correct Sounds and the 'Phags-pa initials of the *Menggu ziyun* are each related to the traditional Chinese *zimu*, laid out in Table 1. The 'Phags-pa sound values used in this table are those used by Mongolists for Mongolian.

Table 2. The ‘Phags-pa and Korean Alphabets, Compared with the Chinese Initial Consonant System

No.	Chinese	Value	‘Phags-pa	Value	Korean	Value
牙音 MOLARS • Velar Stops & Nasal						
1.	見	k	ꡂ	g	ㄱ	k
2.	溪	k‘	ꡁ	k‘	ㅋ	k‘
3.	群	g‘	ꡀ	k	ㄲ	kk
4.	疑	ng	ꡃ	ŋ	ㆁ	ng
舌頭音 APICAL LINGUALS • Dental Stops & Nasal						
5.	端	t	ꡊ	d	ㄷ	t
6.	透	t‘	ꡉ	t‘	ㅌ	t‘
7.	定	d‘	ꡈ	t	ㄸ	tt
8.	泥	n	ꡋ	n	ㄴ	n
舌上音 RAISED LINGUALS • Palatal Stops & Nasal						
9.	知	t̂				
10.	徹	t̂‘				
11.	澄	d̂‘				
12.	孃	ń	ꡇ	ñ		
脣音重 LABIALS HEAVY • Bilabial Stops & Nasal						
13.	幫	p	ꡎ	b	ㅂ	p
14.	滂	p‘	ꡍ	p‘	ㅍ	p‘
15.	並	b‘	ꡌ	p‘	ㅃ	pp
16.	明	m	ꡏ	m	ㅁ	m
脣音輕 LABIALS LIGHT • Dentilabial Spirants						
17.	非	(f)	ꡤ	f(h^1w)	ㆄ	ph
18.	敷	(f‘)	[illegible]			
19.	奉	(v‘)	ꡤ	v(h^2w)	ㅹ	pph
20.	微	(m^w)	ꡓ	w	ㅱ	mh
齒頭音 APICAL INCISORS • Dental Affricates						
21.	精	ts	ꡒ	dz	ᅎ ᅐ	c
22.	清	ts‘	ꡑ	ts‘	ᅔ ᅕ	c‘
23.	從	dz‘	ꡐ	ts	ᅏ ᅑ	cc
24.	心	s	ꡛ	x	ᄼ ᄾ	s
25.	邪	z	ꡕ	z	ᄽ ᄿ	ss
正齒音 UPRIGHT INCISORS • Palatals and Retroflexes						
26.	照	tś / tṣ	ꡆ	ǰ	ᅐ	(ć)
27.	穿	tś‘ / tṣ‘	ꡅ	c‘	ᅕ	(ć‘)
28.	牀	dź‘ / dẓ	ꡄ	c	ᅑ	(ćć)
29.	審	ś / ṣ	ꡮ	s^2	ᄾ	(ś)
30.	禪	ź	ꡚ	s^1	ᄿ	(śś)
喉音 LARYNGEALS • Laryngeals						
31.	影	·	[illegible]	y^1<u>h</u>	ㆆ	·
32.	曉	χ	ꡜ	h^1	ㅎ	x
33.	匣	γ	[illegible]	h^2y	ㆅ	xx
34.	喻	j/i̯	[illegible]	y^{2}’(a)	ㅇ	h
半舌音 SEMILINGUALS • Liquid						
35.	來	l	ꡙ	l	ㄹ	l
半齒音 SEMI-INCISORS • Dental Nasal Sibilant						
36.	日	ńź	ꡔ	ź	ㅿ	z

Note: Chinese and Korean sound values are the same as in Table 1. The ‘Phags-pa values are those of Clauson 1959. The ‘Phags-pa letters linked with the “wholly clears” (voiceless unaspirated in Chinese) were used to transcribe voiced unaspirated consonants in Mongolian, in much the same way as the voiced consonants of the roman alphabet are used to transcribe the voiceless unaspirated initials in the modern Pinyin system. The ‘Phags-pa equivalents in the laryngeal class are too complicated for description here, but reflect among other things the fact that Mongolian has no glottal stop and that syllables beginning with a vowel require different initials depending on whether the vocalic onset was plain or yodized. On line 34, the two Mongolian letters more or less reflect the same distinctions Karlgren registered in his reconstructions: “smooth vocalic ingress” (*i̯*-) and “consonantal ingress” (*j*-). Applications of this distinction in the *Menggu ziyun* are inconsistent, however, and present many problems.

Both systems provided letters for the velar and dental stops and nasals (nos. 1–8). Both systems accepted that the Chinese supradental stops (nos. 9–11), having long since merged with the palatal affricates (nos. 26–28), needed no alphabetic notation. Even though the presumed supradental nasal *ṇ*- had merged with the regular dental nasal *n*-, the 'Phags-pa system assigned a letter to it anyway, creating for Yuan times a nondistinctive distinction that we shall see attracting some exasperated attention from Ch'oe Sejin. As for the dentilabials, these were especially important in Chinese dialects and required special letters in 'Phags-pa. Sino-Korean lacked dentilabials, but Sejong created a set of so-called "light" labials for this group so that the Chinese sounds could be transcribed when required. (One of these, the bilabial spirant ㅸ [ph], or /β/, also filled a need in Sejong's pure Korean orthography, although this sound was short-lived in Middle Korean and this letter was abandoned before the end of the fifteenth century.) Finally, the palatal/retroflex series (nos. 26–30) had a full series of 'Phags-pa graphs, reflecting the viability of these sounds in Chinese. In Sino-Korean there may never have been any such consonants, but if there had been, they had merged with the regular dental affricates long before Sejong's time. But here too, special Korean letters were adapted for Chinese transcription situations. Table 2 demonstrates clearly that the inventors of the 'Phags-pa and Korean systems were both attentive to their own respective needs. Although between 'Phags-pa and Korean the consonantal letters themselves were very different (we will come back to the question of graphic correspondences later), their respective *systems* show the overriding influence of the traditional Chinese consonantal categories.[27]

This parallel application of the Korean and 'Phags-pa alphabetic systems to the transcription of the Chinese *zimu*, and in particular the firm fact that Sin Sukchu used the Mongol Rimes in his phonological work, makes it useful to review anew the phonological projects launched under Sejong's orders. The first one in need of clarification is Sejong's reported plan to transliterate the *Yunhui*.

Many scholars have been puzzled by this project of Sejong, which as we have seen was ordered in the second lunar month of 1444, not too long after the announcement of the invention of the alphabet. After provoking the opposition of Ch'oe Malli's group and an outraged retort by Sejong, however, nothing more is heard of any work on the *Yunhui*. My own belief is that mention of the

Yunhui was dropped while work instead proceeded on the *Menggu yunlüe*, which shared—and perhaps was responsible for—some of the *Yunhui*'s peculiarities. In his table of the *zimu* of the *Yunhui*, Ch'oe Sejin commented on the *Yunhui*'s relationship to the 'Phags-pa alphabet, referring to the *zimu* by the names they bore in the *Yunhui* (the sound of each initial being marked by the first sound in the respective names).

> [Initial] *ngu* equals *ngi*; *niang* equals *ni*; *·wa* equals *·ing*; and *fei* equals *fu*. These [four] initials should not have been divided into two. That the *Yunhui* split them arose from the fact that, although the pair *ngu* and *ngi*, [for instance,] were the same in the *Mongol Rimes* (*Mengyun*), the Mongol *letters* for them were different. It was the same situation for *ni/niang*, *·wa/·ing*, and *fei/fu*. Only for *ni/niang* was a special argument offered. I have never been able to understand why [the *Yunhui*] so sharply distinguished them and considered them different.[28] (Emphasis added; · = glottal stop)

Ch'oe Sejin thus opines that the *Yunhui* maintained such nondistinctive distinctions because the 'Phags-pa alphabet, which had a pair of letters for each, made the same false distinctions. Ch'oe was not the first to notice this. The congruity of the *Menggu ziyun* initial consonantal system with that of the *Yunhui* had been pointed out already in 1297, in the prefatory material to the *Gujin yunhui juyao*,[29] and in 1308 in one of the prefaces to the *Menggu ziyun*.[30] It has also been remarked by modern investigators.[31] Since the *Menggu ziyun* or its ancestor was almost certainly compiled before the *Yunhui*, it is likely that the two initial systems are not only similar, but that the *Yunhui* was under 'Phags-pa consonantal influence. But regardless of which one influenced which, any relationship between the two systems puts in a different light the fact that Sejong's *Yunhui* project was seemingly dropped, while Sin Sukchu's *T'onggo*, "fixed" by Sejong, seemingly appeared out of nowhere. The best way to explain this situation is that the *Yunhui* project in fact turned into an examination of the "Mongol Rimes," which because of their systematic arrangement and alphabetic advantage provided a more efficient way to study the *Yunhui* in particular and Yuan-period Chinese pronunciation in general.

The abandonment of the *Yunhui* could also have resulted from the political sensitivity, both for Ming-Chosŏn relations and for internal opinion in Korea, of republishing a work originally patronized by the Mongols. In addition, since the *Yunhui* was very bulky, with rich definitions, etymological notes, and abundant citation of literature, the cost of a Korean edition would have been high. And although the *Yunhui* had some "modern" features, such as reflecting the loss of the final consonants *-p*, *-t*, and *-k* in Entering Tone syllables, its use of the rime classification of the *Libu yunlüe* placed it clearly with the "old" rime books.

The *Hongwu zhengyun* was only apparently more modern. It had a streamlined organization, with fewer initial and rime classes, but its pronunciations had many "old" features. The Entering Tone final consonants, for instance, were fully reflected, in spite of the Hongwu emperor's injunction to use modern northern Chinese pronunciation as the base. Phonologically, the choice between the *Yunhui* and the *Hongwu zhengyun* was a toss-up between two conservative rime books, each with a few modern tendencies. But the political viability of the latter was beyond question, and it was much more modest in size. Without any sure evidence on the point, it can be inferred that not too long after the original order to translate the *Yunhui*, the project was dropped in favor of the Ming work, and the *T'onggo* project was launched as a preparatory study for it.

In the *T'onggo*, as we know from Ch'oe Sejin, the four tonal classifications of Chinese syllables were grouped all together under their common Correct Sounds heading. But while it owed its structure to the *Mongol Rimes*, its purpose was to serve as an organized listing of Chinese pronunciations and as a reference guide for the projected edition of the *Hongwu zhengyun*, which in the *T'onggo*'s prolegomena is referred to as "the main rimes" (*pon'un*). When the completed *Hongmu chŏng'un yŏkhun* was published in 1455, the *T'onggo* was placed at the beginning as a kind of alphabetic index.

The structural influence of the *Mongol Rimes* can be inferred in the *T'onggo* and seen in the *Tongguk chŏng'un*. Traditional Chinese rime books had arranged all lexical items first by tone, so that in a set of words like *dōng* 'east', *dǒng* 'manage', and *dòng* 'freeze' (written here in modern Chinese pronunciation with tonal indications added) each would have to be looked up in a different volume of the dictionary. In the *Menggu ziyun* and similar "Mongol rimes," however, these were all listed in the same place, under a single 'Phags-pa syllable *dong*, with each of the words in its respective tonal subgroup. Sin Sukchu followed this principle in both the *Tongguk chŏng'un* and the *T'onggo*, as did Ch'oe Sejin in his *T'onghae*. Such an arrangement was much better for non-Chinese users of rime books, since in many cases it would have been precisely the tone that they needed to know. Uncertain, for example, whether *dong* meaning 'freeze' was in the Rising or Departing Tone, they could look under the general heading dong and quickly determine that it was the latter. But Sin did not slavishly follow all of the Mongol practices. He retained a strong preference for the theoretical inclusion of the corresponding Entering Tone syllables with the homorganically appropriate rimes, so that, for instance, he also listed the syllable dok (modern Mandarin *du*) 'alone' with the various *dong* words. This also had a practical advantage for Korean users, since the Entering Tone words still possessed their final consonants in Sino-Korean and the homorganic relationship between *-ng* and *-k* was still clear. The Mongol rime books, in contrast, included the word for "alone" with other non–Entering Tone words pronounced *du*, reflecting the fact that in northern China these final consonants had dropped.

Another influence of 'Phags-pa practices is reflected in the unusual Korean treatment of words in Chinese rimes of the type *-ao* and *-ou* (*Menggu ziyun* nos. 10–11). In Chinese pronunciation, either of Yuan times or of the present day, such syllables have a noticeably labialized offglide, which the *Menggu ziyun* identified with the sound of the labialized vocalic initial [w], historically a former *m-* that had changed under certain conditions of yodization and vocalization to *β-*. The 'Phags-pa letter for this initial was ꡤ. In Sino-Korean this change never occurred. For example, while in northern Chinese the word *wei* 微, the *zimu* name for this initial, went through the transformation *my(w)ei* > **βʷei* > *wei*, the Korean pronunciation of it had evolved to, and today remains, *mi*. In applying this letter to the *final* element of syllables of the type *-ao* and *-ou*, the 'Phags-pa phoneticians were creatively using their resources to meet the need for a labial offglide in the finals *-au* and *-ou*. But in Korean, such finals had long lost, or had never had, such a feature and were pronounced simply *-o* and *-u*, respectively, with no distinctive labial offglide. They were in no way different from the finals *-o* and *-u* descended from the completely different Middle Chinese rimes *-uo* and *-əu*.

And yet, Sin Sukchu adapted this Mongol orthography not only for his transcriptions of Chinese (where it made some sense), but even for his spellings of the corresponding Sino-Korean syllables in the *Tongguk chŏng'un*. The Korean letter corresponding to 'Phags-pa ꡜ was ㅱ, which Sejong had made by adding the null (ㅇ [h]) to the regular labial ㅁ [m]. Sin's application of this letter ㅱ [mh] in Sino-Korean syllabic finals like 곰 [komh] and 굼 [kumh] for *Tongguk chŏng'un* rimes 16 (高, etc.) and 17 (鳩, etc.) introduced an artificiality into his system but exactly reflected a 'Phags-pa–Chinese orthographical practice.

To be sure, the Sino-Korean orthography of *Tongguk chŏng'un* required that *all* syllables have a final consonant. Even those ending in a vowel were given a zero terminal by adding the null, or ㅇ [h]. Thus the names for *Tongguk chŏng'un* rimes 23 (孤, etc.) and 25 (拘, etc.) were written 공 [koh] and 궁 [kuh], respectively. Although this practice could be defended as a historical orthography that helped graphically to discriminate syllables that involved large numbers of homonyms, it is still a fact that there was no difference at all in the actual pronunciation of [komh] and [koh], or between [kumh] and [kuh], and that this theoretical distinction was quickly abandoned. That the final consonant chosen in the former case was exactly parallel to the one chosen by the 'Phags-pa orthographers for the same group of characters shows the clear influence of the 'Phags-pa script in this instance.

Another probable legacy of 'Phags-pa may be detected in the way Sejong analyzed the syllable. It was emphasized earlier that traditional Chinese theory had broken it down into an initial consonant and a rime—the latter consisting of the vowel, the final consonant if any, and the tone. Thus, in a syllable like nan 難 , Chinese phonologists had recognized the initial *n-* but had never associated it with the final *-n*. But the 'Phags-pa orthographers had separated the vowel from the final consonant, recognizing in this example both the independent vowel *-a-* and the phonemic unity of the consonant *n*, whether it occurred at the beginning or the end of the syllable. For them, the syllable now had three parts, an initial, a vocalic unit, and a potential final consonant. This was a genuinely alphabetic breakthrough. (However, there was some irregularity in the way this new syllabic principle was applied. For instance, there was still the inclination, common to the Indic alphabets and to Tibetan, to regard the vowel *-a-* as implicit in any initial consonant, so that 'Phags-pa orthography for Chinese syllables like *nan* and *gao* showed no vowel: they were respectively spelled simply [nn] and [gw].) Sejong removed this problem and ignored the rather awkward array of 'Phags-pa vowels in general by carrying out his own highly sophisticated vocalic analysis and by his rigorously consistent engraphment of that analysis. Yet in spite of the imperfect 'Phags-pa realization, the 'Phags-pa inventor can take the credit for having clearly established the principle of the tripartite division of the Chinese syllable, and in Korea this principle became the cornerstone of Sejong's orthography.

The inventors of each alphabet developed their respective vowel notations, getting no help whatsoever from a Chinese system that knew nothing of discrete vowels. The 'Phags-pa Lama, here as with the consonants, relied first on adapting the vowels of the Tibetan alphabet, then invented other letters or orthographic devices as needed. Sejong, in contrast, analyzed vowel sounds phonologically (speaking of lips "contracted" or "spread," the position of the tongue, the quality of the sound as "deep" or "shallow," and so forth) and, going beyond mere letters, invented a *vowel system*.

Although there is no direct written record that Sejong personally consulted the *Menggu yun* or a similar book of variant title, there is certain evidence that Sin Sukchu used such an edition. Given Sejong's personal role as the inventor of the Korean alphabet, his interest in the *Yunhui* and other rime books, and his "fixing" (i.e., authorizing) of the *Sasŏng t'onggo*, it is exceedingly unlikely that this wisest of all Korean kings could have been ignorant of the history and uses of the 'Phags-pa script in connection with Chinese phonology. Indeed, given the central role of Sejong not only in the alphabet and phonological projects but in virtually all of the intellectual activity of the Korean court, it is much more likely that Sin Sukchu learned of the *Menggu yun* from Sejong than vice versa.

In addition to the standard monuments of the Chinese phonological tradition, Sejong also consulted Chinese scholarly opinion through interviews at every available opportunity. In 1445 and on other unspecified occasions, Sin Sukchu and Sŏng Sammun (1418–1456) were sent to Liaodong to consult a Chinese scholar, Huang Zan, said to have been well versed in phonological matters,[32] and the same team interviewed the Chinese scholar Ni Qian, who was in Seoul as the member of a Chinese diplomatic mission in early 1450.[33] The intensity of these efforts can best be seen in Sin Sukchu's remarks in his preface to the *Hongmu chŏng'un yŏkhun*:

> So we were given the royal command to search out the correct [pronunciations] among the teachers and learned men of China. We went and returned as many as seven or eight times and questioned many people. The metropolis of Yan [Peking] is the common meeting place of the world, and though the road going and coming is long, not a few things were explained and clarified by our friends there. In our effort to get to the end of the deviations between standard and popular pronunciations, we met with all kinds of people, even the envoys from different quarters and strange regions, even people as insignificant as Buddhists and Daoists and rank-and-file soldiers. Moreover, when ambassadors from the Son of Heaven came to our country and there was a learned man among them, we also approached them and sought the correct. . . . But never once did we meet a man who clearly understood rime studies, and who could distinguish for us the fine points of tonal rules and of consonants and rime tables. All we could do, by relying on the remains in his own speech and reading pronunciations, was to retrospectively seek precision in some detail of clear-and-muddy or open-and-closed. The hardest thing of all was this: that we exerted ourselves so hard and for so long, and came up with so little.[34]

Students of Korean linguistic activity in Sejong's court have often been so concerned with the dramatic development of the Korean alphabet that they have either not noticed or have forgotten the broad international dimension in which this work took place. In the initial period of development, almost as much effort went into understanding *Chinese* phonology as Korean. Indeed, an investigator who looks at the whole picture gets the strong impression that success in solving Korean, particularly Sino-Korean, problems was seen to require understanding of the Chinese situation first. As we can appreciate from Sin's moving remarks, he and Sejong exhausted every available resource in their pursuit of understanding the Chinese sound system. But in spite of everything, the linguistic phenomena themselves were extremely complicated. Traditional Chinese scholars had been so torn between loyalty to the classical system, on the one hand, and awareness of fundamental diachronic change, on the other, that by Sejong's time their work as a whole had increased rather than resolved the confusion. This situation was perhaps the natural result of the fact that Chinese phonology was locked in a circular trap: it could not explain variable and contradictory historical data on the pronunciation of Chinese characters without resorting to those same Chinese characters as a phonetic medium. The only way out was via an independent phonetic script, not necessarily as a replacement for Chinese characters, but at least as an analytical tool. To the extant that the phonetics of the 'Phags-pa script, at least as applied in the *Menggu (zi)yun*, were tied to the Chinese sound system through the *zimu*, it provided only an imperfect means of escape from the traditional difficulties, and China spurned even that tool as soon as the Mongols were out of the way. But in Korea, in spite of its own long and oppressive Mongol interlude, a much more open attitude had enabled investigators to recognize the usefulness of the 'Phags-pa materials. Sin Sukchu used the new Korean alphabet to transliterate 'Phags-pa readings and to record thousands of popular Chinese pronunciations from actual speech, all of which he used to supplement the transliterated *fanqie* spellings (often hopelessly out of date) in the *Hongwu zhengyun*. From the objectivity of the outside and with the powerful tool of an independent system of phonetic notation, he, and later Ch'oe Sejin, produced the most systematic and well-reasoned phonetic descriptions of the sounds and tones of northern Chinese attempted through the end of the sixteenth century.

OTHER EAST ASIAN LANGUAGES AND SCRIPTS KNOWN IN SEJONG'S TIME

Compared with the relatively large numbers of people in Korea who could read classical Chinese, those with knowledge of other neighboring East Asian languages were vastly fewer in number. Yet these languages were important for Korea's foreign relations, and the government maintained a language school whose responsibility it was to see that the nation's military officials and diplomats never lacked for necessary language assistance. Colloquial Chinese was the most in demand, but Japanese, Ryukyuan, and Jurchen were also studied for the ongoing needs of diplomacy and commerce. Mongolian had been widely known in Korea during the thirteenth and fourteenth centuries. Even though Ming northern expansion in Yongle times (1402–1424) had effectively insulated Korea from contact with the Mongols, study of the Mongolian language continued throughout the Chosŏn dynasty.

Insofar as most of these languages and scripts are concerned, no impact on the Korean alphabet is either discernible or likely to have existed. But it is highly unlikely that people involved with the alphabet were unaware of these other writing systems. In the various accounts of Sin Sukchu's career included in the appendix to his collected works, *Pohanjae chip*, it is said that Sin could speak Chinese, Japanese, Mongol, and Jurchen.[35] Although there is undoubtedly some exaggeration here, it is a fact that Sin in 1443 went on an extended diplomatic mission to Japan, was responsible for Korea's Japanese diplomacy for many years, and later in life wrote an excellent book on Japan and Ryukyu.[36] He noted the Japanese syllabaries and was probably familiar with them. As we have seen, he went to Peking and frequently to Manchuria on diplomatic business or scholarly inquiry on behalf of Sejong; thus claims for some Chinese speaking ability probably had some foundation. There is probably not much to the assertion of a knowledge of Jurchen, although Sin did have high military responsibilities on the northeastern frontier in the early 1460s. As for his knowledge of Mongol, given his frequent citation of the *Menggu yun*, it is obvious that he could at least read the 'Phags-pa script.

I believe that any influence on the Korean alphabet from these neighboring scripts, apart from 'Phags-pa, would have been negative in character. A syllabic script of the Japanese open-syllable type made no sense for Korean, with its great variety of closed syllables; thousands of graphs would have been necessary to write Korean unambiguously with a syllabary. Such a script would have had no practical utility.

The so-called Jurchen script was more a code than a writing system; to this day its complete decipherment is unattained and probably unattainable given the few written texts that still exist. Although what exists is often partly decipherable because of surviving Sino-Jurchen glossaries, no one yet has figured out the *principle* of this writing—indeed it may not have had any. If it did no more than discourage Koreans from imitating it in developing their own writing, it made a noble contribution.

Apart from direct graphic influence, the Mongolian and Japanese phonetic scripts could have served as examples of a more broadly based literacy. In this connection it is especially interesting that Sin Sukchu, in his single reference to the Japanese *kana* syllabaries, said nothing about phonetics or graphics but rather emphasized widespread literacy, "without regard to male or female."[37]

Some Western writers of the nineteenth century believed that, given Korea's long Buddhist history, the Korean alphabet had probably been influenced by some variety of writing used in the writing of Sanskrit. As reasonable as that supposition seemed to them, I am unaware of any evidence suggesting that any Korean of the Koryŏ or Chosŏn periods read Sanskrit. More fundamentally, the political weakness of Buddhism in the Chosŏn state would have made such a situation unlikely, in spite of Sejong's own personal respect for Buddhism. Usually written with the Devanagari letters, Sanskrit was also written with the Brahmi and Gupta scripts. All of these would have been very exotic as far as Korea was concerned. In addition there was another script, the Siddham, that was elaborated from a Brahmi base in China and was used by East Asian Buddhists to write prayers or other religious invocations known as *dhāraṇī.* Sejong surely was aware of this form of writing, since there was a Siddham *dhāraṇī* on the ceiling beam of his own audience hall. In 1426, Confucianists demanded that it be removed, and it was.[38] But no one has ever suggested any connection between Siddham and the Korean alphabet, and there is none.

THE MONGOLIAN 'PHAGS-PA SCRIPT

There were two Mongolian alphabets. The Uighur script was borrowed from the Central Asian Uighur Turks early in the thirteenth century. It was quickly domesticated to Mongol use and remains in use today (except in the Republic of Mongolia itself, where, however, many now clamor to disestablish the Soviet-imposed Cyrillic script and readopt the Uighur). But the Uighur script, however beautiful calligraphically, was grammatologically limited. Khubilai Khan felt the need for a more richly endowed script to write not only Mongolian but the other major languages of his empire as well. Early in his reign he ordered his personal preceptor and adviser, the Buddhist priest 'Phags-pa Lama, to design a new script that would be used to write the major languages of the Mongol empire, and in 1269, the learned Lama delivered what has come to be called the 'Phags-pa script. It was promulgated by Khubilai's decree in that year as the "New Mongol Script" (*Menggu xinzi*).[39]

The 'Phags-pa Lama based his script mainly on the Tibetan alphabet, making adaptions or inventing new letters where needed. For the remainder of the Yuan dynasty, these "Mongol Letters" (*Menggu zi*) were widely used in formal edicts, seals, and monumental inscriptions, and also in some religious applications. But with the fall of Yuan in 1368, they passed quickly out of use. Today most surviving texts in 'Phags-pa are in Mongolian, but true to its intended international role, there are also some in Chinese, Turkish, Tibetan, and Sanskrit.[40] During the Mongol period, the Koryŏ court routinely received edicts and seals using this script,[41] and even in Sejong's day the historical archives probably contained Mongolian documents written in 'Phags-pa.

Both Mongolian scripts were taught in the Language Academy from the beginning of the Chosŏn dynasty. By 1423, the 'Phags-pa course was in decline, but special measures were taken in that year to maintain it in the curriculum.[42] On this occasion the Korean name for 'Phags-pa was given as "*Ch'ŏbawŏlchin* (Ch. *Tie'eryuezhen*) letters." This is a transcription of the Mongol word *dörbeljin*, reflecting the widely used informal name *dörbeljin üsüg*, "square writing," after 'Phags-pa's squarish appearance. A book titled *Ch'ŏbwŏlchin t'o* ('Phags-pa Particles) is mentioned in 1469 in a list of the Language Academy's Mongolian textbooks.[43] Thus Korean records document the existence of 'Phags-pa in Korea at exactly the period of the invention of the Correct Sounds.

In addition to the grammatological relationship of 'Phags-pa–Chinese materials to the early Korean projects relating to Chinese and Sino-Korean phonology and rime-book compilation, there is the question of 'Phags-pa influence on Korean letter shapes. A Canadian scholar, E. R. Hope, published a seriously argued case for a 'Phags-pa–Korean alphabetic correspondence in 1957. His arguments suffered much from being pushed too far and were gravely weakened by his inability to handle an already large Korean literature on the alphabet's origin. He treated the question not as a cultural historian, but in the manner of an armchair orientalist comparing one alphabet with another. Like many alphabetic comparatists, he emphasized letter shapes over everything else and appears to have believed that, whatever the historical circumstances of the supposed cultural contact might have been, they would not, when ultimately learned (that could be left to others), be able to invalidate the putatively hard graphic facts.[44] He also ignored the role of King

Sejong as sophisticated phonologist and as the active, designing intelligence behind the Correct Sounds.

After the discovery of the text of the *Hunmin chŏng'ŭm haerye* in 1940, and especially after its full photolithographic publication in 1946, any Korean doubts (and there had been some) over the origin of the letter shapes were dissolved by the *Haerye*'s revelation that the letters had been designed to depict the outline of speech organs involved in the articulation of the various classes of consonants (translated above).[45] Along with general scholarly opinion in Korea and internationally, I accept the *Haerye*'s testimony as both convincing and authoritative. I consider it to be an unmovable rock of fact that is not only strongly documented but makes sense in its own terms. Yet I have already established that 'Phags-pa alphabetic transcriptions of Chinese together with the *Menggu ziyun* or a similar book had a palpable influence on Korean rime-book compilation and orthographical practice in the 1440s and 1450s. Against this background, I can proceed with an investigation of 'Phags-pa and Korean letter shapes, recognizing that any conclusions must accommodate the *Haerye*'s speech-organ explanation of the Korean letter shapes.

The essence of the *Haerye* explanation is that letter shapes were established not on a letter-by-letter basis, but on the basis of one basic shape per consonant class. Once that basic shape was determined, it was modified to create graphs for other sounds in the same class. On this criterion, one needs only one convincing correspondence *per class* to begin serious comparison. Furthermore, any graphic correspondence that involves two different consonant classes must be excluded from consideration. This is the case with the 'Phags-pa letter ㄹ [ŋ], which has exactly the same shape as the Korean letter [l], and also with 'Phags-pa ㅌ [j], which is identical to Korean [t']. These pairs cut across classes while offering little or no comparison phonetically, and therefore can be safely removed from consideration as cases of 'Phags-pa graphic influence on Korean.

On a class-by-class basis, then, let us look at some of the more plausible graphic correspondences between 'Phags-pa and Korean letters. This can best be done by examining Table 2 above, referring to both the Korean and the 'Phags-pa letters by the Chinese *zimu* number at the far left.

In *zimu* no. 1 (a molar), the Korean shape will be the same as the 'Phags-pa shape if the hanging box in the 'Phags-pa letter is dropped.

In *zimu* no. 5 (a lingual), the two shapes are virtually the same, the lower stroke in the 'Phags-pa letter needing only a bit of straightening. Of particular note is the slight left-overhang of the top horizontal stroke in the Korean letter, which was pointed out to me by a Korean scholar as a special feature in the original design of this letter in the *Haerye*. Whereas given Korean geometricism we might expect a pure right angle, the slight overhang in the original Korean letter draws special attention to the 'Phags-pa letter, which has this same feature.

In *zimu* no. 13 (a labial), the 'Phags-pa letter, when turned and made to stand upright, will resemble the Korean letter. The basic Korean shape for the labial class is a closed square that is then altered by extending two of the sides. The 'Phags-pa letter, if geometrically simplified in accordance with the general graphic style of the entire Korean alphabet, can be matched with its mate in the Korean column.

In *zimu* no. 16 (the labial nasal), the 'Phags-pa letter could be straightened and closed into a box to match the Korean letter, as suggested by Hope (1957), but it is not very neat. Moreover, given the more convincing correspondence in no. 13, no further match is needed for the labial class.

In *zimu* no. 24 (an incisor), the 'Phags-pa shape bears plausible comparison to Korean no. 21. However, the foundation letter for the incisor class is Korean no. 24, with which 'Phags-pa no. 24, with further cropping, can also be brought into correspondence. Hope suggests matching 'Phags-pa no. 27 with Korean no. 21. While strictly speaking this pair satisfies the condition of common class membership—both are incisors—the match jumps across subclass boundaries; and whereas up to now the most plausible correspondences have been between 'Phags-pa and Korean letters that were both of the wholly clear type (see Table 1), the 27–21 matchup is between a Korean wholly clear and a 'Phags-pa partly clear. One must hesitate over such a suggestion.

Among the laryngeal *zimu* (nos. 31–34), there is no correspondence worth mentioning. Hope concocts a preposterous triple link involving the modern Korean letter ㅇ (now used as a null in syllabic initial position and for [ng] in syllabic final position), which he defines as "NG or null," unaware that in Sejong's original scheme this letter was two letters, ㅇ [h] and ㆁ [ng]; he uses the modern double identity to link up, on the one hand, with ꡖ, one of the 'Phags-pa nulls, and, on the other, with the Tibetan "headless" form ཿ for [ng]. Here he departs even from 'Phags-pa to grasp a match. It is clear in the first place that the 'Phags-pa orthographers had great difficulty dealing with the "laryngeal" *zimu* (the situation is even more complicated than suggested in Table 2), and in the second place that Sejong's circular letter corresponds graphically to nothing on the 'Phags-pa side.

Finally, the two single-member classes are represented by *zimu* nos. 35 and 36. In the case of no. 35 (semilingual), the 'Phags-pa letter bears comparison with the Korean either by turning it upright and straightening out the middle bar, or by cropping both its left and right sides to leave what essentially is the Korean [l]. In the case of no. 36 (semi-incisor), the 'Phags-pa and Korean letters are completely dissimilar. But strictly speaking, both of these Korean letters build on the basic shape for their respective main classes—the open right angle for the linguals and the V-shaped form with the apex on top for the incisors. The semilingual and semi-incisor therefore do not need to be individually accounted for in investigating 'Phags-pa–Korean correspondences, since their shapes accord with the basic shapes of their respective parent classes. In the words of the *Haerye*: "The semilingual ㄹ [l] and the semi-incisor ㅿ [z] likewise depict the outline of the tongue and the incisor, only the form is altered; in these cases the principle of adding strokes does not apply."

The suggested correspondences are summed up in Table 3, which shows the most graphically plausible matchup in each of the traditional consonant classes. The suggested graphic development within the class is shown at the right. The first thing to emphasize about this table is that four out of the five major consonant groupings in this table are represented by a 'Phags-pa–Korean matchup. Only in the case of the laryngeals is there no plausible corresponding letter.

In each of the four represented classes, the 'Phags-pa-Korean matchup involves the wholly clear letter. In the original Chinese scheme, the wholly clear category comprised unaspirated, voiceless

Table 3. Some 'Phags-pa–Korean Letter Correspondences

Sound and Sign / Consonant Class	Zimu	'Phags-pa	Korean	Development: Neither Clear nor Muddy	Development: Wholly Clear	Development: Partly Clear
Molar	見	ꡂ	ㄱ	┌ - → ㆁ	ㄱ →	ㅋ
Lingual	端	ꡊ	ㄷ	ㄴ ←	ㄷ →	ㅌ
Semilingual	來	ꡙ ↗	ㄹ	ㄹ ↙		
Labial	幫	ꡎ ↗	ㅂ	ㅁ ←	ㅂ →	ㅍ
Incisor	精 心	ꡛ ↗ →	ㅈ ㅅ		ㅈ → ↑ ㅅ	ㅊ
Semi-incisor	日		ㅿ	ㅿ ↙		
Laryngeal	喻		ㅇ	└ - - ㅇ →	ㆆ →	ㅎ

Note: The progressions indicated in the "development" column are proposed by me and imply, except in the laryngeal class, where there is no 'Phags-pa–Korean correspondence, a starting point in the "wholly clear" letters. The development as explained in *Hunmin chŏng'ŭm haerye* was discussed earlier.

consonants. (For the situation in Mongolian, see the note to Table 2.) Even in the incisor class, where one 'Phags-pa letter is suggested as a match for two Korean letters, both Korean letters are wholly clear. The incisor is the only class to have two wholly clears, and for that reason it is of particular interest that both of the Korean wholly clears can be derived from the 'Phags-pa letter.

In all of the correspondences, one can see the operation of a principle of geometric reduction in the adapted Korean letters. If there were to be a single master principle for a good writing system, simplicity would be the leading candidate for the role. Any observer looking at the 'Phags-pa alphabet can see that although the 'Phags-pa Lama carried out a general straightening of the Tibetan letters he was imitating—enough to earn the nickname "square writing" for his script—he did not achieve much simplicity. But Sejong kept things very simple, and for that reason his script was practical and workable from the beginning. Critics of the correspondences suggested here might say that some of the matchups require too much adapting. But in view of the overall geometric simplicity of the Korean letters, drastic simplification is *in itself* an applicable principle in comparing the Korean shapes.

The most striking departure from the development scheme described by the *Haerye* is that whereas the latter expressed the intraclass development as one of adding strokes to the simpler letter to make the "more severe" letter, the scheme suggested here implies, in the lingual and labial classes, also a *reduction* of strokes in the direction of the *less* severe. In fact, the *Haerye*'s stroke-addition rule is inconsistently applied. While it works according to plan in the linguals, incisors, and laryngeals, there are glitches in the labials and molars. In the former, strokes are not added, but extended. Had a true addition been effected while maintaining the basic closed, rectangular shape for this class, we might have letters like * ⊟ for [p] and * 目 for [p']. In the case of the molar class, the exceptional form for the neither-clear-nor-muddy letter ㆁ [ng] called forth a special discussion from the *Haerye* editors themselves. The corollary of the principle of adding strokes for more severity is reducing them for less severity. In stating the principle, it was neater and more efficient for the *Haerye* writers to state it in one direction only, and this is what they did. But given the likelihood of 'Phags-pa graphic influence on most of the wholly clear initials, it is reasonable to suppose that in the actual designing of the letters strokes were reduced in the direction of the neither-clear-nor-muddy, while added in the direction of the partly clear. I suspect that the reduction principle operated even in the exceptional case of the letter ㆁ [ng], the neither-clear-nor-muddy representative in the molar class. Consider the *Haerye*'s explanation of this situation:

> As for ㆁ [ng], the root of the tongue blocks the throat and the breath of enunciation passes through the nose. Nonetheless, the pronunciation resembles that of ㅇ [h]. Thus in the rime books the *zimu* 疑 [ng] and 喻 [h] are often confused with each other. [So in this case] we have also taken the depiction [for ㆁ] from the throat and not made [this letter] the primary form for designing the letters of the molar sounds. The throat is assigned to Water, while the molars are assigned to Wood. Although ㆁ stands with the molars, it resembles ㅇ. It is analogous to the buds and shoots of a tree that, produced in water, are soft and pliant and still have much of the material force of water. With ㄱ [k], the tree becomes solid substance; with ㄲ [kk], the tree flourishes and grows; and with ㅋ [k'], the tree ages and matures. Therefore in these cases we have taken all the depictions from the molars.[46]

The clever application of Confucian cosmological thought—in this case Five Agents (*wuxing/ohaeng*) theory—is found throughout the *Haerye*, but here it seems especially forced. The phonological situation, however, is very adroitly handled in the *Haerye* treatment. What the editors said of the Chinese rime book situation was true, and it was especially true of the *Menggu ziyun*, where the confusion caused by *ng*- initials becoming nulls was ubiquitous and out of control. In Korean and Sino-Korean, the situation was much clearer: there was no initial *ng*- at all. But to maintain the historical distinction in transcriptions of Sino-Korean, Sejong ingeniously contrived to make the letters for [ng] and [h] look like each other, while mindful that in initial positions they both represented a null in fact. For this, his basic shape had to be the null, from the laryngeal class. Yet, in his letter ㆁ, is there not a trace of a "reduced" molar letter ㄱ in that perky hair that stands up from the circular null? With only two strokes in ㄱ, a reduction can yield either ㅡ or ㅣ. We could speculate that Sejong chose the vertical stroke to suggest the original molar character of this consonant. (Choosing the horizontal alternative would have produced a letter too easily confused with the pure laryngeal series and also with the vowel ㅡ [ə].) This would silently reflect that the original letter in this series was in fact the wholly clear ㄱ —itself a "reduction" of the 'Phags-pa ꡂ.

In the case of the semilingual class, in which [l] is the sole member, there was no wholly clear member. Whether Sejong "altered" his basic lingual shape to create ㄹ [l] or made it by borrowing and geometrically simplifying the 'Phags-pa letter ꡙ is not of great importance as far as the present discussion is concerned. Sejong needed a letter that would look like it was built on the lingual baseshape, and he could have it one way or the other.

The hypothesis that most of the wholly clears of the Korean alphabet were adapted from 'Phags-pa forms can accommodate the *Haerye*'s discussion of the "least severe" letters as depicting the outlines of the various speech organs. It is no less cogent and ingenious as an ex post facto rationalization than as a formula for graphic design. In explaining such simple and reduced forms, the very arbitrariness of the exercise would have been an asset to Sejong. The reduced, elemental forms Sejong ended up with were perfectly susceptible of rationalization as depictions of speech organs. Still more important, they were easily distinguishable as letters. The *Haerye* editors also make much of Yin-Yang, Five Agents, and "Three

Powers" (*sancai*, that is, Heaven, Earth, Man) manipulations to explain the letters, but few would doubt that all of this is ex post facto, even though highly interesting. Likewise, making the speech-organ analogy also ex post facto in no way compromises the keen phonetic imagination that lies behind it. Those who insist that the speech-organ explanation is the only possible one must rather explain how it is that four key 'Phags-pa letters, each an exact *zimu* analog to its Korean correspondent, could have closely similar shapes even though invented far away in another country 175 years earlier. Such an alignment goes beyond coincidence.

To sum up, Korean letters for most of the wholly clear initials are noticeably similar in basic shape to their 'Phags-pa counterparts. Influence by these on the Korean wholly clears can be reasonably inferred. In adapting these letters, Sejong subjected them to geometric simplification. These letters, each in its respective consonant class, would then have become the basic graphic forms on which the other letters in the class were built, either by the reduction of a stroke in the direction of the "less severe" or the addition of a stroke in the direction of the "more severe." In the laryngeal class no 'Phags-pa letters were borrowed; Sejong adopted a circle as the basic shape and in this class probably actually began with the "least severe." The idea that certain key Korean letters were influenced by 'Phags-pa forms can be accommodated fully within the structure of the *Haerye*'s explanations and analyses. Finally, it is not a valid criticism that so few 'Phags-pa–Korean matchups can be proposed. Given the facts that are known from the *Haerye*, there is room for only five extrinsic shapes; that four of them are available from 'Phags-pa shows an 80 percent rate of accommodation.

THE OLD SEAL

As everyone who has studied the Correct Sounds knows, the earliest references to the Korean alphabet say that it "imitated the old seal [script]" (*pang kojŏn*).[47] There has probably been more puzzlement over these three syllables than on any other problem connected with the origin of the Korean alphabet. This chapter cannot end without one more attempt to crack this old conundrum. Furthermore, there is a 'Phags-pa dimension to it.

It is natural enough that most of the discussion so far has taken the phrase "old seal" in its most transparent sense and focused on the ancient Chinese seal script. In antiquity, its forms were presumably close to the actual script in use in China. From the time of the invention of the seal, perhaps in the fourth or third century B.C., these characters began to be imaginatively redrawn, often with exaggerated elongation and curving, into the varied forms that have become traditional on seals. The arguments to relate this or that Korean letter to this or that seal character have usually convinced no one beyond their respective makers.[48] The task of relating the simple and rigidly regular geometric lines of the original Korean script to the most elongated, tortuous, serpentine graphic style in the entire Chinese calligraphic repertoire is hopeless, and in fact it has been abandoned for some time, leaving only the original, unsolved mystery.

However, investigation of materials relating to the 'Phags-pa script in China during the Yuan period yields rather striking evidence that the seal script (Ch. *zhuan*, Kor. *chŏn*) was on several occasions associated directly with the 'Phags-pa letters—evidently because of a perceived graphic similarity—and that in some cases the 'Phags-pa letters were even referred to as *zhuan* characters. Furthermore, we see the phrase *Menggu zhuanzi*, "Mongol seal characters," and we see the second syllable of *Menggu*, meaning "old," used in the sense of "Mongol" in discussions of 'Phags-pa letters. Let us look at some of these textual usages.

Earlier I mentioned the preface of Wang Yishan to a now lost early edition of the *Menggu ziyun*, referred to by him as *Menggu yunlei* and identified as the work of a certain Li Hongdao, about whom nothing can be learned. Wang's preface plays games with the word *gu*, "old." Because he is clearly punning, I avoid translating it and simply romanize all instances.

> Master Li Hongdao has shown me his compilation of *Mongol Rimes* (*Menggu yun*). Now, if it is a matter of *gu* graphs, none are more *gu* than these. . . . In Hongdao's rime compilation, he uses the most *gu* of *gu* graphs; he uses the *gu* to teach men of modern times about *gu*! [In standard modern rime books there are 205 rimes,] but when I look for them in these *gu* rimes, there are only fifteen headings, which is not very many! Speaking in general, there are only thirty-two *zimu*. Indeed, if you speak of them as a group there are thirty-two, but when dispersed [in words] they can be counted in the

> tens, hundreds, thousands, myriads![49] As for *gu* graphs, none are more *gu* than Meng*gu*. However, in saying this I mean only the *gu*-ness of the graphic style.
>
> In the *Zhou li*, among the "locality officers," the "controller of the crowd" handles teaching for the state. The Bao Clansman works under him; his duties are to use the six kinds of writing to teach the children of the kingdom. Now Hongdao also teaches people, with his Meng*gu* rime compilation. He wants modern people who already know graphs [Chinese characters] to know *gu* graphs. He uses only thirty-two graphs yet comprises tens, hundreds, thousands, myriads of words. Comprising tens, hundreds, thousands, myriads of words, he teaches tens, hundreds, thousands, myriads of people. If one regards the merit of the Bao Clansman to be outstanding, certainly Hongdao's merit in graphic studies is not trifling either. Were [the great Tang commentator] Kong Anguo to be born again today, he would not have to end up exclaiming that our contemporaries don't include some of competence and wisdom.
>
> Yes indeed, graphs [characters] are but the writing of speech; rimes are the sounds of speech. Were it not for graphs, there would be no completion of the rimes; were it not for rime compilations, there would be no way to look up the graphs. Even so Hongdao's use of a rime compilation for the instruction of others is [really] a reapplication of the *Qieyun* method that began with Lord Sima [Guang].[50]

In reading these words of Wang Yishan, who, like Sejong later, found inspiration for language and literacy teachers in the *Zhou li* (although they cited different passages), one begins to see that one must pay as much attention to the "old" of "old seal" as to the seal itself: "Nothing is more *gu* than Meng*gu*." When, at the beginning, he says, "none are more *gu* than these," he is speaking of the graphs in Li Hongdao's book, which are Mongol 'Phags-pa consonantal letters. When he says "*gu* rimes," he is explicitly talking of the *Mongol Rimes* as a book title. In this passage, in no sense can all of these *gu* phrases be interpreted as merely referring to old or ancient characters, nor can "*gu* graphs" mean anything other than 'Phags-pa letters.

Another important use of *gu* in the sense of "Mongol" occurs in a printed Korean edition of the *Gujin yunhui juyao*, Xiong Zhong's 1297 abridgment of the original *Yunhui*. We have already noted the observation by Zhao Yintang that in a Chinese edition of Xiong's work it is asserted that the initial consonants in its prefatory tables and those in the *Menggu ziyun* are identical. The exact wording is *Meng gu zi yun yin tong* 蒙古字韻音同 , "same as the initials of the *Menggu ziyun*." In a Korean edition of the *Gujin yunhui juyao*, the corresponding phrase begins with *ju* 據 instead of *meng*, yielding "according to the old (*gu*) *ziyun*, the initials are the same."[51] This makes for a grammatically awkward sentence; it does not read naturally. The modern scholar Yu Ch'anggyun has therefore explained *ju* as a misprint for *meng*.[52] But this seems farfetched either graphically or phonetically. I rather suspect a calculated attempt to cover up the Mongol contribution to the *Yunhui*'s phonology. However it came about, the "old" (*gu*) can only mean "Mongol."

Wang mentions nothing about seal characters, but other writers do. The British Library manuscript of the *Menggu ziyun* contains, in its prefatory material, a table of *zhuan zimu*, "seal initials."[53] The list of ninety-eight 'Phags-pa letters that follows the caption contains thirty-eight standard and sixty-two variant 'Phags-pa letters, all in the same style and all giving the appearance of seal-style Chinese characters. A casual reader not closely familiar with the standard 'Phags-pa forms would not be likely to distinguish the standard and variant forms on stylistic grounds. Clearly, these 'Phags-pa letters were seen to resemble, or perhaps imitate, the classical Chinese seal style.

In the 'Phags-pa versions of the *Baijia xing*, or "Hundred Surnames," which are found in the various editions of the *Shilin guangji*, a fourteenth-century compendium of classified topics and essays,[54] there are more direct references to 'Phags-pa letters as seal characters. Luo Changpei and Cai Meibiao illustrate two separate texts of the *Baijia xing* in their study of 'Phags-pa. The *Shilin guangji*'s introduction (first published in 1325) to the first reads as follows:

> Aside from the [classical] old seal (*guzhuan*, Kor. *kojŏn*) there is another seen in the world: we have now obtained the text of the "Hundred Surnames," put into seal by the Mongols. The written forms, as each is seen in its place [in the *Baijia xing* text], are such as the world has never seen. We carefully publish it here, following the [section devoted to the classical] old seal. Once brush wielders study these, lo! their brush will run like a dragon or a snake![55]

It can be seen from these lines that not only was "old seal" used to allude to the 'Phags-pa script, but that this "Hundred Surnames" text was actually placed in the *Shilin guangji* in the section immediately following the essay on the genuine, ancient "old seal" writing. Another edition of the *Shilin guangji* (1340), containing a slightly different version of the *Baijia xing*, also has a special introduction, this one entitled *Menggu ziti*, or "Mongol Graphic Forms":

> The Mongol writing is something that earlier scholars had not seen. Recently, customs and culture have moved from the north to the south, and the new learning esteems [this style]. [In ancient times,] after the tadpole writing was discontinued, the seal (*zhuan*) and clerical (*li*) styles became prevalent. These styles were both old (*gu*). Later on, the true (*zhen*) and the grass (*cao*) styles shared popularity. Now in our time, the royal transformations again are close to those of old, and customs and usages are returning to the pure. Mongol studies have been established as a field for specialization. If beginners will copy this piece again and again, they might use it as a shortcut to official position.[56]

Here the connection with the seal writing is indirect but clear in context, and we see the allusive use of "old" similar to that in Wang Yishan's preface. It is likely that during Khubilai's time and afterward, individuals would have found it useful and occasionally necessary to have a personal seal with one's name in the 'Phags-pa script. No doubt this is one of the reasons for the popularity of transcriptions of the "Hundred Surnames" in 'Phags-pa.

Another reference to the "seal" and "clerical" styles in application to 'Phags-pa can be found in an essay on the 'Phags-pa script in the *Shushi huiyao* (Essentials of the History of Writing), a treatise on calligraphy compiled by Tao Zongyi (1320–1400) in 1376. Although the immediate interest of this description of 'Phags-pa regards its placement immediately following notice of a calligrapher noted for expertise in the "seal and clerical" (*zhuan li*) scripts, it is also worthy of note for its reference to the ultimate Indian, or "Brahman" (*fan*), ancestry of the 'Phags-pa alphabet.[57]

A similar text on 'Phags-pa is found in another treatise on calligraphy, the *Fashu kao* (Investigation of Writing Models) by Sheng Ximing, first published in 1331. Its list of the 'Phags-pa letters and account of their use is also in the context of a general discussion of *fan* writing. This section concludes with the following remarks by Sheng Ximing:

> I respectfully observe that although the various barbarian scripts have changed and become quite different from each other, there are none that do not go back in origin to the Brahman Sounds (*fanyin*). The reason I now say "Brahman Sounds" and not "Brahman Writing" (*fanshu*) is that [in these scripts] sounds and pitches combine to make words [or syllables—*zi*]: one supplies the sound in order to bring forth the idea. It is not like our Chinese writing, with its Six Principles [of logographic composition]. Zheng Qiao once said that in the *fan* letters there was a "representation of forms" [*xiangxing*—one of the Six Principles], but that was just his speculation. The *zimu* [that is, separate consonantal sounds] are similar to the old writing (*guwen*) of Cangjie [the reputed inventor of Chinese writing]: their sounds and rimes join together to form words, just as the old writing diversified and evolved to become the seal characters (*zhuan*). The evolution of the *zimu* into the scripts of the various barbarians is also analogous to the change of the seal characters into the various clerical forms and the running and cursive scripts.[58]

Although this reference to *zhuan* writing directly follows an exposition of the 'Phags-pa alphabet, Sheng Ximing does not suggest any explicit association of seal writing and the Mongolian script. But he does suggest another interesting way that we might interpret the statement that the Correct Sounds "imitated the old seal" (*pang kojŏn*). Just as the seal forms represent a joining together of primitive graphs ("old writing, *guwen*), he says, the "barbarian scripts" represent a combination of discrete sound signs (*zimu*) into words. Unlike Chinese characters, which consist of various combinations of semantic elements with each other or with phonetic elements (the Six Principles), phonetic scripts combine sounds to make words, and these words "bring forth the idea." This kind of explanation may seem to a modern reader to stray far from the point, but to a person who knew only Chinese characters and had no concept of alphabetic writing, this would have been an effective way to explain it.

Still, the expression "imitate the old seal" would seem to be an unnecessarily recondite way to get such an idea across, and to some this observation must also apply to *pang kojŏn* as an allusion to the 'Phags-pa script. But while there would have been no problem in directly discussing the seal script (Sejong, in fact, had in 1440 approved special incentives to develop more widespread calligraphic expertise in this form of writing),[59] it was something else to suggest openly that the Correct Sounds were in some way connected to Mongol writing. The people of Sejong's age were less than a century removed from the era of Mongol domination in Korea. Mongol culture was seen by many China-oriented literati of the time as synonymous with barbarism. Had not Ch'oe Malli made the connection explicit in his famous anti-alphabet memorial of 1444? His remarks suggest that he too was aware of some literary or textual connection between *ko* ("old, antiquity" = Ch. *gu*), the Mongols, and seal writing (*kojŏn*):

> Let us assume that the graphs of the vernacular script are all based on old (*ko*) characters and are not new characters. But even if the graphic forms imitate the old seal writing (*pang ko chi chŏnmun*), the combining of the graphs according to sound is utterly opposed to what is old (*ko*); there is truly no basis for it. If these graphs should flow into China and people there adversely criticize them, how could we be without shame, considering our service toward the great (*sadae*) and our affection for China? Although from ancient times customs and local usages have differed within the Nine Lands [of the Chinese ecumene], there has never been a case of one of them separately making a script based on local speech. Only the Mongolians, Tanguts, Jurchen, Japanese, Tibetans, and others of that ilk have their own graphs. But these are the matters of barbarians, not worth talking about.[60]

How naturally Ch'oe's rhetoric flows from a critique of the comparison with old seal writing into a denunciation of the degenerate scripts of the barbarians, the Mongols listed first! Whether or not he had some idea of "old seal" meaning something else beneath the surface, his opposition to the new writing on the grounds of civilization was deeply felt and widely shared. In the Korean system of government (very differently from China's at that time), the ruler's power was not so unqualified that Sejong could stir up a political storm without fear of the consequences. It would have been prudent to keep "barbarian" influence, if any there was, to oneself. It cannot be proven that Sejong was aware of the 'Phags-pa/Old Seal literary references that I have cited, but it is hard for me to imagine that he was not. But at least, Ch'oe's words suggest that at the time of the first announcement of the Correct Sounds in late 1443 or early 1444, some creative public relations had been employed to diffuse opposition to the alphabet and to put a Chinese "spin" on it, so that it would not alarm people who were nervous and defensive about the association of non-Chinese peoples (that is, themselves) and non-Chinese writing with barbarism. Assuming Sejong knew of the 'Phags-pa/Old Seal association, he could say that he was imitating the Old Seal and be slyly suggesting the truth. Those who recognized the reference and liked the alphabet could wink and exult in what a clever king they had, while if the hostile group picked up on the reference, it could be dismissed as an innocuous nod to ancient Chinese culture.

One last matter remains to be noted. We have seen above that some Chinese calligraphy experts discussed 'Phags-pa in the context of Indian (*fan*) writing. In this context it is more than interesting that Sŏng Hyŏn (1439–1504), a widely recognized writer on poetry and the arts in the generation after Sejong's reign, wrote in his collection of essays, the *Yongjae ch'onghwa*, a short notice on the Korean alphabet—which he called the "vernacular script" (*ŏnmun*)—that ended with the sentence "The shapes of the letters were made by relying on *fan* letters."[61] It is hard to believe that Sŏng Hyŏn, one of Korea's best-known connoisseurs of calligraphy in the late fifteenth century, had not read Yuan treatises on calligraphy such as the *Shushi huiyao* and the *Fashu kao*, much less Zheng Qiao's famous essay on the elements of writing, with its characterization of *fan* writing systems. Sŏng was born eleven years before Sejong's death and knew many of the people who had worked with him, including Sin Sukchu. His testimony as a near contemporary is important.

SEJONG AND 'PHAGS-PA

The Korean alphabet was at the center of a complete strategy of language and literature development. The new letters were the product of careful research and deliberation by Sejong (1443–1444). When promulgated, they were accompanied by an intelligent description and rationale (*Hunmin chŏng'ŭm haerye*, 1446). They were immediately used in composing a cycle of Korean poems in honor of the founders of the Chosŏn state (*Yongbi ŏch'ŏn ka*, 1447) and in the compilation of a dictionary of Sino-Korean pronunciations (*Tongguk chŏng'un*, 1447). These projects were followed by the list of Chinese pronunciations of characters classified by rime groups (*Sasŏng T'onggo*, ca. 1450), itself only preparation for the complete Korean edition of the Ming riming dictionary *Hongwu zhengyun* (*Hongmu chŏng'un yŏkhun*, 1455). All of these were official projects ordered by Sejong. On the unofficial level, Sejong and his son Prince Suyang—later King Sejo—were busy composing in Korean impressive collections of Buddhist narratives and poetry (*Sŏkpo sangjŏl*, 1447–1448; *Wŏrin ch'ŏngang chi kok*, 1448; *Wŏrin sŏkpo*, 1459). In the broader picture, this entire cluster of works was itself but a complement to the great number of institutional and cultural projects that spanned Sejong's reign. All of these were marked by their adherence to the general values and standards of East Asian civilization and the confirmation of an original and self-asserted Korean legitimacy within it, as demonstrated in particular by the *Yongbi ŏch'ŏn ka*.

In the total picture of the creation of the Correct Sounds, the role of the 'Phags-pa script and of the *Mongol Rimes* is of relatively modest import as compared to Sejong's general language strategy and his own creativity and originality. Foreign alphabets have been copied and adapted to other languages on numerous occasions in world history and in every corner of the globe, but in no other instance has the adaption of a few alien letters been accompanied by so much intellectual inquiry and such a revolutionary alphabetic theory as in the Korean case.

A comparison of the accomplishments of the 'Phags-pa Lama and Sejong is perhaps instructive. The learned Lama performed a workmanlike service in adapting the letters of the Tibetan alphabet to a wider international use, but he did not thereby earn any particular distinction in the history of writing. Sejong may have adapted four or five 'Phags-pa letters, but in doing so he took their bare patterns as graphic and phonological building blocks and transcended the 'Phags-pa Lama's alphabet completely. The 'Phags-pa script is a genuine alphabet with discrete letters for consonants and a small selection of vowels, but its inventor could not escape from the Indic principle that all consonants contained an implicit vowel *a* that did not need expression; Sejong, as we have seen, not only made letters for all his needed vowels, but he conceived them as parts of an interdependent vocalic system.

The 'Phags-pa Lama simplified and straightened some Tibetan letters, whereas Sejong conceived and applied a principle of geometric simplicity and a principle of graphic symbolism. These not only provided for practically distinguishable letter shapes but made the script easier to grasp and learn. The 'Phags-pa Lama was able to change writing directions by adapting the horizontally written Tibetan into the vertically written 'Phags-pa; this was evidently seen as a necessary change if the new script was to have any effectiveness as a medium for Chinese. Sejong, who felt a similar need, invented an alphabet written in syllabic blocks so that it could be used in complete harmony with Chinese writing, whether written vertically or horizontally, and if horizontally, whether from the left or from the right. In this feature the Korean alphabet was, and still remains, unique in the world. While some later critics, even in the Korean language community, have thought that a syllabically written alphabet made too many difficulties for printing, the grammatological thinking and printing practices of Sejong's own time made his solution the only viable one. In recent times the computer and a revolutionary new printing technology have liberated Korea's alphabet from the tyranny of the line, and we hear no more about "writing side by side" (*karo ssŭgi*).

These thoughts on the close comparison of the two scripts also suggest broader contrasts on the level of cultural policy. The emperor Khubilai ordered a polygraphic script for a polyglot empire, whereas Sejong was concerned only with Korean national needs under the broader canopy of China's universalistic cultural reach. While I have no disposition either to criticize Khubilai for having an empire or to praise Sejong for having no more than a kingdom, the closer connection between language and script in the Korean case was a factor in its greater success in the long run. While the Greek, Latin, Arabic, and Indic alphabets had dramatic success on the international level, the phenomenon owed much more to the established cultural strength of those civilizations and to natural evolutionary process than to any edicts or directives. Khubilai had his script designed specifically for the efficient circulation of orders and edicts and for other public uses, such as on personal seals, identification badges (*paizi*), coins and paper money, and monumental inscriptions. The spread and use of the 'Phags-pa script was a matter of the projection of power; when ultimately Mongol power was lost a century later, its new script, which had never gained much cultural authority, was discarded with relief.

The contrast with the Korean alphabet is dramatic. Sejong never once issued an edict requiring the use of the Correct Sounds, although he was not above once using them in an official document and presenting it to his puzzled subordinates, almost certainly to embarrass them.[62] Rather than use the alphabet in orders and edicts and other displays of power, he ordered the compilation of dynastic hymns and dictionaries. Even his extensive use of the new script for the development of Buddhist literature was his own family affair, carried out by his son and done in memory of his departed wife; it went almost unnoticed in the public record. He urged his officials to consider translating the Confucian classics into Korean but did not force the issue.

Sejong let off those who had protested the alphabet in 1444 with light and transitory punishment. Ch'oe Malli's criticism represented a hatred of the new writing that by all appearances was widely shared by officials and scholars, but Sejong never suppressed this dissent, and his royal anger at Ch'oe and his colleagues was gone the next day. Such restraint probably was instrumental in the success of the Correct Sounds in the long run. Sejong might have pushed his new script more aggressively, but he seems to have appreciated that kings come and go while ruling classes go on and on. Arbitrary force might well have provoked violent reaction later, perhaps even the obliteration of the script from human memory. Sejong and Sejo let sleeping dogs lie, and after their deaths a still-hostile bureaucracy let a sleeping script lie. It took over a century for the Correct Sounds to take social root, mainly among women, Buddhists, and others not greatly empowered in the world, to assure survival.

In such a vast and cohering context of language and history, the effort made in this chapter to establish a Mongolian dimension in the alphabetic and lexical projects emphasizes a rather small and limited part of the whole. Much more space could profitably have been devoted to the Chinese dimensions of the work, as represented especially by the *Yunhui* and the *Hongwu zhengyun*, or the Korean dimension as seen in the literary and orthographic debut of the Correct Sounds in the writing of pure Korean. But the Mongolian dimension, though a significant part of the Correct Sounds' background and interesting in itself, has not received much attention from other scholars and is not generally seen as a part of the alphabet's history, either in Korea or internationally. The present chapter is an attempt to throw some light into this corner and draw some new attention to a little known part of a very great story.

NOTES

1. This translation is considerably revised from that in my Ph.D. dissertation (Ledyard 1966: 259), which includes a complete translation of *Hunmin chŏng'ŭm haerye*.

2. Since the alphabet was announced in the last month of lunar 1443, it is often written that it was made in "late 1443." However, most of the last month of Sejong's twenty-fifth lunar year (cyclically *kyehae*) occurred in the first solar month of 1444 (Julian calendar); consequently I mention both 1443 and 1444 to be on the safe side. See *Sejong sillok*, 102.42a (Sjg 25/12/siwŏl=1443 Dec. 21 to 1444 Jan. 19).

3. *Sejong sillok*, 103.19b (Sjg 26/2/kyŏngja). In the reference here cited, Sejong was being criticized by Ch'oe Malli for suggesting such a thing, indicating that some announcement to this effect had been made by Sejong. His wishes in this regard are also mentioned by Chŏng Inji in his postface to *Hunmin chŏng'ŭm haerye*.

4. *T'aejong sillok*, 28.44a (Tjg 14/12/kihae); *Sejong sillok*, 105.25a–26b (Sjg 26/7'/im'in). Here and elsewhere, an apostrophe after the month indicates an intercalary month (*yunwŏl*).

5. *Sejong sillok*, 7.19a (Sjg 2/1'/muja); 26.30a (Sjg 6/12/ pyŏngjin); 61.54b (Sjg 15/9/sinmyo).

6. *Sejong sillok*, 56.33a–34b (Sjg 14/6/pyŏngsin); 59.32b (Sjg 15/2/musin).

7. See *Zhou li shu* section "Spring Officers," 31.8b (commentary by Jia Gongyan, seventh century, *Shisanjing zhushu* edition). Sejong has actually combined part of the *Zhou li* text with part of the commentary to it by the Han commentator Zheng Xuan. The probable reason for this is that Zheng gave two different interpretations of the phrase *shu ming* (my "written word"), and Sejong wanted to make clear which one he was following. The Zheng interpretation that Sejong preferred reads: "Some hold that in antiquity we said 'names' (*ming*) for what we now call 'graphs' (*zi*); that [the clerk] causes the Four Quarters to know the characters (*wenzi*) of books, so that the people may be able to read them."

8. *Sejong sillok*, 64.19a–19b (Sjg 16/4/kapsul).

9. *Sejong sillok*, 103.21b (Sjg 26/2/kyŏngja).

10. See Lee 1975.

11. The full evidence on this point can be omitted here, as it is amply developed in the essay by Ki-Moon Lee in this volume.

12. See Karlgren 1954. This work systematically sums up most of Karlgren's earlier work on the reconstruction of what people now prefer to call

"Middle Chinese" and "Old Chinese." During the past half century, many great scholars have worked to extend, reject, or revise Karlgren's work, but today one still has to begin with Karlgren himself in order to follow this literature.

13. Some of the principal monuments of the Chinese phonological tradition were mentioned in an order of 1412 to send to Seoul, from the Ch'ungju branch archives, such classics as the *Yupian*; Lu Deming's famous collection of phonetic glosses on the classics, *Jingdian shiwen* (first half of the seventh century); the *Guangyun*; and the *Wuyin zhizhang tu* (if this is not another title for the well-known *Qieyun zhizhang tu* attributed to Sima Guang, it may be rime tables associated with Han Daozhao's *Wuyin jiyun* of 1211). See *Taejong sillok*, 31.30a (Tjg 12/8/kimi, 12 Sept. 1412). The recall of these books would probably have been too early to involve Sejong (he was at that time a relatively obscure fifteen-year-old prince, still six years from the demotion of his brother and his own sudden and unexpected promotion to crown prince in 1418), but all of these works and no doubt others would have been available to him when, in later years, he began to acquire his mastery of this difficult field.

14. In the total scheme of the *Haerye*, it is necessary that a full letter serve as transliteration for this "null" initial. Consider this a "silent" h. The full system of roman transliterations is given in tables 1 and 2.

15. *Hunmin chŏng'ŭm haerye* (reprint, 1946). The original text of 1446, photolithographically reprinted in this edition, is unpaginated, but this passage would be on pp. 1b–2a. See full translation (here slightly revised) in Ledyard 1966: 229.

16. *Sejong sillok*, 122.5a (Sjg 30/10/kyŏng'o). A complete copy of the *Tongguk chŏng'un* of 1447 has survived intact and is in the Kŏn'guk University Library, Seoul. See *Tongguk chŏng'un* (photolithographic reprint, 1973).

17. The *Libu yunlüe* simplified the traditional list of 206 rimes to 106, and this arrangement generally held the field until modern times. An early edition bears a preface by Liu Yuan dated 1252. Since Liu was from a town named Pingshui, his short list of rimes was often referred to as the "Pingshui Rimes." But there is good evidence that this rime arrangement had already been in existence since 1231. See Wang Li 1957: 472–477. On page 475, Wang's date "Zhida eighth year=1329" is an error. The correct date is "Zhengda eighth year=1231."

18. *Sejong sillok*, 103.19a (Sjg 26/2/pyŏngsin). It was this project that stirred Ch'oe Malli to write his famous anti-alphabet memorial, in which he charged Sejong with, among many other things, "lightly revising the rime books already perfected by the ancients, interpolating into them the unattested vernacular script (*ŏnmun*)." See *Sejong sillok* 103.21a (Sjg 26/2/kyŏngja).

19. *Sejong sillok*, 14.9a (Sjg 3/11/kyemi). In this instance, Sejong was reading Zhu Xi's conversations on the *Daxue* (The Great Learning), which were recorded partly in the colloquial.

20. *Sejong sillok*, 64.3b (Sjg 16/4/kyech'uk); 64.28a (Sjg 16/5/kab'o).

21. On Yi Pyŏn's prowess in Chinese and his popularity as a teacher, see *Sejong sillok*, 63.17a (Sjg 16/2/ kab'in).

22. The *Sasŏng t'onggo* (hereafter abbreviated *T'onggo*) does not survive and seems to have been unmentioned in the records of Sejong's time. But its contents are largely known through the *Sasŏng t'onghae*, compiled in 1517 by Ch'oe Sejin, who states that Sin's work was done during Sejong's reign. The *Hongmu chŏng'un yŏkhun* (1455), in sixteen *kwŏn*, survives in an incomplete copy, with the first two *kwŏn* missing and with significant textual damage to the Korean readings in *kwŏn* 3 to 8. See *Hongmu chŏng'un yŏkhun*. The 1973(?) reprint includes "restoration" of missing or damaged parts by the modern editor, Pak Pyŏngch'ae. Sin Sukchu's original preface to the *Yŏkhun* is found in Sin's collected works, *Pohanjae chip*, 15.24a (photolithographic ed., 1937). In this preface, Sin says that the *T'onggo* was "fixed" (*chŏng*) by Sejong.

23. I use a photocopy of a mid-seventeenth-century reprint of the *Sasŏng t'onghae*, given as a royal gift to Assistant Right Royal Secretary (*ubu sŭngji*) Sim No on September 6, 1656 (Shunzhi 13/7/18). This copy was later owned by the Japanese bibliophile Maema Kyōsaku and is now in the Tenri University Library in Tenri, Japan.

24. *Sasŏng t'onggo* prolegomena (*pŏmnye*), 1b and 2b (paragraphs 4 and 8). For a valuable and wide-ranging study of the impact of "Mongol rimes" on Korean phonological studies in the fifteenth and sixteenth centuries, see Yu Ch'anggyun 1974. Yu deals with many of the issues raised here but does not consider graphic comparisons of the Korean and 'Phags-pa alphabets.

25. *Sasŏng t'onghae*, second set of prolegomena, 1b and 2b (paragraphs 4 and 8).

26. The *Menggu ziyun* has been photolithographically reprinted in Luo Changpei and Cai Meibiao 1959: 93–127. There are separate notes on the work by both Luo and Cai (pp. 83–91). They report the British Library number, OR.6972, and the information that it was acquired from a "Mrs. Rushell" in 1909, but do not provide any information on the origins of the *Menggu ziyun*. The British Library copy was clearly made during the Qianlong reign (1736–1796), since the names of all Qing emperors up through Qianlong appear in their standard taboo-avoiding forms. However, the copyist left no other sign of his work on the text. As copied, the text contains two prefaces, both dated 1308. The first is by a man named Liu Geng, who describes the editor, Zhu Boyan (=Bayan, a Mongol name), as having made an important contribution in correcting earlier editions of this work. The second is by the editor, who signs with his Chinese name, Zhu Zongwen. He also refers to earlier editions and identifies two of them by name—a "Hubei" edition and a "Zhedong" edition. Unfortunately, neither is given any kind of date. There can be no doubt, however, that the *Menggu ziyun* appeared long before 1308. In the collected writings of Wang Yishan (1214–?1286), the *Jiacun leigao* (*Siku quanshu zhenben* ed., fascicle 469), there is an undated preface (5.12a–13b)

Wang wrote for a book called the *Menggu yunlei* (Mongol Rime Classes) compiled by a certain Li Hongdao. From Wang's remarks that Li's book has only fifteen rime headings and that the characters are classified under these headings regardless of tone, it is clear that the *Menggu yunlei* is the same book, or the same kind of book, as the *Menggu ziyun*. Just when the *Yunlei*—or *its* predecessor—first appeared can only be guessed. The *terminus post quem* would be the date of Wang's death, which is not precisely known. But in 1286, Wang left a number of writings suggesting he was a dying man putting his affairs in order: in that year, he wrote the preface to his collected works, his own autonecrology (29.15b–19a), and a note on his old family homestead, in which he charged his son to keep up its maintenance (7.9a–11a). It would not seem that he would have lived much longer. A scanning of his entire literary collection finds no date after 1286. This evidence makes it doubtful that his preface to the *Menggu yunlei* would have been written later than this. The *terminus ante quem* would be no earlier than 1269, when the 'Phags-pa script was promulgated (*Yuan shi*, 6.122 and 202.4518). But it was probably later. A good guess would be 1275, when Khubilai established a branch of the Hanlin Academy to deal exclusively with the 'Phags-pa script (*Yuan shi*, 8.165). My guess is that the earliest version of the *Mongol Rimes* would have appeared between 1275 and 1286.

It is presumed that some version of the *Menggu yunlei* or *ziyun* reached Korea during late Koryŏ times, when the 'Phags-pa script became well known in connection with Yuan dynasty imperial decrees and other formal documents sent to Koryŏ (see below, note 41), and when there would have been genuine need for reference material on the 'Phags-pa script. However, I have found no mention of it in any Koryŏ source. The earliest Korean record would be the *Menggu yun* mentioned by Sin Sukchu no later than ca. 1450; the latest would be the references made by Ch'oe Sejin. In addition to those of 1517 already mentioned, there are three others, in 1527, in connection with the well-known Korean textbooks of colloquial Chinese the *Nogŏltae* (The Old Cathayan) and *Pak T'ongsa* (Interpreter Pak). Ch'oe's prolegomena to his editions of these works are also affixed to the beginning of the second fascicle of the 1656 edition of the *Sasŏng t'onghae*; in these, three references to *Menggu yun* or *Mengyun* are found on page 5b (paragraph 7).

27. It might be more accurate to say here "the *adapted* system of 'Phags-pa letters," since originally the 'Phags-pa letters were derived from the letters and sounds of the Tibetan alphabet. As suggested by Sir Gerard Clauson, the refining of the 'Phags-pa alphabet for purposes of Chinese transcription may have been the responsibility of the branch of the Hanlin Academy established in 1275, mentioned in the preceding note. See Clauson 1959: 303.

28. *Sasŏng t'onghae*, note at the end of the second table (following the preface), which lays out the *Yunhui*'s initials.

29. The *Yunhui* has long been lost, but its general outline is known through

the *Gujin yunhui juyao*, an abridgment edited by Xiong Zhong in 1297. The Chinese scholar Zhao Yintang, in remarks quoted by Luo and Cai (1959: 84), points out that in the general tables of initials in the prefatory matter of the abridgment, there is a note saying "same as the initials of the *Menggu ziyun.*"

It is important to note that although the project to gloss the *Yunhui* was dropped, the Koreans did later produce their own printed editions of the *Gujin yunhui juyao*—a direct republishing of the Chinese text, with no intrusion or mention of Korean alphabetic glosses—in which this same information is found. However, between the Chinese edition as quoted by Zhao and at least one of the Korean editions, there is an important difference in wording, which I will examine later in discussing the "Old Seal." One Korean edition, which superficially appears to be a movable type edition of the sixteenth or seventeenth century, but which is not dated or identified by the modern publisher, has been photolithographically reprinted in Korea: see *Kogŭm unhoe kŏyo* (1975). See also note 51 below.

30. Zhu Zongwen's preface to the *Menggu ziyun* also emphasizes the special relationship of the Mongol consonants to the initial system used in the *Yunhui.*

31. Ligeti, for example, believes that the *Menggu ziyun* sound system is in effect a transcription of the *Yunhui*'s (1956: 37, note). But given that the *Menggu ziyun* or its ancestor most probably predated 1286 and the *Yunhui* was not compiled until 1292, I argue that the situation was reversed.

32. *Sejong sillok*, 107.3a (Sjg 27/1/sinsa). The Liaodong trips are mentioned in various accounts of Sin's career written by Sin's friends after his death in 1475. These are included in the appendix (*purok*) to the *Pohanjae chip*, 10, 22a, and 29a. The missions are also noted in connection with Sŏng Sammun in *Yuk sŏnsaeng yugo* (Literary Remains of the Six Gentlemen; ed. Pak Sunggo, 1878), 1.18a. Huang Zan (?1413–?1448) was a Ming academician who had been banished, first to a frontier post in Shanxi, then to Liaodong, as the result of a political involvement in the middle 1430s. For what little biographical material can be found on him, see Ledyard 1965: 129–138. Interestingly enough, some later Chosŏn dynasty scholars believed Huang Zan's contribution to be the transmission of the 'Phags-pa alphabet to Sin Sukchu. See *Sŏngho sasŏl*, comp. Yi Ik (1681–1763), vol. 1, p. 553, and *Ŏnmun chi*, comp. Yu Hŭi (1773–1837), pp. 11 and 45–47. Yi Ik seems to have known of the 'Phags-pa script only through literary references. It is clear from what he says that he did not understand the difference between the 'Phags-pa and Uighur scripts used for Mongolian, and we cannot be sure that he had ever seen a sample of 'Phags-pa writing.

33. *Sejong sillok*, 127.22a (Sjg 32/1/musin). Ni Qian received his literary degree in 1439 and died in 1479. He wrote an account of his mission to Korea, *Chaoxian jishi* (Notes on Chosŏn), but it contains no mention of any phonological discussions.

34. *Pohanjae chip*, 15.24b.
35. *Pohanjae chip*, appendix, 18b, 25a, 32a.
36. *Haedong cheguk ki* (1933), preface dated 1471.
37. *Haedong cheguk ki*, 37b.
38. *Sejong sillok*, 34.3a (Sjg 8/10/kyeyu).
39. *Yuan shi*, 6.122 and 202.4518.
40. For general information on 'Phags-pa, see Poppe 1957; Clauson 1959; and Luo and Cai 1959. Poppe's work considers mainly materials in the Mongolian language; Clauson explores the phonetic problems of 'Phags-pa with reference both to Mongolian and to the *Menggu ziyun*. Given Luo and Cai's emphasis on documenting the history of 'Phags-pa as a transcription medium for Chinese, their work is most pertinent to the issues discussed here.
41. Just a few years after the invention of the 'Phags-pa script, a decree in the new writing arrived in the Koryŏ capital, Kaegyŏng, from Khubilai, but no one could then read it; see *Koryŏ sa*, 27.36a (Wŏnjong 14/1/imsul=1273 Jan. 28). Koryŏ quickly got used to this script, and many 'Phags-pa documents accumulated in its archives. In a gesture of accommodation to Ming, the Koryŏ government in 1385 "returned" eight patents that had been written in 'Phags-pa and conferred upon Koryŏ kings by Yuan emperors. *Koryŏ sa*, 135.46a. The 'Phags-pa script is also mentioned in one of King Ch'ungsŏn's famous conversations with Chinese scholars, this one concerning the erection of 'Phags-pa inscriptions in honor of Confucius. *Koryŏ sa*, 34.6b–7a. On these inscriptions, see Luo and Cai 1959: 33–34 and plates 4–8.
42. *Sejong sillok*, 19.9b (Sjg 5/1/kiyu); 19.11b (5/2/ŭlmyo).
43. *Kyŏngguk taejŏn* (1934), 3.5b.
44. The same remarks could be applied to those who have argued that the Korean letters are derived from the Tibetan. If these scholars had known of the 'Phags-pa script and its relationship to Tibetan, they would undoubtedly have adopted a 'Phags-pa–Korean theory. A short list of publications by such theorists would include Rosny 1864; Taylor 1883; Lacouperie 1892; and Hulbert 1892 and 1896. The dates of these articles belong to the dark ages of Korean scholarship in the West, and few today would accept either their methodology or most of their conclusions. However, what these people saw was partly what Hope saw, and however attenuated, there was something to it.
45. See Ledyard 1966: 15–16.
46. *Hunmin chŏng'ŭm haerye* (unpaginated, but the passage translated would be on pp. 3b–4a). Translation adapted from Ledyard 1966: 233.
47. The first is in the original announcement of the Korean alphabet, in early 1444: "Its letters imitate the Old Seal" (*ki cha pang kojŏn*). *Sejong sillok*, 102.42a (Sjg 25/12/siwŏl). The second is in Ch'oe Malli's attack on the alphabet, which I will consider below. The third is in Chŏng Inji's postface to *Hunmin chŏng'ŭm haerye*, p. 31b: "While depicting outlines [of speech organs], these letters imitate the Old Seal" (*sang hyŏng i pang kojŏn*). Beyond

these three unelaborated statements, no other remark on the "Old Seal" connection by people close to the event can be found in presently available sources.

48. For the guesses of the *sirhak* scholar Yi Tŏngmu (1741–1793), see his volume of essays and studies, *Ch'ŏngjanggwan chŏnsŏ*, *kwŏn* 54 (unpaginated, but the tenth page). For those of a dedicated Western investigator, who for his time wrote a very good study of the alphabet, see Gale 1912: table 12.

49. The *Guangyun* dictionary contained 206 rimes, but many editions linked two of them with only a small number of characters into one, making 205. Wang's mention of fifteen rime headings is crucial to the linking of Li Hongdao's book *Menggu yunlei* with the presently surviving *Menggu ziyun*, which also has fifteen. In specifying only thirty-two *zimu*, Wang Yishan has subtracted from the traditional list the "raised linguals," which by his time had merged with the "upright incisors." Unaware of vowels and how they work, Wang does not count the 'Phags-pa vowels, and of course without them he could not make his "tens, hundreds, thousands, myriads" of words.

50. Wang Yishan, *Jiacun leigao*, 5.12a–13b.

51. I rely for this information on Yu Ch'anggyun 1966: 206, note 1. Yu uses a Korean edition of the *Gujin yunhui juyao* that has a postface by Yi Sik (1584–1647) and is now in the Tōyō Bunko in Tokyo. The same passage, presumably also on the basis of the Tōyō Bunko copy, is also discussed in a later study by Yu Ch'anggyun (1974). The passage in question also occurs in the reprint, *Kogŭm unhoe kŏyo*, p. 3 in the modern pagination, but since in the original a seal (what an irony!) had been impressed over this very spot and because the quality of the photolithographic reproduction is poor, it is not possible to determine whether the character in question is *ju* or *meng*. The original date of this Korean edition of the *Gujin yunhui juyao* is unclear, and the question is not even addressed in the explanatory matter (written by Steffan Rosén) provided by the modern publisher. Korean bibliographies list five or six surviving copies of this work, some of them incomplete, which are evidently not all of the same printing.

52. In his *Monggo ullyak*, Yu refers to the same passage as if the character was *meng*, without discussion of any misprint (1974: 66).

53. *Menggu ziyun*, 1.6a–b (Luo and Cai 1959: 98).

54. The *Shilin guangji* is today quite rare; there are some copies in Japan, some in Beijing, and some fragments in the Vatican Library. I have never seen more than photographs of the pages in 'Phags-pa published in Luo and Cai 1959 and in Ligeti 1956. Even these show great differences. Luo and Cai have plates from two editions illustrating texts of the *Baijia xing*, the first (pp. 57–68) from a 1340 edition now in the Beijing University Library, the second from a recut Japanese edition of 1699 based on a Yuan xylograph of 1325 (pp. 69–82). Ligeti publishes a *Baijia xing* text he says is from the 1699 edition, but it does not match the one shown in Luo and Cai; in fact it corresponds more closely with their 1340 edition. In checking out this book in various bibliogra-

phies, both Chinese and Japanese, I have observed many differences of title, number of *juan*, section numbers, and so on. It needs a thorough study. As for Korean holdings, I know only of the copy available in Sejong's time. There is a notice of the book being brought to Seoul by a returning envoy in 1402 in *T'aejong sillok*, 2.23a (Tjg 2/1/kyehae). T'aejong's citation of the *Shilin guangji* is attested twice: once in 1411, *T'aejong sillok*, 21.6a (Tjg 11/1/pyŏngja), and once by retrospective reference in Sejong's time, in 1440, *Sejong sillok* 88.1b (Sjg 22/1/ sinhae). Sejong's bell-casting center referred to the *Shilin guangji* in 1431: *Sejong sillok*, 50.38b (Sjg 12/12'/kapchin). It is cited in the *Oryeŭi* (Monograph on Ritual) in *Sejong sillok*, 128.8a and 9b. As far as I can determine, the copy used by T'aejong and Sejong has not survived, unless it is one of those now in Japan, where Japanese bibliographies place three Yuan editions. See *Toshoryō kanseki senbon shomoku* (Tokyo, 1930), 3.40a, and *Naikaku bunko kanseki bunrui mokuroku* (Tokyo, 1956), 293–294.

55. *Shilin guangji* (1325 xylograph recut in Japan in 1699), section 4, 10.53a, reproduced in Luo and Cai 1959: 71. The phrase "text of the 'Hundred Surnames' put into seal by the Mongols" (*Menggu suo zhuan Baijia xing*) does not mean a *Baijia xing* written in ancient seal-style characters. The text as printed in the *Shilin guangji* in all three illustrated cases has the Chinese characters of the text—a riming list of surnames—in normal *kaishu* style and underneath each surname its transliteration in normal 'Phags-pa letters.

56. *Shilin guangji* (1340 edition), (juan unknown), p. 10b, reproduced in Luo and Cai 1959: 59.

57. *Shushi huiyao* (photolithographic reprint of a Hongwu period [1368–1398] xylograph, in *Wujin Taoshi yiyuan*, 1929), 21b–23a. Speaking of the versatility of Indian phonetics, the text quotes the Song encyclopedist Zheng Qiao as saying: "Whether the cry of the crane, the sound of the wind, the cackle of fowl or the barking of dogs, whether Heaven-shaking thunder and lightning, or the buzz of a mosquito or a gadfly passing your ear—all can be transcribed" (22b). This is most curious, since Chŏng Inji's postface to *Hunmin chŏng'ŭm haerye* says of Sejong's Correct Sounds: "Even the sound of the wind, the cry of the crane, the cackle of fowl, and the barking of dogs—all may be written." Perhaps he thought it was going too far to add the thunder, lightning, and bugs. In any case, this language makes it likely that Chŏng Inji—one of the three contemporaries to make reference to the "old seal"—was familiar at least with Zheng Qiao's essay, but perhaps also with the *Shushi huiyao*.

58. *Fashu kao*, 2.3b.

59. *Sejong sillok*, 88.2a–b (Sjg 22/1/kyech'uk).

60. *Sejong sillok*, 103.20a (Sjg 26/2/kyŏngja).

61. *Yongjae ch'onghwa*, 7.178–179.

62. *Sejong sillok*, 114.12a, 13b (Sjg 28/10/kapchin and chŏngmi).

REFERENCES

Primary Sources and Traditional Editions, by Title

Ch'ŏngjanggwan chŏnsŏ 青莊館全書 (Writings of Yi Tŏngmu 李德懋). 71 *kwŏn*. Compiled by Yi's son Yi Kwanggyu 李光葵, 1795. Manuscript, Seoul National University Library.

Fashu kao (An investigation of calligraphic models). 8 *juan*. Comp. Sheng Ximing 盛熙明, 1331. Reprinted in series Lianting shi'er zhong 楝亭十二種, ed. Cao Yin 曹寅, 1712.

Haedong cheguk ki 東海諸國紀 (Notes on the countries in the Eastern Sea—Japan, Ryukyu Kingdom). 1 *kwŏn*. Comp. Sin Sukchu 申叔舟, 1471, with minor supplementary material added by others up to 1501. Movable type ed., ca. 1506. Photolithographically reprinted in *Chōsen shiryō sōkan* 朝鮮史料叢刊, no. 2. Seoul: Chōsenshi henshūkai, 1933.

Hongmu chŏng'un yŏkhun 洪武正韻譯訓 (Transliterated readings of the Hongwu zhengyun, The Correct Rimes of the Hongwu period [1368–1399]). 16 *kwŏn*. Comp. Sin Sukchu 申叔舟, 1455. Photolithographic reprint of *kwŏn* 3–16, with *kwŏn* 3–8 partly damaged; "restoration" of damaged parts by Pak Pyŏngch'ae 朴炳采. Seoul: Koryŏ University Press, ?1973.

Hunmin chŏng'ŭm 訓民正音 (Correct sounds for the instruction of the people). Comp. King Sejong 世宗大王. Original xylographic ed. 1446, together with *Hunmin chŏng'ŭm haerye* (see next). Photolithographic reprint, Seoul: Chosŏn'ŏ hakhoe, 1946.

Hunmin chŏng'ŭm haerye 訓民正音解例 (Explanations and examples for the Correct Sounds for the Instruction of the People). Comp. Chŏng Inji 鄭麟趾, Sin Sukchu 申叔舟, et al. Original xylographic ed. 1446, together with *Hunmin chŏng'ŭm* (see preceding). Photolithographic reprint, Seoul: Chosŏn'ŏ hakhoe, 1946.

Jiacun leigao 稼村類藁 (Classified draft of the writings of Wang Yishan 王義山 [1214–?1286]). Hand copy (ca. 1770s), photolithographically reprinted in *Siku quanshu zhenben* 四庫全書珍本 (Taipei, n.d.), vol. 469.

Koryŏ sa 高麗史 (History of Koryŏ). 139 *kwŏn*. Comp. Chŏng Inji 鄭麟趾 et al., 1454. Photolithograpic reprint, 3 vols., Seoul: Yŏnhŭi [later Yŏnse] University, Tongbanghak yŏn'guso, 1955.

Kyŏngguk taejŏn 經國大典 ([Chosŏn] Administrative Code). 6 *kwŏn*. Comp. Sŏ Kŏjŏng 徐居正 et al., 1469. Reprint, Seoul: Chōsen sōtokufu Chūsūin, 1934.

Menggu ziyun 蒙古字韻 (Mongol rimes). Ed. Zhu (Bayan) Zongwen 朱(伯顏)宗文, 1308. Photolithographic reprint of mid- or late-eighteenth-century hand copy in Luo Changpei and Cai Meibiao 1959.

Ŏnmun chi 諺文志 (History of Ŏnmun). Comp. Yu Hŭi 柳僖, 1824. Edited with commentary by Yu Ch'angdon 柳昌惇. Seoul: Sin'gu munhwasa, 1958.

Pohanjae chip 保閑齋集 (Collected writings of Sin Sukchu 申叔舟 [1417– 1475]). Expanded and supplemented by Sin Suk 申洬 1645. Photolithographically reprinted in *Chōsen shiryō sōkan* 朝鮮史料叢刊, no. 14. Seoul: Chōsenshi henshū kai, 1937.

Sasŏng t'onghae 四聲通解 (Complete explanation of the Four Tones). 2 *kwŏn*. Comp. Ch'oe Sejin 崔世珍, 1517. Photocopy of a mid-seventeenth-century reprint, presentation copy of 1656, now in Tenri University Library, Tenri, Japan.

Sejong sillok. See Sejong taewang sillok.

Sejong taewang sillok 世宗大王實錄. 163 *kwŏn*. Comp. Chŏng Inji 鄭麟趾, Hwangbo In 黃甫仁, et al., 1452–1454. First movable type edition, 1466– 1472. Photolithographic reprint in vols. 2–6 of *Chosŏn wangjo sillok* 朝鮮王朝實錄, 48 vols. Seoul: National History Compilation Committee, 1955– 1958.

Shushi huiyao 書史會要 (Essentials of the history of calligraphy). 9 *juan*. Comp. Tao Zongyi 陶宗儀 (1320–1400). Photolithographic reprint of a Hongwu period (1368–1398) xylograph in the series Wujin Taoshi yiyuan, 1929.

Sŏngho sasŏl 星湖僿說 (Sŏngho's frivolous ideas). 30 *kwŏn*. Comp. Yi Ik 李瀷 (1681–1763, ho Sŏngho). Manuscript kept by Yi Ik's descendants, photolithographic reprint, 2 vols. Seoul: Kyŏnghŭi ch'ulp'ansa, 1967.

T'aejong sillok. *See* T'aejong taewang sillok.

T'aejong taewang sillok 太宗大王實錄. 36 *kwŏn*. Comp. Pyŏn Kyeryang 卞季良, Yun Hoe 尹淮, et al., 1423–1430; rev. Maeng Sasŏng 孟思誠, Hwang Hŭi 黃喜, et al., 1430–1431. First printed edition (movable type), 1603–1604. Photolithographic reprint in vols. 1–2 of *Chosŏn wangjo sillok*, 48 vols. Seoul: National History Compilation Committee, 1955–1958.

TaeMyŏngnyul chikhae 大明律直解 (Direct interpretation of the *Da Ming lü* [Ming penal code]). 1395. Reprint, Seoul: Chōsen sōtokufu Chūsūin, 1935.

Tongguk chŏng'un 東國正韻. 1973. (The correct rimes of Korea). 6 *kwŏn*. Comp. Sin Sukchu 申叔舟 et al., 1447. Photolithographic reprint of the original movable type edition. Seoul: Kŏn'guk University Press, 1973.

Yongjae ch'onghwa 慵齋叢話 (Yongjae's miscellany). 3 *kwŏn*. Comp. Sŏng Hyŏn 成俔 (1439–1504). Collected in *Taedong yasŭng* 大東野乘 (Great Korean collection of unofficial histories), compiled by persons unknown during the seventeenth century, printed in 13 vols. Vol. 7. Seoul: Chōsen kosho kankōkai, 1909.

Yuan shi 元史 (History of the Yuan dynasty). 210 *juan*. Comp. Song Lian 宋濂 et al., 1369. Modern edition, 15 vols. Beijing: Zhonghua shuju, 1976.

Yuk sŏnsaeng yugo 六先生遺稾 (Literary remains of the Six Gentlemen [among them Sŏng Sammun 成三問, 1418–1456]), Ed. Pak Sunggo 朴崇古, 1878.

Zhou li shu (Commentary on the *Zhou li* [Rites of Zhou]). Comp. Jia Gongyan 賈公彥 (seventh century). Shisanjing zhushu 十三經注疏 edition. Taipei, 1976.

Modern Scholarly Literature

Clauson, Gerard. 1959. The *h*P'ags-pa alphabet. *Bulletin of the School of Oriental and African Studies* 22, part 2, 300–323.

Gale, James S. 1912. The Korean alphabet. *Transactions of the Korea Branch of the Royal Asiatic Society* 4: 13–61.

Hope, E. R. 1957. Letter shapes in the Korean Onmun and Mongol *h*P'ags-pa alphabets. *Oriens* 10: 150–159.

Hulbert, Homer B. 1892, 1896. The Korean alphabet. *Korea Review* 1 and 3: 233–237.

Karlgren, Bernhard. 1954. Compendium of phonetics in ancient and archaic Chinese. *Bulletin of the Museum of Far Eastern Antiquities* (Stockholm), 22: 211–367.

Lacouperie, Terrien de. 1892. On the Corean, Aino, and Fusang writings. *T'oung Pao* 3: 440–465.

Ledyard, Gari. 1965. Biographical notes on Huang Tsan 黃瓚. *Asea yŏn'gu* 亞細亞研究 (Koryŏ University), 8/1: 129–138.

———. 1966. The Korean language reform of 1446: The origin, background, and early history of the Korean alphabet. Ph.D. dissertation, University of California, Berkeley, 1966. Reprint, Ann Arbor: University Microfilms International (catalogue no. 66-8333).

Lee, Peter H. 1975. Songs of flying dragons: A critical reading. Cambridge: Harvard University Press.

Ligeti, L[ouis]. 1956. Le Po kia sing en écriture 'phags-pa. *Acta Orientalia Hungarica* 6: 1–52.

Luo Changpei and Cai Meibiao. 1959. Basiba-zi yu Yuandai Hanyu [Ziliao huibian] 八思巴字與元代漢語〔資料彙編〕(The 'Phags-pa script and Yuan period Chinese [Collection of source materials]). Beijing: Kexue chubanshe.

Poppe, Nicholas. 1957. The Mongolian Monuments in hP'ags-pa Script. Tr. from the Russian by John R. Krueger. Wiesbaden: Otto Harrassowitz (Göttinger Asiatische Forschungen, Band 8).

Rosny, Léon de. 1864. Aperçu de la langue coréenne. *Journal Asiatique*, 6th series, 3: 287–325.

Taylor, Isaac. 1883. *The Alphabet*. 2 vols. London.

Wang Li. 1957. *Hanyu yinyunxue* 漢語音韻學 (Phonology of Chinese). Beijing: Zhonghua shuju. 2nd printing.

Yu Ch'anggyun 兪昌均. 1966. Tongguk chŏng'un yŏn'gu [Yŏn'gu p'yŏn] 東國正韻研究〔研究篇〕(A Study of the Tongguk chŏng'un). Seoul: Hyŏngsŏl ch'ulp'ansa 螢雪出版社.

———. 1974. Monggo ullyak kwa Sasŏng t'onggo ŭi yŏn'gu 蒙古韻略 과 四聲通考 의研究 (A Study of the Menggu yunlue and the Sasŏng t'onggo). Seoul: Hyŏngsŏl ch'ulp'ansa.

CHARACTER GLOSSARY

Except in the cases of a few frequently mentioned individuals, the following listings do not include books and their authors or editors cited in the notes for whose names the characters are provided in the reference list. Nor do they include characters for common place names, sexagenary cyclical designations, or publishers.

Persons

Cangjie 倉頡
Ch'oe Malli 崔萬里
Ch'oe Sejin 崔世珍
Chŏng Inji 鄭麟趾
Gu Yewang 顧野王
Han Daozhao 韓道昭
Huang Gongshao 黃公紹
Huang Zan 黃瓚
Kong Anguo 孔安國
Li Hongdao 李洪道
Liu Geng 劉更
Liu Yuan 劉淵
Lu Deming 陸德明
Luo Changpei 羅常培
Maema Kyōsaku 前間恭策
Ni Qian 倪謙
Sejo [taewang] 世祖大王
Sejong [taewang] 世宗大王
Sheng Ximing 盛熙名
Sima Guang 司馬光
Sin Sukchu 申叔舟
Sŏng Sammun 成三問
Sŏngjong [taewang] 成宗大王
Suyang [taegun] 首陽大君
Tao Zongyi 陶宗儀
T'aejo [taewang] 太祖大王
Wang Yishan 王義山
Wŏnjong [taewang] 元宗大王
Yi Ik 李瀷
Yi Pyŏn 李邊
Zheng Qiao 鄭樵
Zheng Xuan 鄭玄
Zhu Boyan 朱伯顏
Zhu Xi 朱熹
Zhu Zongwen 朱宗文

Book Titles

Baijia xing 百家姓
Chaoxian jishi 朝鮮紀事
Ch'ŏbawŏlchin to 帖兒月真吐
Ch'ŏbwŏlchin to 帖月真吐
Da Ming lü 大明律
Daxue 大學
Guang yun 廣韻
Gujin yunhui 古今韻會
Gujin yunhui juyao 古今韻會舉要
Haerye 解例
Hongwu zhengyun 洪武正韻
Hunmin chŏng'ŭm 訓民正音
Jingdian shiwen 經典釋文
Libu yunlüe 禮部韻略
Menggu yun 蒙古韻
Menggu yunlei 蒙古韻類
Menggu yunlüe 蒙古韻略
Menggu ziyun 蒙古字韻
Mengyun 蒙韻
Nogŏltae 老乞大
Nongsa chiksŏl 農事直說
Nongsang jiyao 農桑輯要
Oryeŭi 五禮儀
Pak t'ongsa 朴通事
Po kia sing 百家姓
Qieyun 切韻
Qieyun zhizhangtu 切韻指掌圖
Samgang haengsil 三綱行實
Sasŏng t'onggo 四聲通考
Sasŏng t'onghae 四聲通解

Shilin guangji 事林廣記
Sŏkpo sangjŏl 釋譜詳節
Taemyŏngnyul chikhae 大明律直解
Tongguk chŏng'un 東國正韻
Wŏrin ch'ŏngang chi kok 月印千江之曲
Wŏrin sŏkpo 月印釋譜
Wujin Taoshi yiyuan 武津陶氏藝苑
Wuyun jiyun 五韻集韻
Wuyun zhizhangtu 五韻指掌圖
Yongbi ŏch'ŏn ka 龍飛御天歌
Yongjae ch'onghwa 慵齋叢話
Yuan shi 元史
Yuk sŏnsaeng yugo 六先生遺藁
Yunhui 韻會
Yunhui juyao 韻會舉要
Yunlei 韻類
Yupian 玉篇
Zhou li 周禮

Other Terms

bi/pyŏk 闢
cao 草
chikhae 直解
chŏng 定
ch'uk 縮
chungsŏng 中聲
Ch'obawŏlchin 帖兒月真
Ch'ungju 忠州
deng 等
dengyun tu 等韻圖
fan 梵
fanqie 反切
fanshu 梵書
fanyin 梵音
fei 非
fu 敷
gu 古
guwen 古文
hap/he 合
Hunmin chŏng'ŭm 訓民正音
hunsŭp 訓習
hyangch'al 鄉札
idu 吏讀
juan 卷
kai 開
kaishu 開書
kana 假名
ki cha pang kojŏn 其字倣古篆
ko/-go 古
kwŏn 卷
li 隸
Menggu 蒙古
Menggu suo zhuan 蒙古所篆
Menggu xinzi 蒙古新字
Menggu zi 蒙古字
Menggu ziti 蒙古字體
mi 微
ming 明
Monggo 蒙古
ngi 疑
ngu (yu) 魚
ni 泥
niang 孃
ohaeng 五行
Ŏnmun 諺文
paizi 牌子
pang ko chi chŏnmun 倣古之篆文
pang kojŏn 倣古篆
panjŏl 反切
Pingshui 平水
pon'un 本韻
pŏmnye 凡例
purok 附錄
pyŏk/bi 闢
sadae 事大
sancai 三才
sang hyŏng i pang kojŏn 象形而倣古篆
Sayŏg'wŏn 司譯院
she 攝
siwŏl 是月
Tie'eryuezhen 帖兒月真

wei 微
wenzi 文字
wuxing 五行
Yan 燕
yŏk 譯
yunwŏl 閏月
Zhedong 折東
Zhengda 正大
zhen zhuan 真篆
Zhida 至大
zhuan li 篆隸
zhuan zimu 篆字母
zi 字
zimu 字母
·ing 影
·wa ム

4

THE PRINCIPLES UNDERLYING THE INVENTION OF THE KOREAN ALPHABET

Pyong-Hi Ahn

The principles used in the design of the letters of the Korean alphabet are explained in the *Hunmin chŏng'ŭm haerye* (Explanation and Examples of the Correct Sounds for the Instruction of the People). In the section of that document titled "Explanation of the Designing of the Letters" (*Chejahae*), the shapes of the letters are said to "depict the outlines [of the forms they represent]" (象形). The term "depict outlines" derives from traditional Chinese graphic science, where it is used in the meaning of "pictographic," one of the "Six Principles of Writing" (*liushu* 六書) found in the construction of Chinese characters. However, only the basic letters of the alphabet used to represent initial sounds can be said to be purely pictographic. The letters used to represent medial sounds (the vowels) can be said to have been formed according to the nonpictorial, more abstract principle known in Chinese lexicography as *zhishi* (指事). The initial letters formed by adding strokes to the basic shapes can be said to have been constructed according to a third principle, that of *xingsheng* (形聲), the "phonetic compound." Medial letters formed by combining basic shapes can be said to have been formed by another of the traditional six principles, the one known as *huiyi* (會意), or "joined meanings." In this way, it can be seen that *liushu*, the traditional graphic analysis of Chinese characters, underlies the construction of the Korean alphabet.

INTRODUCTION

The principles used in inventing the original twenty-eight letters of the Korean alphabet are explained in detail in the section of the

Hunmin chŏng'ŭm haerye (Explanation and Examples of the Correct Sounds for the Instruction of the People; hereafter called *Haerye*) titled "Explanations of the Designing of the Letters" (*Chejahae*). The many hypotheses about the invention of the alphabet formulated before the *Haerye* text was found, therefore, must be reconsidered in this light.

To understand how the Korean alphabet was created, we must take into account the intellectual circumstances out of which it arose and that led up to the writing of the *Haerye*.[1] The orthographic principles underlying this unique writing system are explained by the scholars who composed the text of the *Chejahae*. There is no reason to question these explanations; the authors, after all, participated in the invention. The problem is how to understand what the explanations mean: whether to be satisfied with the words of the explanations themselves or to find possible hidden meanings by reading between the lines. Taking the latter point of view, I think that the men who wrote these explanations were influenced by the graphic analysis found in the traditional study of the Chinese script and that the *liushu*, the "Six Principles of Writing" used to classify the graphic structure of Chinese characters, lie behind the explanations of the *Chejahae*.[2]

Though my own analyses are to be presented in the latter part of this chapter, I would like to point out, first of all, that the letters to be discussed in this study of the principles used in inventing the alphabet are limited to the original twenty-eight letters. King Sejong created seventeen initial and eleven medial letters. These letters are referred to by the king as the "newly created twenty-eight letters" in his preface to the *Hunmin chŏng'ŭm*, and they are called the "twenty-eight letters of the Correct Sounds" in the *Chejahae*. To be sure, the *Haerye* also provides descriptions of certain orthographic principles for combining symbols: initials and medials are written together to form syllables; two of the basic consonant symbols are combined vertically to represent a bilabial fricative; consonants are written side by side to form clusters. Needless to say, however, these combinatory principles do not constitute the creation of new letters. They are clearly secondary. For this reason, I restrict my discussions to Sejong's basic twenty-eight letters and their relationship to the *liushu*.

THE "SIX PRINCIPLES"

The *Chejahae* text describing the construction of the alphabet is well known and readily available elsewhere.[3] There is therefore no need to repeat the body of the text here. Instead, the explanations given there are summarized in tables 1 and 2.

The first thing to be noted about these explanations is that five of the letters for the initials and three of the letters for the medials (the vowels), were made first; the rest of the letter shapes were devised based on those first eight shapes. Thus, not all twenty-eight letters were constructed separately. Only the basic eight letters were constructed independently of the other letter shapes, while the remaining twenty were devised by adding one or more strokes to the basic graphs or by using shapes associated with them.

These processes used in the construction of the letter shapes are well known. Less clear to linguistic scholars today, however, is the

Table 1. Seventeen Initial Letters

Basic Letters	Explanation of Shape	Adding Strokes		Different Body
ㄱ k	root of the tongue closing epiglottis		ㅋ kh	
ㄴ n	the tongue touching the hard palate	ㄷ t	ㅌ th	ㄹ l
ㅁ m	mouth	ㅂ p	ㅍ ph	
ㅅ s	teeth	ㅈ c	ㅊ ch	ㅿ z
ㅇ* o	throat	ㆆ ?	ㅎ h	ㆁ ng

*This letter, called a laryngeal in the *Haerye*, functioned in most cases as a "zero phoneme" used to maintain the canonical shape of an initial consonant for syllables that actually began with a vowel. However, it has also been shown by philologists to have represented a voiced velar fricative in certain phonological environments; see Lee Ki-Moon 1977: 15–26.

Table 2. Eleven Medial Letters

Basic Letters	Explanation of Shape	Arising first		Arising Second	
ㆍ o	Heaven/Round	ㅗ wo	ㅏ a	ㅛ ywo	ㅑ ya
ㅡ u	Earth/Level	ㅜ wu	ㅓ e	ㅠ ywu	ㅕ ye
ㅣ i	Man/Standing				

significance of these processes. What the relevant passages in the *Chejahae* text mean to us today is not necessarily the same as the nuanced meaning they would have had in the Korean intellectual world of the fifteenth century. In order to grasp the true meaning of the *Chejahae* explanations, we must reexamine them in light of the scholarship of the time. Only then can we begin to understand the actual principles underlying the letter shapes.

In what follows, I will show how closely the Korean letter constructions fit into the traditional graphic categories used in the analysis of Chinese characters. This correspondence could not have been accidental. In my view, the intellectual processes used to make the letter shapes of the Korean alphabet followed the principles thought to underlie the construction of Chinese graphs.

In China, the traditional "science of writing" (文字學) began with the appearance of the dictionary *Shuowen jiezi* (說文解字) in the Han dynasty. In that work, which provided the framework of graphic analysis used in East Asia until modern times, all characters were divided according to their composition into two general categories, *wen* (文) and *zi* (字). *Wen* is a "single body" character that cannot be reduced (or separated) further, and *zi* is a "combined body" character analyzable into two or more simpler elements, usually *wen*. The character 文, for example, is considered an elemental, *wen* character (in origin, the graph is thought to be a pictographic representation of a man with tattooing on the breast); the "combined body" character 字, in contrast, is composed of two elements, the *wen* character 子 under a "roof."

Within this bipartite framework, all characters were further classified according to the *liushu*. Of these six principles, four are used to explain the compositional structure of characters. The first two, the *xiangxing* (pictographic) and *zhishi* (roughly, ideographic) principles, refer to the structure of elemental, *wen* characters. Composite, *zi* characters were analyzed as either *huiyi* (joined meaning) or *xingsheng* (phonetic compound) graphs. The two remaining principles, *zhuanzhu* (轉注) and *jiajie* (假借), have nothing to do with the original structure of the graphs; they refer instead to graphs secondarily adapted to write words different from the words they were originally devised to represent.[4]

The division of Chinese characters into *wen* and *zi* clearly corresponds to the division of Korean symbols into two types: the basic letters and the letters made by adding strokes or combining shapes.

This is not a coincidence. The correspondence becomes clearer when the *xiangxing*, *zhishi*, *huiyi*, and *xingsheng* principles of the *liushu* are compared to the methods used to construct the letters of the Korean alphabet. The basic letters of the Korean alphabet, which are "single body" graphs, are structured according to the *xiangxing* and *zhishi* principles of elemental, *wen* characters. The other Korean letters are "combined body" graphs put together according to the *huiyi* and *xingsheng* principles of composite, *zi* characters.

As explained in the *Chejahae*, the basic letters of the initials were made according to the *xiangxing* principle—they depict shapes. The only difference is that whereas Chinese characters like 日 (sun) and 月 (moon) were made by depicting the shape of the objects in question, the letters of the Korean alphabet were made by depicting the characteristic shape of the speech organs involved in the articulation of the sounds. This difference results from the fact that Chinese characters are a logography while the letters of the Korean alphabet are phonetic symbols.

It appears that two methods of *xiangxing*, pictography, were used in constructing the basic letters of the initials. In the basic letters representing the five basic series of sounds (see Table 1), the so-called molar (in modern terms, the velar) ㄱ (*k*) and lingual ㄴ (*n*) are constructed differently from the labial ㅁ (*m*), the incisor ㅅ (*s*), and laryngeal ㅇ consonants. The latter three depict the shape of the speech organ involved (labial ㅁ represents the outline of the mouth, incisor ㅅ the outline of a tooth, laryngeal ㅇ the outline of the throat). In contrast, the molar and the lingual letters graphically depict not the organ alone but the articulatory gesture (the graph for the "molar" ㄱ schematically represents the root of the tongue blocking the throat; lingual ㄴ shows the tip of the tongue touching the upper palate). The explanation for this difference may be simply that it is more difficult to depict the speech organ schematically in the case of the molar or lingual sound. In any event, in spite of this remarkable contrast, all of the basic shapes for the initial consonants were devised according to the *xiangxing* (pictographic) principle of traditional graphic analysis.

According to the *Chejahae*, the basic letters for the "medials" (the vowels) were also constructed according to the *xiangxing* principle. The descriptions of the three basic vowel letters state that their shapes were meant to depict Heaven, Earth, and Man (see Table 2). While the initial letters imitate the speech organs involved in the articulation of sound or the speech organ at the articulation, the medial letters were made by symbolizing the articulatory associations represented by Heaven, Earth, and Man. In Neo-Confucianism, Heaven and Earth are symbols of Yang (陽) and Yin (陰), respectively, and Man is a symbol combining both Yin and Yang. The basic letters of medials, then, ultimately represent these abstract concepts. Whereas the initial letters were made by the *xiangxing* method of imitating concrete entities, the medial letters were constructed using the ideographic, *zhishi* principle of representing abstract concepts.[5] The medial letters represent not real-world objects, but symbolic abstractions.

The letters made by adding one or more strokes and the letters made by combining shapes correspond to Chinese characters in the *zi* category. A letter made by adding strokes is analyzed as the basic letter made by *xiangxing* plus one or more strokes. For example, the letter ㅋ (*kh*) is constructed by adding a stroke to the basic letter ㄱ (*k*) representing the place of articulation. The extra stroke is said to represent a "strong sound"—meaning that the sound is articulated at the same place but with a stronger sound. Similarly, the letter ㄷ (*t*) is constructed by adding a stroke to the basic letter ㄴ (*n*) to "strengthen" the sound. Therefore, since letters like ㅋ and ㄷ are constructed by adding an element to a graph with which they share phonetic features, they can be said to follow the *xingsheng* principle of the *liushu*—they form a phonetic series. The basic letter contained in the composite graphs (e.g., the ㄱ part of ㅋ) appears to correspond to the phonetic (*shengfu* 聲符) of a composite Chinese character, and the added stroke appears to correspond to the signific (*yifu* 義符) (sometimes called the "radical") of the character.

Scholars of the Chinese script might argue that letters formed by adding strokes, such as ㅋ and ㄷ, cannot be considered composite letters because the stroke is not itself a separate letter. (The analogous part of a composite Chinese character, the signific, or radical, is a form of an independent character.) If the Korean letter is not a composite body, then it cannot be said to constitute a graph constructed by the *xingsheng* principle. Following this line of reasoning—again, using arguments developed in the study of Chinese graphs—it might be asserted that the basic letters for the initials are regular examples of the *xiangxing* principle, and the letters formed by adding strokes are modified examples of the *xiangxing* principle. Note that a Chinese character considered to be a "modified" example of *xiangxing*, such as 果 (*guo* 'fruit'), cannot be a *wen* character, since it can be analyzed into simpler units (木 *mu* 'tree' and 日); the entire graph is a pictographic imitation of a real object, with the added element indicating the fruit of the tree. However, the Korean letters formed by adding a stroke cannot be considered this kind of modified *xiangxing*; the added stroke in these complex letters contains the meaning of "strong sound," like the signific in a *xingsheng* Chinese character. However, as explained in the *Chejahae*, there are no individual strokes that have the meaning of "strong sound" in the letters made by changing the basic shape (ㄹ, ㅿ, ㆁ). The extra strokes mean that the graph represents a sound related to that of the basic letters. Therefore, letters made by adding strokes correspond not to the modified examples of *xiangxing*, but to the regular examples of *xingsheng*, and letters with a modified shape to the modified examples of *xingsheng*.

According to the explanation given in the *Chejahae*, all medial letters except the three basic ones can be called "combination characters." Therefore, these letters correspond to Chinese characters in the *zi* category. For ㅗ (*wo*), for example, the *Chejahae* states that "its shape is formed by the combination of · and ㅡ " (其形則 · 與ㅡ 合而成); for ㅏ (*a*), "its shape is formed by the combination of ㅣ and ·" (其形則 · 與 ㅣ 合而成). In other words, two basic medial letters are combined in the cases of the complex letters ㅗ (*wo*), ㅏ (*a*), ㅜ (*wu*), and ㅓ (*e*); and three basic medial letters are combined in the cases of ㅛ (*ywo*), ㅑ (*ya*), ㅠ (*ywu*), and ㅕ (*ye*). This process is the same as in Chinese characters formed by means of the *huiyi* principle. The explanation in *Chejahae* is that ㅗ (wo) represents the companionship of Heaven and Earth, and ㅏ (*a*) represents the work of Heaven and Earth appearing in things, but waiting for Man for their completion. From these statements, we see clearly that the three basic letters · (*o*), ㅡ (*u*), and ㅣ (*i*) retain their representational meaning of Heaven, Earth, and Man not only when alone but also when combined to form ㅗ (*wo*) and ㅏ (*a*).

These combination letters were not created because they were thought to combine the phonetic characteristics of the constituent graphs. Phonetics, per se, was not the primary consideration. The *Chejahae* explanations make this fact unmistakably clear. Rather, the graphs were constructed to combine the meanings of Heaven, Earth, and Man as these concepts were perceived in Neo-Confucian philosophy. This same principle of combining meanings can be found in the way Chinese characters such as 武 (*wu*) and 信 (*xin*) are analyzed. Chinese philologists thought that 武, the character for the word *wu* 'military', was a combination of 止 'stop' and 戈 'dagger-ax' and inferred that the word "military" itself originally meant "stop dagger-axes." Similarly, since the character for the word "trust," 信, seemed to be formed from a combination of 人 'man' and 言 'speak', they reasoned that the word "trust" must have originally signified a man and his word. Complex characters formed in this way were what philologists saw as examples of the *huiyi*, "combined meaning," principle. Though the Korean letters secondarily derived from the three basic letters (ᆢ ywo, ㅑ ya, ㅠ ywu, and ㅕ ye) can be thought to have some relationship with the phonetic value of the letters first derived from the three basic letters (ㅗ wo, ㅏ a, ㅜ wu, and ㅓ e)—the difference is clearly the addition of an initial glide /y/—the former was not made by merely adding · (*o*) to the latter (remember that · represented the vowel /o/, not /i/). According to the *Chejahae*, combining two basic letters leads to the latter, and combining three basic letters leads to the former. Therefore, all of these combination letters, were constructed using the *huiyi* principle.

In studying the principles underlying the invention of the Korean alphabet, one needs to understand that not only does the construction of initial and medial letters follow different *liushu* principles—*xiangxing* for initials and *zhishi* for medials, for example—but they also are completely independent of each other. For instance, though the basic letter ㅡ (*u*) of the medials has the same shape as the horizontal stroke added to make composite initial letters, there is no relationship between the two. In other words, ㄷ (*t*) is a letter made by adding a stroke to ㄴ (*n*), but it is not made by combining ㄴ with the medial ㅡ. The construction of the initial system and the construction of the medial system were conceived to be totally independent of one another. They have no more relationship to one another than either does to the system of "side dots" (傍點) Sejong devised to represent pitches, where, for example, the dot used to represent a high pitch has the same shape as the medial letter · (*o*).

It can be understood from the above explanations that the principles used in inventing the twenty-eight letters of the Korean alphabet correspond well to the classification of Chinese characters into *wen* and *zi*, and to their structure according to the *liushu* principles. Those relationships are summarized in Table 3.

Table 3. Six Principles of Writing in the Structure of the Korean Alphabet and of Chinese Characters

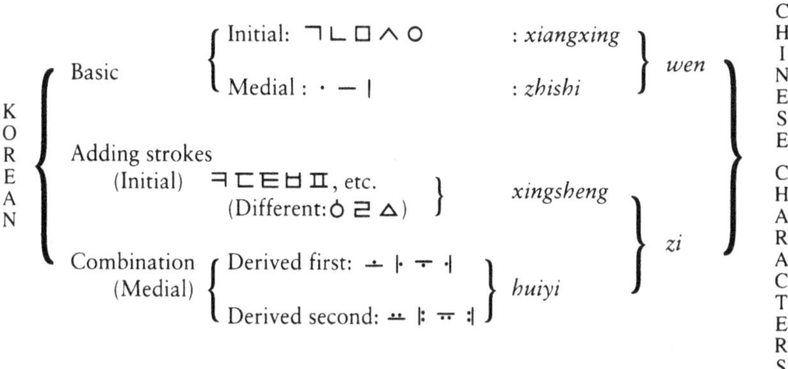

The above explanations are based on the assumption that the scholars participating in the creation of the Korean alphabet knew well the concepts of *wen* and *zi* and that they had an understanding of the *liushu*. When we look for direct textual attestation of this knowledge, not only is one of the *liushu* principles, *xiangxing*, found conspicuously in the *Chejahae* descriptions, but it is also mentioned in the famous line from Chŏng Inji's postface to the text: "while depicting outlines (象形), these letters imitate the 'Old Seal' (篆書) [a style of calligraphy]." Discussion of the other principles (*wen*, *zi*, *zhishi*, and so forth) cannot be found in the *Chejahae*. But understanding and knowledge of the science of Chinese characters was a fundamental part of the education of Korean scholars at the time. Once these men decided to make new letters, it would have been impossible for them to disregard the principles with which Chinese characters were constructed. Chinese characters were, after all, the only writing system used in Korea at that time. Moreover, the above explanations and tables show too clean a correspondence to be considered a coincidence. Nor is it a coincidence that the number of Chinese characters in each category increases in the order of *zhishi*, *xiangxing*, *huiyi*, and *xingsheng*; the twenty-eight letters of the Korean alphabet are similarly allocated among the categories. Furthermore, the historical facts discussed below support the assumption.

First, it is to be noted that junior bureaucrats read the *Hanshu* 漢書 (The History of the Han Dynasty). According to the *Kyŏngguk taejŏn* 經國大典 (The Grand Code of Managing the Nation), the public officers working for the Royal Secretariat (*Sungmunwŏn* 承文院) were supposed to receive lectures from the director (*chejo* 提調) on the books they read every ten days, and the *Hanshu* was one of those books.[6] In the "Yiwenzhi" (藝文志) of the *Hanshu* there appears a passage about the *liushu*: "the so-called depiction of shapes (象形), the depiction of things (象事), the depiction of meaning (象意), the depiction of sounds (象聲), the borrowing of meaning (轉注), and the borrowing of sound (假借), all of which are the bases of making characters." This passage has been always referred to for elucidating the meaning of the *liushu*. Although not all bureaucrats had the experience of serving as public officers working for the Royal Secretariat,[7] it is clear that the book was in general circulation among bureaucrats and scholars, since it was a fundamental part of liberal education at that time. At the very least, scholars of that age were well aware of the "Six Principles of Writing" through the *Hanshu*. Acquaintance with the principles was unavoidable, and knowledge of them is almost certain to have been good.

Next, there is evidence that Sejong's counselors read the *Liushu lüe* (六書略) of the *Tongzhi ershi lüe* (通志二十略) written by Zheng Qiao (鄭樵) of the Song dynasty. This fact is clear from the latter part of this passage in Chŏng Inji's postface to the *Haerye*: "Presumably because the outer kingdoms have their sounds but lack characters for them, they have borrowed Chinese characters to take care of their needs. . . . In fact, things are all at ease in accordance with where they are situated; they cannot be forced to be the same [as things elsewhere]." The phrasing at the end of this passage is an allusion to a passage from the "Shuwen zonglun" (殊文總論) of the *Liushu lüe*.

Looking one step further, it can be shown that the "Qiyi chengwen tu" (起一成文圖) found at the beginning of the *Liushu lüe* has a close relationship with the basic letters of the Korean alphabet. It has been inferred that this chapter had a profound effect on the creation of the alphabet because not only is the graph 一 and its modified characters found in that chapter similar to the letter shapes of the Korean alphabet, but also all the basic letters of the alphabet appear there.[8]

Given that the principles by which the letters of the alphabet were formed have such a relationship with the *liushu* of Chinese characters, why is this fact not clearly described in the *Haerye* text? The expression *xiang* 'depict' (象) is found in such phrases as "depicting their outline" (象其形) in the *Chejahae*; "depicting outlines" (象形) in Chŏng Inji's postface; and "the Correct Sounds [the alphabet] esteem their outlines in designing the letters" (正音制字尚其象) and "the eleven medial sounds are also made by depicting their outlines" (中聲十一亦取象) in the *Chejahae*. However, the principles of the *liushu* other than *xiangxing*, such as *zhishi* and *huiyi*, are not found in the *Haerye*. This fact might cast doubt on the hypothesis presented in the present essay. But the absence of such testimony could also be the result of the nature of understanding and knowledge of scholars in Sejong's day about the *zhishi*, *huiyi*, and *xingsheng*. In the "Yiwenzhi" of the *Hanshu*, from which it is believed Korean scholars' knowledge of *zhishi*, *huiyi*, and *xingsheng* derives, these three principles were called, respectively, "depiction of things" (象事), "depiction of meaning" (象意) and "depiction of sound" (象聲); therefore, these terms all have *xiang* 'depiction' in common with of *xiangxing* (象形). It is also to be noted that there appears the passage "As for the *liushu*, they are all modifications of *xiangxing*" in the preface of the "*Xiangxing* 1" (象形第一) of the *Liushu yüe*, showing that *xiangxing* was regarded as the basic principle of the *liushu*. In view of this fact, the Korean scholars might have understood *zhishi*, *huiyi*, and *xingsheng* to be principles for making letters that are not very different from *xiangxing*, or to be modified versions of *xiangxing*; therefore, they would have considered mention of *xiangxing* and *xiang* to be enough of an explanation of how the letters of the alphabet were made.

From the above discussion, it can be seen that the scholars participating in the creation of the alphabet had knowledge of the *liushu* and of the difference between *wen* and *zi* as used in the traditional science of Chinese characters, and that these scholars used such knowledge in deciding the shapes of the Korean letters. The principles used in inventing the Korean alphabet, which are now widely known through the explanations found in the *Chejahae*, cannot be understood without knowledge of the four graphic principles *xiangxing*, *zhishi*, *huiyi*, and *xingsheng*, and of the difference between *wen* and *zi*.

CONCLUSION

We have examined the relationship between the principles used in making the twenty-eight letters of the Korean alphabet and the principles used in the traditional study of Chinese characters. Based on this line of investigation, we have reached the conclusion that in developing the Korean alphabet, knowledge of Neo-Confucianism and Chinese phonology was used to a great extent, as was knowledge of the "Six Principles of Writing" found in the structure of Chinese characters. In inventing new characters, Sejong and his counselors thought it necessary to refer to the writing systems of peripheral nations, including 'Phags-pa, Sanskrit, Mongolian and *kana*. In this context it was all the more essential to study Chinese characters, since they were, after all, the "universal writing system" of the East Asian world and the only means of writing used in Korea in Sejong's day.

Imagine a nation that did not have its own writing system and wrote using the Roman alphabet instead. Now suppose that certain scholars of that nation were going to invent their own alphabet: Does it not stand to reason that in this task they would automatically make use of their knowledge of the usages and principles of the Roman alphabet? It follows, then, that Korean scholars would first turn for inspiration to the writing system they had grown up with and with which they were most familiar. The fact that the twenty-eight letters of the Korean alphabet fell into two distinct categories, simple and composite, shows that the creators of that system had internalized the central idea of the Chinese system, in which graphs were divided into *wen* and *zi*. Furthermore, it can be no accident that the basic letters of the Korean initials are structured according to the *xiangxing* principle, the basic Korean medials by the *zhishi* principle, the combination letters of the medials by the *huiyi* principle, and the letters formed by adding strokes or altering the shape according to the *xingsheng* principle. Hence, the four principles of the *liushu* found in the structures of Chinese characters were also found to be the principles used in creating the shapes of the Korean alphabet.

Commenting on the alphabet in his postface to the *Haerye*, Chŏng Inji said, "While depicting outlines, these letters imitate the Old Seal; they follow their sounds and harmonize with the seven series of sound, containing all the meaning of Heaven, Earth, and

Man, and the delicacy of Yin and Yang." The fact that the tripartition of letters—shape, sound, and meaning—corresponds to the three elements of Chinese characters (形 , 音 , 義) also supports our present conclusion.

I have proposed elsewhere in treating the *kugyŏl* (口訣) of Middle Korean that there was a continuity between the Korean alphabetic system and the Korean use of Chinese characters borrowed to write native words (Ahn 1977: 128–129).[9] The hypothesis was based on the fact that, although the borrowed characters used as *kugyŏl* were unrelated to the construction of the alphabetic letters, the way they were used was analogous. The example in the *Hapchahae* (Explanations of Letter Composition) section of the *Haerye* states that in mixing Chinese characters with the alphabet, "there are cases where Chinese characters, depending on their pronunciation, may be supplemented with [isolated] medial and terminal sounds; for example, 孔子 ㅣ 魯 ㅅ :사ᄅᆞᆷ (Kwongca i LWO s salom) 'Confucius (is) a man of Lu.' " The Korean particle *i* (the subject marker) in this example is used in a way that was directly deduced from the usage of the *kugyŏl* characters 是 and 伊 : According to *kugyŏl* convention, 是 or 伊 could be used to represent the Korean subject marker and inserted into a Chinese text when the preceding nominal ended in a vowel—just as is the Korean letter ㅣ (*i*) in the *Haerye* example. Similarly, the genitive s (ㅅ) in the example follows the usage of the *kugyŏl* character 叱 . There is also a *kugyŏl* precedent for the treatment of glides in the alphabetic system. In the Korean alphabet, onglides are incorporated into the letter itself; for example, ㆉ (*ywo*) and ㅑ (*ya*). In contrast, vocalic elements with offglides, such as ㅐ (*ay*) and ㅔ (*ey*), are treated as separate letters. This difference in treatment cannot be unrelated to the fact that onglides were not analyzed and spelled out separately in the Korean tradition of borrowing characters.

There were also many other conventions and principles that derived from earlier Korean usage of Chinese characters. I have argued that the tradition of borrowing characters, both for use as *kugyŏl* and for transcribing extended Korean passages,[10] was the inspiration for much that is found in the alphabetic system (Ahn 1984).

Before the invention of the alphabet, Koreans had already established a stable and unified tradition of writing. The continuity between this system of borrowing Chinese characters to write

Korean and the newly created alphabet shows how strong the tradition was. The scholars participating in the invention of the alphabet could not help but make use of their knowledge of this system and of the *liushu* in establishing the principles for the new writing system.

The fact that the principles used in the invention of the alphabet are related to earlier traditions in no way diminishes the originality of Sejong's achievement. As was conspicuously shown in Ch'oe Malli's anti-alphabet memorial to the throne, the way in which a syllable is analyzed into phonemes and shown to be composed of initial and medial letters is radically different from Chinese writing. The shapes of the basic letters of the alphabet, though all of them appear in the "Qiyi chengwen tu," were explained as depicting the speech organs and the Three Great Absolutes (Heaven, Earth, and Man); the medial letters were made with extremely simple dots and lines or combinations of these elements, while initial letters were made by adding strokes or combining shapes; and all of these letters fit together into a well-ordered system. Such a system could not have been brought into being without great originality and genius, as Chŏng Inji made clear in his postface to the *Haerye*.

I have claimed in the present essay that knowledge from the scientific study of Chinese characters was used in inventing the alphabet and that this knowledge came directly through the Korean tradition of borrowing characters for the purpose of transcription. I have argued for intellectual continuity: it was both natural and unavoidable that traditional resources be used, and without taking such factors into consideration, we cannot begin to understand the magnitude of the Korean achievement. By studying the principles used in inventing the alphabet, we find that the scholars who produced it did not merely imitate traditional theory; rather, they creatively used the resources of that tradition to produce an original, Korean writing system.

NOTES

The Korean version of this chapter was published in *Kang Sinhang kyosu hoegap kinyŏm nonmunjip* (Ahn 1990). That published article is presented here with minor revisions. Yale romanization is used for linguistic forms.

1. A representative work on this topic is Kim Wanjin 1983.

2. Other scholars have also suggested a connection between the principles used in the invention of the Korean alphabet and the *liushu*. Referring to a cru-

cial phrase in the *Chejahae*, "Each of the twenty-eight letters of [the alphabet] was made by imitating a shape respectively," Kang Sinhang (1987) interprets the phrase in a way that meant the letters were not made in imitation of the 'Phags-pa alphabet or any other such characters, but rather according to the principles of the *liushu*.

Yu Ch'ang-gyun (1966) went further, suggesting a direct relationship between the alphabet and the four *liushu* categories *xiangxing*, *zhishi*, *xingsheng*, and *huiyi*. Although this claim sounds superficially similar to what I propose in the present chapter, it is based on a fundamentally different interpretation. Therefore, I accept the conceptual understanding of Professor Kang but, with regret, not the line of reasoning of Professor Yu.

3. See, for example, the English translations given in Ledyard 1966. Most of the translations from the *Hunmin chŏng'ŭm* and the *Haerye* used in this chapter are adapted from those given in that source.

4. *Jiajie* characters are graphs borrowed to represent a word with a similar sound. *Zhuanzhu* characters are believed, by some, to represent words with a similar meaning; but other scholars dispute this interpretation, and the significance of this last category remains controversial.

5. Yu Ch'ang-gyun (1966) presents a similar interpretation of the "medial" letters. However, Yu's explanation that the *zhishi* principle is used for the first four composite letters, while the second four composite letters are synthesized by using the three basic letters, does not seem to me to be properly substantiated.

6. The publication of the *Kyŏngguk taejŏn* was much later than the invention of alphabet. But since the work was a revision of already existing codes of laws such as the *Kyŏngje yukchŏn* 經濟六典 (The Six Codes of Governance), the regulations on these lectures are believed to have been enforced before the publication of the *Kyŏngguk taejŏn*.

7. There is no written record that scholars participating in the creation of the alphabet such as Sin Sukchu had served in this position. The only witness that such was the case is found in the 1442 work *Xiao-Xing bajing shijuan* 瀟湘八景詩卷 (Poems on the Eight Scenic Views of the Xiao and Xiang Rivers) by Prince Anp'yŏng, which contains poems by Chŏng Inji, Sin Sukchu, and Sŏng Sammun. In this work there appears a statement that Sŏng Sammun was an officer in the office of the Royal Secretariat. If the record on the scholars who took part in the creation of the alphabet had been more extensive, the names of other scholars who had served in the position would almost surely have been found.

8. These influences have been referred to over and over again in articles and books related to the creation of the alphabet, e.g., Hong Kimun 1946, Kong Chaesŏk 1967, and Kim Yŏngman 1987.

9. *Kugyŏl* is a term referring to the Chinese characters borrowed to represent Korean syntactic elements, usually particles, intercolated in a Chinese text to elucidate its meaning. Since few early *kugyŏl* texts have been preserved, the

origins of the *kugyŏl* tradition are largely obscure. Still, it is clear that one of the main principles for borrowing a Chinese character and using it in this fashion was that it was associated with a sound similar to a native Korean morpheme.

10. This type of writing, in which Chinese characters are used to transcribe a completely Korean passage, was known as *hyangch'al* (鄕札) and had been used in Korea at least since the sixth or seventh century.

REFERENCES

Ahn, Pyong-Hi. 1977. Chungse kugŏ kugyŏr-ŭi yŏn'gu (A study of the *kugyŏl* of Middle Korean). Seoul: Iljisa Publishing Co.

———. 1984. Han'gugŏ ch'aja p'yogipŏb-ŭi hyŏngsŏng-gwa t'ŭkching (The formation and characteristics of borrowed characters in Korean). In *Chesamhoe kukche haksulhoeŭi nonmunjip* (A collection of papers from the Third International Conference of the Academy of Korean Studies), 621–635.

———. 1990. Hunmin chŏng'ŭm-ŭi chejawŏlli-e taehayŏ. (On the principles used in creating Hummin chŏng'ŭm letters). In *Kang Sinhang Kyosu hoegap kinyŏm kugŏhak nonmunjip* (Papers in Korean linguistics in commemoration of the sixtieth birthday of Professor Kang Sinhang). Seoul: T'aehaksa, 135–145.

Hong, Kimun. 1946. Chŏng'ŭm paltal-sa (A history of the Korean alphabet). Vol. 2. Seoul: Seoul Newspaper Publishing Co.

Kang, Sinhang. 1987. Hunmin chŏng'ŭm yŏn'gu (A study on the *Hunmin chŏng'ŭm*). Seoul: Songgyungwan University Press.

Kim, Wanjin. 1983. Hunmin chŏng'ŭm cheja kyŏng'wi-e taehan sae koch'al (A new investigation into the circumstances surrounding the construction of the letters of the Korean alphabet). In *Kim Ch'ŏl-jun paksa hwan'gap kinyŏm sahak nonch'ong* (Historical studies: A festschrift in honor of the sixtieth birthday of Dr. Kim Ch'ŏl jun), Seoul: Chisik Sanŏpsa Publishing Co., 353–366.

Kim, Yŏngman. 1987. Hunmin chŏng'ŭm chahyŏng-ŭi wŏnhyŏng-gwa saengsŏng ch'egye yŏn'gu (A study of the prototypes for letter shapes and the system of production for the Korean alphabet). In *Chang T'ae-jin paksa hoegap kinyŏm kugŏ-kungmunhak nonch'ong* (Papers on Korean language and literature: A festschrift in honor of Dr. Chang T'aejin), 43–70. Seoul: Samyŏngsa Publishing Co.

Kong, Chaesŏk. 1967. Han'gŭl kojŏn kiwŏnsŏr-e taehan koch'al (A study of the hypothesis that the origin of the Korean alphabet is in the shape of the Old Seal forms of Chinese characters). *Chungguk hakpo* 7: 45–54.

Ledyard, Gari Keith. 1966. The Korean language reform of 1446: The origin, background, and early history of the Korean alphabet. Ph.D. dissertation, University of California, Berkeley. University Microfilms 66-8333.

Lee, Ki-Moon. 1977. Kugŏ ŭmun-sa yŏn'gu (A study of the history of Korean phonology). Seoul: Tower Press.

Lee, Kwangho. 1988. Humin chŏng'ŭm sinje isipp'alcha-ŭi sŏngkyŏg-e taehan yŏn'gu (A study on the characteristics of the newly invented twenty-eight letters of the Korean alphabet). *Paedal mal* 13:47–66.

Yu, Ch'ang-gyun. 1966. "Sanghyŏng i chabang-gojŏn"–e taehayŏ (On the phrase "while depicting outlines, these letters imitate the Old Seal"). *Chindan hakpo* 29 and 30: 371–390.

5

GRAPHICAL INGENUITY IN THE KOREAN WRITING SYSTEM: WITH NEW REFERENCE TO CALLIGRAPHY

Sang-Oak Lee

Although some scholars have attempted to draw coincidental and nonsystematic connections between a few of the letters in *Hunmin chŏng'ŭm* (the Korean alphabet) and those of neighboring writing systems, these apparent similarities are the result of the limited nature of the set of strokes (vertical, horizontal, and slanted lines, and circles) frequently used in an alphabet. Ledyard (1966) and Yu Ch'ang-gyun (1966) have suggested 'Phags-pa script as a possible model for the Korean alphabet, in particular, the 'Phags-pa consonants ꡊ [d] and ꡙ [l] for Korean ㄷ [t] and ㄹ [l]. However, other letter shapes, like Korean ㄹ [l], ㅅ [s], ㅈ [č], and ㅌ [t'], do not have the same sound value as the similar 'Phags-pa letters ꡃ [ŋ], ∧ [o], ㅈ [o], and ꡈ [ǰ]. With only this much coincidental similarity, nobody can safely claim that there is systematic correspondence.

It is explained in the book *Hunmin chŏng'ŭm*, published at the time the alphabet was created, that the consonant letters are based on the shape of various speech organs, and the vowel letters are based on the three philosophical symbols for Earth, Heaven, and Human. Two additional unique characteristics of the Korean alphabet are (1) the creation of related letters by the addition of strokes to basic letters and (2) writing words in syllabic units, combining more than two letters within three blocks as found in Chinese characters, for example, 碧 .

In addition to these characteristics, some calligraphic principles are applied. They are (3) writing from left to right and from top to bottom, (4) maintaining equidistance in adding strokes and in creating syllabic units, and (5) limiting the size of syllabic units to the inside of squares in equal sequence. All these give a feeling of symmetry and stability (see Figure 1). As shown in Figure 1, there are several degrees of density in paralleling the strokes: six strokes in the horizontal direction and seven in the vertical direction are the most complex.

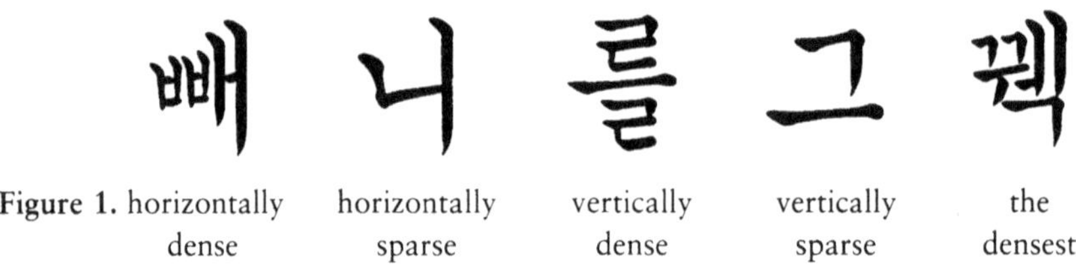

Figure 1. horizontally dense; horizontally sparse; vertically dense; vertically sparse; the densest

HOW WERE THE GRAPHEMES OF *HUNMIN CHŎNG'ŬM* DESIGNED?

Hitherto uninvestigated aspects of the Korean writing system include graphemes and calligraphy. The first question that has never been asked is *how* King Sejong the Great, who invented the alphabet, experimented with various possible strokes and characters on a blank piece of paper. (Although his sons and leading court scholars helped him at various stage of this project, let us assume that the king was the initiator of all ideas, since an individual should come up with an embryonic idea at the outset and it is unlikely that the whole project was initiated through brainstorming.)

As we know, thirty-six initial letters were used in Chinese rime books, as shown in Table 1, but only twenty-three in Korean. Since Sejong already knew the Chinese version quite well, it is likely that he started by analyzing the Korean sound system with reference to that of Chinese and consequently came up with twenty-three consonants that forced some mergers, as shown by braces in Table 1.

Table 1. The Thirty-Six Initial Consonants of Middle Chinese (the left side of braces) and the Twenty-Three Initial Consonants of Middle Korean (the right side of braces)

MANNER / PLACE	全淸 chŏnch'ŏng	次淸 ch'ach'ŏng	全濁 chŏnt'ak	不淸不濁 pulch'ŏng pult'ak
牙音 aŭm	見 } 君 ㄱ	溪 } 快 ㅋ	群 } 虯 ㄲ	疑 } 業 ㆁ
舌音 sŏrŭm	端, 知 } 斗 ㄷ	透, 徹 } 呑 ㅌ	定, 澄 } 覃 ㄸ	泥, 娘 } 那 ㄴ
唇音 sunŭm	幫, 非 } 彆 ㅂ	滂, 敷 } 漂 ㅍ	竝, 奉 } 步 ㅃ	明, 微 } 彌 ㅁ
齒音 ch'iŭm	精, 照 } 即 ㅈ 心, 審 } 戍 ㅅ	淸, 穿 } 侵 ㅊ	從, 牀 } 慈 ㅉ 邪, 禪 } 邪 ㅆ	
喉音 huŭm	影 } 挹 ㆆ	曉 } 虛 ㅎ	匣 } 洪 ㆅ	喩 } 欲 ㅇ
半舌音 pansŏrŭm				來 } 閭 ㄹ
半齒音 panch'iŭm				日 } 穰 ㅿ

In this sequence of preparation, I am sure that he used the "trial and error" method and was not mysteriously inspired with a mature idea for the entire set of characters at once, as his court scholars claimed. Evidence for this can be seen in the fact that dots were originally used for the vowels but were later changed to short strokes when the dots proved to be impractical (e.g., ㅣ· becomes ㅏ). Thus was the inventor willing to revise and improve the letters even after the "final" set was made public.

Another significant change is that the original set of letter shapes was composed of straight lines and right angles not suitable for brush writing but was later modified to forms easier to write with a brush. Sejong probably used a brush to draw a draft of scripts and felt the difficulty of writing dots from the beginning but in the initial period stuck to the philosophical symbol of a round dot for Heaven.

Economy of Calligraphy

In the case of ㄱ, ㅋ and ㄴ, the reason why the inventor did not choose ┌, ⊨ and ┘ is that the latter require one more stroke apiece in brush writing. This may be regarded as another calligraphic principle: (6) minimization of strokes. Another interesting example of economy of calligraphy is the later development of shapes like ㅅ, ㅈ, ㅊ and ㅅ, ㅈ, ㅊ from original ㅅ, ㅈ, ㅊ. There is a visible reduction in the number of strokes from 2, 3, 4 to 1, 2(1), 3(2).

Avoiding Calligraphic Similarity

When King Sejong invented the consonant letters, he may have ended up with several similar characters, as marked by a dotted line in Figure 2. It is well known that ㅌ and ㄹ printed in small type are often misread even today. Two problem areas were avoided: one is ヨ and the other 日. Thus, (7) calligraphic similarity must be avoided by introducing different shapes.

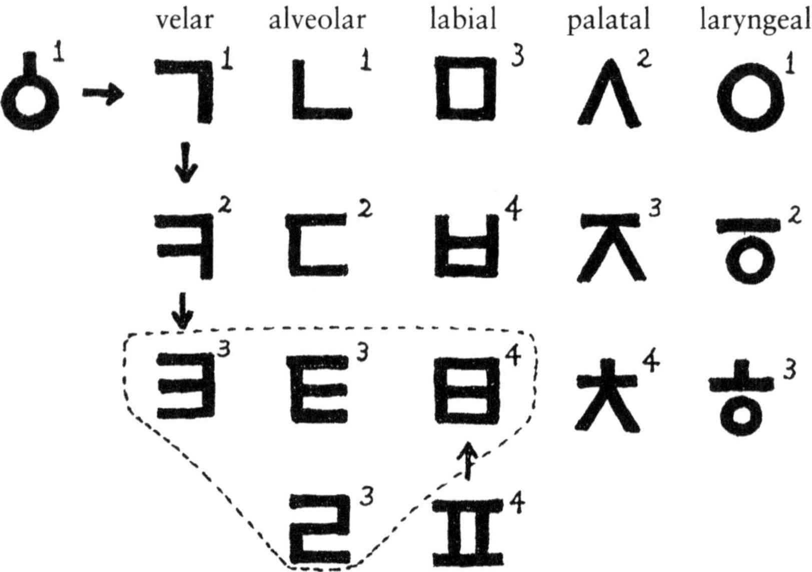

Figure 2. An Imaginary Draft for Designing the Korean Alphabet

It is my assumption that King Sejong avoided the graphic jam by eliminating ヨ, shifted ㄱ and ㅋ down to fill a blank, and newly introduced ㆁ as an exceptional measure (ㆁ was made by adding ', probably the top part of ㅊ, to ㅇ.) He considered ㆁ similar to ㅇ because of confusion between these two sounds in the Chinese rime books. In early Chinese, there was one letter for [ŋ] and another letter for [ɦ] or [j], according to Kang (1990). After the Yuan dynasty, [ŋ] disappeared and merged with [ɦ] or [j], but King Sejong, who was well versed in early Chinese phonology, invented ㆁ and ㅇ to equate with [ŋ] and [ɦ, j], respectively. He intentionally assigned a common shape, that is, a circle, to both letters in spite of violating the regularity of ㄱ and ㅋ.

Kim (1975) has criticized Sejong for mistakenly trying to rectify the general confusion between ㆁ and ㅇ based on earlier Chinese sounds. Yet I interpret the introduction of ㅇ as a probable means of avoiding a graphic jam, an interpretation more in line with other ingenious aspects of *Hunmin chŏng'ŭm*.

However, it is ironic to assign two distinct sound values to ㆁ and ㅇ while mentioning the "similarity" of the sounds represented by ㆁ and ㅇ. Furthermore, Sejong was mistaken in describing [ŋ] as the closing of the "throat" by the tongue root (in *Hunmin chŏng'ŭm haerye chejahae*), because we cannot pronounce [ŋ] closing the throat, but by opening it while closing the "velar" area. It is understandable that he could not see the back part of the oral cavity clearly and mislocated the "velar" closure to the throat. Sejong, though a prominent phonetician of his era, could not experiment with optical instruments.

Although I do not advocate the hypothetical connection between 'Phags-pa and the *Hunmin chŏng'ŭm*, it could be suggested that ㄱ might have originated from 'Phags-pa ꡂ and that the remaining shape like a dipper ㅂ developed to ㆁ. However, ㅁ was a basic labial consonant, while ㅇ was another basic letter symbolizing the throat. Therefore, this assumption is based on two different shapes that cannot be intermingled.

As described by Kim (1975), many scholars believe that ㅂ has two additional strokes on the top of ㅁ, but that is wrong. ㅁ has three strokes and ㅂ only four in brush writing. Thus, there is but one additional stroke.

As for 日, this shape looks not only like the Chinese character 日 but also like the other Korean letters ㅌ, ㄹ, and ㅋ. Therefore, to avoid the jam in Figure 2, ㅍ was introduced, probably by turning ㅐ by 90 degrees. ㅐ is a more natural way of adding strokes to ㅁ and ㅂ, but there may have been problems in composing shapes like ㅐㅐ and ㅐ.

Graphemes with Maximal Distinction

Last but not least, ㅋ was chosen over ⊐ to avoid the probable confusion with ㄷ. ⊐ is a possible shape after adding a stroke to ㄱ. Likewise, ⊨ is a possible shape after adding a stroke to ㄴ. It is likely that either the set ㅋ and ㄷ or the set ⊐ and ⊨ would be selected to keep (8) maximal distinction between graphemes. Maximal distinction together with avoidance of calligraphic similarity are aspects of a general principle of calligraphic distinctiveness.

HOW HAVE WE BENEFITED BY FORMALIZING THE PRESENT SHAPES OF VOWELS?

Before the new alphabet was proclaimed, the king and his sons may have tested two possibilities for assigning letters to the vowel sounds. The version they decided on was to make the long strokes of the vowels [a, ja, ɔ, jɔ, i] vertical and those of the vowels [o, jo, u, ju, ɨ] horizontal. They probably chose this arrangement because the former vowels are used more frequently (see Table 2 below), and the long vertical stroke creates a vertical axis in brush writing and is calligraphically convenient. I would like to call this aspect (9) calligraphic convenience or easy movement of a brush.

Table 2 below is based on three different investigations by professors Chŏng In-sang (fifteenth-century texts), Kim Hŭng-kyu (sixteenth- to nineteenth-century texts), and Yu Chae-wŏn (twentieth-century texts). The first two columns on the fifteenth-century texts with and without Sino-Korean words contain the most relevant data; the latter two are for reference.

As shown in Table 2, vowel group A with vertical axes has quite higher frequencies than B with horizontal axes throughout the three periods. Therefore, if the shapes of vowel letters were opposite (i.e., ㅏ for [o], ㅗ for [a], and so on) to the present formalization, it would be quite awkward to write with a brush.

Table 2. Frequency of Vowel Letters in Three Different Periods

		Fifteenth-century Pure Korean Texts Only		Fifteenth-century Texts with Sino-Korean		Sixteenth- to Nineteenth-century Texts		Twentieth-century Pure Korean Texts	
A. Letters with vertical axes									
ㅏ	a	4532	14.14%	6252	15.33%	85555	19.93%	28580	24.23%
ㅐ	ɛ	922	2.88%	1291	3.17%	7777	1.81%	6171	5.23%
ㅑ	ja	548	1.71%	674	1.65%	6957	1.62%	828	0.70%
ㅒ	jɛ	26	0.08%	26	0.06%	10	0.00%	11	0.01%
ㅓ	ɔ	1803	5.62%	2935	7.20%	31995	7.45%	15652	13.27%
ㅔ	e	694	2.16%	929	2.28%	11819	2.75%	2208	1.87%
ㅕ	jɔ	1184	3.69%	1817	4.46%	33743	7.86%	2466	2.09%
ㅖ	je	359	1.12%	426	1.04%	3825	0.89%	185	0.16%
ㅣ	i	7043	21.97%	8200	20.11%	63103	14.70%	21785	18.47%
ㆎ	ʌi	730	2.28%	730	1.79%	10762	2.51%	—	—
Subtotal			55.65%		57.09%		59.52%		66.03%
B. Letters with horizontal axes									
ㅗ	o	3612	11.27%	4669	11.45%	53392	12.44%	11413	9.68%
ㅛ	jo	221	0.69%	368	0.90%	5696	1.33%	314	0.27%
ㅜ	u	1015	3.17%	2096	5.14%	31251	7.28%	14189	12.03%
ㅠ	ju	77	0.24%	186	0.46%	6957	1.62%	155	0.13%
ㅡ	ɨ	2520	7.86%	2806	6.88%	33795	7.87%	10299	8.73%
ㆍ	ʌ	5582	17.41%	5585	13.70%	18064	4.21%	—	—
Subtotal			40.64%		38.53%		34.75%		30.84%
C. Letters with both axes									
ㅘ	wa	302	0.94%	567	1.39%	7889	1.84%	718	0.61%
ㅙ	wɛ	45	0.14%	51	0.13%	231	0.05%	200	0.17%
ㅚ	ø	274	0.85%	340	0.83%	2946	0.69%	899	0.76%
ㅝ	wɔ	56	0.17%	131	0.32%	3092	0.72%	246	0.21%
ㅞ	we	6	0.02%	6	0.01%	86	0.02%	74	0.06%
ㅟ	y	154	0.48%	272	0.67%	2993	0.70%	1304	1.11%
ㅢ	ɨi	355	1.11%	422	1.03%	7359	1.71%	233	0.21%
Subtotal			3.71%		4.38%		5.73%		3.13%
Total			100.00%		100.00%		100.00%		100.00%

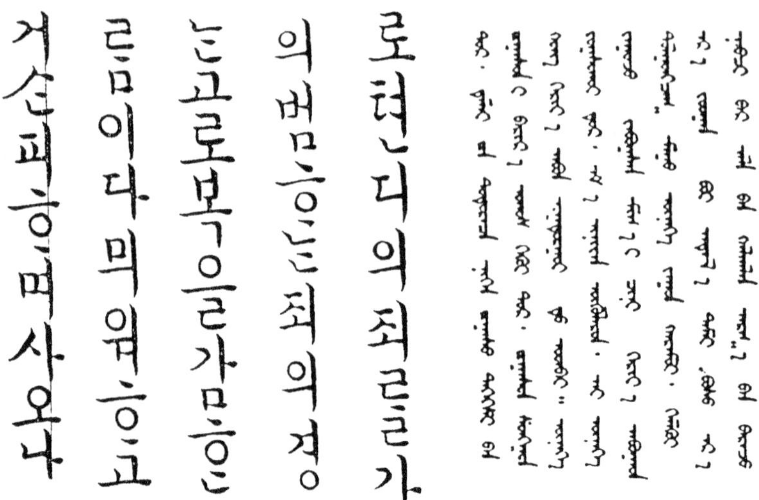

Figure 3. *Kung-ch'e* (*left*) and Mongolian Writing

As presented in Figure 3, the so-called *kung-ch'e* (the court style of writing the Korean script) and the Mongolian script have very distinct vertical axes. In this kind of writing style, it is very desirable to allot the vertical strokes to the most frequently used sounds (i.e., "vowel group" in the Korean case; Mongolian has vertical strokes all through its alphabet).

Whether or not Sejong and his sons experimented with or were aware of this relationship between the frequency of sounds and the assignment of vertical strokes, formalizing the present shapes of vowels has benefited calligraphers and brush writers at various levels of skill. One would think that the opposite arrangement would be more convenient nowadays, when most people write horizontally, but actually the current system is more practical even for nonbrush calligraphy with a quill or a pen. See Figure 4. Horizontal writing for the Korean script retains the tradition of vertical strokes for the frequent vowel group, and this mismatch between vertical strokes and horizontal stream of writing agrees well with the schematic representation of quill writing shown at the bottom of Figure 4. With a brush or a pen it is easier to move our fingers vertically.

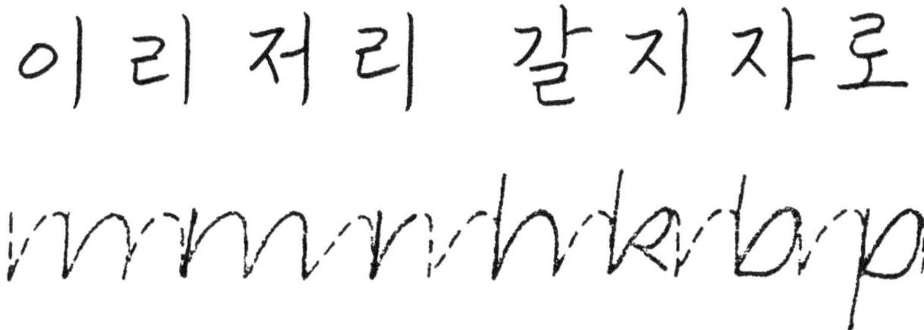

Figure 4. Comparison between Korean Horizontal Writing and Quill Writing

For vowels, as shown in Figure 5, Sejong did not suggest possible combinations like ㆇ and ㆊ, although these letters were seemingly necessary in Middle Korean. We presently find ᄃᆄᆻ 다 in a dialect and 바 ᄁᆑᆻ 다 as a contracted form.

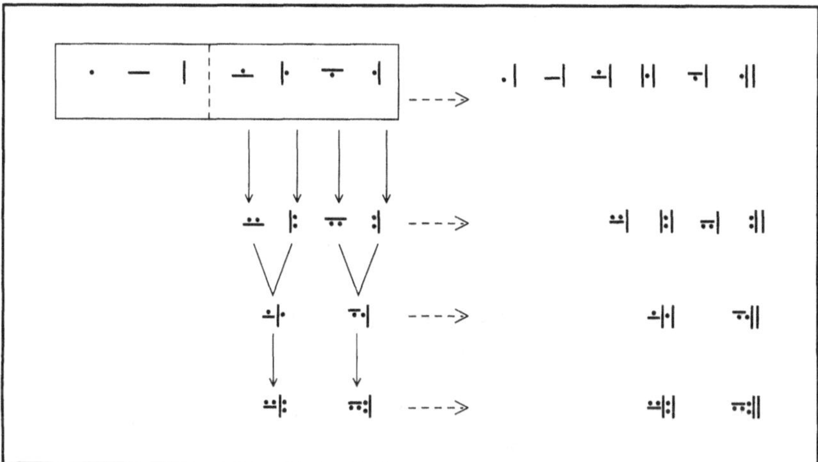

Figure 5. A Flow Chart of Developing Vowel Letters

AFTERWORD

Professor Ahn Pyŏng-hi has noted in his chapter that Korean characters in the book *Hunmin chŏng'ŭm* show a similar shape to *chŏnsŏ* (篆書), "seal" characters in Chinese writing styles. As shown in Figure 6A, they were carved very delicately with slight curves at the beginning and end of each stroke. Note also that the vowel [ʌ] was given the shape of a round dot in this, the first book written with the Korean alphabet. It was possible to make the effort to carve these curvy and round shapes because it was the first publication to use Korean script and it was manageably small.

However, as mentioned above and shown in Figure 6B, the curves were changed to right angles and the round dots to short strokes, probably for the convenience of carving. Later these curves were again changed to a more natural shape for brush writing, as shown in Figure 6C.

Figure 6. A. Hunmin chŏng'ŭm B. Sŏkpo sangjŏl C. Wŏrin sŏkpo

REFERENCES

Kang, Sinhang. 1990. Hunmin chŏng'ŭm yŏn'gu (A study of *Hunmin chŏng'ŭm*), Revised ed., Seoul: Sung Kyun Kwan University Press.

Kim, Wanjin. 1975. Hunmin chŏng'ŭm chaumja-wa kahoek-ŭy wŏlli (The consonant letters in *Hunmin chŏng'ŭm* and the principle of adding strokes). *Ŏmunyŏn'gu* 7 and 8; also in Lee Ki-Moon 1977: 217–227.

Ledyard, Gari. 1966. The Korean language reform of 1446: The origin, background, and early history of the Korean alphabet. Ph.D. dissertation, University of California, Berkeley.

Lee, Ki-Moon. 1974. Hunmin Chŏng'ŭm-e kwallyŏndoen myŏt munje (Some problems in relation to *Hunmin chŏng'ŭm*). *Kugŏhak* 2: 99; also in Lee Ki-Moon 1977: 200–216.

———, ed. 1977. Muntcha (Scripts). *Kugŏhak nonmunsŏn* (Selected papers in Korean Linguistics 7. Seoul: Minjung sŏgwan.

Yu, Ch'ang-gyun. 1966. "Sanghyŏng-i chabanggojŏn"–e taehayŏ (On the meaning of "Symbolization and Imitating the Old Letter Style." *Chindan hakpo* 29 and 30; also in Lee Ki-Moon 1977: 153–179.

6

THE VOWEL SYSTEM OF THE KOREAN ALPHABET AND KOREAN READINGS OF CHINESE CHARACTERS

Sinhang Kang

In order to create the Korean alphabet, King Sejong and his counselors made extensive analyses of the phonemes of fifteenth-century Korean. But, in addition, they seem to have made maximum use of their knowledge of Chinese phonology in the design of this writing system.

Koreans borrowed Chinese characters and began writing Chinese in the Han dynasty. But in assimilating the character readings that the Chinese used, both in the Old Chinese period (seventh century B.C. to third century A.D.) and, later, in the Middle Chinese period (sixth to tenth centuries A.D.), the Koreans modified the readings to fit the phonological system of their own language. These distinctively Korean readings subsequently changed and developed as the Korean language did, along lines different from Chinese. The result was that, from very early on, the Koreans used readings for the characters that did not match up with those used by the Chinese.

In China and the rest of East Asia, the study of phonology traditionally meant the study of how Chinese characters were read. When Koreans created their alphabet in the fifteenth century, they naturally used this phonological science to analyze the phonological system of Middle Korean, and for them this meant using the Korean readings of Chinese characters.

THE COMPILATION OF THE *TONGGUK CHŎNG'UN*

While the Korean alphabet was being created, the same persons involved in its development compiled the *Tongguk chŏng'un* in 1447. In this rime dictionary, the character readings were transcribed in the Korean alphabet and arranged in such a way as to show clearly the initial consonants, the vowels (medial and principal vowels), and the endings of the finals. Putting aside some partial prescriptiveness, the arrangement of the readings in this dictionary corresponded to the phonological system of initials, vowels, and final endings found in the promulgation document of the Korean alphabet, the *Hunmin chŏng'ŭm* (The Correct Sounds for the Instruction of the People).

THE SYSTEM OF INITIALS IN THE *HUNMIN CHŎNG'ŬM* AND THE *TONGGUK CHŎNG'UN*

King Sejong and his advisers knew that languages vary according to geographical circumstances and that they change over time. We can see this knowledge at work when Chŏng Inji, one of the king's principal advisers, expresses the following opinion in his postface to the *Hunmin chŏng'ŭm haerye* (Explanations and Examples of the Correct Sounds for the Instruction of the People): "The winds and soils of the Four Quarters diverge, one from the other, and enunciations and breaths, following them, are likewise different. Therefore, languages outside [of China] have their own pronunciations [different from those of Chinese]." In his introduction to the *Tongguk chŏng'un*, Sin Sukchu expresses a similar view: "From a geographical viewpoint, the mountains and rivers of our nation form a separate division, and hence our climate and pronunciation are different from those of China. Because of this, the sounds of Chinese characters have also naturally changed according to our pronunciation."

Because of these differences, Sin went on to say, some of the distinctions found in the thirty-six initials of the Chinese rime tables were not reflected in the Korean consonants, and thus, he said, there was no need to be bound to this system of thirty-six initials. Reasoning along these lines, Sin and the others compiled the *Tongguk chŏng'un* as a rime dictionary with twenty-three initials, and the system by and large corresponded to that of the *Hunmin chŏng'ŭm*. Underlying this twenty-three-initial system that the compilers of the *Tongguk chŏng'un* came up with were the following facts we know to be true about Sino-Korean initials:

1. The sound originally pronounced as k'- in China was usually pronounced as k-.

2. There were also some sounds pronounced as h- that were originally pronounced as k‘- in China.
3. There was only one character, 快 , read with an initial k‘-.
4. There was no difference between apicals (舌頭音) and laminals (舌上音).
5. There was no difference between bilabials (脣重音) and labiodentals (脣輕音).
6. There was no difference between dentals (齒頭音) and palato-alveolars (正齒音).
7. There were no voiced consonants (全濁音) at all.

Because of these facts, the initial consonants of fifteenth-century Sino-Korean were as follows:

p	t	ts	s	k	
p‘	t‘	ts‘		k‘	h
m	n			ŋ	
	r		z		

However, in trying to organize the Korean readings of Chinese characters, the compilers of the *Tongguk chŏng'un* presented a system of twenty-three initials that smacked of prescriptivism:

p	t	ts	s	k	ʔ
p‘	t‘	ts‘		k‘	h
$p^ʔ$	$t^ʔ$	$ts^ʔ$	$s^ʔ$	$k^ʔ$	$h^ʔ$
m	n			n	(zero)
	r		z		

The creators of the *Tongguk chŏng'un* tried to harmonize the actual Korean readings of Chinese characters in the fifteenth century with this twenty-three-initial system. In doing so, for example, they often represented consonants as voiced consonants or as *k*‘-, when in fact they were not.

SINO-KOREAN READINGS OF FINALS IN THE FIFTEENTH CENTURY

In the introduction to the *Tongguk chŏng'un*, the initials of Sino-Korean are explained in detail, but the finals (the vocalisms) are not mentioned. That is why few have dealt with the relationship between the vowel system of the *Hunmin chŏng'ŭm* and the final system of the *Tongguk chŏng'un*. However, there is a very close relationship between the two.

In the *Chejahae* (Explanations of the Designing of the Letters) of the *Hunmin chŏng'ŭm*, the seven principal vowels are explained as follows:

ㆍ	舌縮而聲深	ʌ (ɐ)
ㅡ	舌小縮而聲不深不淺	ɨ (ɯ)
ㅣ	舌不縮而聲淺	i
ㅗ	與ㆍ同而口蹙	o
ㅏ	與ㆍ同而口張	a
ㅜ	與ㅡ同而口蹙	u
ㅓ	與ㅡ同而口張	ə

ㆍ [ʌ] is pronounced with the tongue constricted, and the enunciation is deep.
ㅡ [ɨ] is pronounced with the tongue slightly constricted, and the enunciation is neither deep nor shallow.
ㅣ [i] is pronounced with the tongue not constricted, and the enunciation is shallow.
ㅗ [o] is like ㆍ [ʌ], but the mouth is constricted.
ㅏ [a] is like ㆍ [ʌ], but the mouth is spread.
ㅜ [u] is like ㅡ [ɨ], but the mouth is constricted.
ㅓ [ə] is like ㅡ [ɨ], but the mouth is spread.

We will now survey the relationship between the phonological system of the *Tongguk chŏng'un* and the actual Korean readings of Chinese characters in order to clarify what this vowel system is based upon. Recognizing that the readings in the *Tongguk chŏng'un* were compiled with the intention of revision, scholars have considered them excessively artificial ones and have made little of their relationships to the actual readings of Chinese characters.[1]

The appendix to this chapter lists the correspondences found in the finals, arranged by the rime groups (攝) of traditional rime tables; each rime group name is given in the leftmost column. The second column gives the *Tongguk chŏng'un* values. The number listed under the *Tongguk chŏng'un* column is the one assigned in the dictionary to that particular set of finals (the finals of the *Tongguk chŏng'un* were classified into twenty-six sets); to the right of the number is the "even tone" (平聲) name, both its alphabetic representation and the Chinese character used in the *Tongguk chŏng'un* to designate the set. The third column shows the readings of Chinese characters actually used in Korea in the fifteenth century. The column on the extreme right represents the same correspondences in "entering tone" syllables—that is, syllables with the same vocalism that ended in consonants other than nasals.

Based on the values in the table in the appendix to this chapter, Table 1 shows the correspondences between the vowels given in the *Hunmin chŏng'ŭm* and the *Tongguk chŏng'un* transcriptions, on the one hand, and the actual Sino-Korean readings, on the other (for comparison, the finals in the Korean translation of a Chinese rime dictionary, the *Hongwu zhengyun*, are also given).

Table 1. The Vowels of the *Hunmin chŏng'ŭm*

	·	ㅡ	ㅣ	ㅗ	ㅏ	ㅜ	ㅓ	ㅛ	ㅑ	ㅕ	ㅠ	ㅘ	ㅝ	ㆇ	ㆊ
	ʌ	ɨ	i	o	a	u	ə	io	ia	iə	iu	ua	uə	ioia	iuiə
Sino-Korean	o	o	o	o	o	o	o	o	o	o	o	o	o		o
Tongguk chŏng'un	o	o	o	o	o	o	o	o	o	o	o	o	o		o
Hongwu zhengyun		o	o		o	o	o		o	o	o	o	o		o

	ㆎ	ㅢ	ㅚ	ㅐ	ㅟ	ㅔ	ㆉ	ㅒ	ㆌ	ㅖ	ㅙ	ㅞ	ㆈ	ㆋ
	ʌi	ɨi	oi	ai	ui	əi	ioi	iai	iui	iəi	uai	uəi	ioiai	iuiəi
Sino-Korean	o	o	o	o	o	o			o	o	o	o		o
Tongguk chŏng'un	o	o	o	o	o				o	o	o			o
Hongwu zhengyun		o		o	o			o	o	o	o			o

From Table 1 we can conclude that the final system of the *Tongguk chŏng'un* corresponds almost completely with the vowel system of the *Hunmin chŏng'ŭm*. In other words, the compilation of the *Tongguk chŏng'un* can be said to have been based on the actual Korean readings of Chinese characters. It is true that the finals of the *Tongguk chŏng'un* are not in complete accord with the actual readings. That is because some finals of the *Tongguk chŏng'un* (-iuiən: -iən, -iuiəŋ:-iəŋ, -uiŋ:-oiŋ, -iui:-iu) were prescriptive readings intended to correct pronunciations. Nevertheless, of the eleven basic medial letters of the Korean alphabet, the symbols · , ㅗ , and ㅛ were not used to represent finals in the Korean translation of the *Hongwu zhengyun*. From this fact we can see that the *Tongguk chŏng'un* better reflected actual Korean readings of Chinese characters than could be expected from a Korean translation of Chinese categories.

THE MEDIAL SYSTEM OF THE *HUNMIN CHŎNG'ŬM*

Nevertheless, the text of the *Chejahae* of the *Hunmin chŏng'ŭm* together with Table 1 are still not adequate to identify how the vowels in the *Hunmin chŏng'ŭm* were actually articulated. It is useful to consider here also the following statement from the "explanatory notes" (*pŏmnye*) to the *Sasŏng t'onggo* (A Complete Investigation of the Four Tones) (the text dates from around 1455):

1. 大抵 本國之音 輕而淺 中國之音 重而深 (The sound of Korean is essentially light and shallow, and the sound of Chinese is heavy and deep.)
2. 故中聲為 ㅏ 之字 則讀如 ㅏ ㆍ 之間 為 ㅑ 之字 則讀如 ㅑ ㆍ 之間 (Therefore, the Chinese sound of the letter ㅏ is read as [a sound] between ㅏ and ㆍ; that of the letter ㅑ is read as [a sound] between ㅑ and ㆍ);
   ㅓ 則 ㅓ ㅡ 之間 ㅕ 則 ㅕ ㅡ 之間 (in the case of ㅓ, as [a sound] between ㅓ and ㅡ; in the case of ㅕ, as [a sound] between ㅕ and ㅡ);
   ㅗ 則 ㅗ ㆍ 之間 ㅛ 則 ㅛ ㆍ 之間 (in the case of ㅗ, as [a sound] between ㅗ and ㆍ; in the case of ㅛ, as [a sound] between ㅛ and ㆍ);
   ㅜ 則 ㅜ ㅡ 之間 ㅠ 則 ㅠ ㅡ 之間 (in the case of ㅜ, as [a sound] between ㅜ and ㅡ; in the case of ㅠ, as [a sound] between ㅠ and ㅡ);
   ㆍ 則 ㆍ ㅡ 之間 ㅡ 則 ㅡ ㆍ 之間 (in the case of ㆍ, as [a sound] between ㆍ and ㅡ; in the case of ㅡ, as [a sound] between ㅡ and ㆍ);
   ㅣ 則 ㅣ ㅡ 之間 (in the case of ㅣ, as [a sound] between ㅣ and ㅡ);
   然後庶合中國之音矣 (when these things are done, we can get the appropriate Chinese sounds.)

However, the commentaries to the Korean translation of the *Hongwu zhengyun*, a fifteenth-century work (1455) intended to standardize readings of Chinese characters, seem to show that the above statements were not applicable to all vowels. This line of reasoning is also supported by the commentaries to the *Sasŏng t'onghae* (1512).

The vowels actually used for the finals of the *Hongwu zhengyun* were ㅡ, ㅣ, ㅏ, ㅜ, ㅓ, ㅑ, ㅠ, ㅕ, ㅘ, ㅝ, ᆑ, ㅢ, ㅐ, ㅟ, ㅒ, ㆌ, ㅖ, and ㅙ, while those used under the criteria given in the explanatory notes to the *Sasŏng t'onggo* were only the endings ㅏ, ㅑ, ㅒ, ㅙ, ㅘ, ㅓ, ㅕ, and ㅝ. Let us look at these facts more closely.

Here are some statements from the commentaries to the *Hongwu zhengyun*:

> **Medial vowels:** ㅏ a, ㅙ uai, ㅒ iai
> The readings for the finals [represented by the characters] 皆, 解, and 泰 that are written with the vowel ' ㅏ ' are somewhat deep, and therefore should be pronounced with a sound between that of [Korean] ㅏ and ㆍ. However, finals that follow labials and palato-alveolars are pronounced as ㅏ.

The commentaries in the text are the same as the above for the vowels ㅏ, ㅑ, ㅘ and the finals 刪, 產, 諫, 割; the vowels ㅏ, ㅑ and the finals 爻, 巧, 效; the vowels ㅏ, ㅑ, ㅘ and the finals 陽, 養, 樣, 藥; the vowels ㅏ, ㅑ and the finals 覃, 感, 勘, 合.

> **Medial vowels:** ㅓ ə, ㅝ uə
> The readings for the finals 歌, 哿, 箇 that are written with the vowel ' ㅓ ' are not in accord with actual pronunciations. Therefore, they should be pronounced as a sound between ' ㅓ ' and ' ㅡ ', using the same tongue shape as that of ' ㅓ '. They come near to the sound ' ㅗ ' [ɤ]. Vowels written with ' ㅝ ' are the same.

> **Medial vowels:** ㅕ iə
> The readings for the finals 蕭, 條, 嘯 that are written with the vowel ' ㅕ ' are not in accord with actual pronunciations. Therefore, they should be pronounced as a sound between ' ㅕ ' and ' ㅡ ' with the same tongue shape as that of ' ㅕ '. [In the *Sasŏng t'onghae*, where the sound series of (the Korean version of) the *Hongwu zhengyun* seem to have been copied down intact, there is a commentary saying that in northern Chinese there is no sound ' ㅕ '. It follows that the above commentary is applicable only for ' ㅓ '.]

The above commentaries can be summarized as follows: (a) the Chinese sound corresponding to ' ㅏ ' is somewhat deep and therefore should be pronounced as a sound between ' ㅏ ' and ' ㆍ ' of Korean; and (b) the Chinese sound corresponding to ' ㅓ ', if pronounced as a sound between ' ㅓ ' and ' ㅡ ', comes closer to ' ㅗ ' [ɤ]. The meaning of (a) can be understood more clearly with the help of the explanatory notes to the *Sasŏng t'onghae*. There it is explained that in the articulation of dental sibilants (齒音), alveolars (齒頭) are pronounced with the tongue raised up to teeth and their sound is shallow, whereas palato-alveolars (整齒) are pronounced with the tongue rolled up to the alveolar ridge and their sound is deep.

The terms "shallow" and "deep" used in these commentaries seem to refer to whether the points of articulation are relatively front or back. Therefore, the indication is that the ' ㅏ ' [a] of Korean is a central vowel, ' ㆍ ' [ʌ] a back vowel, and the *a* of Chinese is a vowel pronounced as a sound between the two.

Statement (b) indicates that the Chinese vowel written with ' ㅓ ' must be pronounced as a sound between Korean ' ㅓ ' and ' ㅡ ' and that, when that is done, the actual sound thus becomes something close to ' ㅗ '. This statement can be interpreted as meaning, for example, that the actual readings of the Chinese final ' 歌 '—which was written with the vowel ' ㅓ ' in the *Sasŏng t'onghae*—were [-ɔ] and [-uɔ] (or [-ɤ]) in the fourteenth and fifteenth centuries. A Chinese ending written as ' ㅝ ' [uə] was also pronounced as something close to ' ㅗ ' [ɤ].

Based on these explanations, it can be concluded that the vowels of Middle Korean were articulated in the following places ('a' and 'ɤ''represent the values of the Chinese vowels):

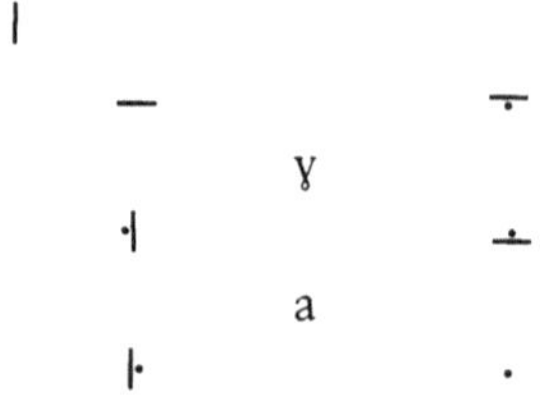

CONCLUSION

In their introductory remarks to the *Tongguk chŏng'un*, the editors stated that the Korean readings of Chinese characters, when compared with the proper Chinese readings, were in great confusion. Therefore, they said, the *Tongguk chŏng'un* was compiled with the intent of correcting these differences. Largely as a result of this statement, modern scholars have tended to dismiss the readings given in that dictionary as wholly artificial and prescriptive, and they have thus underestimated the true linguistic achievement represented by the *Tongguk chŏng'un*. The oversight is unfortunate. The *Tongguk chŏng'un* is, on the contrary, an extremely valuable work not only for interpreting the Korean readings of Chinese characters, but also for understanding Middle Korean and the Korean alphabet in a much broader sense.

When we compare the phonological system of the actual Sino-Korean readings with the readings of Chinese characters given in the *Tongguk chŏng'un*, we find many obvious correspondences, and these correspondences are especially striking in the two vowel systems. Thus we may conclude that the *Tongguk chŏng'un* was based on the true Korean readings of Chinese characters in the fifteenth century and that the analysis of these Sino-Korean readings contributed to the creation of the Korean alphabet as a phonemic framework of twenty-three initial consonants and eleven principal vowels.

APPENDIX

RIME	*TONGGUK CHŎNG'UN* Final No.	Name	Reading	SINO-KOREAN VALUES	ENTERING TONE EXAMPLES*
山	10	간 干	-an	-an	-al : -al
			-uan	-uan	-ual : -ual
	12	건 鞬	-ən	-ən	-əl : -əl
				(-an)	(-al)
			-uən	-uən	-uəl : -uəl
				(-uan)	(-ual)
			-iən	-iən	-iəl : -iəl
			-iuiən	-iən	-iuiəl : -iəl
咸	14	감 甘	-am	-am	-ap : -ap
				(-ʌm)	(-iəp)
				(-iəm)	
	15	검 箝	-əm	-əm	-əp : -əp
				(-am)	
				(-ɨm)	
			-iəm	-iəm	-iəp : -iəp
				(-ʌm)	
梗	1	긍 揯	-ʌiŋ	-ʌiŋ	-ʌik : -ʌik
					(-ak)
				-iəŋ	: -iək
				(-iŋ)	
	2	굉 觥	-oiŋ	-oiŋ	-oik : -oik
					(-uk)
	7	경 京	-iəŋ	-iəŋ	-iək : -iək
					(-ik)
					(-ʌik)
					(-ɨk)
			-iuiəŋ	-iəŋ	-iuiək : -iək
曾	1	긍 揯	-ɨŋ	-ɨŋ	-ɨk : -ɨk
				(-ʌŋ)	(-ʌk)
				(-iŋ)	(-ək)
					(-iək)
					(-ʌik)
					(-ik)

Continued on next page

APPENDIX—*Continued*

Rime	*Tongguk chŏng'un* Final No.	Name	Reading	Sino-Korean Values	Entering Tone Examples*
			-iŋ	-iŋ	-ik : -ik
				-iŋ	-ʌik : -ʌik
	2	굉 觥	-oiŋ	-oiŋ	-oik : -ok
	3	귕 肱	-uiŋ	-oiŋ	-uik : -uk
				-uŋ	
	7	경 京			-iək : -iək
					-iuiək : -iək
宕	5	강 江	-aŋ	-aŋ	-ak : -ak
					(-uak)
			-iaŋ	-iaŋ	-iak : -iak
				(-aŋ)	
			-uaŋ	-uaŋ	-uak : -uak
				(-aŋ)	(-ak)
江	5	강 江	-aŋ	-aŋ	-ak : -ak
					(-ʌk)
果	24	강 歌	-a	-a	
				(-ua)	
			-ua	-ua	
				(-a)	
				(-o)	
假	24	강 歌	-a	-a	
				(-ia)	
				(-ai)	
			-ia	-ia	
				(-a)	
				(-iə)	
			-ua	-ua	
蟹	20	갱 佳	-ai	-ai	
				(-oi)	
				-ʌi	
				(-ai)	
				(-iəi)	
			-uai	-uai	
				(-ua)	
	18	ᄌᆞᆼ 貲	-ʌi	-ʌi	
				(-ɨi)	
				(-ai)	
				(-oi)	
			-i	-i	
	19	굉 傀	-oi	-oi	
				(-ui)	
				(-ʌi)	
				(-ɨi)	
	22	곙 鷄	-iəi	-iəi	
				(-əi)	
				(-iə)	
				(-i)	
				(-ʌ)	
				(-ɨi)	
			-iuiəi	-iəi	
				-iu	
				(-uəi)	
				(-iuiəi)	

APPENDIX—*Continued*

RIME	*TONGGUK CHŎNG'UN* Final No.	Name	Reading	SINO-KOREAN VALUES	ENTERING TONE EXAMPLES*
效	16	고ᇢ 高	-ow	-o (-u)	
				(-io)	
				(-oi)	
			-iow	-io	
				(-o)	
臻	8	ᄀᆞᆫ 根	-ʌn	-ʌn	
				-ɨn	
			-ɨn	-ɨn	-ɨl : -ɨl
				-ən	-əl
				(-in)	
			-in	-in	-il : -il
					(-ɨul)
					-ɨl
	9	곤 昆	-on	-on	-ol : -ol
					(-ɨl)
				-un	-ul
	11	군 君	-un	-un	-ul : -ul
				(-on)	(-ɨl)
			-iun	-iun	-iul : -iul
深	13	ᄌᆞᆷ 簪	-ʌm	-ʌm	
			-ɨm	-ɨm	-ɨp : -ɨp
				(-am)	
				(-um)	
			-im	-im	-ip : -ip
				(-ʌm)	(-ɨp)
通	4	공 公	-oŋ	-oŋ	-ok : -ok
				-uŋ	
			-ioŋ	-ioŋ	-iok : -iok
				(-oŋ)	
	6	궁 弓	-uŋ	-uŋ	-uk : -uk
			-iuŋ	-iuŋ	-iuk : -iuk
				(-ioŋ)	
止	18	ᄌᆞᆼ 貲	-ʌ	-ʌ	
				(-ɨi)	
				(-i)	
				(-ʌi)	
				(-ai)	
			-i	-i	
				(-ʌ)	
				(-ʌi)	
				(-ɨi)	
				(-iəi)	
			-ɨi	-ɨi	
				(-ʌ)	
				(-ʌi)	
				(-i)	
				(-uəi)	
	21	귕 媯	-ui	-ui	
				(-oi)	
				(-iu)	
				(-iuiə)	
				-uəi	
				(-i)	

Continued on next page

APPENDIX—*Continued*

RIME	TONGGUK CHŎNG'UN Final No.	Name	Reading	SINO-KOREAN VALUES	ENTERING TONE EXAMPLES*
			-iui	-iu	
				(-iəi)	
				(-oi)	
				(-io)	
				(-iui)	
				(-ui)	
				(-iuiəi)	
流	17	구ㅱ 鳩	-uw	-u	
				(-o)	
				(-iu)	
				(-iui)	
			-iu	-iu	
				(-iui)	
遇	23	공 孤	-o	-o	
				(-oi)	
				(-u)	
				(-io)	
	26	겅 居	-ə	-ə	
				(-əi)	
			-iə	-iə	
				(-iəi)	
				(-ia)	
	25	궁 拘	-u	-u	
				(-o)	
				(-iu)	
			-iu	-iu	
				(-u)	
				(-iui)	

*In these entering tone forms, the letter ㄹ, which is elsewhere in this chapter represented as /r/, is written as -l, since the phoneme is assumed to have been phonetically realized as a lateral in syllable-final position.

NOTE

1. Yu Ch'ang-gyun (1963), however, claims that the vowel letters of the *Hunmin chŏng'ŭm* originated from the *Tongguk chŏng'un* system.

REFERENCES

Kang, Sinhang. 1973. *Sasŏng t'onghae* yŏn'gu (A study of the *Sasŏng t'onghae*). Seoul: Sinasa.

———. 1990. *Hunmin chŏng'ŭm* yŏn'gu (A study of the *Hunmin chŏng'ŭm*). Revised ed. Seoul: Sŏnggyun'gwan University Press.

Lee, Ki-Moon. 1972. Kugŏ ŭmunsa yŏn'gu (A study of the phonological history of Korean). Seoul: Seoul National University Han'gungmunhwa Yŏn'guso.

Pak, Pyŏng-ch'ae. 1983. *Hongmu chŏng'un yŏkhun*-ŭi sinyŏn'gu (A new study of the Korean translation of the *Hongwu zhengyun*). Seoul: Koryŏdae Minjongmunhwa yŏn'guso.

Yu, Ch'ang-gyun. 1963. Hunmin chŏng'ŭm chungsŏngch'ege kusŏng-ŭi kŭn'gŏ (The basis for the formation of the principal vowel system of the *Hunmin chŏng'ŭm*). Ŏmunhak, vol. 10: 24–43.

———. 1966. *Tongguk chŏng'un* yŏn'gu (A study of the *Tongguk chŏng'un*). Taegu, Korea: Hyŏngsŏl Publishing Co.

7

THE INVENTION OF THE ALPHABET AND THE HISTORY OF THE KOREAN LANGUAGE

S. Robert Ramsey

The invention of the Korean alphabet took place during an unusual time in the history of Korean. With his alphabet Sejong recorded a stage of the language characterized by consonant clusters and a complex system of tones. Both structural features were short-lived. Changes in the clusters began almost immediately—some may well have had alternate pronunciations as single phonemes even at the time of Sejong's invention. Within a century or so, clusters had developed into the well-known "reinforced" consonants found in all later-known varieties of the language. The tone system also soon disappeared in the central dialects. Reflexes of its distinctions can be found in the pitch accent and vowel length of some modern dialects, but no dialect of Korean today has a system of suprasegmentals quite like that attested by the tone marks of Sejong's writing system.

SEJONG'S PHONEMICS

Today we rightly marvel at the fact that Sejong invented an alphabet incorporating graphic representation of features. But the greater wonder is that he was able to invent an alphabet at all, given the theoretical framework within which he had to work.

Chinese phonological theory, which underlay Korean thinking about language, began with the syllable as the basic unit of phonology. Up until Sejong's day, the greatest discovery of this phonological science had been the realization that the syllable could be divided into two smaller units, an "initial" and a "final." The initial was the initial consonant (if the syllable began with a vowel, the initial was zero), and the final contained everything else—the medial vowel, the nuclear vowel, the ending or coda, and the tone. This discovery made Chinese phonological science possible, for out of it came the *fanqie* ("turning and cutting") system of indicating pronunciation, with which Chinese scholars were able to record, after a fashion, the phonological system of their language.[1]

In Korea the Chinese division of the syllable into two parts was changed into a three-way analysis. This new, Korean analysis appears for the first time in the *Humin chŏng'ŭm*, where the syllable is analyzed into an initial, a medial, and a terminal. In our phonemic analyses, initials and terminals have equal standing as phonological units, since they are all consonants. But for Sejong the initials were the departure point provided by a Chinese-style framework. His innovation was that he realized the initials could be equated to the sounds that ended the syllable: "For the terminal sounds, one again uses the initial sounds," he wrote (see Appendix 2). That was all he said about the terminals. Since the initials had all been listed and explained, the terminals did not need to be given again because they were the same. The remainder of the syllable was the "medial sound," which we recognize as the vocalic element. Thus arose the discovery of the vowel, for which separate symbols were devised, making the new writing system into a true alphabet.

Representation of Clusters

But Sejong also recognized that a tripartite division of the syllable was not enough to represent Korean fully. His Korean analysis was not completely bound by any theoretical framework. The editors of the *Hunmin chŏng'ŭm haerye* outlined the workings of this much more complex Korean system in the section "Explanation of the Combining of the Letters." What we call initial clusters are introduced as follows: "With the initial sounds, two or three letters may be used together and written side by side. For example, in the colloquial language [i.e., Korean], *·sta* 'land', *pcak* 'one of a pair', and *·pskum* 'crack, opening'." With these three examples, the *Haerye* succinctly introduces the three kinds of initial clusters generally recognized for Middle Korean: (1) those clusters that begin with *s*-, (2) those that begin with *p*-, and (3) those that begin with *ps*-.

Geminates

But there was also another group of complex initials. The *Haerye* section on combining letters continues: "[Some letters] can be written side by side with themselves. For example, vulgar colloquial *·hye* 'tongue', but *·hhye* 'to pull'; *kwoy·Oye* 'I love someone', but *kwoy·OOye* 'someone loves me'; *swo·ta* 'overturning something', but *sswo·ta* 'to shoot it'." The *Haerye* editors tell us nothing more. The minimal pairs show that the geminate symbols represented real phonemic contrasts in the language, but what were they? Linguists and philologists have puzzled over these examples.

The curious geminate *OO* is rare in Middle Korean texts. It is found only after a causative/passive verb stem and before /y/ or (orthographically) *i*. It is variously thought to have represented *-yy-*, a "narrowing and tensing" of this semivowel, a juncture marker, or perhaps a special occurrence of the velar fricative *G*. In any event, the geminate did not occur in word-initial position. The geminate *hh* has an even more restricted occurrence. It only occurred in the one etymon meaning "to pull." The third geminate, *ss*, in contrast, represents much more than a marginal distinction. It occurred widely in the early texts and increased in frequency thereafter.

The Phonemic Status of Middle Korean *ss*

What is represented by *ss* is generally assumed to have had the same phonological value in Sejong's day that it has now; that is (along with *hh*), *ss* was a reinforced, or tense, consonant, and by this feature of tensity it is thought to have contrasted with the plain sibilant *s*. By this line of (probably correct) reasoning, *ss* was the precursor of the modern series of distinctively reinforced obstruents.

But Sejong was not intentionally using a digraph to write a unit phoneme. He clearly saw *ss* as a combining of two phonemic units, just as the editors of *Haerye* said it was. What it represented was phonemically two separate *s*'s. The segmental phonemes had already been introduced, and this entire section of the *Haerye* was meant as an explanation of how those phonemes, which had all been explained in the previous section, were combined to form syllables and words. There is no reason to believe that Sejong was anticipating later orthographic convention by using digraphs to represent phonemes with distinctively tense articulation.

Sejong had a deep understanding of phonemic analysis. Ki-Moon Lee is surely right in saying (in another context) that Sejong closely identified the *s* found at the beginning of complex initials with the *s* of the Middle Korean genitive marker, the so-called *sai-siot* (1972: 123). Whatever phonetic value *ss* may have had in initial position, its occurrences in medial position were enough to establish its identity as a geminate, or cluster of two *s*'s—two separate phonemes.

An Etymological Source for Initial ss-

Part of the reason for questioning the double *s* at the beginning of words seems to be the existence of Middle Korean doublets like *sip-* ~ *ssip-* 'chew'. Such doublets are considered early evidence for the marking of words with emphasis by tensing the initial (see Kim-Renaud 1977). Martin, however, suggests that these initials had incorporated an "emphatic prefix," which probably had a sibilant pronunciation (1991: 44). This solution would help explain why most authentic occurrences of initial *ss* in Middle Korean were found in verb forms;[2] the emphatic marking of words began in the verbs (Ki-Moon Lee 1977: 53; Ramsey 1978), extending only later to noun forms. Examples of *ss* include:

ssip- 'chew'	·*sso-* 'be valuable'	·*sso-* 'pile up, build'
·*ssu-* 'write'	·*ssu-* 'wear (a hat)'	·*sswo-* 'shoot, sting'

All of the above Middle Korean verb stems had variants with a single *s* as the initial consonant (e.g., ·so- 'be valuable'). It is curious that these forms with a single-*s* initial were recorded later than those with the double symbol *ss* (for example, ·*ssu-* 'write' is found in the *Sŏkpo sangŏl* of 1447; ·*su-* 'write' is found in the *Wŏn'gak-kyŏng ŏnhae* of 1465). But there is little reason to believe that the forms were therefore any less authentic. They still constituted doublets, despite the relatively later dates of attestation.

There is another piece of evidence that at least two of the above six verbs were morphemically complex. As described in Ramsey 1986 and 1991, verb stems with complex initials were accompanied by other morphological peculiarities. Such monosyllabic stems were regularly characterized by (1) a high pitch, (2) a "minimal vowel" (*o*/*u*) or *i*, and (3) an open syllable. The verb stem *ssip-* 'chew' was low-pitched and closed by a consonant; the stem ·*sswo-* 'shoot' has as its vowel /wo/.[3] Thus both forms appear not to belong naturally to the class of stems with complex initials. The evidence seems strong that in both cases a prefix was added.

What about the other four stems? They have the canonical shape we expect of stems with complex initials. Thus, if they are also morphemically complex (as Martin's evidence suggests), the prefix was probably added at a relatively early date. That is certainly the case with ·*ssu*- 'to write'. In an important, recent discovery, Ki-Moon Lee has found that this verb was transcribed in the *Jilin leishi* (A.D. 1103–1104) with phonograms indicating a reading of **husu*- (1991: 18).[4] The prefix (if that is what it is) was already present in the twelfth century.

Lee's reconstruction is extremely interesting. For my own research, it is important because of the support it lends to my suggestion, on the basis of internal evidence from the fifteenth-century materials, that we reconstruct dissyllabic forms for such stems (Ramsey 1986, 1991). In the case of this particular verb, I had reconstructed **su·su*- (with the second syllable automatically assigned a high pitch). But now Lee has shown that I was probably wrong in my assumption that the initial consonant was a sibilant. Instead, the consonant appears to have been a velar fricative. If this is right, the lone Middle Korean occurrence of *hh* (in the verb ·*hhye*- 'to pull') can be explained as an example of that same element. But this one solution raises other, more difficult problems. If **hu*- and not **su*- were found to be the original form of Martin's "emphatic prefix," we would be hard pressed to explain why the emphatic variant of *kuzu*- 'lead' is *skuzu*- and not ˣ*khuzu*- (see below, for discussion of the aspirates).

Representation of Tones

The nature of Korean phonological analysis becomes especially clear in the way the tones are treated. The categories of the analysis are Chinese, at least in form, as we see from the terse description at the end of the main text of the *Hunmin chŏng'ŭm*: "One dot added to the left [of the syllable] indicates the Going Tone. Two indicate the Rising Tone. If there are none, then it is the Even Tone. For the Entering Tone, the adding of dots is the same, while [the pronunciation is] hurried and tense." The traditional four tones, the terms in which this description is couched, were not the natural distinctions of Korean. Sejong used them because they were the departure point for any discussion of suprasegmentals. But within the confining framework of these categories he was still able to represent Korean in a way that did not distort the data. His thinking rose above the limitations of theory.

In the Chinese phonological system of traditional analysis, pitch distinctions were neutralized in syllables ending in an unreleased voiceless stop, *-p*, *-t*, or *-k*. Such syllables were therefore classified in a separate "tonal" category called the "Entering Tone." But Sejong realized that, in the Korean language, pitch distinctions obtained for such syllable types. This is why he added the phrase "for the Entering Tone, the adding of dots is the same." Further on, in the *Haerye*, Sejong's commissioners added examples showing all the possible pitch distinctions found in "entering tone" syllables.

Not all of the tones recorded in Middle Korean texts were distinctive. After the first high pitch in a verb stem or noun, distinctions tended to be ignored or overridden by automatic rules of prosody (see Ramsey 1978 and the references cited there to works by Kim Wanjin and Chŏng Yŏnch'an). Martin calls the typical string of nondistinctive pitches "an automatic 'sing-song' tune of alternating accents" (1991: 61).

But, distinctive or not, the "tones" were marked consistently. The conventions for affixing diacritic dots were followed faithfully, and apparently with very few mistakes, for a good century and a half. It was a remarkable achievement. Few societies, even in modern times, have managed such strict orthographic standards, especially regarding the use of diacritics. Though we have no record of it, there must have been rigorous, standardized training for typesetters and editors.[5]

MIDDLE KOREAN AND INTERNAL RECONSTRUCTION

Because of Sejong's consistent system of transcription, particularly of the suprasegmental pitches, the phonological system reflected in the *Hunmin chŏng'ŭm* and the subsequent texts of the Middle Korean period can be known in extraordinary detail. The texts provide the most fertile kind of ground for phonological analysis.

In a number of articles, most recently Ramsey 1991, I have described ways in which earlier stages of the Korean language can be reconstructed by using these materials. These attempts have relied on paradigmatic and distributional irregularities in the phonological system, supplemented by comparative evidence from the modern dialects.

Aspirates as Clusters

In addition to plain initials and clusters, Middle Korean also had aspirates. Though Sejong analyzed these as unit phonemes, it is clear that, in origin at least, the aspirates were also complex (for discussion see Ramsey 1991).

As mentioned above, three series of clusters were transcribed in Middle Korean texts. To these, let us now add the third series of complex consonants, the aspirates:

sp-	st-	sk-	(ss- hh-)
pt-	pth-	ps-	pc-
pst-	psk-		
ph-	th-	ch-	kh-

Sources for Complex Initials

The correlation between patterns of accent and canonical shapes of morphemes shows clearly, in my view, the origins of consonant clusters and most other complex initials. The basic distributional facts are listed in Ramsey 1991 and need not be repeated here.

I would but add that, for the purposes of internal reconstruction, the shapes that do not occur are as important as those that do. In Middle Korean, unaccented occurrences of the so-called *minimal* vowels *o* and *u* are rarely found between voiceless obstruents.[6] Those missing syllable types were, in my view, the sources of most complex initials found in the fifteenth century. Low-pitched minimal vowels had occurred between voiceless obstruents at an earlier stage of the language, but these were subsequently lost through syncope before the fifteenth century. Once such a vowel was lost, the obstruents formerly separated by that vowel came together to form a cluster. Stems that had originally been two syllables long became monosyllables. The location of high pitches, which had largely been predictable, became distinctive.

Dating the Changes

Internal reconstruction, like the comparative method, tells us nothing about when the changes took place. There is at most, in the abundance of evidence, only the hint that some of the changes may not have taken place long before Sejong's day.

The adoption of Chinese vocabulary into Korean provides at least an approximate reference point. Unfortunately, Sino-Korean contains no information about clusters. But, as is well known, its distinctions do at least give clues about the sequence in which the aspirates emerged. Sino-Korean *th-* and *ch-* (versus *t-* and *c-*), on the one hand, reflect well original Chinese distinctions in the dentals and dental affricates; *ph-*, on the other hand, does not reflect the aspiration of Chinese; and *kh-* is extremely rare in Sino-Korean, being found only in the readings of four characters.

On the basis of this and other evidence, Ki-Moon Lee argues that Old Korean (the language of Silla) probably had aspiration distinctions in the dentals and dental affricates (1977: 89–91). A few occurrences of the labial aspirate *ph* may have by then already been distinct from *p*; but the velar aspirate *kh* had a marginal existence, if it existed at all, in Old Korean.

The emergence of clusters and the growth of aspirate vocabulary through vowel syncope seem to have taken place much later—at least after the twelfth century. From phonograms used in the *Jilin leishi*, Ki-Moon Lee reconstructs **posol* as the twelfth-century form of *·psol* 'rice' (1977: 60–61). The phonograms used for **potol* 'daughter' are further evidence that vowel syncope had not yet taken place. Finally, from other phonograms in the same text, the *Jilin leishi*, Lee has now found evidence enabling him to reconstruct as twelfth-century forms **hoto-* and **huku-* for *·tho-* 'ride' for *·khu-* 'be big' (Lee 1991: 17–18).

The Role of Internal Reconstruction

The last two forms highlight both the strengths and the weaknesses of internal reconstruction. Based on internal evidence alone, I suggested (Ramsey 1986: 193) somewhat different reconstructions:

Ramsey 1986	Lee 1991	Middle Korean
*.to·Ho-	*hoto-	·tho- 'ride'
*.ku·Hu-	*huku-	·khu- 'be big'

In these forms I reconstructed an ambiguous **H* because the structure of Middle Korean did not give enough information to decide what voiceless velar obstruent was the source of aspiration. Moreover, as Lee's evidence makes clear, my ordering of the two consonants involved was incorrect. Now we see that (in addition to vowel syncope) the creation of aspirates at least sometimes required metathesis (or assimilation of aspiration). Lee's reconstructions also raise the possibility that Martin's "emphatic prefix" may have been involved in the process.

Still, internal reconstruction enables us to determine the pitches of the earlier forms and to specify more precisely which vowels were subject to syncope. More important, internal reconstruction allows us to work with the entire corpus of Middle Korean. Because of internal reconstruction, we can say with confidence that the entire class of verb stems with the canonical shape of the above two verbs originated through the same phonological processes. By contrast, the *Jilin leishi* phonograms, precious though they may be, do not yield this kind of systematic information. The two methods are best used in a complementary way.

The Initials *pst-* and *psk-*

Most words beginning with *pst-* and *psk-* (and *pth-*) appear to be compounds. Once we have restored the vowels lost through syncope, the forms become at least three syllables long, too long to be single Korean morphemes. (As a rule, Korean morphemes generally do not exceed two syllables in length.)

The majority of these words form a semantic word family having to do with breaking, cracking, piercing, and so on. Here are ten examples:

1. pskay- 'to break'
2. ·psketi- 'to collapse, fall in'
3. :pskey- 'to penetrate, go through'
4. ·psku- 'to cut off'
5. ·psko- 'to peel (a shell, etc.)'
6. ·pski- 'to stick in'
7. ·pskul 'a chisel'
8. ·pskum 'a crack, interstice'
9. psto·li- 'to break'
10. pstilG- ~pstilu- 'to pierce, gore, stick, poke'

I believe all of these words are compounds containing the verb *pozo-~poso-~pozG-~posG-~puzu-* 'break, shatter'. As can be seen, this (pre-)verb had many variants in Middle Korean; its modern reflexes are even more varied: *puswu-*, *pusu-*, *paswu-*, *peswu-*, *pus-*, *pu(s)-* (with *pue* as the infinitive), and probably still other forms in the dialects. If we apply reasoning along the lines developed in Ki-Moon Lee 1977 (pp. 15–25), a velar can be reconstructed for this verb; an earlier form may have been something like **pozgo-* or **pozog-*. But the ancestor of the form that appears in the ten compounds given above must have had voiceless consonants (at least **s* in place of **z*); otherwise, the interceding minimal vowel would not have been lost, since syncope seems to have taken place only between voiceless obstruents. Thus, at some point in the history of the word, there must have also been a variant with the form **pos(k)o-* or **poso(k)-*. The modern reflexes support such a reconstruction.

Compare, especially, number (9) with a modern verb of similar meaning, *puse-ttuli-* 'to smash', which is a compound with *-(t)tuli-*, an auxiliary verb that intensifies transitivity. Example number (10) had as a synonym *tilG-*~*tilu-*; this latter verb was apparently the uncompounded form. Perhaps *:pskey-* 'to penetrate, go through' (3) is related to *:ey-* 'go around'. It does not take a big stretch of imagination to see that *·pskul* 'a chisel' is a tool for breaking or cracking; the noun must therefore be a nominalization of the verb in question. The noun *·pskum* 'a crack, interstice' is an even more obvious nominalization.

Here are some words with *psk-* or *pst-* initials that are possibly also related:

11. ·psko- 'to hatch'
12. pskuley 'bundle'
13. ·psku 'time, occasion'
14. ·pski 'time, occasion'
15. ·pskini 'meal(time)'
16. ·pstay 'time, occasion'

The verb *·psko-* 'to hatch' (11) was another form of example (5); hatching an egg was another way of breaking a shell. Number (12) appears in a hapax from *Kugŭppang ŏnhae* (1466?) in the context '(divide into two) bundles'; the meaning may have been 'divisions' rather than 'bundles'. Numbers (13) and (14) may be nominal forms of the verb *·psku-* 'cut off' (4)—a time or occasion can be thought of as a juncture in time. Number (15), *·pskini* 'meal(time)', is probably a compound containing number (14), *·pski* 'time, occasion'. Number (16), *·pstay* 'time, occasion', appears to be a compound of (13) plus a variant of (-)*·toy* 'time (when)'.

Words that do not appear to be related include

17. ·pskwu- 'to borrow'
18. psku·li- 'to envelope, wrap, embrace'
19. ·pskwul 'honey'
20. psti- '(water) steams'
21. pstu·li 'smallpox, pustule, or pimple'

Number (17) is not well attested; it usually appears, especially in early texts, as *·skwu-*. It is possible to imagine water steaming (20) as somehow involving bursting; but wrapping or embracing (18) is a bit farther away semantically. The two nouns *·pskwul* 'honey' and *pstu·li* 'smallpox' must have other etymologies. The latter, especially, may well be a loanword of some sort—unless pustules are thought of as things bursting through the skin.

There are a number of words with *pth-* initials in Middle Korean. Though it is not yet clear how they might be related etymologically to the other word family, some of these also have meanings involving breaking or bursting:

22. ·ptho- 'to split, crush'
23. ·pthu- 'to crack open'
24. ·ptheti- 'to burst'

Other examples of words with this initial include

25. ·ptho- 'to pluck (a zither)'
26. ·pthut- 'to pluck out (hairs, etc.)
27. ·ptho- 'to clap (hands)'
28. pthwuy- 'to spring, bound'
29. :pthwuk (onomatopoeia)

CHANGE AND TRANSITION

We tend to view phonological change as a slow, inexorable process, but such may not be the case. Our awareness of systematic change grew out of nineteenth-century philology, a time when Lyell's theory of ponderous, glacial change as the mechanism for shaping geological history still very much held sway. Darwinian theory, the scientific model on which linguistic theorists drew more direct analogies, also stressed the slow, smooth, and imperceptible nature of change. However, in more recent decades the biological and geological sciences have begun to accommodate less gradual models of historical change. These days one hears of sudden environmental or climatic shifts, of "catastrophe" theories (meteorites, for example, decimating life forms, reminiscent of Whiston's late-seventeenth-century theory of life-destroying comets), or of the evolution of species in fits and starts and relative bursts of sudden change after long periods of genetic stability. Such models are richer and more interesting than ones describing change as the slow ticking of a clock.

Language, too, must surely, at times, change rapidly after relatively long periods of stability. In our field one sees evidence that this idea is gaining acceptance. Gradualism is receding. Glottochronology, for example, so popular thirty or forty years ago, is generally felt to be discredited, not just because of arguments against its mathematics but, I believe, because the rigidity of the model does not fit well the spirit of our times.

The ideas about the Korean language I have tried to develop in this chapter fit a more punctuated model of language change. The sound system reflected in the early alphabetic texts appears to represent a transition stage of the language. Sejong documented structural features resulting from extensive phonological change; soon after his day, these features were leveled. In particular, the last set of examples, the family of words with the peculiar initial clusters *psk-* and *pst-*, seem especially out of place in Korean. Few in number, these words have the appearance of fleeting, transitional forms. The rich Middle Korean system of initial clusters and tones characterized a relatively short and atypical stage of Korean phonological history.

NOTES

1. The splitting of the syllabic atom remained a highly theoretical analysis that never became part of Chinese writing. It was never (until the *zhuyin fuhao* spellers of modern times) made into a usable orthography.

2. Or, in nouns, were transparently cases of morphemic complexity, usually involving *sai-siot;* e.g., *s ·non ·ni sswo·li ·ni,...* '"s," being a tooth sound,...' (*Hunmin chŏng'ŭm ŏnhae*, 7b).

3. This verb is recorded as having a low pitch in the *Haerye*. If true, there would be an additional divergence from the canonical shape. But since in other texts the verb is attested with a high pitch, it is likely that this one instance in the *Haerye* was either a slip or an overzealous effort to create a perfect minimal pair with *swo·ta* 'overturning something'.

4. Lee presents his reconstruction in han'gŭl. Here, as throughout this chapter, Yale romanization is used to transcribe Korean linguistic forms. The Korean Vowel Shift has not been taken into account.

5. This observation about premodern standardization of Korean orthography comes out of discussions with Professor Ki-Moon Lee.

6. See Ramsey 1991: 232 for an interesting class of exceptions. There are also a small number of as yet unexplained exceptions, such as *poto·thi-* 'to hit' and *potoy* (part of a loom).

REFERENCES

Kim, C.-W., and Soo-Hee Toh. 1980. Rule reordering in Middle Korean phonology. *Language Research* 16: 75–86.

Kim-Renaud, Young-Key. 1977. The syllable in Korean phonology. Paper presented at the Korean Symposium, 1977 Institute of the Linguistic Society of America, Honolulu, Hawai'i. In *Papers in Korean Linguistics*, ed. Chin-W. Kim, 85–98. Columbia, S.C.: Hornbeam Press.

Lee, Ki-Moon. 1972. Kugŏ-sa kaesŏl. Revised ed. Seoul: Minjung Sŏgwan.

———. 1977. Kugŏ ŭmun-sa yŏn'gu. Seoul: Tower Press.

———. 1991. Kugŏ ŏhwi-sa yŏn'gu. Seoul: Tong' a ch'ulp'ansa.

Lee, Sung Nyong. 1961. Chungse kugŏ munpŏp. Seoul: Ŭr'yu munhwasa.

Martin, Samuel E. 1992. A reference grammar of Korean. Rutland, VT.: Charles E. Tuttle Company.

Ramsey, S. Robert. 1978. Accent and morphology in Korean dialects. Seoul: Tower Press.

———. 1986. The inflecting stems of proto-Korean. *Language Research* 22:2: 183–194.

———. 1991. Proto-Korean and the origin of Korean accent. In *Studies in the historical phonology of Asian languages*, ed. William G. Boltz and Michael C. Shapiro, 215–238. Amsterdam: John Benjamins Publishing Company.

8

THE STRUCTURE OF PHONOLOGICAL UNITS IN HAN'GŬL

Chin W. Kim

Five and a half centuries after its historic invention and after at least one half century's scholarship probing into its origin and background, the true nature of han'gŭl's graphic structure is yet to be fully appreciated. There has been much praise but little appraisal. Like a beautiful work of art or literature, han'gŭl has been admired but not been critically analyzed. It is fitting therefore that a special symposium on han'gŭl was organized at the eighth biennial meeting of the International Circle of Korean Linguistics. I will examine three of its many virtues here.

HAN'GŬL AS A FEATURAL SCRIPT

The universal praise of han'gŭl usually centers on two points: (1) it is the world's first invented, not evolved, writing system currently in use, and (2) it is a system based on the principle of one character per phoneme. However, han'gŭl has more merit than these two points suggest. I contend that it is the only writing system in which graphic shapes are designed in such a way that subsegmental phonetic features are systematically correlated.

It is, of course, far different from the representational format of Jakobsonian Distinctive Features that we are familar with. In han'gŭl, there is no matrix with rows and columns, and there are no binary feature coefficients. The lack of such notations, in fact, has prevented people from recognizing han'gŭl as a featural script. I will show below that han'gŭl characters are constructed with strokes that represent phonetic features.

In the case of the consonantal system, the han'gŭl script represents at least seven or eight phonetic features, namely, labiality, dentality, velarity, sibilancy, laryngeality, occlusivity, aspiration, and tensity, as shown in Table 1.

Table 1. Componential Classification of Original Han'gŭl Consonants

	Continuants	Occlusives	Aspirates	Tense	Others	Common Shape
Labials	ㅁ [m]	ㅂ [p]	ㅍ [pʰ]	ㅃ [p']	ㅸ [β]	ㅁ
Dentals	ㄴ [n]	ㄷ [t]	ㅌ [tʰ]	ㄸ [t']	ㄹ [r/l]	ㄴ
Sibilants	ㅅ [s]	ㅈ [c]	ㅊ [cʰ]	ㅉ [c']	ㅿ [z]	ㅅ
Velars	ㆁ [ŋ]	ㄱ [k]	ㅋ [kʰ]	ㄲ [k']		ı
Laryngeals	ㅇ [ɦ]	ㆆ [ʔ]	ㅎ [h]	ㆅ [x]		ㅇ
Stroke Principle	Basic Shape	One Extra Stroke	Two Extra Strokes	Doubling		

I have taken some liberty in the terminology and arrangements in Table 1: (1) I labeled the first column, which includes nasals, "Continuants" because they have continuous air flow and their articulation can be prolonged. (2) I have also relabeled the second and third rows "Dentals" and "Sibilants"; their original names in the *Hunmin chŏng'ŭm haerye* (Explanations and Examples for the Correct Sounds for the Instruction of the People, 1446) were *sŏrŭm* 'tongue sounds' and *ch'iŭm* 'tooth sounds', respectively. There is no misnaming here, however. Since labials involve lips, velars the tongue back, and laryngeals the pharynx, only dentals are involved in articulation with the tongue blade. And if we interpret "tooth" in "tooth sounds" as meaning "air stream turbulence at the teeth," then relabeling them "Sibilants" is reasonable. (3) A more complex issue is the relation between the circle in ㆁ, the character for velar nasal [ŋ], and the circle common in the characters for laryngeal consonants.

It is quite apparent that Sejong regarded ㆁ [ŋ] as belonging to the laryngeal group, since it has the same basic circle shape common in all laryngeals. What is not apparent is whether he saw that ㆁ [ŋ] and ㅇ [ɦ] were in complementary distribution and thus were justifiably allographs sharing the same circle shape. This would be an intriguing topic to pursue. In any event, the letter shape ㆁ is not quite out of place as a velar segment. If we compare the first and second columns for each row in Table 1, namely, ㅁ [m] versus ㅂ [p], ㄴ [n] versus ㄷ [t], ㅅ [s] versus ㅈ [c], and ㅇ [ɦ] versus ㆆ [ʔ], it is clear that one extra stroke represents "interruption" or "occlusivity" as opposed to "continuity" (and two extra strokes "rough interruption," i.e., "aspiration"). Now if we take the common stroke in velars to be a short vertical line, then certainly "the stalk" in ㆁ can be said to represent velarity. (In the case of labials, there are some variations. Given ㅁ [m] as the basic labial, the parallel logic would dictate ㅂ for [p] and ㅍ for [pʰ]. Still, the principle of extra strokes is discernible in ㅂ [p] and ㅍ [pʰ].)

As for the vowel system, *Hunmin chŏng'ŭm haerye* gives the following description of seven basic (simple) vowels:

- ㆍ [ɔ] depicts the (round) heaven; the tongue is retracted, and its voice is deep. (舌縮而聲深)
- ㅡ [ɨ] depicts the (flat) earth; the tongue is slightly retracted, and its voice is neither deep nor shallow. (舌小縮而聲不深不淺)
- ㅣ [i] depicts a (standing) man; the tongue is not retracted, and its voice is shallow. (舌不縮而聲淺)
- ㅗ [o] is the same as ㆍ, but the mouth is contracted/rounded. (ㅗ 與 ㆍ同而口蹙)
- ㅏ [a] is the same as ㆍ, but the mouth is stretched/spread. (ㅏ與 ㆍ同而口張)
- ㅜ [u] is the same as ㅡ, but the mouth is contracted/rounded.
- ㅓ [ə] is the same as ㅡ, but the mouth is stretched/spread.

If we disregard Chinese cosmology from the description of the letter shapes for the three basic vowels and rewrite the original definitions of "retracted tongue" as [+back], "not retracted" as [+front], "deep voice" as [+grave], "shallow voice" as [+acute], "contracted mouth (= lips)" as [+round], and "stretched mouth" as [-round], then we can easily see that han'gŭl's design of vowels is also componential, like Distinctive Features, as Table 2 shows.

Table 2. Componential Classification of Han'gŭl Vowels

		ㆍ	ㅡ	ㅣ	ㅗ	ㅏ	ㅜ	ㅓ
TONGUE								
back	(縮)	+	-	-	+	+	-	-
front	(不縮)	-	-	+	-	-	-	-
GRAVITY								
grave	(深)	+	-	-	+	+	-	-
acute	(淺)	-	-	+	-	-	-	-
MOUTH								
contracted/round	(蹙)				+	-	+	-

The letter shapes for complex vowels involving glides and diphthongs also show the componential nature of han'gŭl's graphic design, for example, ㅐ /ai/ = [ay], ㅔ /əi/ = [əy], ㅚ /oi/ = [oy], ㅟ /ui/ = [uy], ㅢ /ɨi/ = [ɨy], and so forth. Note that English diphthongs, for example, /ei/, /ai/, /au/, /ou/, and so on, are transcribed in the same way by Daniel Jones, the eminent British phonetician, that is, with two vowels. Rising diphthongs beginning with [w] are also written as complex vowels in han'gŭl: ㅘ *oa* for [wa], ㅝ for *uə* [wə], and so on. Especially noteworthy is that this practice for representing complex vowels observes the rules of vowel harmony in Korean. Korean has two harmonic classes commonly known as "light" vowels (*o*, *a*) and "dark" vowels (*u*, ə). Although vowel harmony is on the decline in contemporary Korean, it is still strictly kept in ideophones and in some parts of verbal morphology. The same glide [w] in rising diphthongs [wa] and [wə] is represented in two different vowel characters in order to conform with the harmonic system. Note in this regard that the neutral vowel ㅣ [i] can form complex vowel nuclei with either a dark or a light vowel, for example, ㅚ [oy] or ㅟ [uy] (now [wi]).

Before proceeding further, I would like to discuss DeFrancis' (1989) objections to Sampson's (1985) and my concurring argument that han'gŭl is a featural script. DeFrancis raises two objections to classifying han'gŭl as featural: (1) "Too few of the features, which one scholar (Kim-Renaud 1974) has estimated as numbering nineteen, are actually represented in the system" (p. 197), and (2) "Koreans do not perceive or learn their script in terms of distinctive features but regard the han'gŭl symbols as separate individual letters rather than as partially identical components" (p. 197). I take up these two objections in order below.

Of nineteen features that Kim-Renaud lists (1974: 5), the first three ([sonorant], [syllabic], and [consonantal]) have the role of classifying speech sounds into major classes, such as consonants, vowels, and glides. Han'gŭl does the same with the shapes of characters and their respective positions in the syllable block, and thus has no need to have separate class features. Several of Kim-Renaud's features are redundant and can be specified with other features. Thus, [+palatal] can be specified as [+coronal, +high], [+labial] as [+anterior, -coronal]; [+occlusive] and [-continuant] are redundant, and so are [+delayed release] and [+strident]. Indeed, features like [palatal], [labial], and [occlusive] are no longer used in the current phonological literature. In addition, [long] is probably unnecessary, since it no longer plays a significantly distinctive role in modern Korean. (Han'gŭl orthography does not represent vowel length in any case.) These mendings remove eight features. Of eleven left, three ([high], [low], and [back]) are mostly for vowels. That leaves eight for consonants. I argued earlier that there are seven subsegmental phonetic features in han'gŭl consonants. Vowels are more readily translatable in terms of five features, as shown in Table 2.

Other featural specifications of Korean segments use fewer features than Kim-Renaud (1974). C. Kim (1967: 164) employs fourteen features to classify Korean consonants and vowels, and Sohn (1987) uses four for vowels (p. 84) and eight for consonants (p. 210), for a total of twelve, for underspecification of all Korean segments. In Jakobson, Fant, and Halle's *Preliminaries to Speech Analysis* (MIT, 1951), in which a distinctive feature theory was originally introduced, twelve features were initially proposed for universal application. Han'gŭl contains ten to twelve features. Is this "too few"?

Actually, a modern distinctive feature system and the han'gŭl script are not comparable, for the compositional and representational principles of the two are different. The former is binary, while the latter is monovalent; the former is analytic and classificatory, while the latter is more synthetic and combinatory; the former has the luxury of matrix representation with as many rows as there are features, while the latter has a tight spatiogeometrical constraint of having to represent characters in mutually distinctive shapes, each with no more than a few strokes.

DeFrancis' second objection is no more tenable than the first. He cites several scholars (two printed sources and two personal communications) who doubt that Koreans learn and read their script by referring to the graphic relationship. Let us assume that this skepticism is well founded, although there is no such experimental evidence. I fail to see how this assumption leads to the conclusion that han'gŭl is not a script based on a subphonemic principle. Since when does the inability to perceive a phenomenon by a lay person constitute evidence for nonexistence of that phenomenon? Can we say that there are no such things as allophones because naive native speakers do not perceive them in their languages? If people do not see seven colors in a rainbow, does it mean that there are not as many shades of colors? Are there no chemical elements just because the lay person does not perceive them in natural objects?

It is then inexplicable that DeFrancis questions Sampson's "approach based on applying a type of linguistic analysis which purports to break down complex speech units into their ultimate components" (p. 197), unless DeFrancis is a linguist who has never done such an analysis but relied solely on native speakers' judgments in linguistic descriptions.

The important question is not whether there are enough features, or whether native speakers are aware of them, but whether the script meets certain conditions for it to be said to be a feature-based writing system. Let's take an example. Suppose we define "sports" as "a competition in physical skills." This definition will exclude chess and GRE exams, on one hand, because these do not involve physical skills, and aerobics and martial arts, on the other, because they are physical exercises, not competitions (except in contests). Neither the number of players nor popular perception is relevant in determining whether an activity is a sport or not. No one would say that basketball is not a sport because it has too few players compared to football, nor can one say that archery is not a sport because many people don't see it as one.

In my view, han'gŭl sufficiently meets the requirement for being a feature-based writing system in that the majority, if not all, of character strokes and shapes represent subsegmental elements. Its principle of representation may not be as coherent and systematic as a modern distinctive feature system, but given the spatiogeometric constraints of a practical writing system, han'gŭl is more featural than the Chinese script is phonetic, DeFrancis' main contention of his 1989 book.

THE HAN'GŬL SYLLABARY AND ITS EFFECT ON READING

I have so far extolled the virtues of han'gŭl by arguing that it is not just the world's first invented alphabet based on a phonemic principle but also the world's only script based on the principle of subsegmental distinctive features. There is, however, one item that is easily forgotten in this line of argument, that is, the readability of such a script.

No matter how scientific and insightful a script might be, it could be a very poor script for the reader. As pointed by Householder

(1967), it is nearly impossible to "read" words written solely in distinctive features. Indeed, as Coulmas cautions in a recent book on writing systems (1989), a phoneticized (or alphabetized) script is neither the end of the evolutionary path of writing systems nor the best system in some absolute sense. A system with the fewest elements is not necessarily the simplest and the best, because it says nothing about the complexity of the mapping relation between graphical signs and linguistic units. In fact, Coulmas argues that the Chinese script, often criticized as cumbersome and uneconomical, is very suitable for the Chinese language, for the script adds a dimension to the visual manifestation of language, thereby giving efficiency and speed to its users, which has no counterpart in purely phonetic writing (1989: 108). Put differently, the fewer the signs in a script, the simpler and more economical it is for the writer and the less efficient for the reader, because such a system presents a very monotonous "scriptscape" with few distinguishing "landmarks"; in contrast, the more signs in a script, the less economical it is for the writer, but the more efficient for the reader, for there are numerous perceptually salient visual cues to aid reading.

Compare the two modes of writing han'gŭl given below: one conventional (in syllable blocks) and the other "deblocked" and linearized:

Blocked: 한주일의 첫째날은 무슨 요일입니까?
Deblocked: 하 ㄴ ㅈ ㅜ 이 ㄹ ㅇ ㅢ 처 ㅅ ㅉ ㅐ 나 ㄹ ㅇ ㅡ ㄴ
ㅁ ㅜ ㅅ ㅡ ㄴ ㅇ ㅛ 이 ㄹ 이 ㅂ 니 ㄲ ㅏ?
Gloss: 'what is the name of the first day of the week?'

The difference in reading efficiency is not just a matter of familiarity. A reading experiment by Kim and Sohn (1986) conducted on students taking Korean at the University of Illinois reports that reading han'gŭl in the alphabetic mode, that is, in deblocked and linearized script, was slower by as much as two and a half times than reading in the syllabic mode. To be more specific, it was found that the average time for twenty-four tokens, of which the above is an example, for all speakers (from level 1 to level 4 students learning Korean) was 199 seconds in the syllabic mode, but 491 seconds in the alphabetic mode.

It is commonly assumed that han'gŭl's being written in syllable blocks is a vestige of the Chinese syllabary. Indeed, there is no evidence that King Sejong took any other factor into consideration in grouping the segments into syllable-size chunks. Whatever the historical origin, King Sejong succeeded in combining the best of the two worlds, by "reconciling two contradictory desiderata for a writing system," according to Sampson (1985: 132), that is, the small number of basic graphic signs makes han'gŭl easy to learn and write; at the same time the large number of different syllable types makes it efficient to read and recognize.

In sum, phonological units represented in han'gŭl are not just segmental ("alphabetic") but also subsegmental ("featural") and supersegmental ("syllabic"). I believe that no other writing system in the world can make this claim.

THE STATUS OF GLIDES IN HAN'GŬL

Now I turn to the position of glides within the syllable structure of Korean. Is a glide part of the syllable onset, or is it part of the syllable nucleus? Han'gŭl is unequivocal in representing glides as part of the nucleus, as the following original descriptions and letter shapes as defined in *Hunmin chŏng'ŭm haerye* attest:

ㅛ [yo] is the same as ㅗ, but rises from ㅣ. (ㅛ與ㅗ同而起於ㅣ)
ㅑ [ya] is the same as ㅏ, but rises from ㅣ.
ㅠ [yu] is the same as ㅜ, but rises from ㅣ.
ㅕ [yə] is the same as ㅓ, but rises from ㅣ.

Apart from the original descriptions given above, what other evidence is there to determine the status of glides within the syllable in Korean in one way or the other? Korean phonologists are not in agreement on a canonical syllable structure. With respect to the position of glides, the syllable structure of Korean can be categorized into several types shown in Figure 1.

Figure 1. Syllable Structures of Korean

a. Flat structure

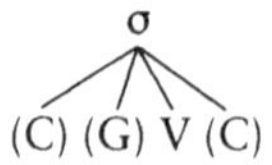

σ

(C) (G) V (C)

Kim and Shibatani (1976)
Y-S. Kim (1984)

b. Glide as onset

i. Right-branching rime

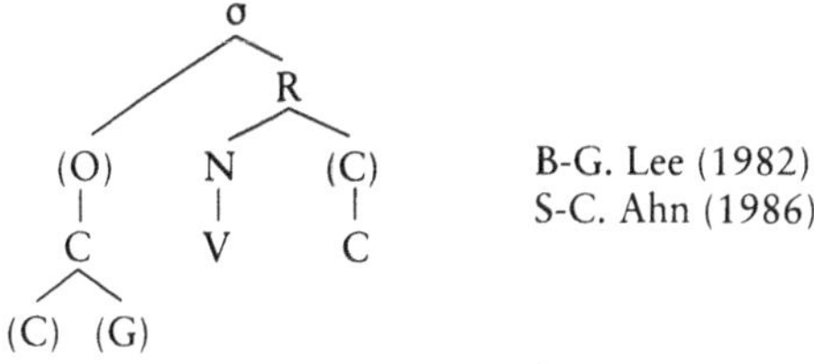

B-G. Lee (1982)
S-C. Ahn (1986)

ii. Left-branching core

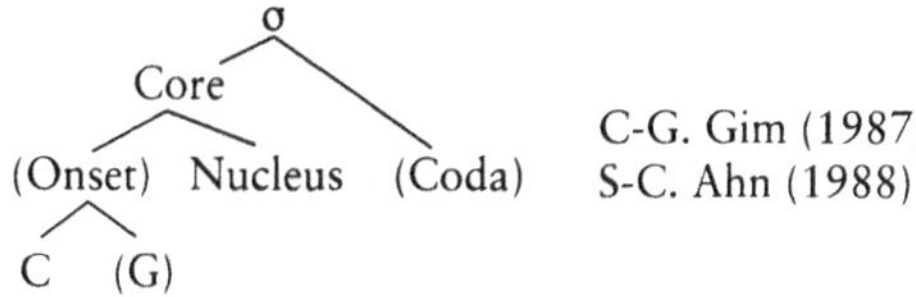

C-G. Gim (1987)
S-C. Ahn (1988)

c. Glide as nucleus

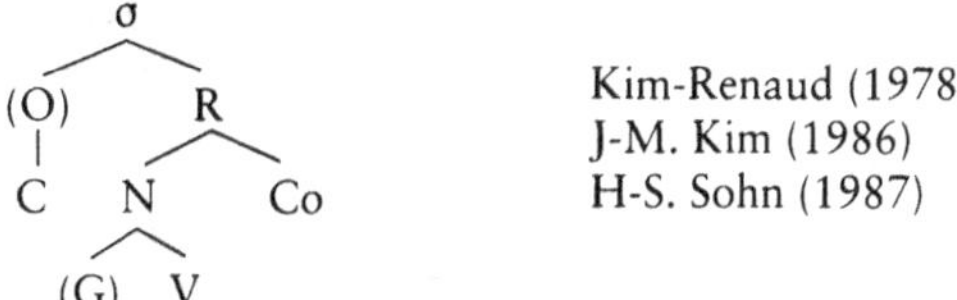

Kim-Renaud (1978)
J-M. Kim (1986)
H-S. Sohn (1987)

Evidence for the glide as part of the syllable nucleus in Korean comes from several phonological phenomena that involve interaction with glides. Much of that evidence was first given by Sohn (1987), who gives excellent arguments for representing complex Korean vowels including diphthongs and glides as a sequence of vowels dominated by the nucleus node. The exact mechanism by which two vowels coalesce to produce surface complex vowels is admirably worked out by Sohn, and I will not go into detail here. But it is worth repeating what she calls the *ex silentio* argument for the nuclear nature of glides.

In many languages where there are consonant clusters, two things are very common: one, severe constraints in the sequencing of segments, what used to be called "phonotactics" or "morpheme structure conditions," and two, a mirror image relation between onset clusters and coda clusters. In English, for example, only non-nasal sonorants may follow stops, which in turn can follow only *s*, for example, *pl-*, *bl-*, *tr-*, *dr-*, *kr-*, *gr-*; *spr-*, *spl-*, *str-*, *skr-*, and so forth. It is also true that for the initial clusters listed above, there are corresponding final clusters in the reverse sequence, *-lp*, *-lb*, *-rt*, *-rd*, *-rk*, *-rg*, *-rps*, *-lps*, *-rts*, *-rks*. Note that there are no final clusters **-wp*, **-wb*, just as there are no initial clusters **pw-*, **bw-*.

Returning to Korean, if we regard the glides *w* and *y* to be parts of the onset cluster, then we might expect that there exist certain constraints in the sequencing of glides with other consonants. But in Korean there are none. Any consonant may precede a glide. A possible exception might be the nonexistence of a sequence of a palato-alveolar and glide *y*. But it is a case of phonetic nondistinction between *cya* and *ca*, rather than a case of nonexistence of the underlying sequence *cya*. Also, if we grant that *Cy* and *Cw* sequences are onset clusters, then we might also expect the corresponding mirror-image sequences, *y*C and *w*C, to occur as coda clusters. But such clusters are simply nonexistent in Korean. Curiously enough, there exist cooccurrence constraints both in permissible coda clusters and in complex nuclei involving glides. In Korean, there are morphemes and words that have two-consonant clusters at the coda position. However, the composition and the order of these clusters are severely constrained, so that only *-ps*, *-ks*, *-lp*, *-lp*^{h}, *-lk*, *-lt*^{h}, *-lk*, *-lh*, *-lm*, *-nh*, and *-nc* are permissible. In complex nuclei, there is a negative condition such that **yi, *yü*, **yɨ*, **wu*, **wo*, **wö*, **wɨ*, and **wü* do not occur, and the only offglide diphthong occurring in Korean is *ɨy*.

This is not the place to explicate the reason for the nonoccurrence of the complex nuclei listed above, nor does this phenomenon by itself constitute evidence for assigning glides to the nucleus rather than to the coda, but on typological grounds alone it makes the former assignment more probable.

Since we are on the subject of consonant clusters, let us examine the phenomenon of consonant cluster reduction in Korean and its relevance to the status of glides. As was mentioned earlier, Korean words may end in one of a small set of two-consonant clusters. When such a word is followed by a vowel, both consonants survive, as the second consonant becomes the onset of the following syllable. But when the next morpheme begins with a consonant, it creates an impermissible three-consonant cluster medially, which prompts deletion of one of the consonants. For example,

kaps 'price',	kaps-i (nom.), but	kap-man 'price only'
nəks 'spirit',	nəks-i (nom.), but	nək-to 'spirit also'
ilk- 'to read',	ilk-əla (imp.), but	ik-ca 'let's read'

cəlm- 'young',	cəlm-ɨn (adj.), but	cəm-ko 'young and'
anc- 'to sit',	anc-ətta (past), but	an-kəla 'sit!' (imp.)

Suppose now that a glide is a part of onset. Then a word-initial consonant followed by a glide should be regarded as a cluster. If such a word is preceded by a word ending in a consonant, we would again have a medial three-consonant cluster, and we should expect the cluster reduction rule to apply to delete one consonant. But this does not happen.

ol-pyə	'this year's crop'
sil-kwa	'fruit'
sok-pyəŋ	'internal illness'
pəp-kwən	'legal power'
kak-p^hyo	'each vote/ballot'

One can argue that this is not a genuine case of a three-consonant cluster by appealing to the intervening CV tier independent of the segmental tier (see Figure 2). In this representation, there is no violation of the canonical syllable structure, and naturally the cluster reduction rule does not apply. But note that this gain is made only at the expense of postulating a large set of complex consonant phonemes in Korean. While there are complex consonants such as affricates and prenasalized consonants in the phonetic inventory of the world's languages, the set is very limited, and a large number of complex consonants involving glides is highly suspect.

Figure 2. Syllable Structure of Glides Viewed as Part of Complex Consonants

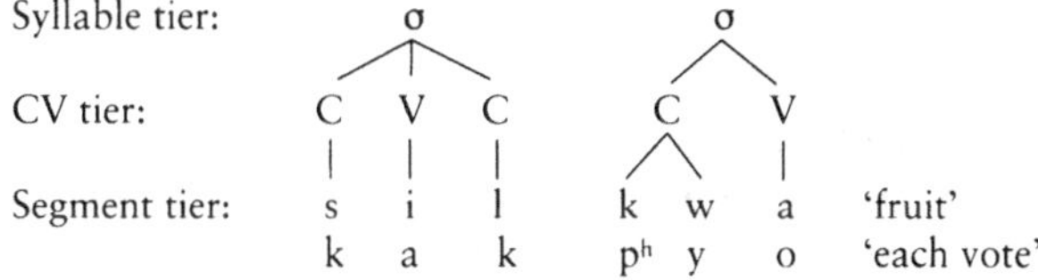

Even if one grants that *Cy* and *Cw* are acceptable complex consonants, one runs into a difficulty when it comes to pre-*y* sonorant deletion in word-initial position in Korean. In Korean, word-initial *l* and *n* are deleted before *y* although they survive in the medial position. For example,

Base form	*Medial*	*Initial*
lyuk 'ground'	tae-lyuk 'continent'	yuk-ci 'land'
lyaŋ 'pair'	yəl-lyaŋ 'ten pairs'	yaŋ-ka 'both houses'
nyə 'female'	su-nyə 'nun'	yə-ca 'woman'
nyo 'urine'	paŋ-nyo 'urination'	yo-to 'urethra'

If *ly* and *ny* are regarded as complex consonants linked to a single C in the CV tier, then deleting the initial segment would be like deleting the first half from affricates or prenasalized stops, that is, the stop component from *ts*, *dz*, and *pf* or the nasal component from *mb*, *nd*, and *ŋg*. It may not be an impossible thing to do, but such a rule would be a complicated one reflecting a rather rare phenomenon.

Sohn also cites a language game to support her argument (1987:108). In this game a melody of CV is copied for every syllable; then the C is prelinked to *p* and V copies the vowel of the preceding syllable. For example,

həkoŋ 'empty sky'	hə-pə ko-po-ŋ
p^hato 'waves'	p^ha-pa to-po
camsil 'a place name'	ca-pa-m si-pi-l

What is noteworthy is that in examples where the syllable contains a glide, this glide is also copied as a part of the nucleus. For example,

kwənse 'power'	kwə-pwə-n se-pe
yaku 'baseball'	ya-pya ku-pu
cwasək 'seat'	cwa-pwa sə-pə-k

If the glide is a part of the onset consonant, then we would not expect the glide to be copied along with the vowel. As Sohn (1987) notes, the fact that it is copied provides substantial evidence that the glide constitutes a prosodic unit with its following vowel rather than with its preceding onset consonant.

There are two pieces of phonetic evidence showing that a glide is a part of the vowel. The first is palatalization of /s/ before /wi/ in such words as *swin* 'fifty', *swi-ta* 'rests', *swip-ta* 'be easy', where the initial consonant [s] is palatalized to [š]. If [w] is a part of the onset cluster /sw/, it is difficult to explain this palatalization phenomenon.

But if [w] is a part of the vowel [i] such that the complex nucleus is a round front vowel [ü], then it is natural for the preceding consonant to be palatalized. (The reason /t/ is not palatalzed to [c] in the same context in such words as *twi* 'back' is probably because the /t/:/c/ distinction is phonemic in Korean, whereas the [s]:[š] distinction is not.)

The most transparent phonetic evidence showing that glides are a part of the syllable nucleus and not of the onset cluster is found in the pronunciation of the liquid phoneme /l/ before a glide. One of the most salient phonetic rules in Korean is the change of [l] to [r] in the prevocalic (syllable-initial) position. For example,

kil 'street', kil-to 'street also', cf. kil-e [kire] (loc.)
tal 'moon', tal-pich 'moonlight', cf. tal-i [tari] (nom.)
pul 'fire', pul-k'oc^h 'flame', cf. pul-ɨl [purɨl] (acc.)

Now, when a glide-initial morpheme follows a morpheme ending in *l*, this *l* uniformly becomes *r* in standard Korean.

il-yo-il [iryoil], *[ilyoil] 'Sunday'
səl-yok [səryok], *[səlyok] 'vindication'
kɨl-wəl [kɨrwəl], *[kɨlwəl] 'writing'
mil-wəl [mirwəl], *[milwəl] 'honeymoon'

If the glides are onset consonants, then the preceding liquid ought to remain as the coda consonant of the preceding syllable retaining the lateral pronunciation [l]. But the fact that it changes to [r] suggests that glides *y* and *w* are a part of the syllable nucleus, allowing the preceding *l* to fill the empty onset position during resyllabification (see Figure 3).

Figure 3. Derivation of [r] via Resyllabification

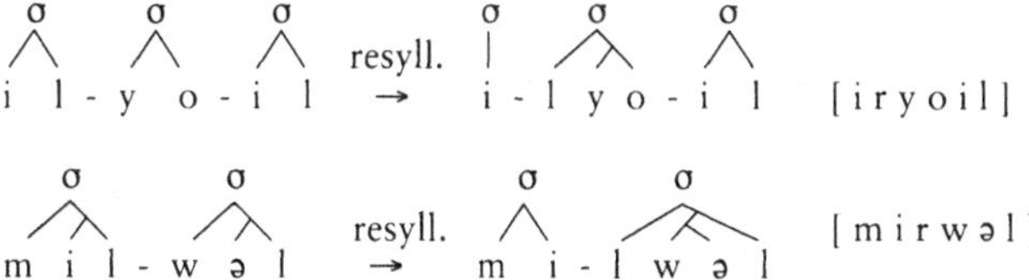

There is in fact a southern (Kyŏngsang) dialect in which the above words are pronounced with lateral [l] ([ilyoil], [milwəl], etc.).

This pronunciation suggests that in this dialect the glides function as the onset consonant, forcing the preceding liquid to remain as the coda consonant. Significantly, it is just in this dialect that we find no nucleus involving a glide after another consonant, that is, there are no such complex nuclei as *wa*, *wə*, *yu*, *yə*, and so forth, postconsonantally. Compare the following sets of words:

Standard dialect	*Kyŏngsang dialect*	*Gloss*
kwaca	kaca	cookie
pwara	para	see (imp.)
kyəul	keul	winter
pyəl	pel	star

This fact is significant, for it shows that there is a nonaccidental relation between the fact that the glides function as onset consonants in the Kyŏngsang dialect and the fact that glides are not found in the nucleus position in the same dialect, for, obviously, glides cannot function both as onset consonants and as nuclei. The fact that the liquid is pronounced as lateral [l] in this dialect indicates that it is in the syllable-final position, with the following glide acting as the onset consonant for the following syllable. In contrast, the fact that the preglide liquid is pronounced [r] in the standard dialect indicates that the glide is a part of the nucleus.

Interestingly, not only do we not find prevocalic glides in the Kyŏngsang dialect, but also there is no postvocalic glide. It might be recalled that there is one diphthong with an offglide in Korean, namely, *ɨy*. As a native suffix, it is a genitive marker, and as a Sino-Korean morpheme, it has a few homophonous meanings, including "justice," "medical," "clothing," and "will." In the Kyŏngsang dialect, all these homophonous morphemes are uniformly pronounced as [ɨ].

CONCLUDING REMARKS

The genius of King Sejong does not lie in the possible but improbable fact that he alone invented the han'gŭl script without any internal help (from his court scholars, for instance) or external input (such as the influence of other writing systems). No one creates something out of nothing. Sejong would have been an unwise man if he ignored all knowledge about the phonologies and writing systems of neighboring languages in devising a new script. His genius lies in the fact that he did not just imitate, but created something totally different and, more important, much better in its linguistic and graphic structures, and in its simplicity and elegance than any existing writing system known at the time, and indeed in the entire annals of writing systems.

Chŏng In-ji, director of the Chiphyŏnjŏn ("Academy of Worthies") during Sejong's reign, who assisted the sage monarch in devising han'gŭl, writes in his postface to *Hunmin chŏng'ŭm haerye* at the time of the royal proclamation of the script: "These twenty-eight letters are so simple and precise that the wise can master them in one morning and even the fool can learn them in ten days. With these letters, writings can be understood, legal appeals can be made, and melodies can be given verses. Indeed, there is nothing that cannot be accomplished. Even the sound of the wind, the cry of a crane, the flutter of a rooster, and the barking of a dog can all be written down." These words are obviously a loyal subject's praise of his lord's accomplishment in very flowery language, but let's give credit where credit is due. King Sejong broke away from the long tradition and bondage of Chinese logography and devised not only a phonemic script, but a script based on phonetic features, that still preserved the syllabic unity in its representation, with all the advantages intact that such a syllabic writing system gives to readers. With truly remarkable insight he perceived the internal relations among both intrasegments and intersegments. He discerned consonantal hierarchy, vowel harmony, the composite nature of diphthongs and contour tones (Sejong transcribed a rising tone as a sequence of a low and a high tone), and the vocalic character of glides. He then devised a graphic system that reflects these internal relations in a simple and systematic way.

Chŏng In-ji concludes his postface: "His Majesty is a god-send, and his wisdom exceeds that of one hundred kings. . . . Though the East has seen many nations come and go, no monarch wiser than His Majesty has existed until today." We can only agree. And so we continue to pay him our humble homage today.

REFERENCES

Ahn, S-C. 1986. Syllabification process in Korean. In *Papers from the 1985 Mid-America Linguistics Conference,* 1-12. Columbia, Missouri: University of Missouri Press.

———. 1988. A revised theory of syllable phonology. *Ŏnŏ* (Linguistic journal of Korea), 13: 333-362.

Coulmas, F. 1989. The writing systems of the world. Oxford: Basil Blackwell.

DeFrancis, J. 1989. Visible speech: The diverse oneness of writing systems. Honolulu: University of Hawai'i Press.

Householder, F. W. 1965. On some recent claims in phonological theory. *Journal of Linguistics* 1: 13-34.

Gim, C-G. 1987. A study of the syllable structure and some processes in its nucleus in Korean [in Korean]. *Mal* (Speech), 12: 25–69.

Kim, C-W. 1967. Some phonological rules in Korean. *Ŏmun-yŏn'gu* (Studies in language and literature), 5: 163–177.

———. 1968. The vowel system of Korean. *Language* 44: 516–527.

———. 1988. On the origin and structure of the Korean script. In *Sojourns in language II*, ed. Chin W. Kim, 721–734. Seoul: Tower Press.

Kim, C-W., and H-Y. Kim. 1991. The *character* of Korean glides. *Studies in the Lingusitic Sciences* 21:2: 113–125.

Kim, C-W., and H. Sohn. 1986. A phonetic model for reading: Evidence from Korean. *Studies in the Linguistic Sciences* 16:2: 95–105.

Kim, J-M. 1986. Phonology and syntax of Korean morphology. Ph.D. dissertation in linguistics, University of Southern California.

Kim, K-O., and M. Shibatani. 1976. Syllabification phenomena in Korean. *Ŏhak-yŏn'gu* (Language research) 12:1: 91–98.

Kim. Y-S. 1984. Aspects of Korean morphology. Ph.D. dissertation in linguistics, University of Texas at Austin.

Kim-Renaud, Y-K. 1974. Korean consonantal phonology. Ph.D. dissertation in linguistics, University of Hawai'i at Manoa.

———. 1978. The syllable in Korean phonology. In *Papers in Korean linguistics*, ed. C. Kim, 85–98. Columbia, South Carolina: Hornbeam Press.

Lee, B-G. 1982. A well-formedness condition on syllable structure. In *Linguistics in the morning calm II*, ed. Linguistic Society of Korea, 489–506. Seoul: Hanshin Publishers.

Sampson, G. 1985. Writing systems. Stanford, Calif.: Stanford University.

Sohn, H-S. 1987. Underspecification in Korean phonology. Ph.D. dissertation in linguistics, University of Illinois at Urbana-Champaign.

9

THE PHONOLOGICAL ANALYSIS REFLECTED IN THE KOREAN WRITING SYSTEM

Young-Key Kim-Renaud

This chapter will discuss various characteristics of the han'gŭl system, each of which reflects a coherent phonological theory bearing on the most important aspects of the sound system of Korean.[1] In several major areas this chapter asserts the existence of a linguistic motivation for some component of the han'gŭl system where previous scholarship has been slow to notice one. These include the shape and structure of the vowel representations, the affinity of the velar and zero/throat consonant series, and the different nature of onglides and offglides.

SYLLABLE STRUCTURE

As Ki-Moon Lee (1972) and many other linguists have pointed out, fifteenth-century Korean scholars, King Sejong in particular, were familiar with the highly developed Chinese phonological tradition that had been influenced in turn by the even older tradition of Pāṇini and the Sanskrit grammarians. The focal point of interest in this theory was the syllable, and that is not surprising, for each Chinese character represents a syllable. The major breakthrough came, however, when it was discovered that Korean syllables could be analyzed as consisting of three distinct subparts, initial, medial, and final. It was noted at once that the initial and final sounds could be identical. Thus was born the alphabetic system. In addition, each subpart could itself consist of more than one segment, as Figure 1 shows.

Figure 1. Syllable Structure

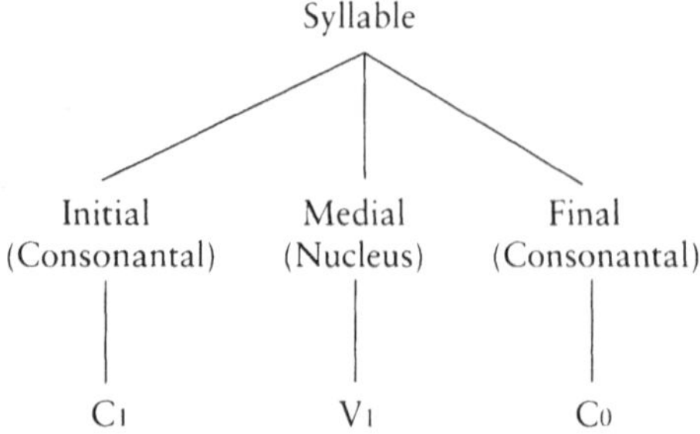

A syllable must consist of at least CV. This canon denotes the optimal nature of the CV syllable. If there is no initial consonant, a circle is written in to indicate that the medial actually follows a syllable boundary, as will be discussed later.[2] Both the initials and the finals could be consonant clusters. Each alphabetic sign was viewed as a subcomponent of a syllable. The prominence of the syllable as a significant phonological unit is based on the Chinese tradition but it is also because of various phonological phenomena in Korean that are best explained in light of the syllable structure (see, for example, Kim-Renaud 1978).

THE PHONOLOGICAL ANALYSIS REPRESENTED BY THE KOREAN WRITING SYSTEM

With the discovery that an initial can also be a final, it became clear to Sejong that the syllable nucleus was distinct from the consonants surrounding it. Sejong divided all sounds into two major groups, consonants and vowels. Consonants and vowel symbols at the time of invention (1446) and in current use are shown in Appendix 1 of this volume. As shown in the inventory, consonants and vowels have distinct shapes easily discernible to anyone. The consonants are geometric shapes with angles and circles, while the vowels are made of long lines and small dots, which later became short lines. More important, these shapes were not arbitrary symbols chosen just to make clear distinctions, but were designed to represent the physiological and psychological reality of the Korean sound system.

Consonantal Phonology

Articulatory and Strength Characteristics of Consonants

The articulatory correlate of the feature [+consonantal] is a narrow constriction at some point in the vocal tract. The inventor of the alphabet, in addition to realizing that the sounds possessing this feature were distinct from those produced without such constriction and inventing two clearly recognizable kinds of graphic representations for them, made another crucial linguistic observation that different but related sounds are produced at the same point of articulation. He decided to create common bases for related consonantal sounds that would actually depict the articulatory characteristics of the group. In addition, a method of *kahoek* 加劃 (stroke addition) was adopted as the fundamental principle in creating consonantal signs.

The basic letters for apicals and dorsals, ㄴ and ㄱ, respectively, imitated the tongue shapes during articulation (with the speaker facing left). Those for labials, dentals, and laryngeals, ㅁ, ㅅ, and ㅇ, respectively, were signs representing shapes of the points of articulation. In the case of labials, the basic letter shape adopted was like the Chinese character 口 'mouth', which originally depicted the shape of the mouth. This is of course only a symbolic representation, as a bilabial articulation is impossible with an open mouth as the graph suggests. It is easy to see, however, that with the speaker facing left, a graphic depiction of bilabial articulation would have had to be just a short line, certainly not a clear representation of the lip activity. Furthermore, it would not have given the graph the geometric look that distinguishes consonantal shapes from vowel forms. With the dentals or sibilants, the narrow escape of air between the teeth is equally hard to depict graphically, and the sign ㅅ, which may be a pictograph of a tooth and which is also a part of the Chinese character 齒 representing the word "tooth," was adopted.

The letter ㅇ (circle or zero) was written in the initial position whenever a syllable started with a vowel. This practice is generally thought to have been an aesthetic one, and some consider it purely a space filler when a syllable starts with no initial consonant (e.g., Huh 1965: 337; Pyong Geun Lee 1988: 68). Samuel E. Martin (personal communication) says that the initial zero represents distinctive smooth vowel onset in Middle Chinese, a bit like the one in Ancient Greek that represented a phoneme. Martin also shows distinctive uses of the initial zero in certain Middle Korean words (1992:

53–57). Others have reconstructed a kind of *alif* or *aleph* having perhaps the value of a voiced fricative [ɦ] produced at the throat or not far from the velar area. Ki-Moon Lee (1972) claims that the zero corresponds to a velar in Middle Korean when it is written in syllable-initial position instead of the preceding consonant, which would normally have onset status. Some pieces of dialectal evidence seem to support this hypothesis, for example, 몰 .애 ([molgae] in many dialects for [morɛ] in Seoul dialect) 'sand' and 울 이 ([ulgi] in NE dialects for [ulli] in Seoul) 'to make cry' (Ki-Moon Lee 1972: 19). Sinhang Kang is probably right in recognizing both kinds (1987: 146), one marking a syllable break and the other a voiced *ɦ* from an earlier velar stop and fricative.

Once the basic consonantal shapes were designed, Sejong did not create related sounds randomly, either. Variations on the basic theme were carried out in a systematic way. In *Hunmin chŏng'ŭm haerye*, abbreviated as *Haerye* (Explanations and Examples [of The Correct Sounds for the Instruction of the People]), the principle of *kahoek* is explained. The five basic letters, chosen from the most gentle/soft series among the consonants, were expanded with a set of systematically added strokes to create related but more *ryŏ* 厲 (rough/strong/severe) sounds:

	→	<u>stronger</u>		
ㄱ /k/	→	ㅋ /kʰ/		
ㄴ /n/	→	ㄷ /t/	→	ㅌ /tʰ/
ㅁ /m/	→	ㅂ /p/	→	ㅍ /pʰ/
ㅅ /s/	→	ㅈ /c/	→	ㅊ /cʰ/
ㅇ /ɦ/	→	ㆆ /ʔ/	→	ㅎ /h/

In *Haerye* there is an authoritative statement about the distinguishing features of various groups of sounds. The principal feature seems to have been the degree of aspiration. For example, the initials were classified into four major groups by features *ch'ŏng* 清 (clear/airy/aspirated) and *t'ak* 濁 (muddy/dense/tense), or *qing* and *zhuo*, respectively, used in traditional Chinese phonology (Ledyard 1966: 144–148). These features were not exactly binary but had a gradient value with another feature, *ch'ach'ŏng* 次清 (even more *ch'ŏng*). Apparently, all the voiced sounds, whether sonorant or obstruent, were regarded as the weakest in their consonantal strength scale.

t'ak	濁	[+tense]	pp, ss, tt, cc, and hh
ch'ach'ŏng	次清	[+asp]	p^h, t^h, c^h, k^h, and h
ch'ŏng	清	[+obst]	p, t, s, c, and ʔ
pulch'ŏng, pult'ak	不清不濁	[+voiced]	m, n, z, l, ng, and ɦ

It seems that Sejong considered the degree of aspiration a determining factor in the famous three-way stop distinction in Korean. According to Chin-W. Kim (1970), who defines aspiration as a function of the glottal opening at the time of release of the oral closure of a stop, the glottal opening is the largest in the case of the heavily aspirated series and smallest in the tense group. Thus, in *Chŏng'ŭm* the slightly aspirated sounds were interpreted as *ch'ŏng* (clear/airy) and heavily aspirated ones even more *ch'ŏng*.[3] Tense sounds were thought to have a close contact at the glottis and possibly also at the point of articulation, giving the impression of being *t'ak* (muddy/dense). It is interesting to note that in Korean the strongest consonants were created either by opening the glottis wide or by narrowing it tightly.[4] Rough *ch'ach'ŏng* sounds were created with an extra stroke, while tense consonants were formed by squeezing the same symbol twice into the consonantal space.[5] Thus, the stronger the consonant, the more complex was its letter shape.

The consonantal strength hierarchy, which is amply and consistently manifested in the letter shapes of the Korean alphabet, is an important notion in such Korean phonological phenomena as intervocalic weakening, extreme weakening in the so-called irregular verbs, unreleasing of syllable-final consonants, and sound symbolism (Kim-Renaud 1974, 1986a; Martin 1962). It is well known that in Korean lenis stops are voiced intervocalically. They are even further weakened in the so-called irregular verbs. I hypothesized in an earlier study (Kim-Renaud 1973, 1974) that the increased degree of sonority of the preceding vowel length causes extreme weakening. Syllable codas are unreleased/weakened: consonant clusters reduce, and stops and fricatives are unreleased. In sound-symbolic or mimetic words, different connotations can be systematically correlated to different degrees of consonantal strength of their variable forms. Thus, plain stops carry the rather gentle and basic meaning of sound symbolism, heavily aspirated sounds give a rough and tough impression, while tense consonants give a tight and intense feeling.[6]

Finer distinctions were made within the lenis obstruant group in terms of their consonantal strength. ㅅ <s> and ㅈ <ch> are both dentals (sibilants) and *ch'ŏng* (slightly aspirated) sounds. However, *Haerye* notes that ㅈ (being an affricate) is stronger than ㅅ. The phoneme corresponding to Middle Korean /c/, designated by the letter ㅈ <ch>, was dental [ts] in the fifteenth century, although it is palatal today in most dialects (Ki-Moon Lee 1972; Ledyard 1966: 167–168). Therefore, the letter ㅈ for the dental affricate /c/ was created by adding a horizontal line, representing the occlusive feature, above the letter ㅅ /s/, graphically demonstrating the relationship between the two sounds.

The reason the glottal *t'ak* letter was formed by doubling the symbol ㅎ <h> and not ㆆ < ʔ > was explained clearly in *Haerye* as follows: "Although /h/ belongs to the *ch'ach'ŏng* series [because of its aspiration force], it is *shallower* [softer] than the ㆆ / ʔ / sound, which cannot *coagulate* to make a *dense* [tense] sound." Ki-Moon Lee interprets this statement as an indication that the letter ㅎ <h> is in fact pronounced at the area of the vowel it cooccurs with, as also observed by other linguists including Chin-W. Kim (1970), and claims that ㅎ <h> should actually have belonged to the plain (slightly aspirated) series. The only reason it was grouped together with the strongly aspirated series, presumably, was to accommodate the sound / ʔ / within the given phonological chart (Ki-Moon Lee 1972: 28–29).

Indeed there is enough phonological evidence to regard the glottal approximant /h/ as one of the weakest among consonants. It often is "invisible" in a phonological environment. For example, it is frequently deleted between vowels. The *l*-weakening occurs between vowels whether there is an intervening *h* or not (Kim-Renaud 1974: 67–68). However, there are other phonological alternations that show that /h/ also behaves like a strongly aspirated consonant, for example, some mimetic contrasts between two related words, 엉클 /əŋkʰɨl/ 'to entangle' and 헝클 /həŋkʰɨl/ 'to entangle in a chaotic and rough way' (Martin 1992: 343). Phonetically, in a strong position such as the utterance-inital one, the phoneme /h/ is commonly pronounced as a velar fricative in very careful or emphatic speech in Korean, for example, [xanarɨm] for /han+alɨm/ 'an armful'. The /h/ sound also represents the voiceless velar fricative [x] in the Korean pronunciation of certain foreign words, which English speakers pronounce as [kʰ], such as 후루시초프 /hurusicʰyopʰɨ/ for the Russian president's name *Khrushchev*, 호메이니 /homeini/ for the Iranian *Khomeini*, and 바하 /Paha/ for the composer's name *Bach*.

The letter ㆅ [xh(?)] was included in the *t'ak* group because of its tensity. The only example with this initial, 〮ᅘᅧ "pull, draw," not only had an alternate spelling of showing tenseness with a combined letter *s*C- but also sometimes developed into *-k*^{h}*y-* in the seventeenth century. These and other facts seem to suggest that it was a tense sound with a position of articulation not too far removed from the velar area (Ki-Moon Lee 1972: 50).

The letter ㆆ /ʔ/ looks like an exception to the velar hypothesis for the "throat" sounds, as a glottal stop cannot be pronounced close to the velar area. However, it was probably only an abstract phoneme, anyway, created to indicate an etymological glottal stop in Sino-Korean (Ledyard 1966: 166), and in the case of Korean to mark a "preglottalizing" feature before a tensed consonant (Ledyard 1966: 188) or a "syllable break," which was achieved by closing the glottis (Huh 1965: 297). In practice, the letter was never phonemic in fifteenth-century Korean.[7] As a tensifier, it often went unwritten and eventually was supplanted by *sai-siot* or *Bindungs-s* (lit. "in-between *s*"), which was originally a genitive marker but later functioned as a "breaker" or a kind of boundary marker between two major class morphemes in compounding.

The "throat" series also displays some unique characteristics. In addition to the double *h*, ㆅ , there are examples of double circles, ㆀ , although these are limited just to a few predictable cases. This occurred in a noninitial syllable when an *i*-final verb was followed by another *i*, typically a causative or passive suffix that is followed by another vowel-initial affix, for example, 괴 〮ᅇᅧ (< 괴 + ㅣ + ㅣ) 'being loved'. Here both vowel nuclei to which these *i*'s belong were complex, and both of the *i*'s were realized as [y]. Huh regards this as a kind of vowel strengthening that was realized as a tense [i] or [y] (1965: 337). It is indeed plausible that the double circle was a syllable break marker representing some kind of unconscious effort to prevent the disappearance of the second [y], which would not have been a desirable result because it carried a heavy semantic load. Thus the double circle did not itself have a palatal value, but the effort to keep the second [y] in spite of its normally weak phonological position resulted in the elongated [y].[8] Martin hypothesizes that a double zero was used to keep...y< ㆀ >y... and...y< ㆀ >i... distinct from...yy... and...y... in causative and passive forms (1992: 22). It would have had a phonemic value of [ɣ] or [ɦ]. Martin's theory seems to be nicely compatible with the graphic shape chosen.

However, the double circle was never considered to be a phonemic representation, as indicated by its failure to be included in the tense consonant group. Furthermore its life was short and limited to certain fifteenth-century texts (Pyong Geun Lee 1988: 71).

Voiced sounds, being neither aspirated nor tense, were characterized as neither *ch'ŏng* nor *t'ak*.[9] Not all "soft" (voiced) consonants were considered equal, however. Because of their limited occurrence in initial position, ㅸ [β], ㅿ [z], and ㄹ [l] were not considered basic but were made by modifying some more basic shapes slightly. For the labial and lingual series, the nasal consonants were chosen as basic, as they were considered the least strong consonants.

Haerye explains that in the case of the velar series, the lax obstruent, and not the nasal, is taken as basic. However, it was clearly understood that the velar nasal was just like other nasals in its consonantal strength. Its close relationship to other velar consonants was also observed. For this reason the text goes into an elaborate explanation of why the expected course was not taken. Clearly, the velar nasal was thought to be closer to the sound represented by a circle, because they were often interchangeable and were confused even in Chinese rime books. In fact, a velar nasal is often dropped after nasalizing the neighboring vowel in fast speech in many languages including Korean. When there is a need to strengthen a nasalized vowel, for example, in singing in French, one can clearly hear a velar nasal following the vowel. This fact as well as the complementary distribution between the velar nasal (syllable final position) and the zero (syllable initial position) surely led to the merging of the two symbols.[10]

The two-way correlation of the velar nasal with the glottal and other velar sounds was skillfully captured by alluding to the Confucian cosmological theory of the Five Agents, *ohaeng* 五行 : in brief, the shape ㆁ <ng> (a tree-shoot) draws its form from the letter ㅇ <∅> (water). ㄱ <k> is a tree that has come into being out of that shoot; ㅋ <k'> is the adult shape of the tree; and ㄲ <kk> represents a venerable stage of that tree. The implication is that the velars and glottals were very closely related in the fifteenth century. It is indeed possible that the inventor of the alphabet perceived the phonetic fact that the glottal sound was a kind of fricative that was pronounced quite close to the velar area. The weaker of the two series were the fricatives. Therefore, contrary to the popular interpretation, the true basic form of the velars appears to have been the circle with a tick, not ㄱ <k>. The velar nasal thus was represented by a sign that includes both the glottal (circle) and velar (small vertical line) markers. When adding the occlusive marker, the horizontal line, above the velar nasal form, the part depicting the throat (that is, the circle) was dropped, deriving the letter ㄱ <k>.

Consonant Cluster Reduction, Tensing

Unlike Modern Korean which allows consonant clusters only in syllable-final position, in the fifteenth century the initials could also be complex and contain up to three consonants. Initial consonant clusters were limited mainly to three kinds, that is, *sC-*, *pC-*, and *psC-* clusters.[11] Whether all members of the clusters were pronounced has been an object of lively discussion among linguists. Huh takes the fact that there was no particular treatment of consonant clusters in *Hunmin chŏng'ŭm haerye* as evidence that each of the consonants was pronounced (1988: 45). Ki-Moon Lee (1972) and others have claimed that not all /s/'s in *s*-clusters actually marked an [s] sound, and that the letter ㅅ <s> was used to mark tensing even in Middle Korean. Martin believes that in early spellings the *s-* usually represented a genuine sibilant, but soon the clusters in various words began to assimilate the initial *s-* or *p-* to the following obstruent, and later *sC-* became only a device to spell the geminates, regardless of their origins (1982: 608–609). He explains the emergence of tense consonants as minimal clusters, "geminates with the disappearance of the *s*." "Like the Cheshire cat that Alice found in Wonderland—[the *s*] appears and disappears, leaving nothing behind but the tension that we expect in the allophones of *p*, *t*, *c*, and *k* after a voiceless consonant" (Martin 1975: 156). Ramsey suggests that they were not always etymologically genuine, either (1978b: 60). For example, there was sporadic tensing for nonphonetic reasons as there is today.

These clusters were a rather transient phenomenon in Korean phonological history. These initial clusters, typologically unusual in Altaic languages, developed from vowel syncope (Ki-Moon Lee 1972: 58; Ramsey, this volume). Such highly marked clusters must immediately have begun to undergo a new change. It seems that the first effort to reduce the consonantal sequence was to release only the last consonant of the cluster. That is why tensing seems to have occurred first in *s*-clusters. When the /s/ is unreleased, something like an unreleased [t˺], it is neither audible nor observable. The only trace would be in the tenseness of the following consonant. Note that when a /p/ is unreleased, even though the sound is greatly weakened and barely audible, there is a visible cue because of the observable position of articulation. The unreleasing of the first parts of the initial consonant clusters seems to explain why these clusters have always reduced to the final consonant of the cluster, never *p* or *s*. In Korean, as in many languages, the initial sound gets stronger enunciation. If everything else were equal, the initial *p* or *s* should have remained rather than the following consonants.

The *s*-cluster tensing was also much more productive because of the post–"*s*-genitive" tensing in compound nouns. Therefore, the letter ㅅ <s> was chosen more often than the ㅂ <p> to express tensed consonants, when the etymological source of the first consonant in the cluster was not clear. Gradually both ㅅ <s> and ㅂ <p> were not phonetically realized and came to be used as an orthographic device to mark tenseness of the following consonant. There must have been variable pronunciations as well, which seems to account for variable orthographic representations.

According to *Haerye*, consonants in syllable-final position were limited to the following eight letters: ㄱ <k>, ㆁ <ng>, ㄷ <t>, ㄴ <n>, ㅂ <p>, ㅁ <m>, ㅅ <s>, ㄹ <l>. In practice, however, there are such clusters as the ones that can be seen in ᄒᆞᆰ [hʌlk] 'soil, earth', ·낛 [naks] 'fishing', and ᄃᆞᆰᆺ ·ᄣᅢ [tʌlks-pstai] 'the hour of the chicken'. The eight final consonants must then have represented actual pronunciation. Fifteenth-century Korean also had neutralization of obstruents in syllable-final position. The only difference from Modern Korean would seem to be that the dental series, ㅈ /c/, ㅊ /cʰ/, ㅉ /c'/, ㅅ /s/, and ㅆ /s'/, were neutralized as ㅅ [s], not as ㄷ [t˺]. So, syllable-final consonants underwent a sort of weakening, but there was no requirement to unrelease the coda totally by keeping firm some contact point in the mouth, as is the case in Modern Korean.[12] Perhaps the degree of unreleasing was less severe. Therefore, all sibilants just weakened to their weakest counterpart [s], not necessarily to a complete closure. This phenomenon could easily be captured by the graphic relationships between all dentals.

Vowel Letters and Vowel Combinations

If we leave out the four iotized vowel nuclei, which will be discussed later, there are seven vowels in *Hunmin chŏng'ŭm*. The most important phonological consideration in their design was the concept of vowel harmony, which is often thought to be one of the most important characteristics of Altaic languages and which has been a subject of lively inquiry in Korean phonology. Since there was no vowel theory developed in Chinese phonology, the design of Korean vowel letters seems to reflect directly an important aspect of Korean phonology that is not shared by speakers of other languages (Taylor and Taylor 1962).

The constraint on the compatibility among different kinds of vowels within a given unit is thought to have been quite rigorous in the oldest form of Korean, though there are numerous violations found in the Middle Korean texts of the fifteenth century. Because of various historical changes, vowel harmony is no longer systematically applied. However, it still is very much alive in sound-symbolic words, which are so prevalent in Korean, as well as in some grammatical alternations (Kim-Renaud 1976). More important, the two harmonic groups carry a distinct, predictable semantic connotation, which Koreans have traditionally called Yang 陽 'bright' and Ŭm (Chinese Yin) 陰 'dark'. Thus bright vowels connote a bright, cheerful, light, diminutive impression, while dark vowels have a dark, melancholic, heavy, and big connotation. The labels *yang* and *ŭm* happen to have been borrowed from Chinese cosmology, but they are not arbitrary markers used just to classify the vowels into two different groups. The traditional concept of opposites is appropriate because the contrasting features are semantically predictable and have a fixed universal interpretation as well as a phonetic definition.

It is often mentioned that the time of the invention of the alphabet was a time of many radical changes in Korean phonological history. One historical change that has drawn much attention of students of vowel harmony is a Great Vowel Shift hypothesized by Ramstedt (1939), Wanjin Kim (1963/1971), Ki-Moon Lee (1969), and others. Wanjin Kim posits the following articulatory positions for vowel symbols as underlying representations for fifteenth-century Korean vowels, preceding the hypothesized Great Vowel Shift.

Front/Neutral	Central/Dark	Back/Bright
ㅣ <i>	ㅜ <u>	ㅗ <o>
	ㅡ <ŭ>	ㆍ <ʌ>
	ㅓ <ŏ>	ㅏ <a>

Kim says that the shift was completed only by the seventeenth century (p. 44). It is hard to prove or disprove an abstract phonemic underlying representation, but it appears that the vowel shift had already been completed by the fifteenth century (see Sinhang Kang's chapter in this volume). In other words, by that time the vowel harmony system was no longer on the vertical (back versus nonback) axis that W. Kim's proposal would suggest. The semantic features that had only been derived features earlier came to assume the primary role. That seems to be exactly why semantic factors played such a key role in the invention of vowel signs (Kim-Renaud 1976).

Haerye starts with a statement on three basic vowels. The letters are drawn from traditional Chinese cosmology. They are stylized symbols of Heaven, Earth, and Man, represented by a dot (·), a horizontal line (—), and a vertical line (ㅣ), respectively. Although arbitrary at first glance, they are given specific articulatory and perceptual (acoustic and sound-symbolic) definitions, as shown below.

> a. In pronouncing · [ʌ], the tongue is contracted (舌縮), and so the sound is deep (聲深). The letter is shaped round, depicting Heaven, which opens at the first time period (子).[13]
>
> b. In pronouncing — [ɨ], the tongue is a little contracted (舌小縮), and so the sound is neither deep nor shallow (聲不深不淺). The letter is shaped flat, depicting Earth, which opens at the second time period (丑).
>
> c. In pronouncing ㅣ [i], the tongue does not contract, and so the sound is shallow. The letter is shaped upright, depicting Man, who is born at the third time period (寅).

The three basic letter shapes thus represented the vowels pronounced at the back, middle, and front of the mouth. Here the deep sounds are reminiscent of the feature [grave], and the shallow sounds of [diffuse]. However, the phonological theory behind the establishment of these three basic letter shapes is that not only can Korean vowels be classified according to their articulatory and acoustic features, but they can also be distinguished by their inherent sound-symbolic meanings. Thus the Heaven sound is characterized by the feature *yang* 陽 (bright), and the Earth sound by *ŭm* 陰 (dark). Man is the third being to emerge but stands between Heaven and Earth. In reality, the vowel *i* in Korean, represented as a human being standing between heaven and earth (ㅣ) is a neutral vowel, although it is an *ŭm* vowel in a word-initial syllable (Kim-Renaud 1976).

In proceeding to design other vowel letters, the inventor did not apply the method of *kahoek* (stroke addition), the fundamental principle used in creating consonantal signs, except in the case of vowel nuclei with *y*-onglides. In the first combinatorial letter shapes, called *ch'och'ul* 初出 ("first derivation"), the horizontal and vertical lines were used as the main axis to which the round dot would be attached. This was symbolized by the round Heaven (dot) interacting with Earth (horizontal line) and Man (vertical line). However, these derived graphs were not arbitrarily assigned sound values, but were designed according to a set of specific phonetic principles. The combinatory horizontal line in *Haerye* represented pursed lips 口蹙 (round/high),[14] and the vertical line stretched lips 口張 (unrounded/low) as shown below.

a. ㅗ [o] is like ㆍ [ʌ] but with pursed lips 口蹙 (rounded/high).

b. ㅏ [a] is like ㆍ [ʌ] but with stretched lips 口張 (unrounded/low).

c. ㅜ [u] is like ㅡ [ɨ] but with pursed lips 口蹙 (rounded/high).

d. ㅓ [ə] is like ㅡ [ɨ] but with stretched lips 口張 (unrounded/low).

ㅗ [o] and ㅏ [a] are like ㆍ [ʌ] in that they are all *yang* vowels. The only difference is that while ㅗ [o] is round and higher than ㆍ [ʌ], ㅏ [a] is lower than ㆍ [ʌ], which is unmarked in terms of such features. ㅜ [u] and ㅓ [ə] are like ㅡ [ɨ] in that they are all *ŭm* vowels, and again it is the roundness and vowel height that distinguish the first two from the basic vowel. Here the choice of the position of the small dot is not random. When the small dot is placed above the Earth, it is bright. When it occurs below the Earth, it is dark. When the small dot is placed to the right of the Man, it is bright. When it is situated to the left of the Man, it is dark. Symbolic iconicity is used to create a logical graphic system to represent the psychological reality of Korean speakers.

It was mentioned above that four of the eleven vowels that appear in *Hunmin chŏng'ŭm* were vowel nuclei that contain *y*-glide onset. These medials were represented by an extra dot placed next to the dot of the first-derivation vowels, that is, ㅑ [ya], ㅛ [yo], ㅕ [yə], and ㅠ [yu]. The creation of these medials was called *chaech'ul* 再出 ("second derivation"). Why this *y*-glide was expressed by an extra small dot has been a mystery, and linguists have considered it largely an exception to otherwise highly iconic principles in letter design and just an arbitrary choice. The second dot, however, represented the high front sound /i/, which was symbolized by Man (ㅣ) in the basic list. This vowel is neutral and can occur with any vowel. This fact was explained in terms of Man's close relationship with the dual nature of the universe.

The *y*-glide onset was not considered a separate segment preceding a vowel but, more likely, a [prepalatalized] feature of the vowel. The two morae are thus written tightly together. Indeed the *y* in the prevowel position is shorter than in postvowel position as in *ŭi*. It is interesting to note that onglides and offglides were graphically distinctive. If a reduction of the nuclei occurs, for example, when following a consonant, it is always the *y* feature that deletes and never the vowel.

It is thus clear that the dot is used in at least three different ways. First, it is one of the three basic vowels and represents Heaven, the *yang* vowel. Second, it is used in creating new vowels manifesting a *yang/ŭm* contrast. Finally, it seems to represent Man, which becomes a coarticulation feature [palatal] or [palatalized] in designing iotized vowel letters.

The medial in fifteenth-century Korean sometimes consisted of other types of complex nuclei. When the vowel nuclei included a *w*-glide onset, one of the rounded vowels was attached to the main vowel. Its choice was strictly constrained by the vowel-harmony principle; ㅗ [o] was chosen before a *yang* vowel and ㅜ [u] was chosen before a *ŭm* vowel. In transcribing these vowel nuclei, the general practice is to transcribe the onglide as /w/, but the phonetic value is slightly different, depending on which vowel follows. It is also interesting to note that the /w/ sound can become an independent syllable in certain emphatic pronunciations, for example, 우이 [ui] for 위 [wi] 'upper side' as well as 보아 [poa] for 봐 [pwa] 'Look!'.[15] Thus, the letter shape was devised to represent such regularities by specifying harmonically appropriate onglide in such nuclei.

Another type of complex medial was a diphthong whose second member was high front vowel. These were considered clearly diphthongs, not a *vowel* + *offglide* sequence. The diphthongs were created so that the two parts of the vowel nuclei were equally visible. The frontness of the second vowel in such nuclei was so strong that over time the diphthongs were monophthongized as front vowels. Accordingly, these letters were reinterpreted as they were reanalyzed as front vowels. Thus emerged a whole array of front vowels, including rounded ones, that did not exist before.

Some of the front vowels that originate from complex vowel nuclei still have earlier forms as alternate pronunciations, dialectal or casual. For example, the word for "a crevice, relationship" is 사이 [sai] (normal pronunciation) or 새 [sɛ] (casual). "Three" is 세 [se] in Standard Korean but 서이 [səi] in some dialects. Front rounded vowels manifest similar phenomena, for example, 외 [ö] 'cucumber' has a variant 오이 [oi]. Thus each of the two moraic vowels has obtained full syllabic status as Korean has come to disallow offglides except in the *ŭi* sequence.[16] In all these combinations, these complex vowel letters reveal Korean speakers' subconscious knowledge about the historical relationship between variant forms.

Suprasegmentals

Middle Korean, like some dialects and unlike Standard Korean today, had a pitch accent system. Korean is not and never was a true tone language, if we follow McCawley's (1968) definition, but the word "tone" was used to indicate Korean pitch accent as well as true Chinese tones in the fifteenth century. *Hunmin chŏng'ŭm* included special tone symbols, called *pangchŏm* 傍點 ([left-] side dots). The low or plain pitch *p'yŏngsŏng* 平聲 is unspecified, the high *kŏsŏng* 去聲 is represented with one dot, and the rising-pitch *sangsŏng* 上聲 by two dots that look like a colon.[17] It is written in *Hunmin chŏng'ŭm ŏnhae* (A Vernacular Translation of The Correct Sounds for the Instruction of the People, 1459) that a rising tone is a tone in which the first part is low and the second high. In *Hunmong chahoe* (Collection of Characters for Training the Unenlightened, 1527), a *sangsŏng* is described as long and raised at the end. For example, 부 텨 /puthyə/ [LL] + ㅣ /i/ [H] was written as 부 :텨 /puthyə-i:/ 'Buddha (subj.)'. Therefore, an extra dot in the rising tone captures the complex nature of that syllable.

Chang (1978) and Sang Oak Lee (1978) hypothesize an underlying two level tones, low and high, although they recognize three tones. Huh (1955), Cha Kyun Kim (1988), and Hur (1991) postulate an underlying contour tone as well. Cha Kyun Kim shows some convincing evidence that not all rising tones were derivable from *low* + *high* tone sequences. Words with rising tones like 말 [ma:l] 'language, speech' and :개 [kai:] 'dog' did not have doublets with *low* + *high* tone sequences (Kim 1988: 142–143). It seems to me that, again, it is a question of how abstract an analysis should be. However, Cha Kyun Kim is plausible in saying that the reason scribes were aware of the rising tone that emerged when a low tone was followed by a high tone was probably that there was a rising tone in the phonemic inventory of the language. Otherwise the change would have been largely unconscious. Still another view is expressed by Ramsey (1978a, 1991), who claims that Middle Korean had an accent system in which only the location of the first occurrence of high pitch was distinctive at the morphophonemic level. Syllables with rising pitch, composed of a low-pitched mora plus a high-pitched mora, were accented on the second mora. After that point pitch variations were nondistinctive. This theory seems to explain the historical demise of tones well.

The orthographic practice of early texts was phonemic, and the written records do not offer conclusive evidence regarding the nature of nonsegmental melody. However, the fact that a distinct symbol was provided for the rising tone and that tone marks were applied regularly would seem to suggest that there was no ambiguity about the usage of these tones. Ramsey (personal communication) is probably right in saying that it is not necessarily true that only unpredictable tones were marked at that time, but it could be that all marked/nonplain tones were specified to make reading easier, whether they were predictable or not from a deeper level. Therefore, one could say that tones were fully specified in Middle Korean.

These side dots were used systematically in the fifteenth and sixteenth centuries and then disappeared as patterns of pitch became predictable and accent marking redundant. There is no pitch accent in Standard Modern Korean, and in modern orthography there exists neither the accent nor the length marker. Vowel length has been phonemic in Standard Seoul dialect, but speakers are becoming more and more confused about it as native speakers of the dialect are becoming a marginal force even in Seoul, where the majority of the population has recently come from somewhere else.

In Modern Korean, words or phonological phrases are separated by space, which represents a possible pause domain, and Western-style punctuation markers are used. In the fifteenth century, however, within a sentence there was no space: instead, small circles were used to mark major phrasal and sentential/clausal endings. The circle placed in the center just below the final syllable marked the end of a major break within a sentence, while the circle in the right corner just below the final syllable of a clause or a sentence marked the end of the sentence. Baek (1987) regards these marks as a pause, but they could also be marking an intonation pattern. Thus the phrasal break would indicate something like a rising intonation, while the sentence-final mark would be something like a period today, representing either falling or rising pitch, depending on the meaning of the sentence.[18]

WRITING CONVENTIONS

The Syllable as the Principal Unit

Although clearly identifiable alphabetic symbols were invented, the basic unit for writing was and is the syllable (see Appendix 1 to this volume). This unit was certainly influenced by Chinese writing, which Koreans used for centuries before devising their own writing system. In fact, many Koreans still prefer writing Chinese characters for Sino-Korean words, to disambiguate, to save space (because of the succinct style of Sino-Korean phrasing), to appear official, or simply to show off.

Aesthetically, the inventor wanted a more balanced, equidimensional look in all syllables. As in Chinese, the size of each of the component letters within the syllable would be adjusted depending on the number of segments within it, in order to arrive at a uniform look. Thus all syllables would have consistent size and (squarish) shape.

Graphically, a minimum syllable consisted of *consonant + vowel*, except that in writing a Sino-Korean syllable the final consonant place was filled, by a zero if there was no final consonant. When the principal shape of the vowel was just a dot or a horizontal line, the initial consonant was placed above the vowel.[19] When a vertical line was the major part of the vowel, the consonant was placed to the left of the vowel. When the syllable had no initial consonant, a small circle belonging to the "throat" class was written in. The requirement to fill the initial consonantal position seems to epitomize the optimum nature of a CV syllable, and a phonetic value might even have been given to that "empty" sign, as discussed above. Final consonants were placed below the vowel, centrally below a dot or a horizontal line and slightly to the right side below a vertical line, which is shortened to accommodate the final consonant (cluster). At the time of invention, the Korean syllable structure allowed syllable-initial consonant clusters in combinations of up to three symbols, although these were thought to be a transient phenomenon. Consonant clusters were written from left to right regardless of their constituent number and their position.

As Korean is written in syllables, texts can be written in two different directions. The first practice was to continue the Chinese tradition of starting from the upper righthand corner and writing down and then moving on to the next vertical line to the left. It is also possible to mix scripts other than Chinese, as syllable blocks, being of equal sizes, are easily transposed as if they were single letters. Today it is common to see Japanese, English, and other scripts mixed with Korean.

The writing system reflects the importance of the notion of syllable in Korean phonology, where the majority of morphophonemic changes are results of trying to maintain a certain syllable shape (Kong-on Kim and Shibatani 1976).

The clustering of the alphabetic signs into a variety of syllable shapes has been both praised and criticized. This mode of assembling constituent letters into syllables is considered by many a definite advantage in facilitating reading, as the alphabet is made of a confusingly simple set of symbols (Iksop Lee 1971; Taylor 1980; Sampson 1985; Kim and Sohn 1986). The most common complaint concerns printing, because strings are nonlinear, and letter shapes and sizes have to be adjusted depending on what else occurs within the syllable (Sampson 1985: 144). Mair also points out problems applying modern information technology, which essentially relies on linear processing methods (Chung 1991, cited in Mair 1994: 738). There is a variety of Korean-language software available already, however, and there has been remarkable progress in both the quality and the quantity of such tools over the last decade or so. Furthermore, according to some engineers, morphophonemic spelling conventions make it easy for a computer, or a human for that matter, to parse letter strings, although this impression should be researched rather than assumed.

The Level of Representation

Yongcharye (Examples of the Use of the Letters) in *Haerye* unfortunately does not include phrases or sentences but just noun morphemes. However, early texts from the period immediately following the invention of the alphabet, such as *Yongbi ŏch'ŏn ka* (Song of the Dragons Ascending to Heaven), as well as *Haerye*, indicate that a phonemic rather than a morphophonemic system of orthography had been adopted.[20]

In a *phonemic writing convention*, an intervocalic consonant belongs to the following syllable as long as it is allowed in that position, i.e. if the following syllable does not start with a consonant. Thus, if a consonant-final stem is followed by a vowel-initial affix, the consonant would be written as the initial consonant of the affix-initial syllable, for example, :ᄉᆡᆷ <sʌim> 'source' + ·ᅵ <i> (Subject Marker) is written :ᄉᆡ ·미 <sʌi-mi> 'the source-Subj.'. The phonemic principle was impelled by the *Haerye* authors, thinking such spelling would be easier for "the simple masses," but Sejong seems to have advocated morphophonemic writing (Ki-Moon Lee 1972: 75). Modern orthography in both South and North Korea has adopted a morphophonemic principle, requiring the string to be written with maximum morphophonemic transparency, and the *Noun + Subject particle* sequence in the above example is written using the two morphemes' underlying representations, 샘이. A *morphophonemic writing convention* is one in which allomorphs are minimized.

The only exception to this convention in Modern Korean concerns irregular conjugations, as follows: Phonological alternants that are irregular are written as pronounced (i.e., when the speakers are aware of the actual phonological alternations, the forms are written as they are pronounced). Thus in Modern Korean, only the automatic alternations are written in their underlying representations. The so-called "irregular verb" alternations, vowel harmony, and various phonologically conditioned allomorphs are written as pronounced, because speakers are aware of their variable shapes.

Sampson discusses the merits and demerits of the two levels of representation (1985: 142–143). He cites opinions of two scholars, Ki-Moon Lee for shallower writing (1963: 23) and Frits Vos for deeper writing (1964: 39–40), as possibly representing native versus nonnative speakers' points of view.[21] The argument goes something like this: Whereas the native speaker would find it easier to write things as they are pronounced because he or she "comes to written language with a perfect grasp of how forms are pronounced," a non-native speaker, however proficient, would not attain "mastery of its rules of automatic phonological substitution," and he or she would prefer a deeper level of graphic representation. However, most native speakers take the position of Vos (see Iksop Lee 1992: 417–421). In any case, it is idealistic to think that there is such a thing as *the* native speaker with "a perfect grasp of how forms are pronounced." There are variations even among Standard Seoul dialect speakers. Even the same speaker can alternate between variant forms.

Rather than speculating on what sort of representation level is easier to learn and to use, one can observe some writing samples by different groups of scribes. Older people who learned to write Korean at the time when school orthography was not strictly imposed during the Japanese Occupation show spelling mistakes that are not consistent. In a two-page six-hundred-word (of which about fifty-two words are Sino-Korean) letter I recently got from a seventy-six-year-old educated woman, I notice an approximately equal number of mistakes involving not writing deeply enough and writing too deeply. The first mistakes include such forms as 가라타고 <ka-ra-t'ago> for 갈아타고 <kar-a-t'ago> 'transferring to another car', 차저 <ch'a-jŏ> for 찾어 <ch'aj-ŏ> 'looking for...'. The verb strings have not been considered as complex structures in these cases. Deeper writing samples included such forms as 어듸 <ŏtŭi> for what is now restructured as 어디 <ŏdi> '(some)where' and 눌어서 <nul-ŏsŏ> for 눌러서 <nul-lŏsŏ> 'pushing down...' where the second *l* is inserted by a morphophonemic rule. The first contains an earlier sound sequence <ŭi>, which historically underwent simplification after a tautosyllabic consonant. In the second case, the writer clearly tried to write down the underlying representation, although in modern orthography irregular phonological alternations are written as pronounced. Another more plausible interpretation is that this writer still regards the zero initial as some kind of syllable-boundary marker, for I know she would have read her own spelling as something like [nulləsə]. If another reader read it with no contextual information, the string would have been ambiguous, with at least two meanings: "pushing down..." and "being yellowish..." There are also some wrong analyses manifested by such spelling as

식히 <sik-hi> for 시키 <sik'i> 'to order/make someone do...'. Although there is a causative meaning in this morpheme, it is a single morpheme. The affix /hi/ is a passive form, and since causatives and passives are often identical, this etymology was hypothesized. My point here is that when people write casually without special attention to spelling, there is a constant effort to decompose a string down to its underlying representations.

As for young learners, there is no clear evidence, even at an early stage of learning, that writing phonemically is easier. Again, I have samples of letters written by a six-year-old. In one letter, there are syllables in which the initial and final consonants are interchanged: for example, 멍마 <mŏng-ma> for 엄마 <ŏm-ma>. Some consonants face wrong sides: ㄷ , ㅌ , and ㄸ are written as ⊐ , Ǝ , and ⊐⊐ , respectively. However, there are few mistakes in morphophonemic writing. Only when a string is interpreted as an indivisible chunk is there phonemic writing. For example, this child consistently wrote 있어 <iss-ŏ> when the word clearly had an existential meaning, but when the verb was part of a greeting it was written, for example, 잘이써 <char-i-ssŏ> 'bye'. Even in this case, the liquid was not written with the following vowel, because the meaning "well" in <chal> is transparent in this phrase. The tendency to simplify allomorphy in spoken language seems also to apply to the written language, as people are natural etymologists. Just notice what happened to the word "hamburger": there are now fishburgers and chickenburgers. The string "a napron," an English article followed by a French noun borrowed into English, was reanalyzed as "an apron." As children progress in their understanding of the paradigmatic networks of derivations, the analysis will gradually become more and more "morphematic and infralexical" (Catach 1987: 172–173). In view of the fact that writing is another representation of language, learning how to read and write is part of the language acquisition process.

Indeed, it does not appear to be easier to write down utterances just as they are pronounced without analyzing a given string. The observations made from the above unusual writing samples apply also to writing by Korean-American students who come to a Korean class speaking the language but with no prior education in written Korean, although it is often hard to decide on the source of mistakes because of the great variability in their competence in the language.

CONCLUSION

The idea behind the invention of the alphabet was that if things were both logical and relational, they were easy to learn and use. The first systematicity found was the fact that the same sound occurred in the initial and final positions of a syllable which could be divided into three major parts. With the discovery of the medial's distinctness from the initial or final, the first broad categorization of sounds was made, vowels versus consonants. The two major categories were given recognizably distinct shapes.

Consonants were subcategorized depending on their place of articulation and their strength hierarchy. Basic shapes were iconic, or "motivated" (Haas 1976), as they were either a depiction of articulatory activity or the symbolic representation of the place of articulation. After that, shapes for related sounds were made, again by a clearly defined system of modification. It is generally held that a given distinctive feature can be represented in a sound with varying degrees of strength (Stevens and Keyser 1989: 81), and the Korean writing system seems to capture this fact nicely. Other notable relationships, such as the one between the sibilant and the affricate and the one between the glottal and the velar, are also captured by the presence of related graphic shapes.

Vowel letters start with a phonetic description of three basic sounds, with an articulatory description and a traditional East Asian cosmological explanation, which would have been easily understood and accepted by the Koreans of the time. However, the new letters were not arbitrary choices made to stand for distinctive sounds in Korean. They were designed to reflect iconically and symbolically the semantic contrast that exists among vowels in Korean. Owing to a historical vowel shift, the major features for categorization of vowels into two harmonic groups, bright and dark vowels, were semantic features that had earlier been redundant (Kim-Renaud 1976).

Semivowels /w/ and /y/ were considered to be essentially vowels, forming an integral part of the nuclei. Their shapes vary depending on their relative position within a syllable, and again there exists a certain degree of iconicity in their form and size, representing their phonological status. Chinese cosmological references were brought in to explain various relationships among different sounds, I believe, to facilitate teaching the populace.

Sejong wanted to invent a writing system first of all for Koreans, as explicated in his preface to *Hunmin Chŏng'ŭm*. However, every effort was made to make the system universally applicable. The alphabet and suprasegmental markers were devised in such a way as to cover Chinese, the language of an area that represented the entire civilized world for Koreans at the time.[22] Some special symbols not necessary for Korean at all were part of the original inventory. Tone marking and punctuation were also devised to make it easier for people to understand written text. With time, many of the symbols that were not necessary in writing Korean disappeared from texts and were forgotten.

Writing in syllable blocks was also a way of facilitating readability. It was a practical way of mixing Chinese characters, which Koreans probably found easier than the alphabet at the time of its invention. According to one source (public discussion following Song 1991 in *Linguistic Journal of Korea* 16.1: 218) there are more than 11,000 syllables in Korean.[23] Therefore, to call the Korean writing system a "syllabary" (Taylor 1980) is absurd, because any syllable could be generated based on the alphabetic inventory and the prescribed combinatory principle.[24]

As the language evolved, some sounds disappeared, as did the graphemes that represented them. Some new sounds that have been created through language change, for example, a rich array of new front vowels, have been effortlessly accommodated by the writing system. Some ongoing changes, such as the merging of mid and low front vowels (Hong 1991) and bisyllabification of front round vowels, may create some distance between the spoken and written languages. However, written forms also influence the spoken language, as shown in the full and careful pronunciation of the *ŭi* sequence by youngsters.

There is a clear structural correspondence between the oral and written media of the Korean language. This relationship was made even more striking by the proclamation of the new writing system, which included explanations with examples. Because its design features are phonetically and semantically motivated, and because the system reflects some important phonological alternations, the alphabet is easy for Korean speakers to learn and to use. Because morphemes are transparent in Korean orthography, it is easy to read. Korean morphophonemics is complex, and consistent shapes for morphemes should eventually facilitate computer treatment of written Korean, although the current technology, which has been developed based on the linear writing of Roman alphabetic systems, may not be easily and efficiently accommodated for processing Korean.

Because of its systematic categorization of sounds, with corresponding graphic interpretation, some linguists (Chin-W. Kim 1980/1988; Sampson 1985) have come to consider han'gŭl a "featural" system. Indeed, one could identify labiality, dentality, velarity, sibilancy, occlusivity, and so on. With just a few exceptions it does appear that one could find a specific distinctive graphic representation for each of these features. However, the "relatedness" in letter forms of various phonetic groupings often rests on a graded rather than a binary scale. One important class, *chŏnch'ŏng* 全清 [+gently aspirated] includes both ㅅ /s/ and ㅈ /c/, one basic and the other derived by adding an extra mark. Sometimes, as in the case of velars and glottals, a basic sound seems to be shared by two different groups of sounds.

There are also cases in which the same symbol was used to represent radically different sounds and concepts. For example, the single dot had at least three different functions. It is first of all one of three basic vowel letters. Second, it was used in designing other letters, but its value was not realized until it was put next to a long horizontal or vertical stroke. In this case, it did not have an inherent meaning by itself, but its comparative position gave a definition to the newly created vowel. Finally, it represented a prevocalic palatality. Given these cases, it would be rather forced and in some ways detracting from the true ingenuity and logical nature of the system to call it a featural system, let alone a Jakobsonian system (Chin-W. Kim 1980/1988: 729).

CHRONOLOGICAL LIST OF TEXTS

Hunmin chŏng'ŭm 訓民正音 / Chŏng'ŭm 正音 (The correct sounds [for the instruction of the people]). By King Sejong (世宗大王). 1446.

Hunmin chŏng'ŭm haerye 訓民正音解例 / Haerye 解例 (Explanations and examples [of the correct sounds for the instruction of the people]). By Chŏng In-ji (鄭麟趾), Sin Suk-chu (申叔舟), et al. 1446.

Yongcharye (Examples of the use of the letters) in Hunmin chŏng'ŭm haerye, 1446.

Yongbi ŏch'ŏn ka 龍飛御天歌 (The song of the dragons ascending to heaven). By Chŏng In-ji (鄭麟趾) et al. 1447.

Wŏrin ch'ŏn'gang chi kok 月印千江之曲 (Songs of the moon's imprint on the thousand rivers). By Sejong (世宗). C. 1448.

Wŏrin sŏkpo 月印釋譜 (The moon's imprint on the record of Sakyamuni). By Kim Suon (金守溫) et al. 1459.

Hunmin chŏng'ŭm ŏnhae 訓民正音諺解 (A Vernacular Translation of the correct sounds for the Instruction of the People) in *Wŏrin Sŏkpo*, 1459.

Hunmong chahoe 訓蒙字會 (Collection of characters for training the unenlightened]. By Ch'oe Se-jin (崔世珍). 1527.

Ŏnmun chi 諺文志 (Treatise on Korean vernacular writing). By Yu Hŭi (柳僖). 1824.

NOTES

1. In this essay, the Korean writing system in general will be referred to as han'gŭl ("The Han [Korean/Great] Script"), the term believed to have been first used by Chu Si-gyŏng in 1910 (Ko 1982). However, when I refer specifically and uniquely to fifteenth-century writing, its original name *Hunmin chŏng'ŭm* (The Correct Sounds for the Instruction of the People) or its abbreviated name *Chŏng'ŭm* will be used. In this study, angle brackets contain graphic representations in original Korean writing or in McCune-Reischauer romanization; and phonemic and phonetic representations, given between / / and [ ], respectively, are essentially the same as those adopted in Kim-Renaud 1974. In transcribing Korean sounds, C^h (a heavily aspirated consonant) and C' (a tense consonant) are single sounds in spite of their complex symbols. In contrast, the basic shape of the affricates, both dental and palatal, is expressed by a single sign C. *C*˺ indicates an unreleased consonant. In writing this chapter, I have received much encouragement and helpful criticism from Samuel E. Martin, S. R. Ramsey, John Whitman, and Young-mee Yu Cho. I am most grateful for their time and interest in my study. Needless to say, however, I am solely responsible for the contents and style of the chapter.

2. In the fifteenth century, all Sino-Korean syllables had to have a CVC graphic structure. When a syllable ended in a vowel, a circle was drawn in below that vowel. According to Samuel Martin (personal communication), the Chinese system for arranging the finals had a corresponding category for the codaless syllables, so that it was natural for the Koreans to write the zero for vowel-ending syllables, despite its redundancy given the syllable boundary.

3. The status of the letter ㆆ /ʔ/ is unclear. It was never used as an initial in Korean words, and even in Sino-Korean pronunciation, it was often confused with ㅇ /ɦ/. In fifteenth-century Korean, it was mainly attached to the prospective-modifier ending *-l*, probably as a signal for a syllable break, which causes the following consonant to tense. Ledyard thinks that it was "an artificial letter, used only to indicate the initial of Sino-Korean words which in Chinese dictionaries were said to begin with a glottal stop" (1966: 166), but finds it convenient to assign the value /ʔ/ to it for other reasons.

4. Young-mee Yu Cho (personal communication) notes that if the feature [aspiration] were the crucial factor, one would expect tense obstruents to be the least marked, the plain series second, and the aspirated series the most marked. In my view, "unmarked" does not always indicate the lack of a certain feature. It should refer to what comes the most naturally with the least effort. Therefore, in the case of obstruents, slightly aspirated lenis obstruents would be the most unmarked. Both the strongly aspirated series and tense series require extra effort, one by opening the glottis widely and the other by squeezing it tightly, which thus constitute marked features for Korean obstruents.

5. The labials show a slight anomaly in the manner in which the strokes are added. I do not have a particular idea how this has come about, other than thinking that it was a matter of making an extension in one direction in obtaining occlusivity and in two directions in arriving at the heavily aspirated stop. Note, however, that in the fifteenth century, the symbol ㅁ was a dominant symbol in both ㅂ [p] and ㅍ [pʰ], in which extensions looked minimal compared to their shapes at present.

6. Young-mee Yu Cho brought my attention to Martin's terminology, referring to the tense series as "intensive" and the heavily aspirated series as "paraintensive" in his treatment of mimetics (1992: 343). The implication may be that there is a scalar relationship between these and lenis obstruents. Martin (personal communication) in fact shares my judgment and says that he uses the term "paraintensive" not to mean "more intensive" but rather "differently intensive" or just "an alternate kind of intensive."

7. There are linguists who believe that the [ʔ] sound is phonemic not only in fifteenth-century Korean but also in Modern Korean. For example, Iksop Lee gives as evidence many examples that show ㆆ < ʔ > attached right next to the prospective-modifier, even when it is followed by a sound that is already tense or that cannot be tensed, such as a nasal or a tense or heavily aspirate consonant (1992: 75). In Modern Korean, Lee claims there is an underlying / ʔ / in verbs ending in a nasal, because affix-initial consonants are tensed after such verbs, for example, /an-/ + /ta/ > [ant'a] 'to embrace'. However, the fact that modern orthography does not require any marking for the tensing element might suggest that / ʔ / is more like a signal for a break between the two units that are normally pronounced closely together, so that the two distinct, semantically important units are not merged in such a way that the second meaning is greatly weakened (Kim-Renaud 1974: 159–170).

8. Woong Huh's examples include ·뮈 ·ᅇᅱ· [mui-wwə] 'moving (causative)' (1988: 46, side dots provided from *Wŏrin sŏkpo* [The Moon's Imprint on the Record of Sakyamuni, 1459], ch. 14, and also from Chang-don Yu 1964: 336). He thus interprets the double circle as a tensifier of the following sound, which can be *i*, *y*, or *u*. However, why it should be so was not contemplated.

9. There are scholars, such as Ch'anggyun Yu (1977: 79–80) and Sinhang Kang (1987: 101), who claim that *t'ak* represented voicing and that in certain dialects of Chinese voiced obstruents were also tense. In northern dialects,

however, tensed obstruents were voiceless (Ramsey, personal communication). In Koreans' ears the important feature was tenseness or lack of aspiration rather than voicing, as there was no voicing distinction among obstruents (Yu 1977: 80; Kang 1987: 101).

10. The reason the simple circle was adopted rather than the circle with a tick may not only be for its simpler shape but also to avoid unwanted confusion. At one time, the zero was used even in a final position for Sino-Korean words. When the velar nasal is placed under a vowel— as in 그ᇰ <kŭng>, it looks very much like a ᅮ followed by a zero, i.e., 궁 <kung>.

11. According to Ramsey, there was no /sC-/ sequence in the fifteenth century (1978b: 62). However, there exist sporadic examples of other consonant clusters in transcribing foreign words, for example, ᄎᄏ [cʰkʰ] in 닌 ᄎ쿼 시 [nincʰkʰwəsi], a Jurchen place name (Ki-Moon Lee 1972: 57) and ᄉ나 ·ᄒᆡ [snahʌi] 'young man' (Huh 1988: 45).

12. I am using the term "released" here, as in my dissertation (Kim-Renaud 1974), to mean "requiring an *oral* contact after articulation and not immediately releasing that contact." Therefore nasals and laterals can also be unreleased, as they are in Korean in contrast to, say, word-final nasals and laterals in certain dialects of French (Iverson and Sohn 1994). In Modern Korean this unreleasing force in syllable-final position is so strong that fricatives *s* and *h* take a stop position [t˺], but in Middle Korean the sibilants did not become completely unreleased.

13. The characters 子 <cha>, 丑 <ch'uk>, and 寅 <in> represent the first three of the Twelve Branches of Horary Characters 十二地支 <sibijiji> in Chinese cosmology.

14. The character 蹙 <ch'uk> literally means "to knit the brow" but is translated here as "to purse (the lips)."

15. S. R. Ramsey (personal communication) notes that in Middle Korean, forms such as ᅴ had an offglide, whereas in Modern Korean they have an onglide. In my view, the same two vowels underlie both forms. Their different phonetic realizations are results of different surface phonetic constraints applying in two different periods. The change came about as vowels monophthongized, and the second mora, the [i] vowel, was no longer independently visible.

16. Strictly speaking, even the *ŭi* sequence is made of two vowels. Its reduction pattern clearly shows that the vowels *ŭ* and *i* have equal weight within the nucleus, as one or the other vowel remains depending on the environment (Kim-Renaud 1986b). Kong-On Kim (1978: 77) claims that the first part of the *ŭi* sequence is actually a glide, [i̯], pointing out that when the sequence is stretched, it is the [i] vowel that is lengthened. It may be so in a noninitial syllable, but in word-initial position it is the first part that is lengthened, for example, [ɨ:isa] 'doctor'.

17. Here we leave aside one "entering" tone, which was perhaps not a marker for a pitch but rather a kind of signal for syllable-final unreleasing. It was probably created just to "deal with a theoretical and artificial conformity with Chinese phonology" (Ledyard 1966: 207).

18. S. R. Ramsey (personal communication) brings to my attention a remark in Morohashi's dictionary, *Daikanwajiten* (Great Chinese-Japanese Dictionary) (Morohashi 1956/1968), vol. 2, p. 746, regarding punctuation conventions in traditional Chinese texts, that is, small circles and commalike brush marks for sentence-final and sentence-internal pauses, respectively. The punctuation marks used in some early Korean texts apparently were inspired by this practice, although the two conventions differed from each other in detail.

19. One exception was that in mixed Chinese and Korean script in Middle Korean, a single vowel or consonant could stand independently when that segment was to be incorporated into the final syllable of a Sino-Korean word. For example, in 孔子 ㅣ 魯 ㅅ :사·ᄅᆞᆷ <khongcʌilossa:rʌm> 'Confucius is a person from Lu', the vowel ㅣ <i>, a subject marker, stands by itself, but in reading it would have been read as part of the preceding syllable, and the consonant ㅅ <s>, a genitive marker, although written by itself, would have been pronounced as the final consonant of the preceding syllable.

20. In reality, however, even *Yongbi ŏch'ŏn ka* is not consistently phonemic, and there are some texts, including *Wŏrin ch'ŏn'gang chi kok* (Songs of the Moon's Imprint on the Thousand Rivers, 1448), the creation of which Sejong supervised himself, that favor morphophonemic spelling (Ki-Moon Lee 1972: 73–75).

21. After writing this chapter, I checked with Ki-Moon Lee about his current position on the subject, as he clearly takes a different view in his later writings (e.g., Lee 1972: 75). Lee refers to his former opinion as having been influenced by "phonemic" thinking of the time when the work appeared.

22. This attitude is clearly noticeable in the anti-alphabet memorial of Ch'oe Malli. Ch'oe, who at the time of invention held "the highest purely academic rank in the College [of Assembled Worthies]" (Ledyard 1966: 100), wrote: "Although from ancient times customs and local usages have differed within the Nine Isles, there has never been a case of one of them separately making a script based on the local speech. Only types like the Mongolians, Tanguts, Jurchen, Japanese, and Tibetans have their own graphs. But these are matters of the barbarians, and not worth talking about" (translation in Ledyard 1966: 104).

23. Martin mentions that others have arrived at similar figures (1992: 7): 10,250 by Yu Hŭi (1824: 18) in his *Ŏnmun chi* (Treatise on Korean Vernacular Writing) and 11,172 by Hyŏng-nyŏng Kim (1965).

24. Taylor (1980) adds that han'gŭl is even a "logography in a limited sense." The observation is based on such monosyllabic words as ᄒᆞᆰ <hŭlk> 'earth, dirt'. Such examples can occur in any language and cannot be called evidence for the existence of a "system."

REFERENCES

Baek, Eung-Jin. 1987. The pause in Middle Korean. In *Harvard studies in Korean linguistics II*, ed. Susumu Kuno, Ik-Hwan Lee, John Whitman, Sung-Yun Bak, and Young-Se Kang, 319–327. Cambridge, Mass.: Department of Linguistics, Harvard University.

Catach, Nina. 1987. New linguistic approaches to a theory of writing. In *Georgetown University Round Table on Languages and Linguistics 1986*, ed. Simon P. X. Battestini, 161–174. Washington, D.C.: Georgetown University Press.

Chang, Namgui. 1978. Aspects of Korean diachronic phonology. Ph.D. dissertation, University of California, Berkeley.

Chung, Won L. 1991. Hangeul and computing. In *Characters and computers*, ed. Victor H. Mair and Yongquan Liu, 146–179. Amsterdam, Oxford, Washington, and Tokyo: IOS Press.

Haas, William. 1976. Writing without letters. Manchester, England: Manchester University Press.

Hong, Yunsook. 1991. A sociolinguistic study of Seoul Korean. Seoul: Research Center for Peace and Unification of Korea.

Huh, Woong. 1955. Pangchŏm yŏn'gu (A study of side dots). *Tongbang hakchi* 2:37–194.

———. 1965. Kugŏŭmunhak (Korean phonology). Seoul: Chŏng'ŭmsa.

———. 1988. 15 segi-ŭi ŭmunch'egye (The phonological system of the fifteenth century). In Sin et al. 1988: 41–57.

Hur, Kwang Il. 1991. Tone in Middle Korean. Ph.D. dissertation, Georgetown University.

Iverson, Gregory K., and Hyang-Sook Sohn. 1994. Liquid representation in Korean. In *Theoretical issues in Korean linguistics*, ed. Young-Key Kim-Renaud, 77–100. Stanford: CSLI.

Kang, Sinhang. 1987. Hunmin chŏng'ŭm yŏn'gu (A study of Hunmin chŏng'ŭm) . Seoul: Sung Kyun Kwan University Press.

Kim, Cha Kyun. 1988. Hunmin chŏng'ŭm-ŭi sŏngjo (Tone in Hunmin chŏng'ŭm). In Sin et al. 1988: 113–182.

Kim, Chin-W. 1970. A theory of aspiration. *Phonetica* 21: 107–116.

———. 1980/1988. On the origin and structure of the Korean script. Lecture delivered on October 9, 1980, at the University of Illinois. In *Sojourns in Korean language II*, ed. Chin-W. Kim, Seoul: Tower Press, 721–734.

Kim, Chin-W., and Han Sohn. 1986. A phonetic model for reading: Evidence from Korean. *Studies in Linguistic Sciences* 16:2:95–105.

Kim, Hyŏng-nyŏng. 1965. Urimal munhwaŏ-ŭi patchime taehan yŏn'gu (On finals in Korean culture language) *Ŏnŏhak nonmunjip* (Linguistic papers) 6: 20–78. Phyŏng'yang: Kwahak paekkwa sajŏn ch'ulp'ansa (Scientific Encyclopedic Publishing Company).

Kim, Kong-On. 1978. Vowel system of Korean revisited. In *Papers in Korean linguistics*, ed. Chin-W. Kim, 75–83. Columbia, S.C.: Hornbeam Press.

Kim, Kong-On, and Masayoshi Shibatani. 1976. Syllabification phenomena in Korean. *Language Research* (Seoul) 12:1:91–98.

Kim, Wanjin. 1963/1971. Moŭmch'egye-ŭi sin'goch'al (A new inquiry into the vowel system). *Chindanhakpo* 24:475–511. Reprinted in *Kugŏŭmun ch'eygye-ŭi yŏn'gu* (A study of the Korean phonological system) by W. Kim, 2–44. Seoul: Ilchogak.

Kim-Renaud, Young-Key. 1973. "Irregular" verbs in Korean revisited. *Language Research* 9: 206–225.

———. 1974. Korean consonantal phonology. Ph.D. dissertation, University of Hawai'i.

———. 1976. Semantic features in phonology: Evidence from vowel harmony in Korean. In 12th CLS *Papers from the Twelfth Regional Meeting of the Chicago Linguistic Society*, ed. S. A. Mufwene, C. A. Walker, and S. B. Steever, 397–412. Chicago: Chicago Linguistic Society.

———. 1978. The syllable in Korean phonology. In *Papers in Korean linguistics*, ed. Chin-W. Kim, 85–98. Columbia, S.C.: Hornbeam Press.

———. 1986a. Studies in Korean linguistics. Seoul: Hanshin Publishing Co.

———. 1986b. Monophthongization of the *ɨ-i* sequence in Korean. *Korean Linguistics* 4:1–15.

Ko, Yong-Kun. 1983. "Han'gŭl"-ŭi yurae-e taehayŏ (On the origin of the word "Han'gŭl") in *Paeksŏk Cho Mun-je kyosu hwagap kinyŏm nonmunjip* (A festschrift for Professor Cho Mun-je), Seoul: The Committee for the Festschrift for Professor Cho Mun-je. 31–42. Reprinted in Kugŏ-wa minjok munhwa (The Korean language and cultures), ed. by Min-su Kim, Yong-Kun Ko, Iksop Lee, and Jae-Kee Shim, Seoul: Chimnundang, 1984. 278–286. Also appears under the title, " 'Han'gŭl'-ŭi yurae" (The origin of the word "Han'gŭl") in T'ong'il sidae-ŭi ŏmun munje (On language and writing in reunified Korea), a collection of articles by Yong-Kun Ko, Seoul: Kilbŏs Publishing Co., 1994. 286–297.

Ledyard, Gari. 1966. The Korean language reform of 1446: The origin, background, and early history of the Korean alphabet. Ph.D. dissertation, University of California, Berkeley.

Lee, Iksop. 1971. Muncha-ŭi kinŭng-gwa p'yogipŏp-ŭi isang (The function of writing and ideology in orthography). In *Kim Hyŏng-gyu songsu kinyŏm nonch'ong* (A festschrift for Hyŏng-gyu Kim). Seoul: Ilchogak Publishing Co. 679–694.

———. 1992. Kugŏphyogipŏp yŏn'gu (A study of Korean orthography). Seoul: Seoul National University Press.

Lee, Ki-Moon. 1963. Kugŏ p'yogipŏb-ŭi yŏksajŏk yŏn'gu (A historical study of Korean orthography). Seoul: Hanguk yŏn'guwŏn (Institute of Korean Studies).

———. 1969. Chungsegugŏ ŭmullon-ŭi chemunje (Problems in Middle Korean phonology). *Chindan hakpo* 32: 133–150.

———. 1972. Kugŏŭmunsa yŏn'gu (A study of Korean historical phonology). Seoul: Seoul National University Press.

Lee, Pyong Geun. 1988. Hunmin Chŏng'ŭm-ŭi ch'ojongsŏngch'egye (The initial/final sound system). In Sin et al. 1988: 59–80.

Lee, Sang Oak. 1978. Middle Korean tonology. Ph.D. dissertation, University of Illinois, Urbana.

Mair, Victor H. 1994. Buddhism and the rise of written vernacular. *Journal of Asian Studies* 53:3: 707–751.

Martin, Samuel E. 1962. Phonetic symbolism in Korean. In *American studies in Altaic linguistics*, ed. N. Poppe, 177–189. Uralic and Altaic Series 13. Bloomington: Indiana University Publications.

———. 1975. Problems in establishing the prehistoric relationships of Korean and Japanese. *International Symposium Commemorating the 30th Anniversary of Korean Liberation: Proceedings*, 149–172. Seoul: National Academy of Sciences.

———. 1982. Features, markedness and order in Korean phonology. In *Linguistics in the morning calm*, ed. The Linguistic Society of Korea, 601–618. Seoul: Hanshin Publishing Co.

———. 1992. A reference grammar of Korean. Rutland, Vt., and Tokyo: Charles E. Tuttle Co.

McCawley, James D. 1968. The phonological component of a grammar of Japanese. The Hague: Mouton.

Morohashi, Tetsuji. 1956/1968. *Daikanwa jiten* (Great Chinese-Japanese dictionary). Vol. 2. Tokyo: Taishukan.

Ramsey, S. Robert. 1978a. Accent and morphology in Korean dialects. The Society of Korean Linguistics. Seoul: Tower Press.

———. 1978b. *S*-clusters and reinforced consonants. In *Papers in Korean linguistics*, ed. Chin-W. Kim, 59–66. Columbia, S.C.: Hornbeam Press.

———. 1991. Proto-Korean and the origin of Korean accent. In *Studies in the historical phonology of Asian languages*, ed. William G. Boltz and Michael C. Shapiro, 215–239. Amsterdam/Philadelphia: John Benjamins Publishing Co.

Ramstedt, G. J. 1939. A Korean grammar. *Memoires de la Société Finno-Ougrienne* 82. Helsinki.

Sampson, Geoffrey. 1985. Writing systems. Stanford, Calif.: Stanford University Press.

Sin, Sang-sun, Ton-ju Yi, and Hwan-muk Yi, eds. 1988. *Hunmin chŏng'ŭm*-ŭi ihae (Understanding *Hunmin chŏng'ŭm*). Seoul: Hanshin Publishing Co.

Song, Ki-jung. 1991. Segye-ŭi muncha-wa han'gŭl (Writing systems of the world and han'gŭl). *Linguistic Journal of Korea* 16:1: 153–180.

Stevens, Kenneth N., and Samuel Jay Keyser. 1989. Primary features and their enhancement in consonants. *Language* 65:1: 81–106.

Taylor, Insup. 1980. The Korean writing system: An alphabet? a syllabary? a logography? In *Processing of visible language*, ed. Paul A. Kolers, Merald E. Wrolstad, and Herman Bouma, 67–82. New York: Plenum Press.

Taylor, Insup, and Maurice Taylor. 1962. Phonetic symbolism in four unrelated languages. *Canadian Journal of Psychology* 16: 344–356.

Vos, Frits. 1964. Papers on Korean studies. In *Papers of the CIC Far Eastern Language Institute*, ed. Joseph K. Yamagiwa, Ann Arbor, Michigan: University of Michigan, Committee on Far Eastern Language Instruction of the Committee on Institutional Cooperation. 29–34.

Yu, Ch'ang-don. 1964. Yijoŏ sajŏn (A dictionary of Yi dynasty language). Seoul: Yonsei University Press.

Yu, Chang-gyun. 1977. Hunmin chŏng'ŭm. Seoul: Hyŏngsŏl Publishing Co.

10

ORTHOGRAPHIC DIVERGENCE IN SOUTH AND NORTH KOREA: TOWARD A UNIFIED SPELLING SYSTEM

Ho-min Sohn

Linguistic divergence between South and North Korea since 1945 has been accelerated mainly by three interrelated factors: complete physical insulation between the two Koreas; polarized political, ideological, and social distinctions; and the different language policies implemented by the two governments.[1] As a result, a thick sociopolitical dialectal division, with two standards of speech, has been superimposed on the long existing historical-geographical dialects. The two standards of speech are Seoul-based P'yojunmal (Standard Speech) in the South and P'yŏngyang-based Munhwaŏ (Cultured Speech) in the North. Linguistic divergence is found not only in the lexicon, phonology, grammar, and usage, but also in orthography. The aim of the present chapter is to examine the extent to which han'gŭl spelling divergence exists, to investigate what has caused the divergence, and to suggest some directions leading to a unified spelling system.[2] Disparities will be observed in two current systems: South Korea's *Han'gŭl match'umpŏp* (MOE 1988a) and North Korea's *Kaejŏnghan Chosŏnmal kyubŏmjip* (KLAC 1988). Extensive reference will be made to such previous works by M. Kim (1985), E. Lee (1989), and Lee and Ahn (1991).

Both *Han'gŭl match'umpŏp and Kaejŏnghan Chosŏnmal kyubŏmjip* were derived from *Han'gŭl match'umpŏp t'ong'ilan* (KLA 1933) through repeated revisions. While only minor modifications were made in South Korea before *Han'gŭl match'umpŏp*, two major revisions were made in North Korea before *Kaejŏnghan Chosŏnmal kyubŏmjip*: *Chosŏnŏ ch'ŏlchapŏp* in 1954 and *Chosŏnmal kyubŏmjip* in 1966. The sharing of the source system and the fact that both systems follow two basic spelling principles stipulated in 1933, however, have prevented extreme diversification. One of the basic principles is the principle of morphophonemic spelling. This principle specifies that the original forms of the roots and affixes in compounds and derivatives should be identified as much as possible and spelled accordingly; but if the etymology is not clear, or if the original sounds are unpredictably changed or fossilized, they should be spelled as they are pronounced (MOE 1988a: 1.1; KLAC 1988, *Match'umpŏp*—General Rule). The other basic principle that North and South Korea share is that of word-based spacing (MOE 1988a: 1.2; KLAC 1988, *Ttŭiŏssŭgi*—General Rule). An external deterrent against radical divergence seems to be the fact that the governments and scholars of both Koreas are keenly cognizant of the adverse effect of linguistic diversification on their reunification efforts. For instance, Kim Il Sung's 1964 and 1966 language-related Teachings (*kyosi*) via dialogues with linguists called for the implementation of Chuch'e-oriented linguistic reforms but warned against radical changes (in regard to a proposed script reform, the teaching of Chinese characters, and spacing conventions) in preparation for national reunification.[3] Such activating and deterring forces have affected spelling differences between the two Koreas, but not to an extreme degree.

The existing differences seem to have been created by three partly interrelated causes: (a) the emergence of two standards of speech, (b) different linguistic analyses of similar or identical phenomena, and (c) different conventions followed in breaking with tradition for the sake of regularization. Two standards of speech have emerged because North Korea has legislated Cultured Speech as standard in pronunciation and spelling, in accordance with Kim Il Sung's 1966 Chuch'e-oriented Teachings.[4] Kim called for preserving and developing the national characteristics of Korean based on the speech of P'yŏngyang, suggesting the term Munhwaŏ (Cultured Speech) rather than P'yojunmal (Standard Speech). Munhwaŏ is defined as "the richly developed national language that is formed centering on the revolutionary capital under the leadership of the proletarian party that holds sovereignty during the socialism-constructing period, and that all people hold as a standard because it has been refined revolutionarily and polished culturally to fit the proletariat's goals and lifestyle" (LIASS 1973). North Korea denounces P'yojunmal, claiming that "it has lost its legitimacy as a national language because it is deprived of national characteristics and popular elements and has become the speech of the bourgeoisie, a jumble filled with Western, Japanese, and Chinese elements owing to American imperialists and their followers' national language erasure policy" (Chong et al. 1981; KISU 1983).[5] In South Korea, P'yojunmal is defined as "the contemporary Seoul speech used by educated people" (MOE 1988b), modified from the definition in KLA (1933, 1936), which read "the contemporary Seoul speech used by middle-class people."

Different linguistic analyses are observed, among other things, in the determination of morphemic fossilization in compounds and derivatives. Although both spelling systems share the morphophonemic principle, the CV principle that requires, for example, the syllable division of V.CV and not of VC.V within a morpheme (e.g., 사람 sa.ram, not 살암 sar.am 'person'), and word-based spacing, the question often arises whether an element should be interpreted as a single fossilized morpheme or as a composite of two or more morphemes, whether a speech sound is morphophonemically significant, or whether a sequence of words is to be analyzed as a compound.

The two systems adopt different conventions in regularizing forms and concepts, breaking with tradition to different degrees, as in the names of letters, treatment of the epenthetic *s* (*sai-siot*), treatment of some Sino-Korean diphthongs, and spacing. It appears that North Korea's system has broken with tradition more frequently, pursuing more formal uniformity. This may be due partly to Kim Il Song's Chuch'e language theory, which is closely tied to Kim's "Anti-Japanese Struggle" during World War II, Marxist-Leninist language theory, and North Korea's Cultured Speech Movement, which has prevailed since Kim's 1966 Teachings (Ko 1990). It has been observed by Ko (1990) and others that North Korea has ceased to applaud KLA (1933) since the late 1960s.

EXTRA-SPELLING CONVENTIONS

In addition to spelling and spacing disparities, the two Koreas disagree on three other conventions, direction of writing, names of han'gŭl letters, and alphabetic order for dictionaries and other purposes.

As for the direction of writing, South Korea follows the tradition allowing both horizontal and vertical writing, whereas North Korea stipulates that horizontal writing be used in principle (KLAC 1988). In South Korea, most newspapers use vertical writing, whereas a recent trend in other publications is to favor horizontal writing, owing to typewriter and computer practices, visual expediency, and Western influence.

Disparity also appears in the names of three consonant letters (ㄱ *k*, ㄷ *t*, ㅅ *s*) and geminate consonant letters (MOE 1988a: 2.4; KLAC 1988: 1.1). In the following, romanized equivalents are given under corresponding han'gŭl expressions as needed.

Names of han'gŭl letters

	ㄱ	ㄷ	ㅅ	ㄲ	ㅃ
SK:	기역 ki.yŏk	디귿 ti.gŭt	시옷 si.ot	쌍기역 ssang.gi.yŏk	쌍비읍 ssang.bi.ŭp
NK:	기윽 ki.ŭk	디읃 ti.ŭt	시읏 si.ŭt	된기윽 toen.gi.ŭk	된 비읍 toen.bi.ŭp

North Korea changed the traditional names of the three letters to conform to the other consonant terms. Whereas South Korea's traditional Sino-Korean term *ssang* 'twin' is a purely letter-based term (for example, twin letters in South Korea), North Korea's newly introduced native term *toen* 'hard, tense' is a sound-based term (for example, tensed sound quality in North Korea). North Korea's use of *toen* might have been urged by Kim Il Sung's 1964 and 1966 Teachings that call for maximum use of native terms.

The alphabetic orders used for dictionary entries and so forth do not agree, as shown below (MOE 1988a: 2.4; KLAC 1988: 1.1).

a. Syllable-onset consonants

SK:	ㄱ	ㄲ	ㄴ	ㄷ	ㄸ	ㄹ	ㅁ	ㅂ	ㅃ	ㅅ	ㅆ	ㅇ	ㅈ	ㅉ	ㅊ	ㅋ	ㅌ	ㅍ	ㅎ
	k/g	kk	n	t/d	tt	l/r	m	p/b	pp	s	ss	ng	ch/j	tch	ch'	k'	t'	p'	h

NK:	ㄱ	ㄴ	ㄷ	ㄹ	ㅁ	ㅂ	ㅅ	ㅇ	ㅈ	ㅊ	ㅋ	ㅌ	ㅍ	ㅎ	ㄲ	ㄸ	ㅃ	ㅆ	ㅉ
	k/g	n	t/d	l/r	m	p/b	s	ng	ch/j	ch'	k'	t'	p'	h	kk	tt	pp	ss	tsh

b. Syllable-nuclear vowels and diphthongs

SK:

ㅏ	ㅐ	ㅑ	ㅒ	ㅓ	ㅔ	ㅕ	ㅖ	ㅗ	ㅘ	ㅙ	ㅚ	ㅛ	ㅜ	ㅝ	ㅞ	ㅟ	ㅠ	ㅡ	ㅢ	ㅣ
a	ae	ya	yae	ŏ	e	yŏ	ye	o	wa	wae	oe	yo	u	wŏ	we	wi	yu	ŭ	ŭi	i

NK:

ㅏ	ㅑ	ㅓ	ㅕ	ㅗ	ㅛ	ㅜ	ㅠ	ㅡ	ㅣ	ㅐ	ㅒ	ㅔ	ㅖ	ㅚ	ㅟ	ㅢ	ㅘ	ㅝ	ㅙ	ㅞ
a	ya	ŏ	yŏ	o	yo	u	yu	ŭ	i	ae	yae	e	ye	oe	wi	ŭi	wa	wŏ	wae	we

c. Syllable-coda consonants (*patch'im*)

SK:

ㄱ	ㄲ	ㄳ	ㄴ	ㄵ	ㄶ	ㄷ	ㄹ	ㄺ	ㄻ	ㄼ	ㄽ	ㄾ	ㄿ	ㅀ	ㅁ	ㅂ	ㅄ	ㅅ	ㅆ	ㅇ	ㅈ	ㅊ	ㅋ	ㅌ	ㅍ	ㅎ
k/g	kk	ks	n	nj	nh	t/d	l/r	lk/lg	lm	lp/lb	ls	lt'	lp'	lh	m	p/b	ps	s	ss	ng	ch/j	ch'	k'	t'	p'	h

NK:

ㄱ	ㄳ	ㄴ	ㄵ	ㄶ	ㄷ	ㄹ	ㄺ	ㄻ	ㄼ	ㄽ	ㄾ	ㄿ	ㅀ	ㅁ	ㅂ	ㅄ	ㅅ	ㅇ	ㅈ	ㅊ	ㅋ	ㅌ	ㅍ	ㅎ	ㄲ	ㅆ
k/g	ks	n	nj	nh	t/d	l/r	lk/lg	lm	lp/lb	ls	lt'	lp'	lh	m	p/b	ps	s	ng	ch/j	ch'	k'	t'	p'	h	kk	ss

Notice in (a) and (b) that complex letters immediately follow each corresponding basic letter in South Korea but are grouped after all basic letters in North Korea. North Korea's onset consonant order agrees with *Han'gŭl match'umpŏp t'ong'ilan* (KLA 1933), but its diphthongal order does not. Thus, for example, the triple letter ㅞ *we* (i.e., ㅜ u + ㅓ ŏ + ㅣ *i*) is placed at the end in North Korea, whereas it is placed before the double letter ㅟ *wi* in South Korea (in the sequence ㅜ *u*, ㅝ *wŏ*, ㅞ *we*, ㅟ *wi*). Further notice the North Korean order among double letters, placing ㅘ *wa* and ㅝ *wŏ* after ㅚ *oe*, ㅟ *wi*, and ㅢ *ŭi*. E. Lee (1989: 155) states that whereas in *Han'gŭl match'umpŏp t'ong'ilan* the order among complex letters is determined on the basis of the first letter of a complex, in the North Korean system the complex letters are arranged on the basis of the added (second) letter, thus in the order ㅣ *i* (ㅐ *ae*, ㅒ *yae*, ㅔ *e*, ㅖ *ye*, ㅚ *oe*, ㅟ *wi*, ㅢ *ŭi*), ㅏ *a* (ㅘ *wa*), ㅓ ŏ (ㅝ *wŏ*), ㅐ *ae* (ㅙ *wae*), and ㅔ *e* (ㅞ *we*). A partially sound-based approach in North Korea is observed in (a) and (c). The letter ㄲ *kk*, for example, is regarded simply as the doubling of ㄱ *k* in South Korea, whereas it is treated as an independent entity that has nothing phonemically to do with ㄱ *k* in North Korea. Thus, the only difference between the two systems in (c) is that ㄲ *kk* and ㅆ *ss* are placed at the end in North Korea. North Korea's order of coda consonants deviates not only from South Korea's system but also from *Han'gŭl match'umpŏp t'ong'iran*, whose order is ㄱ *k* . . . ㅎ *h*, ㄲ *kk*, ㄳ *ks*, ㄵ *nj* . . . ㅄ *ps*, ㅆ *ss*.

Let me make a few comments on the above North-South disparities. With regard to the direction of writing, although North Korea hardly practices any vertical writing in publications, its use is allowed in exceptional cases. Since a definite trend in South Korea is to prefer horizontal writing, this divergence is not a major issue. As for the names of the letters ㄱ *k/g*, ㄷ *t/d*, and ㅅ *s*, North Korea's regulation, which is a deviation from tradition, is preferred for its simplicity. Between South Korea's letter-based term *ssang* and North Korea's sound-based term *toen*, the latter is preferable in that all the simple letters describe respective sound qualities in word-initial and word-final positions. Compared to *ssang*, which does not provide any phonological information, *toen* not only implies the independent phonemic status of geminate letters, but also gives information on the tenseness feature of the sounds.

With regard to alphabetic order, later versions of *Han'gŭl match'umpŏp t'ong'ilan* regulated the order of the twenty-four basic letters without specifying where complex letters were to be placed in relation to the basic letters. As a result, there have been inconsistent dictionary entry orderings in South Korea, as illustrated below:

Martin et al.: *A Korean-English Dictionary* (1967)

가	까까머리	가까이	까까중
ka	*kkakkamŏri*	*kakkai*	*kkakkajung*
가가호호	가깝다	가건물	가격
kagahoho	*kakkapta*	*kagŏnmul*	*kagyŏk*
가난	까마귀	굴뚝	
kanan	*kkamagwi*	*kulttuk*	

Hyŏnmunsa (현문사): *Han'gugŏ taesajŏn* (1976)

가	가가호호	가건물	가격
ka	*kagahoho*	*kagŏnmul*	*kagyŏk*

가까이	가깝다	가난	굴뚝
kakkai	*kakkapta*	*kanan*	*kulttuk*
까까머리	까까중	까마귀	
kkakkamŏri	*kkakkajung*	*kkamagwi*	

Martin et al. (1967) and several other well-known dictionaries belong to the first type, where tensed consonant letters are not given independent status but are considered ancillary to their corresponding basic letters.[6] Hyŏnmunsa (1976) and many other recently edited dictionaries are of the second type, where all the words with an initial tense consonant are entered only after all the corresponding lax-consonant initial words. The Ministry of Education (MOE 1988a) has declared the second type to be the standard, as in (a) above. As for vowels and diphthongs, almost all existing dictionaries in South Korea follow the order given in (b).

Although North Korea's order is to some extent phonologically motivated, South Korea's purely graphically oriented order is preferable. In South Korea, for example, ㅐ *ae* is regarded as a combination of the letters ㅏ *a* and ㅣ *i* irrespective of its phonological value; hence it is placed right after ㅏ *a*. In North Korea, it is viewed as a single phonemic unit /ɛ/, which has nothing to do with the phoneme /a/; hence it is placed after all the basic vowel and related diphthong letters. For one thing, the general public perceives ㄲ *kk*, ㅃ *pp*, ㅐ *ae*, ㅔ *e*, and so on, to be related to ㄱ *k/g*, ㅂ *p/b*, ㅏ *a*, and ㅓ *ŏ*, respectively. They are linguistically naive, being concerned more with letters than with the sounds represented by the letters. Graphic orientation of dictionary users and compilers is also observed in English, where words like *philosophy* and *pneumonia* are entered under P, and not under F and N, respectively. Second, South Korea's order is easy to remember, because the ordering rule involved is simply that all the complex letters with arbitrary initial X must follow the basic X in the alphabetic order of the component noninitial letters, as in ㅓ *ŏ*, ㅔ *e;* ㅜ *u*, ㅝ *wŏ*, ㅞ *we*, ㅟ *wi*; and ㄱ *k*, ㄲ *kk*, ㄳ *ks*. Thus, mnemonically, South Korea's system is superior to North Korea's. The mnemonic complexity of North Korea's order of vowel and diphthong letters is reflected in C. Kim's (1991) statement that simple letters come before double letters, which in turn come before triple letters, and that among double letters, complex letters ending in ㅣ *i* precede complex letters beginning with ㅗ *o* and ㅜ *u*. Third, North Korea's order among vowel and diphthong letters appears to be based on quite an unmotivated principle. Why should the added letter, rather than the first letter, be given the head status? Why the unusual order of ㅣ *i* followed by ㅏ *a,* ㅓ *ŏ,* ㅐ *ae,* and ㅔ *e*? Finally, other things being equal, tradition is to be followed. As pointed out in Nam (1987), in *Hunmin chŏng'ŭm* ㄲ *kk,* ㄸ *tt,* and so forth, are explained immediately after their corresponding simple letters. Also, it is well known that in Middle Korean, ㅐ */ay/,* ㅔ */ŏy/*, and ㅚ */oy/*, for example, were phonemic diphthongs composed of ㅏ *a,* ㅓ *ŏ,* ㅗ *o, and* ㅣ *i. Han'gŭl match'umpŏp t'ong'ilan* (KLA 1933) and its later versions also implied that ㅐ *ae* and ㅒ *yae*, for example, are combinations of ㅏ *a* + ㅣ *i and* ㅑ *ya* + ㅣ *i.*

Like South Korea's tradition, North Korea's current system also treats the letter ㅇ occurring in a vowel-initial syllable as a consonant letter, despite its silent quality, and orders it after ㅅ *s. Han'gŭl match'umpŏp* (MOE 1988a) gives all complex letters independent status, stipulating that, for example, words with the initial ㄲ *kk* be entered only after all the words with the initial ㄱ *k*. This is a step toward North Korea's system, where ㄲ *kk* and so forth are given independent status. Dictionary users in the two systems need only be aware of the locational difference of the geminate consonant letters as far as the onset and coda consonants are concerned. However, the serious fact remains that the divergent orders of syllable nuclear vowels and diphthongs cause great confusion to dictionary users.

SPELLING DIVERGENCE AND STANDARDS OF SPEECH

The following sets of examples of spelling divergence are essentially the result of phonological differences existing between Standard Speech and Cultured Speech.

Sino-Korean ㄹ *l/r*

In Standard Speech, Sino-Korean word-initial ㄹ is not pronounced before the vowel sound [i] and the semivowel sound [y] and is pronounced as [n] elsewhere (a). Word-medial (but morpheme-initial) Sino-Korean ㄹ also frequently becomes silent before [i] and [y] (b). In Cultured Speech, this ㄹ is pronounced and is spelled as such. Sino-Korean words with ㄹ that are phonetically identical in Standard and Cultured speech are spelled identically (c).

a. SK:	이발,	역사,	노동,	내일,	누누이
	ibal,	*yŏksa,*	*nodong,*	*naeil,*	*nunui*
NK:	리발,	력사,	로동,	래일,	루루이
	ribal,	*ryŏksa,*	*rodong,*	*raeil,*	*rurui*

b. SK:	나열,	비율,	역이용
	nayŏl,	*piyul,*	*yŏngniyong*
NK:	라열,	비률,	역리용
	rayŏl,	*piryul,*	*yŏngriyong*

c. SK:	분리,	인류,	실례
	pulli,	*illyu,*	*sillye*
NK:	분리,	인류,	실례
	pulli,	*illyu,*	*sillye*

Sino-Korean ㄴ *n*

In Standard Speech, all word-initial and some definable word-medial (but morpheme-initial) Sino-Korean ㄴ's become silent before [i] and [y] and thus are not spelled, whereas Cultured Speech requires them to be pronounced and spelled.

SK:	이탄,	여성,	요소,	연령,	신여성
	it'an,	*yŏsŏng,*	*yoso,*	*yŏllyŏng,*	*sinnyŏsŏng*
NK:	니탄,	녀성,	뇨소,	년령,	신녀성
	nit'an,	*nyŏsŏng,*	*nyoso,*	*nyŏllyŏng,*	*sinnyŏsŏng*

Vowel Harmony

While vowel harmony is strictly observed in Cultured Speech, there is slight deviation from it in Standard Speech. The deviation is in polysyllabic ㅂ *p/b* irregular predicates followed by an infinitive suffix, in which *w* (from ㅂ *p/b*) and the suffix are pronounced as ㅝ *wŏ*, regardless of the bright/dark quality of the preceding vowel, as in (a). Monosyllabic ㅂ irregular predicates in Standard Speech observe vowel harmony, as in (b).

a. SK: 아름다워, 고마워, 가까워서, 괴로웠다
arŭmdawŏ, komawŏ, kakkawŏsŏ, koerowŏtta
NK: 아름다와, 고마와, 가까와서, 괴로왔다
arŭmdawa, komawa, kakkawasŏ, koerowatta

b. SK: 도와, 고와요, 구워
towa, kowayo, kuwŏ
NK: 도와, 고와요, 구워
towa, kowayo, kuwŏ

Sporadic Lexical Disparities

Only Cultured Speech shows umlauting in certain words (a), whereas only Standard Speech shows vowel fronting in certain other words (b).

a. SK: 지푸라기, 부스러기, 호루라기
chip'uragi, pusŭrŏgi, horuragi

NK: 지푸래기, 부스레기, 호루래기
chip'uraegi, pusŭregi, horuraegi

b. SK: 뼉다귀, 귀절, 쇠고기, 외양간
ppyŏktagwi, kwijŏl, soegogi, oeyangkan

NK: 뼉다구, 구절, 소고기, 오양간
ppyŏktagu, kujŏl, sogogi, oyangkan

Only Cultured Speech has aspiration in words like those below.

SK: 수범, 수곰, 아내, 갈치,
subŏm, sugom, anae, kalch'i,
가뜩이, 축축이, 똑똑지, 거북지
kattŭgi, ch'ukch'ugi, ttokttokchi, kŏbukchi

NK: 수펌, 수콤, 안해, 칼치,
sup'ŏm, suk'om, anhae, k'alch'i,
가뜩히, 축축히, 똑똑치, 거북치
kattŭk'i, ch'ukch'uk'i, ttokttokch'i, kŏbukch'i

Numerous other native words are pronounced differently in Standard and Cultured speech:

SK:	우뢰,	긁어모아,	퍽이나,	달걀,
	uroe,	*kŭlgŏmoa,*	*p'ŏgina,*	*talgyal,*
	원수,	햅쌀,	크낙새,	네째
	wŏnsu,	*haepssal,*	*k'ŭnaksae,*	*netchae*
NK:	우레,	그러모아,	퍼그나,	닭알,
	ure,	*kŭrŏmoa,*	*p'ŏgŭna,*	*talgal,*
	원쑤,	햇쌀,	클락새,	넷째
	wŏnssu,	*haetssal,*	*k'ŭllaksae,*	*nettchae*

Sino-Korean Words with Popular Pronunciation (俗音 *Sogŭm*)

Both systems stipulate that Sino-Korean words with popular pronunciation (as distinct from their regular pronunciation) are to be spelled as they are pronounced. Thus, many such words are spelled identically in South Korea and North Korea, such as 나팔 *nap'al* (from 라팔 喇叭 *rap'al*) 'bugle', 남색 *namsaek* (from 람색 藍色 *ramsaek*) 'indigo', 요기 *yogi* (from 료기 療飢 *ryogi*) 'relieving hunger', and 희로애락 *hiroaerak* (from 희노애락 喜怒哀樂 *hinoaerak*) 'joy, anger, sorrow, and pleasure'. There is, however, phonetic/spelling divergence in some words:

SK:	곤란,	논란,	한라산,	유월,	폐렴
	kollan,	*nollan,*	*hallasan,*	*yuwŏl,*	*p'yeryŏm*
NK:	곤난,	론난,	한나산,	류월,	폐염
	konnan,	*ronnan,*	*hannasan,*	*ryuwŏl,*	*p'eyŏm*

Loanword Spelling

Spellings of loanwords are considerably different in South Korea and North Korea. The following examples are from Chong et al. (1981), Chon and Choy (1989: 258-270), and Lee and Ahn (1991). North Korea's spellings of terms for general objects are influenced by Russian and Japanese, whereas South Korea's spellings reflect English pronunciations.

	balance	cover	dilemma	cup	dance	minus
SK:	밸런스,	커버,	딜레마,	컵,	댄스,	마이너스
	paellŏnsŭ,	*k'ŏbŏ,*	*tillema,*	*k'ŏp,*	*taensŭ,*	*mainŏsŭ*
NK:	바란스,	카바,	지렌마,	고뿌,	딴스,	미누스
	paransŭ,	*k'aba,*	*chirenma,*	*koppu,*	*ttansŭ,*	*minusŭ*

	missile	candle	jack	jelly	studio	radio
SK:	미사일,	캔들,	잭,	젤리,	스튜디오,	라디오
	misail,	*k'aendŭl,*	*chaek,*	*chelli,*	*sŭt'yudio,*	*radio*
NK:	미싸일,	간데라,	쟈끼,	쩰리,	스타지오,	라지오
	missail,	*kandera,*	*chyakki,*	*tchelli,*	*sŭt'ajio,*	*rajio*

As for place names, North Korea's spellings follow the pronunciations used in the respective countries, apparently in accordance with Kim Il Sung's suggestion in his 1964 Teachings. South Korean spellings follow the English tradition.

	Jakarta	Congo	Hungary	Cairo	Vatican
SK:	자카르타,	콩고,	헝가리,	카이로,	바티칸
	chak'arŭt'a,	*k'onggo,*	*hŏnggari,*	*k'airo,*	*pat'ik'an*
NK:	쟈까르따,	꽁고,	웽그리아,	까히라,	바띠까노
	chyakkarŭtta,	*kkonggo,*	*waenggŭria,*	*kkahira,*	*pattikkano*

	Sweden	Mexico	Canada
SK:	스웨덴,	멕시코,	캐나다
	sŭweden,	*meksik'o,*	*k'aenada*
NK:	스웨리예,	메히꼬,	카나다
	sŭweriye,	*mehikko,*	*k'anada*

SPELLING DIVERGENCE AND LINGUISTIC ANALYSIS

The following contrastive sets are the result of different linguistic analyses of similar or identical phenomena. Although South Korea and North Korea share the morphophonemic spelling principle, there are numerous cases where phonetically similar or identical compounds and derivatives receive different morphemic analyses in terms of phonological, morphological, or semantic fossilization, and hence spelling divergence occurs. In some cases, South Korea's spellings are more faithful to morphemic etymology; in others, North Korea's are.

ㅗ/ㅛ o/yo, ㅓ/ㅕ ŏ/yŏ

After ㅣ *i*, ㅐ *ae*, ㅔ *e*, ㅚ *oe*, ㅟ *wi*, ㅢ *ŭi*, or after the verb 하 *ha* 'do', South Korea's ㅗ *o* and ㅓ *ŏ* frequently contrast graphically with North Korea's ㅛ *yo* and ㅕ *yŏ*, respectively, as manifested in the spellings of the blunt level suffix (a), the infinitive suffix (b), and the adverbial suffix (c).

a. SK:	아니오,	가시오,	학생이오	
	anio,	*kasio,*	*haksaeng'io*	
NK:	아니요,	가시요,	학생이요	
	aniyo,	*kasiyo,*	*haksaeng'iyo*	
b. SK:	되어,	띄어쓰기,	비었다,	하였다
	toeŏ,	*ttŭiŏssŭgi,*	*piŏtta,*	*hayŏtta*
NK:	되여,	띄여쓰기,	비였다,	하였다
	toeyŏ,	*ttŭiyŏssŭgi,*	*piyŏtta,*	*hayŏtta*
c. SK:	드디어,	도리어,	구태여	
	tŭdiŏ,	*toriŏ,*	*kut'aeyŏ*	
NK:	드디여,	도리여,	구태여	
	tŭdiyŏ,	*toriyŏ,*	*kut'aeyŏ*	

The above words are usually pronounced with the semivowel [y] inserted in both Standard and Cultured speech. South Korea treats this semivowel as phonologically predictable, whereas North Korea treats it as a part of restructured morphemes. South Korea's practice seems to be preferable in (a) and (b) above in view of native speakers' psychology and the morphemic regularity involved in the blunt level suffix and the infinitive suffix. North Korea's practice appears favorable in (c), however, in that, for instance, 어/여 in the adverb 드디어/드디여 *tŭdiyŏ* 'finally' is not different in pronunciation from 여 *yŏ* in the adverb 구태여 *kut'aeyŏ* 'deliberately', and native speakers no longer perceive 어/여 *ŏ/yŏ* and 드디 *tŭdi* as two separate morphemes.

Tensing

After the prospective suffix ㄹ/을 *l/ŭl*, lax stops (ㄱ *k/g*, ㅂ *p/b*, ㄷ *t/d*, ㅈ *ch/j*, ㅅ *s*) become tensed stops in both Standard and Cultured speech. In both South Korea and North Korea, these lax stops were spelled in single (lax) stops until 1957, when in South Korea a decision was made at a Korean Language Society general meeting to spell certain fossilized suffixes with geminate letters, as shown below. North Korea's practice is to follow tradition and spell them consistently as single letters.

SK: -을까, -을꼬, 을쏘냐, -을지라도, -을수록
-ŭlkka, -ŭlkko, -ŭlssonya, -ŭlchirado, -ŭlsurok
NK: -을가, -을고, -을소냐, -을지라도, -을수록
ŭlka, -ŭlko, -ŭlsonya, -ŭlchirado, -ŭlsurok

It is important to consider grammaticalization phenomena in legislating spelling conventions. Frequently, however, it is not easy to determine to what extent forms need to be grammaticalized in order to be considered morphological units for spelling. We need to take into account such criteria as psychological reality, phonological and grammatical regularity, simplicity, naturalness, and tradition. For example, spelling the simple ㄱ *k* in ㄹ/을게 *l/ŭlkke* 'I promise' in South and North Korea can not be sufficiently justified despite its diachronic grammaticalization from ㄹ/을 것이어 *l/ŭl kŏsiŏ*, in view of its complete structural, formal, and semantic restructuring. South Korea's spelling change of ㄹ/을가 *l/ŭlkka* to ㄹ/을까 *l/ŭlkka*, in contrast, might be somewhat premature in that it is still in the process of restructuring, manifesting the regular sense "whether," the partly restructured sense "I wonder," and the fully restructured sense "shall I/we?" In the first two senses, the spelling of ㄹ/을까 *l/ŭlkka* loses parallelism not only with 은/는 가 *ŭn/nŭn ka* but also with ㄹ/을지 l/*ŭlichi*.

Compounds

Different etymological considerations are given to certain compounds. Below, (a) illustrates the cases where South Korea is more faithful to etymology and (b) the cases where North Korea is more faithful.

a. SK: 넋두리, 넓적코, 넓죽한, 몸닭달,
nŏkturi, nŏpchŏkk'o, nŏpchukhan, momdaktal,
가죽나무, 벚나무
kajungnamu, pŏnnamu

NK:	넉두리, *nŏkturi,*	넙적코, *nŏpchŏkk'o,*	넙죽한, *nŏpchukhan,*	몸닥달, *momdaktal,*
	가중나무, *kajungnamu,*		벗나무 *pŏnnamu*	

where 넋 means 'soul, spirit', 넓 'wide', 닦 'polish, clean', 가죽 'tree-of-heaven', and 벚 'cherry.'

b. SK:	앞니, *amni,*	닭조림, *takchorim,*	돌맞이, *tolmaji,*	멋쩍다, *mŏtchŏkta,*
	잠깐, *chamkkan,*	손뼉, *sonppyŏk,*	눈썹 *nunssŏp*	
NK:	앞이, *amni,*	닭졸임, *takchorim,*	돐맞이 *tolmaji,*	멋적다, *mŏtchŏkta,*
	잠간, *chamkan,*	손벽, *sonpyŏk,*	눈섭 *nunsŏp*	

where 이 means 'tooth', 졸 'get boiled down', 돐 'one full year', 적 'small, little', 간 'space', 벽 'wall', and 섭 'brow'.

If no regular phonological pattern is violated, it may be preferable to retain generally known etymological information as much as possible, as in South Korean 넋두리 *nŏkturi* 'speaking on behalf of the dead, a complaint', because such spellings have an ideographic function and thus facilitate morpheme recognition, not to mention their compliance with tradition. Between South Korean 넓적코 and North Korean 넙적코 'flat nose', both pronounced *nŏpchŏkk'o*, however, the latter is preferable, because the consonant cluster *lp* in 넓 *nŏlp* is usually simplified to *l* in pronunciation before a consonant.

Derivatives

Different morphemic interpretations of phonetically identical derivatives are illustrated below.

a. SK:	널따랗다, *nŏlttarat'a,*	걸쭉하다, *kŏltchuk'ada,*	좁다랗다, *choptarat'a,*	빛깔, *pitkkal,*
	일꾼, *ilkkun,*	떠버리, *ttŏbŏri,*	각성바지 *kaksŏngbaji*	

NK: 널다랗다, 걸죽하다, 좁다랗다, 빛갈,
nŏltarat'a, kŏlchuk'ada, choptarat'a, pitkal,
일군 떠벌이, 각성받이
ilkkun, ttŏbŏri, kaksŏngbaji

b. SK: 쌕쌕이, 오뚝이, 홀쭉이, 개구리,
ssaekssaegi, ottugi, holtchugi, kaeguri,
일찍이 더욱이, 생긋이
iltchigi, tŏugi, saenggŭsi

NK: 쌕쌔기, 오뚜기, 홀쭈기 개구리,
ssaekssaegi, ottugi, holtchugi, kaeguri,
일찌기, 더우기, 생그시
iltchigi, tŏugi, saenggŭsi

SK: 스무남은, 그렇지, 어떻지, 한사코,
sŭmunamŭn, kŭrŏch'i, ŏttŏch'i, hansak'o,
아무튼
amut'ŭn

NK: 스무나믄, 그러치, 어떠치, 한사코,
sŭmunamŭn, kŭrŏch'i, ŏttŏch'i, hansak'o,
아무튼
amut'ŭn

Let us take two examples of divergent stipulations on the matter of fossilization. According to South Korea's system, when a root in question (e.g., 쌕쌕 *ssaekssaek* 'hissing') occurs with either the verb 하 *ha* 'do' or the derivational suffix 거리 *kŏri* 'keep doing', it must be spelled in its original morphemic form. Thus, although this morpheme does not occur with *ha*, it does occur with *kŏri*; hence 쌕쌕이 *ssaek.ssaeg.i* 'a jet plane'. North Korea's system regulates that only when a root in question occurs with the *ha* verb must it follow morphemic spelling. Since 쌕쌕 *ssaekssaek* cannot occur with the *ha* verb, 쌕쌔기 *ssaek.ssae.gi* is chosen.

In pairs like South Korean 이렇지 *irŏch'i* versus North Korean 이러치 *irŏch'i* 'to be like this', South Korea interprets the stranded ㅎ *h* (from 하 *ha*) as belonging to the preceding syllable as a coda, apparently in view of its morphosemantic independence, whereas North Korea imposes it on the onset consonant of the following syllable, probably in view of its phonetic blending with the following consonant. Like North Korea, however, South Korea spells 한사코 *hansak'o* 'persistently', 기필코 *kip'ilk'o* 'by all means', 여하튼 *yŏhat'ŭn* 'at any rate', 아무튼 *amut'ŭn* 'anyhow', and 예컨대 *yek'ŏndae* 'for example' instead of 한상고 *hansak'o*, 기필고 *kip'ilk'o*, 여할든 *yŏhat'ŭn*, 아뭏든 *amut'ŭn*, and 옝건대 *yek'ŏndae*. Thus, North Korea's practice attains more formal uniformity, if not functional generality.

DIVERGENCE AND CONVENTIONS

Orthographic divergence may occur when the same or similar pronunciations that receive identical linguistic analysis are still spelled differently, owing to the different conventions followed in South Korea and North Korea.

Epenthetic ㅅ s (*sai-siot*)

It is well known that the so-called epenthetic *s* has been spelled variously in both North and South Korea. It is spelled in South Korea only when the preceding noun root ends in a vowel (a) in native and a small number of Sino-Korean compounds and is left out otherwise (b). In North Korea (since 1966), it is left out everywhere, except when the preceding root is interpreted as a prefix (c).

a. SK:	냇가, *naekka,*	빗물, *pinmul,*	숫자, *sutcha,*	셋집, *setchip,*
	나뭇잎 *namunnip*			
NK:	내가, *naekka,*	비물, *pinmul,*	수자, *sutcha,*	세집, *setchip,*
	나무잎 *namunnip*			
b. SK:	강가, *kangka,*	길가, *kilka,*	논일, *nonnil,*	안고, *anko,*
	감소, *kamso,*	굶지 *kumchi*		

NK: 강가, 길가, 논일, 안고,
kangka, kilka, nonnil, anko,
감소, 굶지
kamso, kumchi

c. SK: 뒷일, 웃집, 샛별
twinnil, utchip, saetpyŏl
NK: 뒷일, 웃집, 샛별
twinnil, utchip, saetpyŏl

Sino-Korean Diphthong C-ye

Both South Korea and North Korea spell 계 *kye,* 례 *rye,* and 혜 *hye* in relevant Sino-Korean words, despite their having been phonetically monophthongized as [ke], [re], and [he], respectively (a). Only South Korea allows two more consonant-initial diphthong letters, 몌 *mye* and 폐 *p'ye*, in Sino-Korean words (b). The original monophthongs are not affected in South or North Korea (c).

a. SK: 계산, 의례, 은혜
kesan, ŭrye, ŭnhe
NK: 계산, 의례, 은혜
kesan, ŭrye, ŭnhe

b. SK: 몌별, 연몌, 폐쇄, 화폐
myebyŏl, yŏnmye, p'eswae, hwap'ye
NK: 메별, 연메, 폐쇄, 화폐
mebyŏl, yŏnme, p'eswae, hwap'ye

c. SK: 게시판, 휴게실
kesip'an, hyugesil
NK: 게시판, 휴게실
kesip'an, hyugesil

Spacing

While morphophonemic spellings have a degree of ideographic function, facilitating morpheme and word recognition, spacing contributes to the recognition of syntactic units. As stated earlier, South Korea and North Korea share the basic principle that spaces be placed between words. While South Korea observes this principle rather narrowly, North Korea's convention is, in many cases, to spell two or more words without spacing, giving them compound status. North Korea's practice may partly result from Kim Il Sung's 1964 and 1966 Teachings, in which Kim indicated that the practice of the time allowed too many spaces. In the examples below (for details, see M. Kim 1985; E. Lee 1989; Lee and Ahn 1991),^ stands for optional spacing.

a. bound nouns

SK:	아는 이,	뜻한 바,	놀 수,	그 밖의,	세 개
	anŭn i,	*ttŭt'an pa,*	*nol su,*	*kŭ pakkŭi,*	*segae*
NK:	아는이,	뜻한바,	놀수,	그밖의,	세개
	anŭni,	*ttŭt'anba,*	*nolsu,*	*kŭbakkŭi,*	*segae*
	'an aquaintance'	*'what is intended'*	*'able to play'*	*'other'*	*'3 items'*

b. Sino-Korean proper nouns and technical terms

SK:	이기선 씨,	이 박사,	6.25사변,	모음조화
	igisŏn ssi,	*ipaksa,*	*yugio sabyŏn,*	*moŭm johwa*
NK:	이기선씨,	이박사,	6.25사변,	모음조화
	igisŏnssi,	*ibaksa,*	*yugiosabyŏn,*	*moŭmjohwa*
	'Mr. I Kisŏn'	*'Dr. Lee'*	*'6.25 Incident'*	*'vowel harmony'*

c. common noun sequences

SK:	여러 해,	시민 모두,	학교 앞,	학생 자신
	yŏrŏ hae,	*simin modu,*	*hakkyo ap,*	*haksaeng chasin*
NK:	여러해,	시민모두,	학교앞,	학생자신
	yŏrŏhae,	*siminmodu,*	*hakkyoap,*	*haksaengjasin*
	'many years'	*'all the citizens'*	*'front of the school'*	*'students themselves'*

d. proverbs and idiomatic expressions

SK:	수박 겉 핥기;	꿩 구어 먹은 자리
	subak kŏt halki;	*kkwŏng gwŏmŏgŭn chari*
NK:	수박겉핥기;	꿩구어먹은 자리
	subak kŏt'alki;	*kkwŏnggwŏmŏgŭn chari*
	'licking the watermelon surface'	*'the place where people ate a broiled pheasant'*
	(superficiality)	*(no trace)*

e. numerals (spacing units: 만 *man*, 억 *ŏk* in South Korea; 백 *paek*, 천 *ch'ŏn*, 만 *man*, 억 *ŏk*, 조 *cho* in North Korea)

SK: 이억 오천삼백오십이만 오천이백이십사
iŏk och' ŏnsambaegosibiman och'ŏnibaegisip'sa
NK: 이억 오천 삼백 오십이만 오천 이백 이십사
iŏkoch' ŏnsambaek osibiman och'ŏn ibaek isip'sa
'253, 525, 224'

f. auxiliary predicates

SK:	보여주다,	주고싶다,	집어먹어 보아라
	poyŏ chuda,	*chukko sipta,*	*chibŏmŏgŏ poara*
NK:	보여주다,	주고싶다,	집어먹어보아라
	poyŏjuda,	*chukkosipta,*	*chibŏmŏgŏboara*

g. verbal and adverbial compounding

SK:	꽃 같다,	하늘 높이,	용서 못 한다
	kkot katta,	*hanŭl nop'i,*	*yongsŏ mot handa*
NK:	꽃같다,	하늘높이,	용서 못한다
	kkotkatta,	*hanŭlnop'i,*	*yongsŏ mot'anda*

CONCLUSION

Let me conclude with some suggestions. Linguistic unification is a key to the recovery of national identity and the reunification of Korea. As an immediate step, it is imperative that Korean linguists from South Korea and North Korea, preferably joined by overseas scholars, get together to discuss the issues involved in containing this ever-growing linguistic diversity and recovering linguistic homogeneity. One general issue is the impact of the ongoing Chuch'e-based language purification movement in North Korea and the more or less laissez-faire policy toward the influx of foreign elements in South Korea.[7] North Korea has been nativizing thousands of Sino-Korean words used by the South Korean public. South Korea, in contrast, has already admitted into its lexicon over ten thousand loanwords from English, while coining numerous Sino-Korean words or introducing Sino-Japanese terms as needs arise.

I have examined the major aspects of orthographic divergence and the relevant issues involved, suggesting solutions in certain cases. Many of them are linguistically intriguing and deserve joint scholarly discussion for resolution. There is no reason why a unified spelling system cannot be legislated. Not only do North and South Korea have nearly the same phonological data, but they also follow the same principles of morphophonemic spelling and word-based spacing. The provisions of *Han'gŭl match'umpŏp* (MOE 1988a) and *Kaejŏng Chosŏnmal kyubŏmjip* (KLAC 1988) are largely terminological variations. For example, the same morphophonemic principle may be defined in different terms. *Han'gŭl match'umpŏp* states, "In principle, han'gŭl spellings follow Standard Speech pronunciations in accordance with grammatical structure" (MOE 1988a: 1.1), whereas *Kaejŏng Chosŏnmal kyubŏmjip* states, "Korean spellings are based on the principle that each meaningful unit in words is spelled the same way wherever it occurs, but in certain cases, spelling words as pronounced or following tradition is permitted" (KLAC 1988, General Rule). An extensive number of such terminological variations can easily be combined into a unified system through joint scholarly deliberations. Furthermore, the most desirable area in which to begin linguistic unification efforts appears to be orthographic divergence, in that the problems involved are relatively free from political and ideological sensitivity.

According to Chon and Choy's (1989) count based on Chong et al. (1981) and H. Lee (1982), (a) 1,400 words have identical pronunciations but different spellings, and (b) 3,130 words have different pronunciations and different spellings. Interestingly, (c) 930 words have different pronunciations but identical spellings, as illustrated in 정열 (SK *chŏng.nyŏl*; NK *chŏng.yŏl*), 창고 (SK *ch'ang.go*; NK *ch'ang.ko*), 넓다 (SK *nŏl.ta*; NK *nŏp.ta*), and 돌배 (SK *tol.bae*; NK *tol.pae*).

With enough scholarly cooperation, there will be no serious problem in unifying the spellings of the (a) group, in view of their phonetic identity. This is the group whose disparities are caused by different linguistic analyses or different conventions. As for the (b) group, which are due to different standards of speech, the majority are Sino-Korean words such as those with the initial ㄹ *l* or ㄴ *n*. In view of the fact that we have many identically spelled words with different pronunciations that belong to the (c) group, some (b) group words may also be unified in spelling without much difficulty.

In general, North Korea's system is oriented toward formal uniformity, as observed in examples such as SK 드디어 versus NK 드디여 *tŭdiyŏ* (cf. SK/NK 구태여 *ku.t'ae.yŏ*); SK 괴로워 *koerowŏ* versus NK 괴로와 *koerowa* (cf. SK/NK 고와 *kowa*); SK 거북지 *kŏbukchi* versus NK 거북치 *kŏbukch'i* (SK/NK 행복치 *haengbokch'i*); SK 바닷가 *padatka* versus NK 바다가 *pada.ka* (cf. SK/NK 바다에 *padae*, 강가 *kang.ka*); SK 일꾼 *ilkkun* versus NK 일군 *ilkun* (cf. SK/NK 농군 *nonggun*); and SK -을까 -*ŭlkka* versus NK -을가 -*ŭl.ka* (cf. SK/NK -는가 -*nŭn' ga*, -을 것 -*ul kŏt*). In all these cases, South Korean linguists have taken different criteria.[8] Joint research is essential to narrow down such numerous discrepancies through intensive linguistic analysis from synchronic and diachronic perspectives, on the one hand, and structural and sociolinguistic perspectives, on the other. Recourse to such criteria as simplicity, generality, naturalness, psychological reality, and tradition, as well as to restructuring and grammaticalization theory, will lead to eliminating many of the disparities.

Until the reunification of Korea is realized, a unified spelling system will have no recourse but to accommodate both standards of speech and treat unresolved disparities as doublets applicable either to both Koreas (e.g., SK 수범 *subŏm* versus NK 수펌 *sup'ŏm*; SK 갈치 *kalch'i* versus NK 칼치 *k'alch'i*) or only to the relevant areas (e.g., SK 이론 *iron* versus NK 리론 *riron*; SK 여자 *yŏja* versus NK 녀자 *nyŏja*). As an alternative way of unifying the spelling systems, Huh (1991) proposes that both South Korea and North Korea adopt the 1948 version of *Han'gŭl match'umpŏp t'ong'ilan*, in that this version, written purely in han'gŭl, was shared by the two Koreas. Simple and ideal as it may be, this solution may not be easily acceptable to North Korea, in that adopting the 1948 version presupposes North Korea's abolishment of Cultured Speech and acceptance of Standard Speech.

Fortunately, there are some indications that both Koreas are endeavoring to approach the other's system. For example, South

Korea has changed C -읍니다 *-ŭmnida* to C-습니다 *-sŭmnida*, given independent status to complex letters, and introduced optionality in many spacing rules. North Korea has abolished the earlier distinction between the velar nasal coda consonant letter ㅇ and the syllable-initial letter ㅇ and become more generous in using spacing than in the 1971 *Kyubŏmjip*.

NOTES

1. Ideological distinctions are reflected in respective educational goals. South Korea aims to develop the nation and the national culture through recognition, development, and fulfillment of each individual's fullest potentialities (National Education Charter). North Korea's goal is to bring up the rising generation as revolutionaries who will fight for a socialist society and the masses (the Constitution). Thus, language is regarded as a means of communication in South Korea, but as a means of thought reform and of strengthening the people's "revolutionary consciousness for continual class struggle" in North Korea. The language policies of the two Koreas are surveyed in Sohn 1991. See also LIASS 1976; C. Kim 1978; Sasse 1980; M. Kim 1985; Chon and Choy 1989; COH 1990; Ko 1990; and Park 1991.

2. In a broad sense, Korean orthography includes Chinese characters and romanization as well. There are still pros and cons regarding the use of Chinese characters in South Korea. The South Korean government repeatedly adopted and abolished the policy of the exclusive use of han'gŭl until 1972, when it fixed the current practice that 1,800 basic characters be taught for reading and writing at intermediate (900) and high (900) schools. This policy does not mean that society (the general public, newspapers, books) is bound by this set of characters. In North Korea, Kim Il Sung's 1946 Teachings and the initiation in 1949 of compulsory education launched, with complete success, the han'gŭl-based literary movement, abolishing Chinese characters altogether. Kim Il Sung's 1964 and 1966 Teachings, however, reinstated character teaching for reading only, to enable students to understand South Korean publications. The major issue in romanization is what sort of alphabetic symbols are to be used for individual sounds and how they are to be spelled. This had been a long-standing question in South Korea until 1984, when the Ministry of Education abolished its 1959 system and enacted a revised system based essentially on the McCune-Reischauer system. It is reported that a recent tentative agreement between South Korea and North Korea is that South Korea's vowel symbols and North Korea's consonant symbols will be used.

3. Kim's 1964 Teachings present the basic directions of his language policies and his 1966 Teachings substantiate them. The areas covered are script reform, Sino-Korean words, loanwords, Chinese characters, spacing and word forms, vocabulary refinement, the campaign for proper language use, and

Korean language education, as well as the concept of Cultured Speech (see Sohn 1991 and other works for details).

4. Some historical justification for the establishment of Cultured Speech is found in Y. Kim 1978. Cultured Speech is also claimed to be the model for the national language that is formed with Kim Il Sung and Kim Chong Il's speech as the nucleus (Chong and Lee 1984). Ki-moon Lee (personal communication) points out that despite North Korea's assertion to the contrary, Cultured Speech is based essentially on Standard Speech, not on the P'yŏng'yang dialect. One example is that Cultured Speech includes palatalized Sino-Korean forms, such as *chŏnggŏjang* 'station' and *ch'ŏnji* 'heaven and earth' rather than the P'yŏng'yang forms *tŏnggŏdang* and *t'yŏndi*. It is premature, however, to subscribe to this view, since Cultured Speech is based on the P'yŏng'yang dialect in many other respects, such as word-initial *l* and *n*.

5. This definition of North Korea's is unwarranted because so-called polluted expressions are excluded from Standard Speech (MOE 1988b; Huh 1991).

6. Nam (1987) illustrates another differently ordered set of this type.

7. While North Korea has been successfully conducting Chuch'e-based language purification, South Korea is achieving only limited success in the ongoing purification efforts of its government, scholars, and language associations.

8. Ko states that South Korea's orthography is "excessively grammatical" compared with North Korea's system and that compromise is needed for a unified orthography (1990:20).

REFERENCES

Chon, Su-tae, and Ho-chol Choy. 1989. Nambukhan ŏnŏ pigyo (A linguistic comparison between South and North Korea). Seoul: Tosŏch'ulp'an nokchin.

Chong, Sun-Ki, et al. 1981. Hyŏndae chosŏnmal sajŏn (A modern Korean dictionary). 2nd edition. P'yŏng'yang: Kwahak Paekkwasajŏn Ch'ulp'ansa.

Chong, Sun-Ki, and Ki-Won Lee. 1984. Sajŏnp'yŏnch'an riron yŏn'gu (A study of lexicography). P'yŏng'yang: Sahoegwahak Ch'ulp'ansa.

Choy, Ki-Ho. 1990. "Hyŏndae Chosŏnmal sajŏn" kwa pukhan ŏnŏjŏngch'aek (A dictionary of Modern Korean and North Korean language policies). *COH* 1990: 277–289.

COH (Chaha ŏmun hakhoe). 1990. Pukhan ŭi Chosŏnŏhak (Korean linguistics in North Korea). Seoul: Hanshin Co.

Huh, Woong. 1991. Nam-buk ŭi mal kwa kul (Speech and writing in South and North). *Han'gŭl saesosik* (Han'gŭl news) 229: 4–6.

Kim, Chin-W. 1978. Linguistics and language policies in North Korea. *Korean Studies* 2: 159–175.

———. 1991. Han'gungmal kwa Chosŏnmal (The South and North Korean languages). *Mal* (Language), 15: 35–47.

Kim, Min-su. 1985. Pukhan ŭi kugŏ yŏn'gu (Studies of Korean in North Korea). Seoul: Korea University Press.

Kim, Young Hwang. 1978. Chosŏn minjogŏ palchŏn ryŏksa yŏn'gu (A study of the development of the national language). P'yŏng'yang: Kwahak Paekkwasajŏn Ch'ulp'ansa.

KISU (Kim Il Sung University). 1983. Ŏŭm mit muncharon (A theory of speech sounds and letters). P'yŏng'yang: Kim Il Sung University Press.

KLA (Chosŏnŏ Hakhoe: Korean Language Association). 1933. Han'gŭl match'umpŏp t'ong'iran (A proposition for unified han'gŭl spelling conventions). Seoul: Chosŏnŏ Hakhoe.

———. 1936. *Chosŏnŏ p'yojunmal moŭm* (A collection of Korean standard words). Seoul: Chosŏnŏ Hakhoe.

KLAC (Kugŏ sajŏng wiwŏnhoe: Korean Language Assessment Committee). 1988. Kaejŏnghan Chosŏnmal kyubŏmjip (A revised collection of Korean language norms). P'yong'yang: Sahoegwahak Ch'ulp'ansa.

Ko, Young-geun. 1990. Chuch'e language theory and North Korean linguistics. *Seoul Journal of Korean Studies* (Seoul National University), 3: 3–20.

Lee, Eun-jong. 1989. Nambukhan ŭi match'umpŏp pigyo yŏn'gu (A comparative study of South-North Korean spelling conventions). *Han-geul* 205: 151–177.

Lee, Huy-sung. 1982. Kugŏ taesajŏn (A great dictionary of Korean). Seoul: Minjung Sŏrim.

Lee, Huy-sung, and Pyong-hi Ahn. 1991. Han'gŭl match'umpŏp kang'ŭi (Lectures on the han'gŭl spelling system). Seoul: Sin'gu-munhwasa.

LIASS (Sahoe kwahagwŏn ŏnŏhak yŏn'guso: Linguistic Institute, Academy of Social Sciences). 1973. *Chosŏn munhwaŏ sajŏn* (A dictionary of Korean cultured speech). P'yŏng'yang.

———. 1976. Uri tang ui ŏnŏjŏngch'aek (The language policies of our party). P'yŏng'yang: Sahoegwahak Ch'ulp'ansa.

MOE (Ministry of Education). 1988a. Han'gŭl match'umpŏp (The han'gŭl spelling conventions). Seoul: Mun'gyobu.

———. 1988b. *P'yojunŏ kyujŏng* (Standard speech regulations). Seoul: Mun'gyobu.

Nam, Ki-Shim. 1987. Kugŏ sajŏn ŭi chamo ŭi ch'arye wa p'yojeŏ ŭi paeyŏlsun e kwanhayŏ (On ordering the alphabetic letters and entries in a Korean dictionary). *Inmun kwahak* (Yonsei University), 57: 1–18.

Park, Youngsoon. 1991. Language policy and language education in North Korea. *Korea Journal* 31.1: 28–40.

Sasse, Werner. 1980. The "cultured language": Implementation of a policy in North Korea. *Korean Linguistics* 2: 67–76.

Sohn, Ho-min. 1991. Language policies and linguistic divergence in the two Koreas. *Sino-Platonic Papers* (University of Pennsylvania), 27: 95–102.

11

EXPERIMENTATION WITH HAN'GŬL IN RUSSIA AND THE USSR, 1914–1937

Ross King

I have demonstrated elsewhere the existence and importance of a large body of written materials in and on Korean from Russia and the USSR. All of these materials contain interesting and diverse data for Korean dialectology, the history of the Korean language, and Korean philology.

It is my purpose here to sketch some of the ways in which Koreans in Russia and later in the USSR went about writing Korean until 1937, when all Soviet Koreans were forcibly deported to Central Asia.

THE PRE-SOVIET PERIOD

Korean Orthography at the Turn of the Century

Before beginning an examination of attempts to write Korean "on-line" in Siberia, I should make some brief remarks about the types of Korean orthography prevailing at the end of the nineteenth century and the turn of our own.[1] Kim Minsu describes five major types of Korean orthography from the fifteenth century to the present: (1) the Chŏng'ŭm twenty-eight-letter system; (2) the Chahoe twenty-seven-letter system (no. 1 minus ㆆ); (3) the Panjŏl twenty-eight-letter system with addition of ㅘ, ㅝ, and ㅣ; (4) the *arae-a* twenty-five-letter system (minus ㆁ and ㅿ); and (5) the Ch'ŏltcha-pŏp twenty-four-letter system (system 4 minus *arae-a*) (1973: 159–160).

The Russian and Soviet sources examined in this chapter contain examples of types 3 to 5, often with interesting quirks and idiosyncrasies. In the pre-Soviet period, the Koreans were using variations on types 3 and 4. The Korean graphs encountered were as follows:

Vowels

Yale	Korean	Yale	Korean
a	ㅏ	ay	ㅐ
e	ㅓ	ey	ㅔ
o	ㅗ	oy	ㅚ
wu (u)	ㅜ	uy (ɨy)	ㅢ
u (ɨ)	ㅡ	ʌy	ㆎ
i	ㅣ	wi/wuy	ㅟ
ʌ	ㆍ	wa	ㅘ
ya	ㅑ	we	ㅝ
ye	ㅕ	(wey	ㅞ)
yo	ㅛ	(way	ㅙ)
yu	ㅠ	(yoy	ㆉ)
(yey	ㅖ)	(yuy/ywuy	ㆌ)
(yay	ㅒ)		

Consonants

p	ㅂ	t	ㄷ	k	ㄱ	c	ㅈ
ph	ㅍ	th	ㅌ	k	ㅋ	ch	ㅊ
(pp/sp	ㅽ	tt/st	ㅼ	kk/sk	ㅺ	cc/sc	ㅾ)
m	ㅁ	n	ㄴ	ng	ㅇ		
						s	ㅅ
				h	ㅎ	ss/ps	ㅆ/ㅄ
		l	ㄹ				

Korean Writing in Russia before 1917 and the *Taehanin Chyŏnggyobo*

Korean writing and orthography at the turn of our century were in a chaotic state, on both sides of the Russo-Korean border. Kim Minsu writes: "Some orthographies from this period are inconsistent from one book to the next, even from one paragraph or one line to the next. But the overall tendency was: a twenty-five-letter system due to loss of the three letters ㆆ, ㅿ, ㆁ, generalization of /sk, st, sp, ps, sc/ for the tense, unaspirated series, and use of the seven *patch'im* (syllable-final consonants) ㄱ, ㄴ, ㄹ, ㅁ, ㅂ, ㅅ, ㅇ" (1973: 226).

After the Kabo Reforms in Korea, which ushered in a change from pure Chinese (*hanmun*) official documents to mixed script writing (*kukhanmun*), Koreans began to turn their attention to the chaotic state of affairs in their native Korean writing. The fundamental question was one of reform versus conservatism, and the most controversial issues were (1) abolition or retention of the *arae a*, (2) whether to write the tense, unaspirates as *s*-clusters or as geminates, and (3) whether to allow new syllable-final *patch'im* or not (alternatively, whether to write phonemically or morphophonemically).

There was little or no coordination in research, and one finds many different eccentric proposals. For example, in 1905 Chi Hŏnyŏng published his *Sinjŏng kungmun* (Newly Amended National Writing), in which he proposed a new letter, "=" (meant to be a combination of /i/ and /ɨ/ > /yɨ/!) and a new diacritic—a dot written to the left of the syllable for a "high, trailing sound" (apparently for long vowels). In fact, Chi Hŏnyŏng's ideas were even decreed (though never implemented) as law, provoking what Kim Minsu calls the first of the "Writing System Upheavals" (1973: 154).

The Kungmun yŏn'guso (National Script Research Institute), formed on July 8, 1907, and attached to the Educational Authority (Hakpu), held a conference in September of 1907 to debate Chi Hŏnyŏng's proposals and two years later submitted a report to the government with its recommendations for Korean orthography. These included a twenty-five-letter system (they rejected the twenty-sixth, *ttan i* ["separated *i/y*"] or " ㅣ " of the old Panjŏl system), writing the tense unaspirated series as geminates, keeping the *arae a*, repudiation of Chi Hŏnyŏng's "=," new rules for syllable-final *patch'im*, and a dot in the upper lefthand corner for long vowels. However, this proposal was never implemented, and the Enlightenment Period ended in as chaotic a state as that in which it began.

Thus, there was nothing like an explicit, agreed orthographic standard for writing Korean until well into this century. My own experience with Korean newspapers published in Vladivostok before the Revolution suggests that the Korean orthography situation in Russia was no less chaotic than that in Korea.

However, while working in the public library in St. Petersburg, I came upon a remarkable Korean journal published in Chita, Siberia, over the course of 1913 and 1914. In three running issues (nos. 9, 10, and 11) in 1914, this journal, the *Taehanin chyŏnggyobo*, or *Journal of the Korean Russian Orthodox Church*, included calls for and experimentation with *karo ssŭgi*, or "on-line" writing in han'gŭl. Because the journal's proposals seem closely linked to contemporary ideas in Korea, let us examine the background in Korea before examining the journal material itself.

History of Proposals to Write Korean "On-Line" in Korea

The idea of abandoning the traditional practice of writing han'gŭl letters in syllable blocks (*moa ssŭgi* 'gather together and write') and writing them on-line instead (*karo p'urŏ ssŭgi* 'linearly take apart and write') is usually attributed to Korea's pioneer grammarian, Chu Sigyŏng (1876–1914).[2]

Kim Minsu links the idea of (*karo*) *p'urŏ ssŭgi* to the influence of Latin writing: "In such a scheme, only the letters are han'gŭl; the system is no different from a kind of romanization. Moreover, when it comes to handwritten or cursive forms of *p'urŏ ssŭgi*, many of the forms imitate the examples of roman letters, and the distinction between han'gŭl and romanization becomes more and more difficult" (1973: 254).

The first evidence of debates on *p'urŏ ssŭgi* in Korea is from 1908 in the National Script Research Institute. In the *Kungmun yŏn'gu an* (National Script Research Draft) produced in December of this year, Song Kiyong came out against it, while Yi Nŭnghwa and Chu Sigyŏng spoke in favor of the idea. Chu Sigyŏng wrote in this draft: "It might seem appropriate in orthography to write online (*hoengsŏ*) each of the consonants and vowels, but of course we should follow the traditional custom and depend upon the precedent of the *Hunmin chŏng'ŭm*. It is my view that it might be possible to write the letters on-line only in cases where it is necessary." From these lines, it would appear that Chu Sigyŏng took a pragmatic view of on-line writing and did not envisage a radical abolition of the traditional *moa ssŭgi* writing.

A year later, in December of 1909, the *Report of the National Script Research Institute* contained more discussion of writing on-line:

> Resolution 11: One method of orthography is to write the initial, medial, and final sounds horizontally, from left to right, on-line (*hoengsŏ*), for example, 텨 ㄴ 하태 펴ㅇ *t'yŏnha t'aep'yŏng*.

> Yi Nŭnghwa: If, in the very beginning, they had written the five letters ㅣ ㅏ ㅓ ㅑ ㅕ below the initials like the European orthography (라ㅁ ㅍ'lamp') (ㅅ티ㅋ 'stick'), it would have been convenient for movable type.

Chu Sigyŏng: In the matter of orthography, we can follow the example of the *Hunmin chŏng'ŭm* and rely upon the traditional method already worked out. But it is also reasonable to write the consonants and vowels separately on-line, whether vertically or horizontally.... This is smoother for the flow of pronunciation, is also convenient pedagogically, and is important for type casting. For example, "Our country is bright and beautiful" would be: (우리 나라 가 밝고 곱다) 우리 나라 가 바ㄹㄱ고 ㄱㅗㅂ다.[3]

However, Resolution 11 was abandoned, and in any case, the Kungmun yŏn'guso was not an official, policy-making body with power or authority to change existing practices.

It was also in 1909 that Chu Sigyŏng, in his "Kungmun yŏn'gu" (Research on Korean Writing), began to elaborate on the idea of on-line writing in his own research. Some of the first known published examples of "on-line" Korean writing are the Chosŏnŏ kangsŭpwŏn's (Korean Language Institute) "Certificate of Completion" (1913) and journals like *Aidŭl poi* and *Mar ŭi sori* (1914) connected with the activities of Chu Sigyŏng. By now, Chu was calling "on-line" writing by the native Korean term *karo ssŭgi* rather than the Sino-Korean *hoengsŏ*. Figure 1 is an example of his "on-line" Korean from *Mar ŭi sori*.[4]

Figure 1. Chu Sigyŏng's "On-Line" Korean (1914)

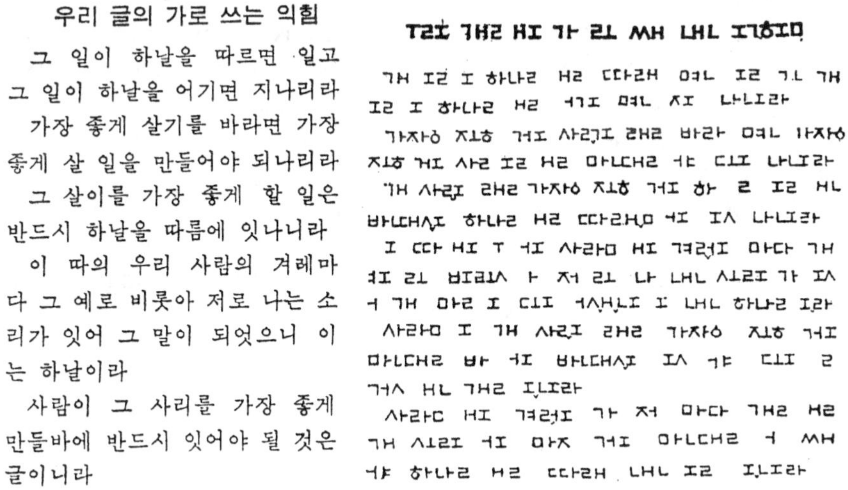

우리 글의 가로 쓰는 익힘

그 일이 하날을 따르면 일고 그 일이 하날을 어기면 지나리라

가장 좋게 살기를 바라면 가장 좋게 살 일을 만들어야 되나리라

그 살이를 가장 좋게 할 일은 반드시 하날을 따름에 잇나니라

이 따의 우리 사람의 겨레마다 그 예로 비롯아 저로 나는 소리가 잇어 그 말이 되엇으니 이는 하날이라

사람이 그 사리를 가장 좋게 만들바에 반드시 잇어야 될 것은 글이니라

사람의 겨레가 저마다 글을 그 소리에 맞게 만들어 쓰어야 하날을 따르는 일이니라

말은 반드시 다듬어야 좋은 말을 이루고 좋은 말을 적어야 좋은 글이 도나니라

그의 가장 좋은 것은 그 가장 잘 다듬은 말을 적은 것이오 또 이를 가로 쓰는 것이니라

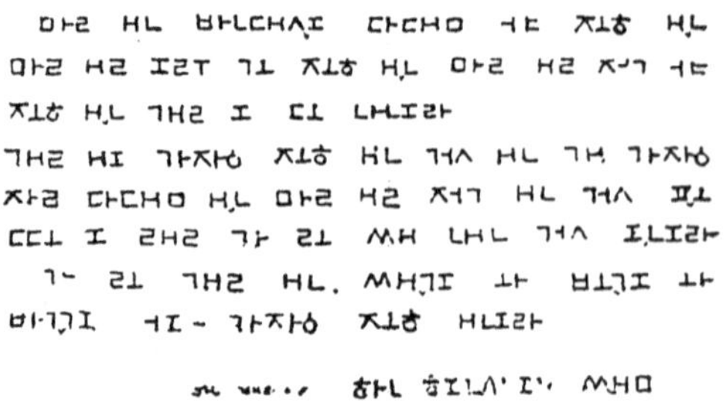

가로 글은 쓰기와 보기와 박기에 가장 좋으니라

ㄹㄷㅁㅈ 한 겨울 날 한 힌샘 씀

ㅁㅏㄹ ㅡㄴ ㅂㅏㄴㄷㅡㅅㅣ ㄷㅏㄷㅡㅁ ㅓㅑ ㅈㅗㅎ ㅡㄴ
ㅁㅏㄹ ㅡㄹ ㅣㄹㅜ ㄱㅗ ㅈㅗㅎ ㅡㄴ ㅁㅏㄹ ㅡㄹ ㅈㅓㄱ ㅓㅑ
ㅈㅗㅎ ㅡㄴ ㄱㅡㄹ ㅣ ㄷㅗ ㄴㅏㄴㅣㄹㅏ
ㄱㅡㄹ ㅡㅣ ㄱㅏㅈㅏㅇ ㅈㅗㅎ ㅡㄴ ㄱㅓㅅ ㅡㄴ ㄱㅡ ㄱㅏㅈㅏㅇ
ㅈㅏㄹ ㄷㅏㄷㅡㅁ ㅡㄴ ㅁㅏㄹ ㅡㄹ ㅈㅓㄱ ㅡㄴ ㄱㅓㅅ ㅣㅗ ㄸㅗ
ㅣ ㄹㅡㄹ ㄱㅏ ㄹㅗ ㅆㅡ ㄴㅡㄴ ㄱㅓㅅ ㅣㄴㅣㄹㅏ
ㄱㅏ ㄹㅗ ㄱㅡㄹ ㅡㄴ. ㅆㅡㄱㅣ ㅘ ㅂㅗㄱㅣ ㅘ
ㅂㅏㄱㄱㅣ ㅔ ㄱㅏㅈㅏㅇ ㅈㅗㅎ ㅡㄴㅣㄹㅏ

ㅎㅏㄴ ㅎㅣㄴㅅㅐㅁ ㅆㅡㅁ

After Chu Sigyŏng's death in 1914, the cause of "on-line" Korean writing in Korea was taken up by his disciples, for example, Kim Tubong (1922) and Yi P'ilsu (1923), and in the Chosŏnŏ hakhoe's *Karo kŭlssi imsi an* (Provisional Plan for On-line Writing) (1936), but not until the 1920s and 1930s.[5]

This is the immediate background to the attempts at writing Korean "on-line" in Siberia in 1914. The experimentation with "on-line" writing in Russia appears to be unknown in Korea,[6] although it is of some importance for the history of Korean writing.[7]

The *Taehanin Chyŏnggyobo*

The *Taehanin chyŏnggyobo* (Russian: *Ezhemesjachnyj zhurnal "Pravoslavie" Rossijskoj imperii, izdanie pravoslavnyx Korejtsev v g. Chite*; Monthly Journal "Orthodoxy" of the Russian Empire, Publication of the Orthodox Koreans in the City of Chita) was published in eleven issues during the years 1913 and 1914. Issues contained editorials, letters from readers, church news, home news, sundry news items from around the world, and information about and from other Korean communities abroad (China, the United States, Japan). The publisher was Mun Yunham and the editor-in-chief Yi Kang.[8]

Volume 9 of March 1914 (Tan'gi 4247) contains one word written on-line, in the table of contents on page 1: *chyŏnggyobo*. The bottom of page 25 starts a section "Uri kŭl" (Our Writing), which sets forth the journal's new position:

Writing On-line (*karo ssŭgi*)

Our people's greatest treasure is our writing; it is the most scientific and most convenient in the world. But even our fine writing is mistaken in its way of writing (*ssŭnŭn pŏp*) and is inconvenient in many ways with respect to education and printing. In this day and age when civilization and culture are advancing by the day, how can we go on like this? Now we shall have to make researches into a new way of writing (*sae ro ssŭl pŏp*). In order for our writing to be as perfect as possible, (1) the letter shapes must be simple, clear, and beautiful; and (2) the number of letters should be small; if the number of letters is too great, it is not only difficult for learning, but also has a great influence on printing technology, which is closely related to cultural progress.

Well then, where can one find letter shapes more geometrical, more simple, and more clear than ㅏ, ㅓ, ㅗ, ㅜ, ㄱ, ㄴ, ㄷ, ㄹ? Compare these to roman letters, which until now have been considered the most perfect: A B X G P R. Isn't it clear even at a quick glance? But the way of writing is mistaken: *stwaeri* ᄯᅫ리. In this way, some letters are written horizontally, others vertically, and the appearance is not only unseemly, but learning it at first is difficult, and furthermore, the letter combinations (*hwaltcha*) [for syllables like] *ka*, *kak*, *skak*, *skari*, *skaek* are in this way not much less than for Chinese characters, and one must compose [characters] in numerous different ways. This has incurred huge losses of time and expense.

But if we now decide to write these vowels and consonants on-line, letter combinations will exceed no more than twenty, we will save no little amount of time in type picking (*ch'aejʌ*) and typesetting (*sikjʌ*), and how clean and easy to read it will be!

But if we are to do this, we shall have to construct rules of grammar (*munpŏp*), and all our fellow countrymen must make efforts to learn to read this writing. Although in the beginning it seems difficult to read, after a little while they will understand that it becomes much easier and more convenient than before.

Figure 2. *Taehanin chŏnggyobo*, Page 26 of Issue No. 9, 1914

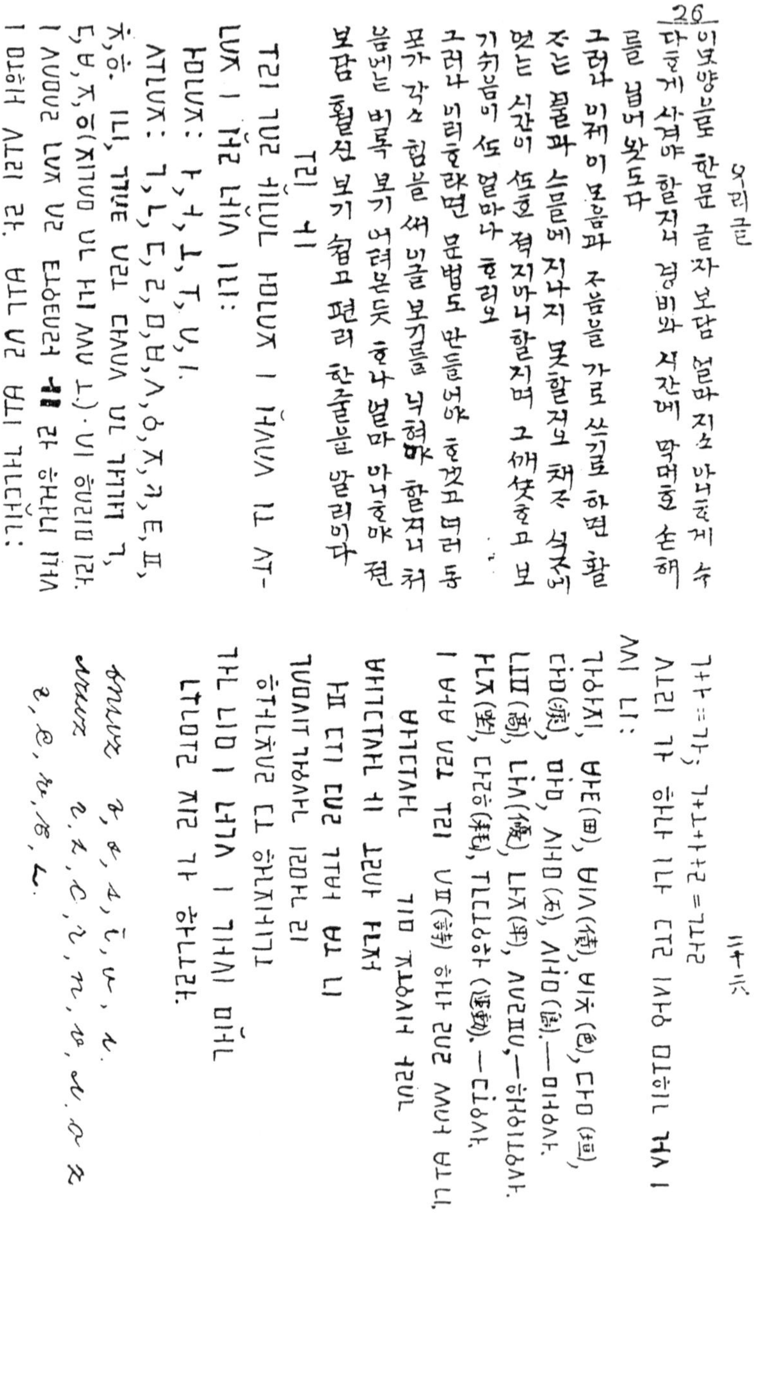

이모양으로 한문 글자 보담 얼마 지소 아니하게 수
다하게 사셔야 할지니 경비와 시간에 막대한 손해
를 넘어 봤도다
그러나 이제 이 모음과 조음을 가로 쓰기로 하면 활
조는 물론과 스믐에 지나지 못할지오 채주 쓰자의
업는 시간이 또한 적지아니할지며 그 애낫하고 보
기쉬움이 또 얼마나 한려오
그러나 이러한략면 문법도 만들어야 하겠고 또러 동
모가 각소 힘을 써 이를 보기를 니혀야 할지니 처
음에는 비록 보기 어려운듯 하나 얼마 아니하야 편
보담 훨신 보기 쉽고 편리 한줄을 알리이다

TZl ㅓl

TZl ㄱUㄹ ㅓlULㄴ ㅏOLUㅈ l ㅣ̆ㅐAUㅅ ㅣㅗ ㅅT-
LUㅈ l ㅣ̆ㅓㄹ ㄴㅓㅣ̆ㅅ ㅣㅗㅣ:
ㅏOLUㅈ: ㅏ, ㅓ, ㅗ, ㅜ, ㅡ, ㅣ.
ㅅTLUㅈ: ㄱ, ㄴ, ㄷ, ㄹ, ㅁ, ㅂ, ㅅ, ㅇ, ㅈ, ㅋ, ㅌ, ㅍ,
ㅊ, ㅎ. ㅣㄴㅣ, ㄱㄱUE Uㄹㅗ ㄷㅓAUㅅ UL ㄱㅓㄱㄱㅓ ㄱ,
ㄷ, ㅂ, ㅈ, ㅎ (ㅈㅣㄱUㅁ UL ㅏㄴㅣ ㅅㅅU ㅗ.) · Uㅣ 하ㄹㅣㅁ ㅣ라.
l ㅅUㅁUㄹ LUㅈ Uㄹ Eㅗ0EUㄹㅓ ㅓl 라 하ㅏㄴㅣ ㅣㅓㅅ
l ㅁㅗ허 ㅅㅗㄹㅣ 라. ㅂㅗL Uㄹ ㅂㅗㅣ ㄱㅓLㄷㅓ̆L:

ㄱ+ㅏ = 가; ㄱ+ㅗ+ㅏ+ㄹ = ㄱㅗㅏㄹ
ㅅㅗㄹㅣ 가 하나 ㅣ나 ㄷTㄹ ㅣㅅㅏㅇ ㅁㅗ히ㄴ ㄱㅓㅅ l
ㅅㅅㅣ ㄴㅣ:
가ㅇ아지, ㅂㅏE(田), ㅂㅣㅅ(債), ㅂㅣㅊ(色), ㄷㅏㅁ(垣),
ㄷㅏㅁ(痰), ㅁㅏㅁ, ㅅㅓㅁ(石), ㅅㅓㅁ(島). — ㅁㅓㅇㅅㅏ.
ㄴㅗㅍ(高), ㄴㅏㅅ(優), ㄴㅏㅈ(平), ㅅUㄹㅍU, — 하ㅓㅇㅣㅗㅇㅅㅏ.
ㅏㄴㅈ(坐), ㄷㅏㄹ하(耗), TㄴㄷㅗㅇㅎㅏE(運動). — ㄷㅣㅇㅅㅏ.
l ㅂㅓㅂ Uㄹㅗ Tㄹㅣ Uㅍ(詩) 하나 ㄹUㄹ ㅅㅅUㅓ ㅂㅗ ㄴㅣ.
ㅂㅏㅣㄷTㅅㅏㄴ ㄱㅣㅁ ㅈㅗㅇㅅㅓ ㅓㄹUL
ㅂㅏㅣㄷTㅅㅏㄴ ㅓㅣ ㅗㄹUㅏ ㅏㄴㅈㅓ
ㅏㅍ ㄷTㅣ ㄷUㄹ ㄱTㅂㅓ ㅂㅗ ㄴㅣ
ㄱUㅁㅅㅣT 가ㅇㅅㅏㄴ ㅣㄹㅁㅏㄴ ㄹㅣ
하ㅓㄴ차Uㄹ ㄷㅗ 하ㄴ지ㅓㅣㄱㅗ
가ㄴ ㄴㅣㅁ l ㄴㅓㄱㅅ l ㄱㅣㅓㅣ ㅁㅓ̆ㄴ
ㄴTㄴㅁTㄹ 지ㄹ 가 하ㄴㅗ라.

ㅎㄴ ㅇㅇ ㅏ, ㅓ, ㅗ, ㅜ, ㅡ, ㅣ.
ㅇ ㅇ ㄱ, ㄴ, ㄷ, ㄹ, ㅁ, ㅂ, ㅅ, ㅇ, ㅈ,
ㅋ, ㅌ, ㅍ, ㅊ, ㅎ.

Resyllabification and Translation of On-line Text in Figure 2

우리 어이
우리 글 에는 암늦 이 여슷 이오 수-
늦 이 열 넷 이니:
암늦: 아, 어, 오, 우, 으, 이.
수늦: ㄱ, ㄴ, ㄷ, ㄹ, ㅁ, ㅂ, ㅅ,
ㅇ, ㅈ, ㅋ, ㅌ, ㅍ, ㅊ, ㅎ 이니,
끝 으로 다슷 은 각각 ㄱ, ㄷ, ㅂ, ㅈ, ㆆ
(지금 은 아니 쓰오.) 의 흐림 이라.

Our Letters
In our writing there are six vowels and ten consonants:
Vowels: *a, e, o, u, ɨ, i*
Consonants: *k, n, t, l, m, p, s, ng, c, kh, th, ph, ch, h*. The last five letters are each the muddy versions of *k, t, p, c,* ʔ (the last not used now).[9]

이 스물 늦 을 통틀어 어이 라 하나니 이것
이 모히어 소리 라. 본 을 보이 건댄:

These twenty letters are all called *ei*. Put together, they are syllables. E.g.:

ㄱ + ㅏ = 가 ㄱ + ㅗ + ㅏ + ㄹ = 괄
소리 가 하나 이나 둘 이상 모힌
것 이 씨니
강아지, 밭, 빗, 빛, 담,
담, 맘, 셤, 셤 -- 명사.
늪, 낫, 낮, 슬프 -- 형용사.
앉, 닳, 운동하 -- 동사.

k + *a* = *ka*, *k* + *o* + *a* + *l* = *kwal*
When one or more syllables join, they are words:
puppy, field, debt, color, wall, phlegm, mind, big sack, island—nouns.
high, better, low, sad—adjectives.
sit, abrade, exercise—verbs.

이 법 으로 우리 읊 하나 를 쓰어 보 니,

In this manner we can write a poem:

박두산 [*sic*] 김 종셔 어른
백두산 에 오르아 앉어
앞 뒤 들 굽어 보 니
금슈 강산 일만 리

훤츨 도 한쟈이고
간 님 이 넋 이 기어시 면
눈물 질 가 하노라.

Mt. Paektu by Kim Chongsyŏ[10]
Sitting atop Mt. Paektu
I overlook the fields below.
Beautiful mountainous scenery extends ten thousand ri. How vast and refreshing!
Were my beloved among the living,
I might shed a tear.

[same *amnɨc* (vowels) and *sunɨc* (consonants) in cursive follow]

Analysis

The shape of ㅡ = *ɨ(ŭ)* has been changed to "U" by pulling up both ends. This is different from Chu Sigyŏng's 1914 shapes in *Mar ŭi sori*, where he writes "H" for ㅡ = /*ɨ(ŭ)*/. Chu Sigyŏng's on-line /i/ was different, too: "I" (probably influence from the Latin script). The shape "U" appears in Kim Tubong's *Kiptŏ Chosŏn malbon* (1922/1934).

ㅓㅣ /ei/ and ㅔ /ey/ are kept apart by writing ˘ over the latter. The same holds for ㅣㅓ /ie/ versus ㅕ /ye/, ㅏㅣ /ai/, and ㅐ /ay/. But /wa/, /we/ (*wŏ*), /oy/ (*oe*), and /uy/ (*ŭi*) do not get the diacritic. This usage does not survive beyond this issue, nor can it be found in Chu Sigyŏng's *Mar ŭi sori*, where Chu simply writes ㅕ /ye/ (*yŏ*), and so on.

Particles are written separately from their noun and verb bases, and "*ɨ* (*ŭ*)-dropping bases" are written with the *ɨ(ŭ)* intact before the infinitive vowel /a, e/: /olua/ 'ascend' versus SS /olla/, /ssue/ 'write' versus SS /sse/. The same can be found in Chu Sigyŏng's *Mar ŭi sori*.

The *iŭng* ㆁ has its old form with the hat, because now it is used only for /ng/ and not as a "zero" before vowels. Likewise in *Mar ŭi sori*.

The tense unaspirated consonants are written as geminates (/kkuth/ 'end'), and not as *s*-clusters.

The grammatical terminology appears to be related to that of Chu Sigyŏng but is nonetheless different. Thus, Chu's /nɨc/ (*nŭt*) corresponded to "morpheme," whereas here it means "letter," with a subdivision of "female letters" (vowels) and "male letters" (consonants). Likewise, in Chu's terminology, the "syllable" was /nasnay, nathnay/ (*nannae*), not /soli/, and I am not aware that he ever used the term /ei/ (*ŏi*) to refer to the Korean script.[11] The word /ssi/ here seems to mean "word," but it could be "part of speech." /ɨph/ (*ŭp*) for "poem" appears to be a neologism from /ɨlph-/ (*ŭlp-*) 'recites/writes a poem'.

The *arae a* has been abandoned in favor of /a/.

A single dot over the vowel indicates length: /tām/ 'phlegm' versus /tam/ 'wall'; /mām/ 'mind', /syem/ 'straw sack' versus /syēm/ 'island', /nās-/ 'be better', /tōngsa/ 'verb'.

The old distinction of syllables /sV, cV/ versus /syV, cyV/ is maintained.

Figure 3. *Taehanin chŏnggyobo*, Volume 10, May of Tan'gi 4247 (A.D. 1914), Page 25

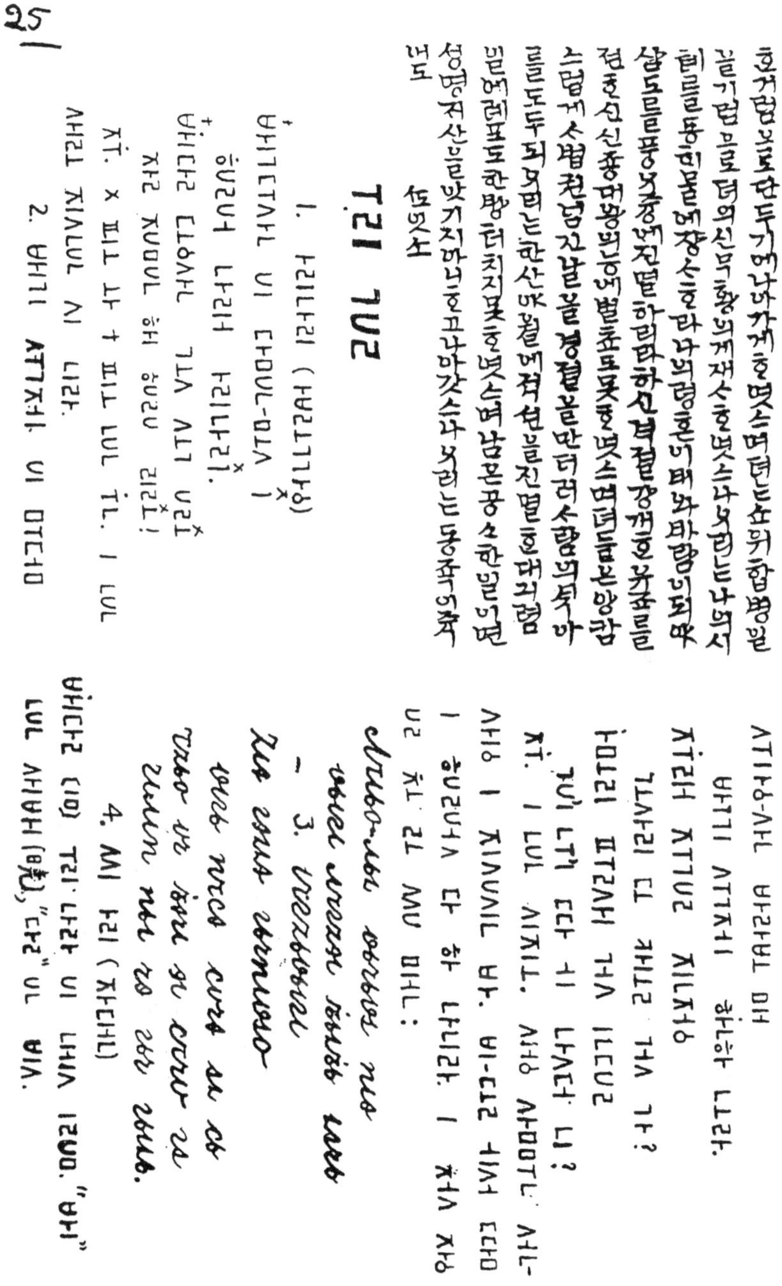

Resyllabification and Translation of On-line Text in Figure 3

우리 글

Our Writing

1. 아리나리 (압록강)
백두산 의 담은-못 이
  흐르어 나리어 아리나리.
배달 동산 곳 속 으로
  잘 즈믄 해 흐르 리로!
주. x 표 와 † 표 는 운. 이 는
새로 짓는 시 니라.

Arinari (Yalu River)
The lake atop Mt. Paektu
  flows down to become the Yalu.
Straight into the bowels of Paedal,
  A thousand years may it flow!
Note: The signs x and † are rhymes.
This is a newly created poem.

2. 백이 숙제 의 무덤
수양산 바라보며
  백이 숙제 한하 노라.
주리어 죽을 진정
  고사리 도 개올 것 가?
아모리 풀새 것 인들
  긔 늬 따 에 낫더 니?

Paek I and Sukche's Grave
Gazing off at Mt. Suyang,
  I lament Paek I and Sukche.
Even though they starved to death,
  would they dig up so much
  as a fern?
Mere grasses though they may be,
  did they not grow on this land?

주. 이 는 시지오. 셩 삼문 선생 이 짓으신 바. 비-돌 에서 땀이 흐르엇 다 하 나니라.

이 첫 장 을 초 로 쓰면:

Note: This is a poem. Written by Sŏng Sammun. They say his perspiration flowed from his tombstone.

The first line in cursive:

[first two lines of (2) in cursive]

3. 육자배기
져 건너 갈미봉
비가 묻어 들어 온 다
우장 을 허리 에 두르 고
기심[13] 매 러 갈 개나

Yukjabaegi[12]
Across the way on Kalmi Peak,
The rain comes pelting down.
Shall I throw on my raincoat and
go out to clear some weeds?

4. 씨 아리 (자뎐)
배달 (임). 우리 나라 의 녯 이름. "배" 는 새배. "달" 은 빗.

Word finder (Dictionary)
Paedal (noun). Ancient name for our country. "*Pae*" is the dawn, "*dal*" is light.

Analysis

The single dot for vowel length we know: note the correspondences with SS–SK (Sino-Korean) /cwū/ 'notes', SK /pāytal/ 'old name for Korea', SK /wūn/ 'rhyme', SK /hān ha-/ 'lament', /cwūli-/ 'starve', /āmoli/ 'no matter how much' = SS /āmuli/. The "note" introduces two new diacritics for "rhyme," but just what the superimposed "x" and "†" do is not clear (perhaps secondary and primary stress, respectively?).

The use of the apostrophe in /kɨ'i nu'i/ is new and must be intended to represent the subject particle /i/ attaching directly to a final vowel.

There is no "*s*-lenition" in /cis-/ 'compose' (SS would have /ciusin pa/). If this is not an ideological position related to the authors' views on orthography (i.e., hard-line morphophonemic writing: keep the shape of the verb base constant, even if it means ignoring sound alternations), it could be a dialect influence. Ditto for the preservation of initial /ny-/ (/nyeys/ = SS /yēys/ 'ancient': we would have expected a long vowel mark in our text).

"Yalu River" /aplokkang/ is written morphophonemically with /-pl-/ rather than phonemically as /-mn-/, as one might expect in a more "alphabetic" scheme. The native Korean for "Yalu River" is interesting. The /nali/ must be cognate with SS /nāy/ 'stream' < MK /:nayh/. The /ali/ is more mysterious and could add fuel to the debate on the etymology of *arirang*, but may be related to SS /oli/ 'duck' (SK /aplok/ is "duck-green"). The /ali/ in /si ali/ 'glossary' is a deverbal noun from /:al-/ 'know'.

The vertical stroke in this on-line scheme is ambiguous between /i/ and /y/ (and zero when one considers its role in, for example, /ay/ [æ] and /ey/ [e]).

The preservation of /tyV/ in /catyen/ (*chadyŏn*) 'dictionary' rounds out our picture of a conservative orthography that preserves /t(h)yV, c(h)V, c(h)yV, sV, syV/.

The text of Sŏng Sammun's *sijo* here diverges from that given by Chŏng Pyŏnguk (1980: 293):

> SWU YANGSAN pʌlapomye I CEY lʌl HAN hʌnola
> cu.lye cu.kɨlcilntɨl CHAYMI to hʌnʌn keska?
> pilok.ay phusay.eys ke.sintɨl kɨy nuy sta.hey nastʌni?

Figure 4A. Volume 11, June of Tan'gi 4247 (A.D. 1914), Page 21

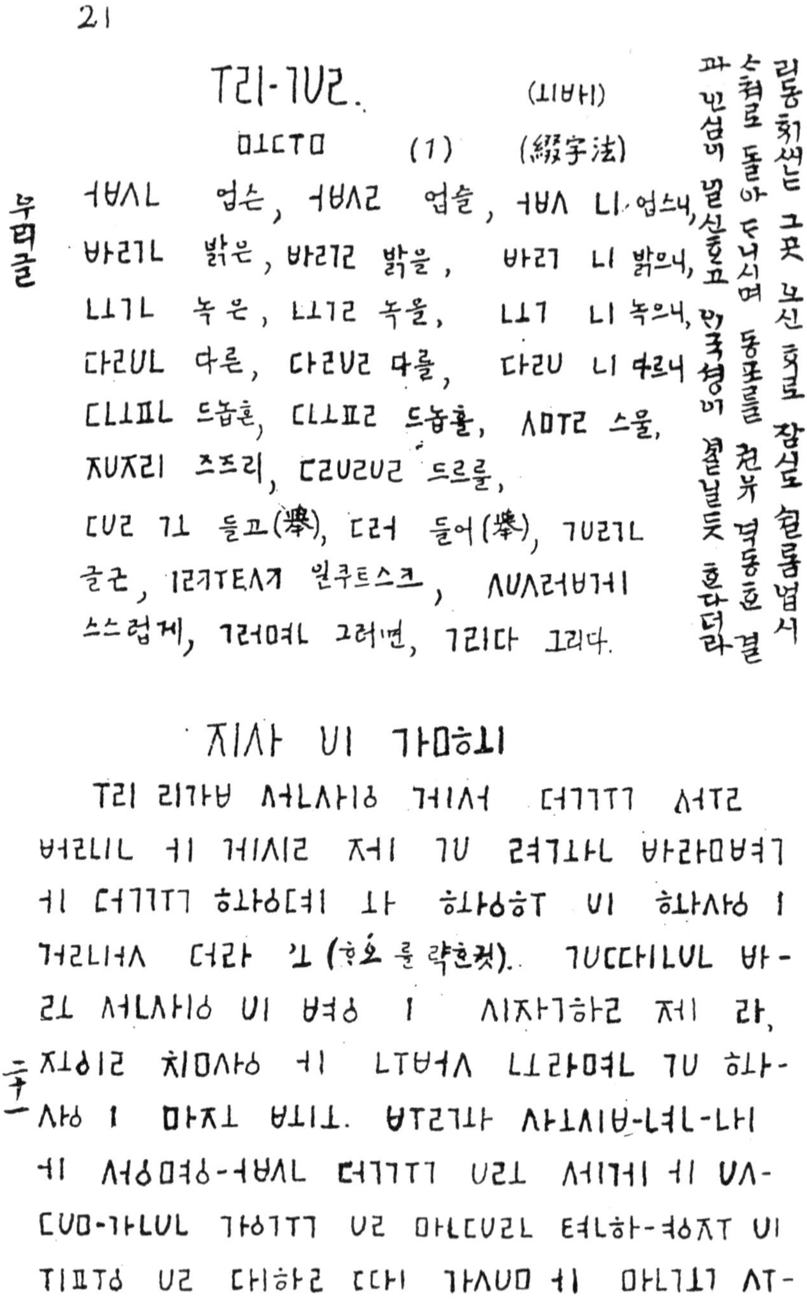

21

우리글

Tㄹㅣ-ㄱUㄹ. (ㅗㅣㅂㅓㅣ)

ㅁㅗㄷTㅁ (1) (綴字法)

ㅓㅂㅅㄴ 업슨, ㅓㅂㅅㄹ 업슬, ㅓㅂㅅ ㄴㅣ 업스니,
ㅂㅏㄹㄱㄴ 밝은, ㅂㅏㄹㄱㄹ 밝을, ㅂㅏㄹㄱ ㄴㅣ 밝으니,
ㄴㅗㄱㄴ 녹은, ㄴㅗㄱㄹ 녹을, ㄴㅗㄱ ㄴㅣ 녹으니,
ㄷㅏㄹUㄴ 다른, ㄷㅏㄹUㄹ 다를, ㄷㅏㄹU ㄴㅣ 다르니
ㄷㄴㅗㅍㄴ 드놉흔, ㄷㄴㅗㅍㄹ 드놉흘, ㅅㅁTㄹ 스물,
ㅈUㅈㄹㅣ 즈즈리, ㄷㄹUㄹUㄹ 드르를,
ㄷUㄹ ㄱㅗ 들고(擧), ㄷㄹㅓ 들어(擧), ㄱUㄹㄱㄴ
글근, ㅣㄹㅋTㅌㅅㅋ 읽쿠트스크, ㅅUㅅㄹㅓㅂㄱㅓㅣ
스스럽게, ㄱㄹㅓㅁㅕㄴ 그러면, ㄱㄹㅣㄷㅏ 그리다.

리동휘씨는 그곳 모신 후로 잠심도 쉬롬넙시
수천로 돌아 두니시며 동포를 권뉴 격동ᄒᆞᆫ 결
과 민심이 빌신ᄒᆞ고 만국형이 볕날듯 ᄒᆞ더라

ㅈㅣㅅㅏ Uㅣ ㄱㅏㅁㅎㅗㅣ

Tㄹㅣ ㄹㅣㄱㅏㅂ ㅅㅓㄴㅅㅏㅣㅇ ㄱㅓㅣㅅㅓ ㄷㅓㄱㄱTㄱ ㅅㅓTㄹ
ㅂㅓㄹㄴㅣㄴ ㅓㅣ ㄱㅓㅣㅅㅣㄹ ㅈㅓㅣ ㄱU ㄹㅕㄱㅗㅏㄴ ㅂㅏㄹㅏㅁㅂㅕㄱ
ㅓㅣ ㄷㅓㄱㄱTㄱ ㅎㅗㅏㅇㄷㅕㅣ ㅗㅏ ㅎㅗㅏㅇㅎT Uㅣ ㅎㅗㅏㅅㅏㅇ ㅣ
ㄱㅓㄹㄴㅓㅅ ㄷㅓㄹㅏ ㄱㅗ (ᄒᆞ오 를 략ᄒᆞᆫ것). ㄱUㄷㄷㅏㅣㄴUㄴ ㅂㅏ-
ㄹㅗ ㅅㅓㄴㅅㅏㅣㅇ Uㅣ ㅂㅕㅇ ㅣ ㅅㅣㅈㅏㄱㅎㅏㄹ ㅈㅓㅣ ㄹㅏ,
ㅈㅗㅇㅣㄹ ㅊㅣㅁㅅㅏㅇ ㅓㅣ ㄴTㅂㅓㅅ ㄴㅗㄹㅏㅁㅕㄴ ㄱU ㅎㅗㅏ-
ㅅㅏㅇ ㅣ ㅁㅏㅈㅗ ㅂㅗㅣㅗ. ㅂTㄹㄱㅗㅏ ㅅㅏㅗㅅㅣㅂ-ㄴㅕㄴ-ㄴㅏㅣ
ㅓㅣ ㅅㅓㅇㅁㅕㅇ-ㅓㅂㅅㄴ ㄷㅓㄱㄱTㄱ Uㄹㅗ ㅅㅓㅣㄱㅓㅣ ㅓㅣ Uㅅ-
ㄷUㅁ-ㄱㅏㄴUㄴ ㄱㅏㅇㄱTㄱ Uㄹ ㅁㅏㄴㄷUㄹㄴ ㅌㅕㄴㅎㅏ-ㅕㅇㅈT Uㅣ
TㅣㅍTㅇ Uㄹ ㄷㅏㅣㅎㅏㄹ ㄷㄷㅏㅣ ㄱㅏㅅUㅁ ㅓㅣ ㅁㅏㄴㄱㅗㄱ ㅅT-

二十一

Resyllabification and Translation of On-line Text in Figure 4A

		우리 - 글		(외배)	
		모둠	(1)	(철자법)	
ㅓㅂㅅㄴ	(업슨),	ㅓㅂㅅㄹ	(업슬)	ㅓㅂㅅ니	(업스니)
바ㄹㄱㄴ	(밝은),	바ㄹㄱㄹ	(밝을)	바ㄹㄱ니	(밝으니)
ㄴㅗㄱㄴ	(녹은),	ㄴㅗㄱㄹ	(녹을)	ㄴㅗㄱ니	(녹으니)
다ㄹUㄴ	(다른),	다ㄹUㄹ	(다를),	다ㄹU니	(다르니)
ㄷㄴ ㅗㅍㄴ	(드놉흔),	ㄷㄴㅗㅍㄹ	(드놉흘),	ㅅㅁㅜㄹ	(스물)
ㅈUㅈ리	(즈즈리),	ㄷㄹUㄹUㄹ	(드르를),		
ㄷUㄹ ㄱㅗ	(들고),	ㄷ러	(들어),		
ㄱUㄹㄱㄴ	(글근),	ㅣㄹㅋㅜㅌㅅㅋ	(일쿠투스크),		
ㅅUㅅ러ㅂ게	(스스럽게),	ㄱ러며 ㄴ	(그러면),	ㄱ리다	(그리다)

지사 의 감회

우리 리갑 선생 게서 덕국 서울
벌닌 에 게실 제 그 려관 바람벽
에 덕국 황뎨 와 황후의 화상 이
걸니엇 더라 ᄒᆞ오. 그때는 바-
로 선생 의 병이 시작할 제 라,
종일 침상 에 눕엇 노라면 그 화-
상 이 마조 보이오. 불과 사오십-넌-내
에 성명-없은 덕국 으로 세게 에 웃-
듬-가는 강국 을 만든 텬하-영주 의
위풍 을 대할 때 가슴 에 만곡 수-

Reminiscences of a Patriot

When our Li Kap[14] was in the German capital of Berlin, there was a portrait hanging on the wall of the inn of the German emperor and empress [they say]. That was just when Li's sickness began, so, because he was laid up in bed all day long, the portrait was in full view across from him. As he faced the imposing presence of an illustrious world leader who had built Germany from nothing into a top-ranking world power,

Figure 4B. Volume 11, June of Tan'gi 4247 (A.D. 1914), Page 22

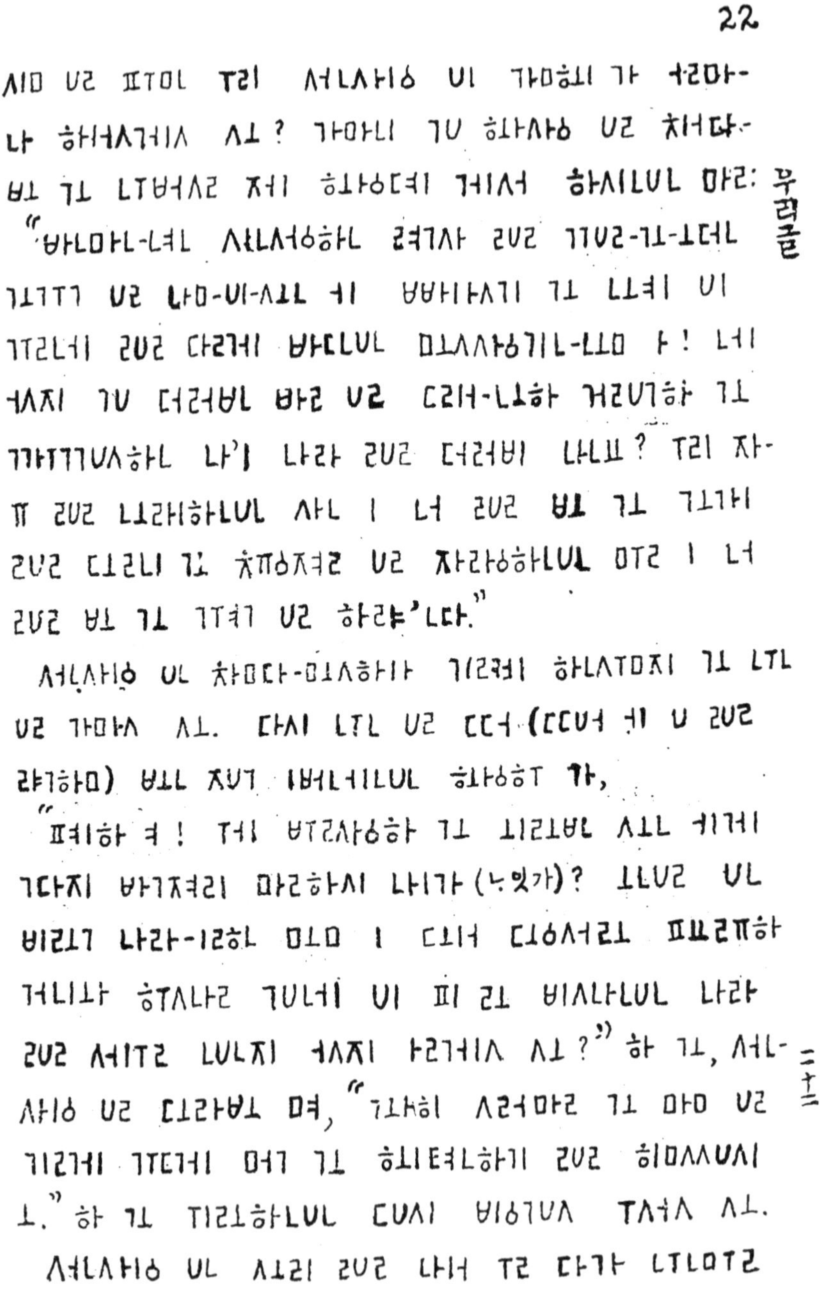

우리글

二十二

Resyllabification and Translation of On-line Text in Figure 4B

심 을 품은 우리 선생 의 감회 가 얼마-
나 하엿겟 소? 가마니 그 화상 을 치어다-
보 고 눕엇을 제 황데 게서 하시는 말:

"반만-넌 신성한 력사 를 끌-고-오-던
고국 을 남-의-손 에 빼앗기 고 노예 의
굴네 를 달게 받는 못상긴-놈 아! 네
엇지 그 더럽은 발 을 드리어-놓아 거륵하 고
깨끗한 내나라 를 더럽이 나뇨? 우리 자-
유 를 노래하는 산 이 너 를 보 고 고개
를 들니 고 충절 을 자랑하는 물 이 너
를 보 고 구역 을 하랸다."

선생 은 참다-못하야 길게 한숨지 고 눈
을 감앗 소. 다시 눈 을 떠 (뜨어 에 으 를
략함) 본 즉 이번에는 황후 와,

"폐하 여! 웨 불상하 고 외굡은 손 에게
그다지 박졀이 말하시 나이가 (ㄴ̣잇가)?
오늘 은 비록 나라-일흔 몸 이 되어 동서로
표류하 거니와 훗날 그네 의 피 로 빗나는
나라 를 세울 는지 엇지 알겟 소?" 하 고,
선생 을 돌아보 며, "과히 슬어말 고 맘 을
길게 굳게 먹 고 회텬하기 를 힘쓰시
오." 하 고 위로하는 듯이 빙긋 웃엇 소.

선생 은 소리 를 나이어 울 다가 눈물

how tortuously grievous must have been his thoughts! As he lay there quietly staring at the portrait, the emperor said: "Hey you, ugly fellow who has had his land stolen away by others, a country with 5000 years of sacred history, you who now wear the fetters of slavery! How dare you lower those filthy feet and dirty my clean and glorious land? Our mountains who sing in praise of freedom look at you and turn their heads, and our waters who extol loyalty look at you and want to vomit." Li Kap, who could bear no more, breathed a sigh and closed his eyes. When he opened his eyes and looked again, this time the empress said: "Your Highness! Why do you speak so cruelly to a pitiful and lonely guest? Though he be a stateless soul drifting East and West, who is to say that in later days they won't create out of their blood a brilliant country?" Then, turning to Li Kap, she gave a big smile as if to console him: "Do not despair too much; take heart and courage, and endeavor to restore your national glory."

Li Kap sobbed aloud for a while,

Figure 4C. Volume 11, June of Tan'gi 4247 (A.D. 1914), Page 23

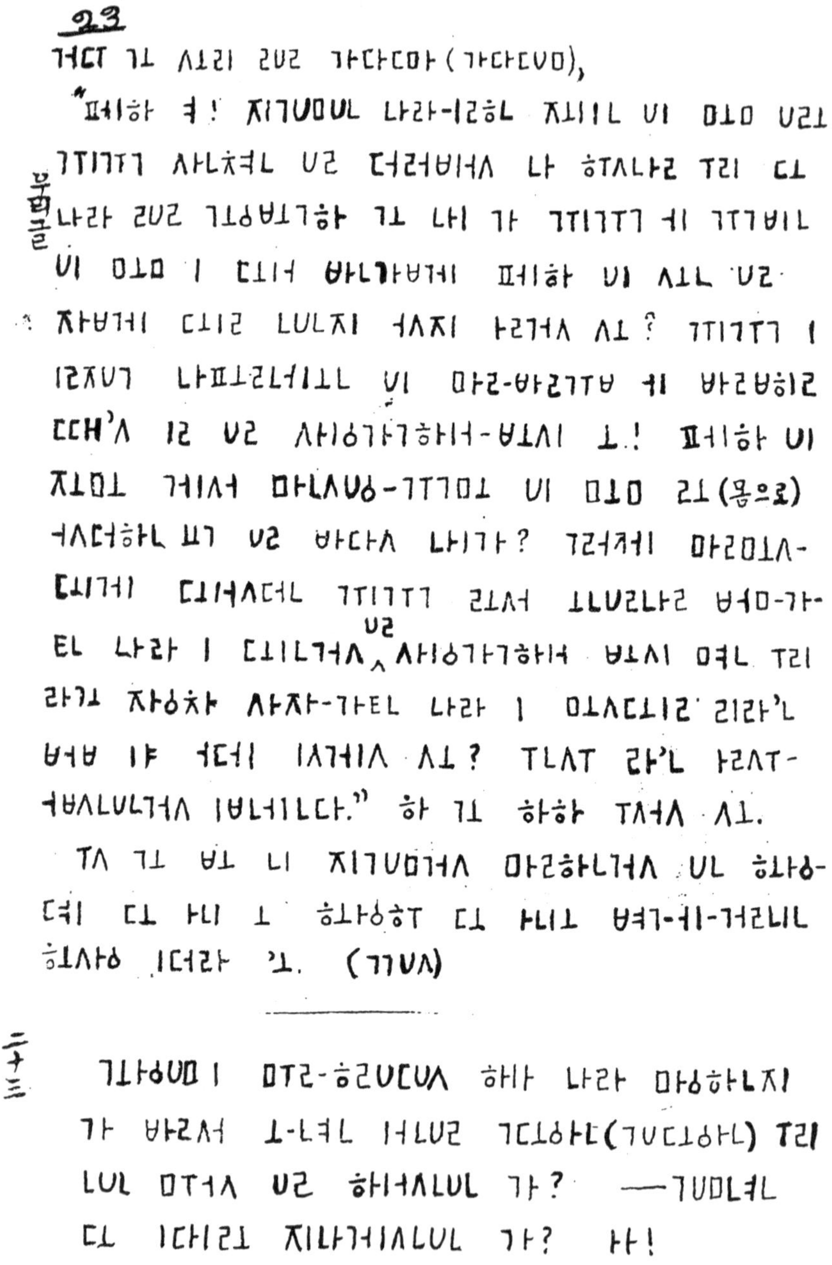

23

거ᄃᄃ 고 소리 루ᄅ 가다ᄃ마 (가다두ᄆ),

"페하 ᅧ! 지구무ᄂ 나라-ᅵᄅᄒᄂ 조ᅵᅵᄂ ᅮᅵ 모ᄆ ᅮ로

구ᅵ구ᄀ 사ᄂ쳐ᄂ ᅮᄅ 더러비ᅥᄉ 나 후ᄉ나ᄅ ᅮ리 도

나라 루ᄅ 고ᅌ보ᄀ하 고 내 가 구ᅵ구ᄀ ᅥᅵ 구ᄀ비ᄂ

ᅮᅵ 모ᄆ ᅵ 도ᅵᅥ 바ᄂ가베 페하 ᅮᅵ 소ᄂ ᅮᄅ

자베 도ᅵᄅ 누ᄂ지 ᅥᄉ지 ᅡᄅ거ᄉ 소? 구ᅵ구ᄀ ᅵ

ᅵᄅ주ᄀ 나포ᄅ너ᅵᅩᄂ ᅮᅵ 마ᄅ-바ᄅ구ᄇ ᅦ 바ᄅ비ᄅ

때'ᄉ ᅵᄅ ᅮᄅ 새ᅌ가ᄀ해ᅥ-보시 ᅩ! 페하 ᅮᅵ

조모 게서 마ᄂ수ᅌ-구ᄀ모 ᅮᅵ 모ᄆ 로(몸으로)

ᅥᄉ더하ᄂ ᄔᄀ ᅮᄅ 바다ᄉ 나ᅵ가? ᄀ러제 마ᄅ모ᄉ-

도ᅵ게 도ᅵᅥᄉ더ᄂ 구ᅵ구ᄀ 로서 ᅩ누ᄅ나ᄅ 버ᄆ-가-

ᄐᄂ 나라 ᅵ 도ᅵᄂ거ᄉ ᅮᄅ 새ᅌ가ᄀ해ᅥ 보시 머ᄂ ᅮ리

라고 자ᅌ차 사자-가ᄐᄂ 나라 ᅵ 모ᄉ도ᅵᄅ 리라'ᄂ

버ᄇ ᅵᅣ ᅥ데 ᅵᄉ게ᅵᄉ 소? ᅮᄂ수 라'ᄂ ᅡᄅ수-

ᅥᄇᄉ누ᄂ거ᄉ ᅵᄇ너ᅵᄂ다." 하 고 하하 ᅮ서ᄉ 소.

ᅮᄉ 고 보 니 지구ᄆ거ᄉ 마ᄅ하ᄂ거ᄉ ᅮᄂ 호ᅡᅌ-

뎨 도 ᅡ니 ᅩ 호ᅡᅌ후 도 ᅡ니ᅩ 벼ᄀ-ᅥᅵ-거ᄅ니ᄂ

호사ᅌ ᅵ더라 고. (ᄀ구ᄉ)

二十三 고ᅡᅌᅮᄆ ᅵ 무ᄅ-ᄒ루두ᄉ 해ᅡ 나라 마ᅌ하ᄂ지

가 바ᄅ서 ᅩ-녀ᄂ ᅵᅥ누ᄅ ᄀ도ᅌᅡᄂ(구도ᅌᅡᄂ) ᅮ리

누ᄂ 무ᅥᄉ ᅮᄅ 해ᅥᄉ누ᄂ 가? —구ᄆ녀ᄂ

도 ᅵ대로 지나게ᅵᄉ누ᄂ 가? ᅡᅡ!

Marginal notes: 붓글 (left margin, beside lines 3–5); 二十三 (left margin, beside the final section).

Resyllabification and Translation of On-line Text in Figure 4c

거두 고 소리 를 가다듬아, "폐하 여!
지금은 나라-일흔 죄인 의 몸 으로
귀국 산천 을 더렵이엇 나 훗날 우리 도
나라 를 공복하 고 내 가 귀국 에 귀빈
의 몸 이 되어 반갑게 폐하 의 손 을
잡게 될 는지 엇지 알것 소? 귀국 이
일즉 나폴네온 의 말-발굽 에 밟힐
땟 일 을 생각하여-보시 오! 폐하 의
조모 게서 만승-국모 의 몸 으로
엇더한 옥 을 받앗 나이가? 그러케 말못-
되게 되엇던 귀국 으로서 오늘날 범-같-
은 나라 이 된것 을 생각하여 보시 면 우리
라고 장차 사자-같은 나라 이 못될 리란
법 이야 어데 잇겟 소? 운수 란 알수-
없는 것 입넨다. [*sic*]" 하고 하하 웃엇 소.

웃고 보니 지금것 말한것 은 황-
뎨 도 아니 오 황후 도 아니오 벽-에-걸닌
호상 [*sic*] 이더라 ᄒᆞ오. (끗)

광음 이 물-흐르듯 하야 나라 망한지
가 발서 오-년 이어늘 그동안 우리
는 무엇 을 하엿는 가? -- 금년
도 이대로 지나겟는 가? 아아!

wiped away his tears, gathered up his courage, and said: "Your Highness! Have I sullied the mountains and streams of your esteemed country with this criminal, stateless body of mine? Who knows, perhaps one day we, too, will restore our nation, and I will come to your good country as a guest of honor and gleefully grasp your hand. Just think of the time when your country was trampled beneath the hooves of Napoleon's horses! What insults did your grandmother suffer as the mother of the Son of Heaven? If you consider that such an indescribably pathetic nation as yours has become a tigerlike state, who is to say that we in future cannot become a lionlike state? Fate is something nobody can predict." So saying, he laughed out loud.

After laughing, he realized that what he had been talking with was neither the emperor nor the empress, but the portrait hanging on the wall. (the end)

Time flies and it is already five years since our country perished. What have we done during this time?—Will we carry on this way this year, too? Alas!

Analysis

The June 1914 issue introduces the use of the hyphen in the following situations:

a. close modifier + modified: 우리-글, 남-의-손
b. close [N + verb]: 성명-없은, 나라-일흔, 범-같은, 사자-같은, 물-흐르듯
c. compound verbs/verb + auxiliary: 끌-고-오던, 들이어-놓아, 참다-못하야, 생각하여-보시 오!
d. other: 반만-년, 오-년, 벽-에-걸닌

The abbreviation of the vowel /-(ɨ)/ is an innovation. It is dropped mostly in the modifiers /-(ɨ)n, -(ɨ)l/, but also in the instrumental /-(ɨ)lo(se)/ and elsewhere. The only rule I can tease out is that it apparently can drop after any consonant except /l/ (perhaps because presence or absence of /ɨ/ determines the difference between phonetic [r] and [l]?). For example, /eps(ɨ)n, eps(ɨ)l, eps(ɨ)ni, t(ɨ)noph(ɨ)n/, and so on, but why /cɨc(ɨ)li/ instead of */c(ɨ)c(ɨ)li/, and why /tɨlko/ but /t(ɨ)le/, /kɨlk(ɨ)n/ but not */k(ɨ)lk(ɨ)n/?

Another new abbreviation, of /hʌ-/, is shown by the apostrophe: /'o/ for /(hʌ)o/, /halya'nta/ for /halya (hʌ)nta/, /toyl lila'n pep/ for /toyl lila (hʌ)n pep/, /unsu la'n/ for /unsu la (hʌ)n/. This issue drops the /ɨ/ of "ɨ-dropping" verbs before the infinitive: /tte/ 'opens the eyes', and not */ttɨ e/.

Of the two other uses of the apostrophe in this issue, one is reminiscent of the previous issue: /na'y/ < /na uy/ 'my'. The other serves to separate a final vowel from *sai-siot* in /palphil ttay's il/ 'the time when was trampled'. The han'gŭl would have been 밟힐 때 ㅅ 일.

This orthography writes the initial /l-/ in Sino-Korean words (e.g., /Li Kap, lyekwan, lyakhʌ-, lyeksa/), ignores the /kk/ in the honorific particle /-(k)keyse/ and question /-(k)ka/, writes /ln/ for /ll/, and tends to write /C + ey/ where SS now writes /C + yey/ (/pheyha, seykey/ versus SS /phyey-, -kyey/).

The lack of lenition of /p/ in "*p*-irregular verbs" (/nup.esnolamyen, telep.(ɨ)n, oylop.(ɨ)n/) must be for the same reason the previous issue wrote /-s-/ in /cis-/ 'create'—influence of the Hamgyŏng dialect(s) spoken by most Koreans on Russian territory and/or strict morphophonemic treatment of verbs.

A more peculiar feature is the preservation of base /-l/ in the modifier form of "*l*-extending verbs" (only one example: /mantɨln/ for /mantɨ-n/). Unlike the previous issues, this one abandons han'gŭl character + V (e.g., /ie/ = /ye, ie/) in favor of reinstating the four graphs ㅠ, ㅛ, ㅕ, and ㅑ on-line.

/motum/ is dialect for /moim/ 'a collection (of examples?)', and /oypay/ appears to be a neologism for "orthography."

On-line Writing in Russia: Summary

The on-line materials from the *Taehanin chhyŏnggyobo* reveal a certain frustration with the vagaries of unstandardized traditional Korean spelling and the often arbitrary conventions imposed by conventional syllabic (*moa ssɨgi*) writing. They also suggest a bold spirit of innovation and experimentation. The *Taehanin chhyŏnggyobo* authors grappled with problems like terminology (neologisms), semivowels and diphthongs (phonetic /yV-, wV-/, orthographic /-Vy/ in the case of /ay/ = [æ], /ey/ = [e]), letter shapes (zero versus the old /ng/ with a hat, the *arae a*, geminated consonants versus *s*-clusters), diacritics (to distinguish /Vy/ from /Vi/, for vowel length, and for abbreviations), spacing, phonemic versus morphophonemic writing (their treatment of Sino-Korean and their rendition of morphophonemic alternations in ɨ-dropping verbs and l-extending verbs suggest they were hard-line morphophonemicists), how closely to mimic the traditional orthography (they kept traditional /ty-, cy-, sy-/), and which variety of Korean to write (the decision to ignore lenition in "*p*-irregular" and "*s*-irregular" verbs was probably related to the dialect of Koreans in Russia). Many of these problems and some of their solutions reappeared in the Soviet period.

THE SOVIET PERIOD

Before examining the Korean orthography of materials published in the USSR until the deportation of the Soviet Koreans in 1937, let us, for the sake of comparison, review the situation in Korea for the same period.

With the annexation of Korea by Japan in 1910, all matters of Korean language policy fell into the hands of the Korean Government-General. In April of 1912, the colonial authorities issued the *Pot'ong hakkyo-yong ŏnmun ch'ŏltcha pŏp*, or "Korean Script Orthography for Use in Elementary Schools," the first official orthography to be implemented since the beginning of the Enlightenment Period. The features of this orthography were

use of *arae a*, but only in Sino-Korean vocabulary (hence, a practical reduction from twenty-five letters to twenty-four);
/sC/ for the tense, unaspirated consonant series;
ten *patch'im*, or syllable-final consonants: /k, n, l, m, p, s, ng, lk, lm, lp/;
dot to the left for long vowels.

This system remained in effect until March of 1921, when the Japanese authorities issued the *Ŏnmun ch'ŏltcha pŏp taeyo* (Summary Korean Script Orthography), but the only significant difference from the 1912 scheme was the abandoning of the dot for long vowels.

A significant change came in February 1930, with the *Ŏnmun ch'ŏltcha pŏp* (Korean Script Orthography), which finally abolished the *arae a* altogether. Other features of this third Korean Government-General orthography were

significant moves toward the morphophonemic principle, for example, new *patch'im*:[15] /t, th, c, ch, ph, kk, ks, nc, lth, lph, ps/;
adoption of the free-standing *sai-siot*: NOUN ㅅ NOUN;
repudiation of palatalization (갈치 versus 같이, 밭치 versus 밭이);
modernization of Chinese character readings (뎍당 > 적당);
use of geminates rather than /sC/ for the tense unaspirates.

The Chosŏnŏ hakhoe (Korean Language Society) announced its own Unified Orthography (the *Han'gŭl ma[t]ch'umpŏp t'ongil an*) in 1933, introducing, for example, the *h -patch'im* for the first time, but its scheme could not be put into practice until after Liberation.

Summarizing the orthography policies implemented under the Japanese, Kim Minsu remarks: "Insofar as our language and writing were the national language of a colonized people, we must first wonder what their [the Japanese rulers'] goal was, but we should recognize that, in orthography, there were no politics or idealism" (1973: 230). This situation contrasts starkly with the situation across the border in the Soviet Far East.[16]

Korean Language and Writing in Their Soviet Context

Western students of Soviet language policy in its first phases are unanimous in their praise for the idealism and above all the progressive ideas behind the sweeping changes ushered in by the Bolshevik Revolution of 1917. Lenin's revolution promised national (ethnic) self-determination and respect for minority rights, and a concomitant struggle against "Great Russian chauvinism."

This implied a reluctance to force the Russian language and writing system on other peoples and a greater emphasis on the role and future of national languages. The first decade of Soviet power emphasized *korenizatsija* ("nativization" or "local rooting"), an ethnic policy that saw language policy as a tool for cultural development, and the Soviets recorded great successes, for example, in the eradication of illiteracy in the 1920s and 1930s.

Few of the languages of the Russian Empire had an established written language before the twentieth century. Crisp lists Kazan' Tatar, Azeri, Chagatai, Georgian, Armenian, and other Slavonic and Baltic languages as exceptions (1989: 41), but Korean belongs here, too. However, it cannot be said that Korean had a well-established (i.e., standardized) written form at this time, and this fact did not escape the attention of Soviet Korean intellectuals, Soviet cultural planners, and pro-latinization zealots (see King ms. 1997).

Baskakov writes that before the October Revolution only four peoples had their own national scripts: the Russians, the Armenians, the Georgians, and the Jews (1972: 6), again omitting the Koreans. On page 9, he outlines the following stages in the development of writing systems in the USSR:

1. 1918–1926: perfection of existing writing systems (no effect on illiteracy)
2. 1926–1936: latinization; rejection of complicated old systems
    a. 1918–1926: transfer in separate national centres
    b. 1926–1929: "unification" advanced as slogan, esp. for Turkic
    c. latinization and unification of huge number of writing systems
3. 1937–1941: "great attraction of the people for the Russian language and Russian culture" leads to a switch to Cyrillic script

Now let us look at the specific case of Korean in the USSR. Period 1, the perfection of existing writing systems, lasts until 1930 in the case of Korean in the Soviet Far East.

Experimentation with Han'gŭl in the Soviet Far East

According to Kim Synxva (Kim Sŭnghwa), the first Soviet book for adults in the Korean language was a Korean translation of the textbook *Doloj negramotnost'* (Away with Illiteracy!) completed in 1924 (1965: 214).[17] The Korean title of this book is *Musik ɨl epsi hanɨn calani ɨy tokpon* (An Adult Reader for Doing Away with Ignorance), published in 1925 in fifteen thousand copies. The preface, dated December 1923, contains the following remarks about orthography and the Korean language:

> In the case of technical terms and phrases that there is no way to express in Korean (e.g., "class struggle"), we had to write them all in Chinese characters. Nonetheless, we believe that if we Koreanize such expressions and put them into use, there will be no difficulties. In any case, from now on we must pay attention to such matters. . . .
>
> In reading this book, the following point should be kept in mind: *we have introduced reforms (though not completely) into the traditional orthography. In Korea, the Korean orthography remains unfixed*, and one can observe that when people commit things to writing each writes in a way different from the next. Thus, if some write /path ey/ [in the field], there are others who write /pas.hey/ or /pat.hey/, etc. We must put right this evil practice at the earliest possible date. . . .
>
> The Russian alphabet has no more than thirty letters, and recently the letters Ѣ and і were abolished to give twenty-eight. The Korean alphabet originally had twenty-eight letters, then twenty-seven and subsequently twenty-five, but recently it was revised again to the point where it has only twenty-four letters. Thus, the history of writing is one of endless change. (Emphasis mine)

This publication contains a few quirks in its orthography and language not found in later Soviet Korean publications: (1) abbreviation of base-final vowel + infinitive vowel as in /payhwasta/ 'learned', as opposed to the later strict isolation of infinitive vowels: /payhoasta/; (2) occasional spelling of /-mnikka, -mnita/ versus later /-pnik(k)a, -pnita/ (though there are also a few occurrences in PC 1926); (3) occasional writing of /sye/ in pure Korean grammatical morphemes, as in /-eysye/ 'at; from', /-myensye/ 'while doing' (also once or twice in SH 1927: /-eysye; kɨlaysye/); and (4) spelling of the copula as both /NOUN-ilta/ and /NOUN-ila/ (rarely in PC 1926).

After the *Adult Reader*, Soviet Korean textbooks (and all other publications) from the period 1923 to 1929 are written in a sometimes inconsistent but nonetheless more or less uniform orthography that strove to adhere to the "morphophonemic principle" rather than to the "traditional" phonemic spelling. That is, the official (though apparently unstated) policy was to write verbal bases consistently (base /mek-/ 'eat' as /mek.nɨn, mek.e/ (먹– everywhere) and not /mek.nɨn, me.ke/ (먹– before following consonants, 머ㄱ– before vowels).

The other salient features of the Soviet Korean orthography after 1923 and up to 1930 are as follows:

1. writing of Sino-Korean word-initial /l/ before all vowels:
/lo.lyek/ 'labor', /la.pal/ 'bugle', /lyen.e/ 'salmon', /lichi/ 'reason', /lyangsik/ 'provisions', /layil/ 'tomorrow' (PA; NB 1929); /lyulichang/ 'window', /lak-tyey/ 'failure', /lyu ha-/ 'to stay at a place' (PA 1927).

2. preservation of word-initial /n/ before /i, y/:
/ni, ni.ppal/ 'tooth' (PA; PC 1926); /nima/ 'forehead' < MK /ni·mah/ (though usually /ima/) (PA 1924; SH 1929); /nyekyesta; nyek.ye, nyekinɨn/ 'consider, deem', /nyemlye/ 'worry' (PA 1927). Occasionally one finds also /ni, ny-/ < SK /li, ly-/: /nithan/ 'peat' (KI 1929).

3. writing of /l.n/ for double /l.l/:
/changphi han ilno/ 'as an embarrassing thing' (NT 1925); /malno/ 'in words', /phalno/ 'with the arms' (PC 1926); /nol.ne kakela/ 'go and play', /kuulne kanta/ 'rolls along' (but also /kuulli-/), /talnang talnang/ 'ding-a-ling', /tɨl-no/ 'toward the field', /talnay/ 'wild garlic', /pulnesta/ 'called', /ilnesta/ 'told', /cintalney/ 'azalea', /kalna/ 'divide', /hɨlne/ 'flows', /malnasta/ 'dried up', /elnɨn/ 'at once', /celnumpali/ 'person with a limp', and so on. Sometimes one also finds /n.l/: /tɨnliesta/ 'could be heard' (PA 1927b).

In the case of "l-doubling bases," the /l/ in forms without doubling is isolated from the /ɨ/: /mol.ɨnɨn/ 'not knowing' (M 1925); /pul.ɨ.myense/ 'while calling' (PA 1924); /kil.ɨnɨn/ 'to raise (animals)' (PA 1924); /ccil.ɨnta/ 'pierces' (PA 1927b); /ccel.ɨta/ 'short' (M 1925; PC 1926); /ccal.ɨn/ 'short' (NB 1929; SH 1929). This is also true of other instances of "hangover" /ɨ/: /alph.ɨta/ 'it hurts', /sɨlph.ɨta/ 'is sad', /oll.ɨta/ 'ascends' (M 1925). Cf. also /kollɨ-/ 'choose' (KI 1929), /ppallɨ-/ 'quick' (SH 1929); and /nallɨ-/ 'to transport' (SH 1929).

4. writing of Sino-Korean /kɨy/ where SS now writes /ki/:
/kɨy/ ‘flag’, /pihayngkɨy/ ‘airplane’, /chunkɨy/ ‘spring season’, /kongkɨy/ ‘air’, /kɨynami/ (boy’s name).

5. writing of /ɨy/ in pure Korean words where SS now writes /i/:
/kɨytali-/ ‘wait for’,[18] /sɨyacɨpeni, sɨyapeni/ ‘uncle-in-law, father-in-law (of woman)’ (M 1925); /ttɨy/ ‘belt’, /otɨy/ ‘mulberry’, /tetɨy; tetɨykey/ ‘slowly’, /kyentɨy-/ ‘endure, stand it’, /kekɨy/ ‘there’, /cekɨy/ ‘yonder’, /yekɨy/ ‘here’, /cohɨy/ ‘paper’, /sɨlkɨy/ ‘wisdom, wits’ (but also /sɨlki/) (PA); /skɨɨl.e tɨyli-/ ‘recruit’, and so forth.

But note also /hɨn/ ‘white’ everywhere (also /hisɨkhisɨk han/ ‘greyish’ in PA 1927); /yuhi/ ‘game, amusement’ (PA; PC 1926); /hi.mang/ ‘hope’ (PC 1926); usually /kei/ for SS /keɨy/ ‘nearly; almost all’.

6. /ay.a/ where SS now has /āy/:
/kay.ami/ ‘ant’, /may.ami/ ‘cicada’, /pay.ami/ ‘snake’, /nay.amsay/ ‘smell’, and /ka.ya.mi/ ‘ant’ (PA 1927).

7. treatment of “*t*-irregular” verbs
Typically, these are treated as being /l/-final underlyingly, with the *t* pronunciation before following consonants noted either as plain /l/ or as the final /-l/ followed by a freestanding /s/(!).[19] Sometimes the sources write simply /-s/ (*t*): /kkaytalko/ ‘realize’ (M 1925); /kelnɨnta, kelnɨn kesi/ ‘walks’, /silko, sil.ɨn, silnɨn/ ‘transports’, /mulnɨnta/ ‘asks’, /talnɨnta/ ‘runs’, /kkaytasci mos hayesta/ ‘did not realize’, /tɨl nɨnta/ ‘listens’; /tɨl.s.ko, tɨl.s.ki lɨl, tɨl.s.ten/ ‘listens’, /mul.s.cianihako/ ‘did not ask, and…’, /mul.s.toy/, /mul.s.ki lɨl/ (also: /mulnɨn/, /tɨl nɨn, tɨlnolako/), /cim to sil.s.ko, sil.s.ci malko/ ‘carries luggage’ (also /silnɨn, silnɨntey/), /kel.s.ci mos hanta/, /kelnɨn kes/ ‘walking’, /kkaytal.s.ko, kkaytal.s.ki lɨl, kkaytal.s.key/ ‘realize’ (PA 1927); /kel.s.ki/ ‘walk’, /talko/ ‘run, and…’ (PA 1927b); /mulnɨn/ ‘ask’, /al.a tɨlkey/ ‘(hear and) understand’ (PC 1926); /musnɨn/ ‘ask’ (Pro 1929); /tɨski/ ‘listen’, /silnɨn/ ‘load’, /kkaytalki/ ‘realize’ (KI 1929); /silko/ ‘load’ (NB 1929); /silnɨnta, sil.ɨlye kanta, silkekcil, silko/ ‘carting, loading’ (SH 1929); and so on.

8. preservation of /c(h)ya, c(h)ye, c(h)yo, c(h)yu/, /t(h)ya, t(h)ye, t(h)yo, t(h)yu/, and /sya, sye, syo, syu/ in some texts:[20]
M 1925 has /honcasye/ ‘alone’, /hamyensye/ ‘while doing’ (also /hamyense/), /musyepta/ ‘scary, frightening’, /syensayng/ ‘teacher’, /musyu ha-/ ‘numerous’, /kopcyel/ ‘double’, /tyek/ ‘enemy’, /cyelkalak, cye.kalak,

ce.kalak/ 'chopstick', /syeng han/ 'healthy, fit', /chyenli/ 'a thousand *li*', /posyen/ 'Korean-style socks', /cyen ey/ 'before', /tyeyil/ 'most, best', /thyenti/ 'Heaven and Earth', and so on. Also: /cyek.ecies.ɨna/ 'got small, but…', /cyulki/ 'stem', /… eysye/ 'at' (once in PA 1927), /cyenyek/ 'evening', /kek-cyeng/ 'worry', /nunsyep/ 'eyebrow', /cyelm.ɨn/ 'young', /cyongyong ha-/ 'quiet', /yekicyeki/ 'here and there', /syu.ken/ 'towel, handkerchief' (PA 1927); /cuk.ɨn chey/ and /cuk.ɨn thyey/ 'pretending to be dead' (PA 1927b); /tyosyen/ 'Korea' (AP 1926). NB 1929 also has /tye, sye/ and so on.

9. writing of /h/:
/cohɨy, cohi/ 'paper', /nonh.a mek-/ 'share and eat', /payhonta, payhoasso/ 'learns', /ssahom/ 'fight', /mohi-/ 'to gather (intr.)' (PA; PC 1926); /nanhu-/ 'divide', /yeho/ 'fox', /ilhey/ 'seven days', but always /nei(tɨl)/ 'you (pl.)' (cf. SS /ne-huy(-tul)/).

10. "difficult" and "happy" have /s.p/:
/paspɨta/, /kisputa, kispue/ (M 1925); /kispehanta/ (PA 1924, but PA 1926 /ki.ppe/).

11. regular lack of "*p*-lenition":[21]
/tulyepɨn kes/ 'frightening thing', /sanap.ɨn/ 'violent, vicious', /musyep.ɨn/ 'scary', /CA.YUlop.ɨn/ 'free', /cɨlkep.ɨmye/ 'enjoyable', (M 1925); /etup.ɨn/ 'dark', /kop.ɨn/ 'pretty', /mukepecesta/ 'got heavy'. But there are occasional deviations: /toɨm/ 'help' (M 1925); /toatalna/ '(asked for) help.'[22]

12. Unumlauted forms (actually more of a dialect problem than an orthographic one):
/talakki/ 'basket with small opening', /ttali-/ 'hit, strike' (PA; PC 1926); /kiltongi lɨl taliko/ 'taking Kiltong-i with him', /ca.mi iss-/ 'is fun, interesting', /kongcungcep.i/ 'somersault' (SS /kongcwung-ceypi/), /kwangi/ 'hoe, pick' (PA 1927); and so on.

13. /C.C; C.h/ versus SS /CC, Ch/:
/kop.pi/ 'reins', /cik.hye cunta/ 'guards for somebody' (PA; SH 1929), /sik.hyesta/ 'made do' (if not /siki-/), /tuk.kepi/ 'toad', /kak.kɨm/ 'from time to time', /utuk.heni/ 'absentmindedly' (PA 1927; SH 1930), /ttuk.keng/ 'cover, top' (PA 1927), /pat.hi-/ 'gives to superior' (cf. SS /pachita/)(PA 1927); /it.hɨnnal/ (PA 1927) 'the next/second day' (SS /i.thut-nal/), /it.hɨl/ (PA 1927b) 'two days' (SS /i.thul/); /mac.huta/ 'to make fit, conform to' (SS /ma.chwu-, macchwu-), /kac.hu-/ 'equips' (SS /kacchwu-/), /kek.kul.ecesta/

'got turned upside down' (SS /ke.kkwule cyessta/) (PA 1927b); /ek.kay/ 'shoulder', /nɨk.kim/ 'feeling' (PC 1926); /tok.ki/ 'ax' (SH 1930), and so on.

14. "roll" (= SS /kwūl-, kwulu-/ < MK /ku[G]ɨl-/):
/kuɨllimyen/ 'if you make roll' (PA 1924); /kuɨlesta/ and /kupɨlmyense/ (PA 1927, SH 1929); /kupɨnɨn/ 'rolling' (SH 1929).

15. Preservation of /ɨ/ after coronals (again, more a question of dialect than orthography):
/kyuchɨk/ 'rules', /achɨm/ 'morning', /maschɨmnay/ 'finally,' /matɨy/ 'joint; counter for songs' (PA; KI 1929); /ilcɨki/ 'early', /kecɨsmal/ 'lie', /ecɨlepɨn/ 'dizzy; messy', /kichɨm/ 'cough' (PA 1927); and so on.

16. unabbreviated negative particle /ani/, often spelled /an.i/: /ISANG hakey ani pointa/ 'do not look strange' (PA 1927); /chipci ani hakeysta/ 'will not be cold' (SH 1929). Also: negative copula /an.ita/.

17. /o/ for SS /wu/ (dialect more than orthography):
/kocho/ 'pepper', /tathom/ 'fight', /ssahom/ 'fight', /potɨlep-/ 'soft', /elkol/ 'face', /so.kkopcil/ 'playing house' (SS /so.kkupcil/), /caco/ 'often', /tomoci/ '(not) at all', /aco/ 'very', /hocho/ 'pepper' (M 1925); /nacong ey/ 'in the end' (PC 1926); and so on.

18. /ɨ/ for SS /wu/ (usually after labials, but also after coronals): /etɨpɨn/ 'dark', /nalsey ka kamɨle/ 'weather is dry' (PA 1927; KI 1929), /tɨmɨn/ 'sometimes', /pata.mɨl/ 'ocean, sea', /wensɨngi/ 'monkey', /a.mɨl CI.PANG/ 'the Amur region', /pɨl/ 'fire' (rarely) (PA 1927); /yemɨnɨn/ 'ripening' (KI 1929), /ppɨli/ 'root' /talɨ-/ 'to treat', /kolɨ/ 'evenly', /memɨl-/ 'stop, stay' (KI 1929); /ocɨk/ 'only', /moksɨm/ 'life', /philsu.phɨm/ 'essentials', /pɨ.the/ 'starting from' (SH 1927); and so on.

19. neutralizations (phonemic spelling slips):
/mis/ 'and' (M 1925; SH 1927); /thako sipta, thako sipci/ for SS /siph-/ (PA 1924); /palam to epta/ 'no wind' for SS /eps-/ (PA 1924; SH 1927); /sut.han/ 'numerous, many' (PA 1924) and /su.than/ (SH 1929) for SS /swuth ha-/; /putcapnɨnta, putcap.a/ 'catch hold of' for SS /puth-/ (PA 1926; PA 1927); /cipsin/ 'straw sandals' for SS /ciph-sin/, /sakcen/ 'wages' for SS /saks-/, /mulɨp kkaci/ 'up to the knee' for SS /muluph/ (PA 1927);[23] /septako malala/ 'Don't say you're sad' for SS /selp-/, /misci ani/ 'reach' for SS /mich-/ (PC 1926); /paywannɨnka/ "did I learn?" for SS /paywessnunka/ (Pro 1929);

/kipci mos ha-/ 'not deep' for SS /kiph-/, /isci mal-/ 'not forget' for SS /ic-/ (KI 1929); /mayskey/ 'so as to tie' for SS /mayc-/, /myes.hay/ 'several years' for SS /myech/, /pisnan/ 'brilliant' for SS /pich/, /pas.e/ 'receive' for SS /pat-/ (SH 1927); and so on.

20. other phonetic spellings, often with spurious *patch'im*:
/kasthi, kasthɨn/ 'together; like', /pusthe/ 'from, since', /kesche/ 'to pass through, experience', /nesnɨnta/ 'puts, places' (for SS /neh-/; cf. also /cis-nɨnta/ 'build, make', which is /cih-/ in all other Soviet materials), /pas.a cuesta, pas.a se, pasnɨnta, pas.tɨl.e/ 'receive/accept,' /skɨsnay-/ 'to finish it', /nas.hananta/ 'appear', /nasthana se/ 'come about' (AP 1926); /ap.phɨlo/ 'in future', /nasko/ 'is low, and...' (NT 1925); /maschɨmnay/ (also /machɨm-nay/) 'finally', /miskkɨle/ 'slippery', /ttɨsttɨs han/ 'warm', /kasche isko/ 'is locked up and...'; /tosci mos-/ 'sprout', /nɨskey/ 'late', /yesnɨn/ 'put, place'; /pasku-/ 'change, exchange' (KI 1929 has /pakk.u-/), /mas.ha; mas.hɨn/ 'be entrusted with' (cf. also /mas.ki-/ 'to entrust to somebody'), /kes.u-/ 'gather up, put in order', /kalɨschim, kalɨschiko/ 'teach', /tosi pota nah.ɨn/ 'better than the city', /noskho/ 'place and...', /sische/ 'wash and...', /pakkhwi/ 'wheel', /pasci; pasnɨn/ 'spit', /eps.say-/ 'get rid of', /ilestha/ 'is like this', /koschi-/ 'fix' (PC 1926); /kotchi-/ 'fix' (KI 1929); /ccosche ka-/ 'go in pursuit', /taschi-/ 'touch against', /noph.hɨkey/ 'high(ly)' (PC 1926); /kɨs.hi-/ 'end, finish', /paschim/ 'final consonant' (Pro 1929); /neschi mos/ 'cannot place', /kasthɨmyen, kasthɨn/ 'seem', /kip.phi/ 'deeply', /pusthe/ 'from' (SH 1927); /hwih.palam/ 'whistling', /myechchɨl/ 'several days' (SH 1929); and so on.

21. use of Chinese characters, even in beginning textbooks
The 1925 *Calani ɨy Tokpon* writes:

> From this chapter on we gradually include in places the simplest and most essential Chinese characters. But since this publication is nothing more than a pamphlet, it is impossible to include the Chinese characters for all things or technical terms, and in any case, even if we did include them all, learning so many of them in a short period would be an uncommonly difficult task.... We acknowledge that, in our society today where Chinese characters still exist, it is expedient to understand the simplest and most essential characters, and so, as far as possible, it is advisable for teachers to take every opportunity to teach, little by little, other essential characters that do not appear in this booklet.

> Chinese characters are much more difficult to learn than our national writing (*kungmun*), and many of them can carry several meanings. Thus, the teacher should be able to explain these and should also teach the correct stroke order and make the students practice the characters often. (P. 34)

One finds indiscriminately frequent use of Chinese characters in M 1925, and sixty-one characters are introduced in PA 1924 (volume 2).

22. velar palatalization (dialect more than orthography):
/cipnɨnta/ 'fixes, repairs' (PA 1924; SH 1930); /citong/ 'pillar', /cis/ 'share, portion', /cilsam/ 'weaving (by hand)' (= SS /kilssam/), /pay.s.cisɨlk/ 'edge/border of stomach' (PA 1927).

23. /a/ for SS /e/ (dialect more than orthography):
/ilh.e palyesta/ 'lost it', /nayye paliko/ 'throw away', /palse/ 'already' (PA 1927). Cf. SS/peli–/< MK/pʌ·li–/.

24. /sC/ for the tense series:
Besides a very few examples in other texts—for example, /pask.ey/ 'outside' (PA 1924; PC 1926);[24] /escay se/ and /e.stekhey/ 'how come' (PC 1926); and /spioneylɨ/ 'pioneer' (once in PS 1926)—the only source I have found that used /sC/ extensively for the tense unaspirates is NT25: /es.te.khey/ 'how; why?', /kɨ stay/ 'at that time', /sto/ 'moreover, in addition', /spulyesta/ 'scattered', /pulskos/ 'spark', /skaci/ 'until', /hamskey/ 'together', /sta.lase/ 'as a result', /skɨsnay-/ 'to finish', /skatalk/ 'reason', /skeytalko/ 'realize', /skɨɨl.e/ 'draw, attract', /skɨs/ 'end', /kas.kewe ci-/ 'get close' (PC 1926; Pro 1929); /pas.ku-/ 'change' (Pro 1929); /us.tuk han/ 'high, lofty' (KI 1929); /hamskey/ 'together', /i.stal.i/ 'Italy', /aphɨli.ska/ 'Africa', /ilskaywucu-/ 'enlighten', /skek.kul.e stɨliko/ 'knock down, overthrow', /stelchi-/ 'throw off', /skok/ 'without fail', /stam/ 'sweat', /skaci/ 'until', /stawi/ 'etcetera', /stɨs/ 'intention', /sca.lɨn/ 'short', /ka.skaun/ 'close', /aski-/ 'be stingy with' (NB 1929); /kis.pɨesta/ 'was happy' (SH 1929; SH 1930), /kas.kap.a onta/ 'is getting closer', /cas.pɨa ciesta/ 'fell on his back', /es.tehkey/ "how?", /esten/ 'some' (SH 1929); and so on.

25. /key/ for SS /kyey/:
/keysinta/ 'is, lives, exists (honorific),' /kwankey/ 'interest; relationship'. Also: /phey/ 'lungs' versus SS /phyey/ (PA 1927).

26. freestanding /-s-/ in compounds:
/hway.s.pul/ 'torch', /cohi.s.cang/ 'sheet of paper', /pha.s.mo/ 'onion shoots' (PA 1926); /tta.s.kulsuk ey/ 'inside the earth', /cay.s.pich/ 'the color of ashes', /twi.s.pal/ 'rear foot', /hwi.s.palam/ 'whistle; birdcall', /mul.s.kay/ 'water's edge' (= SS /mul-ka/), /yel.s.kay/ 'ten pieces', /twi.s.san/ 'mountain at the rear', /aphse.s.tal/ 'preceding month', /moy.s.pul/ 'forest fire', /kil.s.ka/ 'side of the road', /tatɨm.s.tay/ 'wooden club for fulling cloth', /u.s.os/ 'clothing', /cha.s.mul/ 'tea', /nay.s.mul/ 'stream', /moy.s.toth/ 'wild boar', /hay.s.pyeth/ 'sunshine', /pata.s.kay/ 'freshwater seal', /mul.s.koki/ 'fish', /mul.s.sal/ 'water current', /pata.s.koki/ 'ocean fish', /mul.s.kyel/ 'waves', /pay.s.meli/ 'prow of a boat', /pa.s.koli/ 'rope with a ring on it (for fishing things out of the water)', /soy.s.tengi/ 'clump of metal', /olay.s.tongan/ 'for a long time', /cem.s.kun/ 'miner', /poksa.s.tem/ 'slag heap in a mine(?)', /ni.s.sai/ 'between the teeth' (PA 1927); /il.s.kun/ 'worker' (PA 1927; KI 1929); /kɨ monci.s.kaontay/ 'among the dust', /cha.s.sul/ 'teaspoon' (PA 1927); /moy.s.cwi/ 'wild mouse' (KI 1929). But NB 1929 spells out a policy of *ignoring* compound fortification.

27. Only one example of *arae a*: /-ey stʌla/ 'according to' (SH 1927).

28. The NB29 distinguishes zero from /ng/ (ㅇ vs. ㆁ).

The following types of unusual spellings appeared.

1. isolation of the infinitive vowel, even in ɨ-dropping bases:
/oll.a kao/ 'goes up', /oll.ela/ 'go up!',[25] /nonh.a meknɨnta/ 'shares and eats', /emeni lɨl ttal.a/ 'following Mother', /capp.ecesta/ 'fell down', /oassɨpnita/ 'came', /khɨeci-/ 'get big', /cɨlkie hanta/ 'enjoys', /ttɨetanninɨn/ 'floating' (but /ttenanta/ 'departs'), /kennɨe/ 'to cross', /motɨala!/ 'Gather!', /simɨesten/ 'that had been planted', /khɨese nɨn/ 'grow up and. . . ', /sɨlphɨe hanɨn/ 'sad', /ki.ppɨe hanɨn/ 'happy', /ssɨe poala/ 'try writing!' (rarely), /ssɨesta/ 'wore a hat', /ssɨenoh.asta/ 'wrote down' (PA 1927); /ssɨe/ 'writes' (Pro 1929); /khɨe/ 'big' (Met 1929); /chie/ 'clear out' (KI 29); /pullɨesta/ 'called', /ollɨa/ 'go up' (SH 1929). NB 1929 declares as policy the isolation of the infinitive vowel in ɨ-dropping bases.

2. underlying etymological /h/ is spelled out:
/suh.talk/ 'cock' and /amh.talk/ 'hen' (PA 1924; SH 1929; but PA 1926 /su.talk, amtalk/); /amh.so/ 'cow' (PA 1924; SH 1929); /su.h.kes/ 'male of species', /am.h.kes/ 'female of species' (PA 1927); /amh.kay/ 'bitch' (SH 1929).

3. treatment of l-extending bases:
/caln mal/ 'small-talk; guff' (but /canmal; kilta, nun men/ in PA 1926), /kiln.ta, kiln.ecinta, kiln, kilnko/ 'long,' /cip eyse meln.ta/ 'is far from home'; /kilko, kilta, kil.mɨlo/ (PA 1927; for the latter ending, cf. also /sal.mɨlo/ 'because they live'). Cf. also /ul.ɨsimyen/ 'if she cries' (PC 1926).

4. new han'gŭl letters:
ㅇㅂ for /v/ in ᄫᅢᆯ라지보스뚝, ᄫᅢᆯ라지보스또크 'Vladivostok'; double initial /ll-/ in /lleynin/ 'Lenin' (PA; NB 1929). NB 1929 notes: "The new letter /ll/ is not used in Korean" (p. 27).[26] NH 1929 also has ㅇㅈ, in the personal name 쬐, 야, ㅇㅈ. (Ja. Tsoi), but it is not clear what Russian letter it represents (probably Ж = /zh/).

5. occasional use of doubled vowels to represent vowel length:
/keeci/ 'beggar', /mulkaam/ 'dye', /peeli/ 'earning', /kkɨɨlko/ 'pulls, and...' (PA 1927). NB 1929 instructs the teacher to give examples of words that are distinguished by vowel length.

6. pseudo-etymological spellings, that is, attempts to keep etymology clear by writing known (or supposed) bases or endings as separate morphs:
/nanh.u-/ 'divide' and /nonh.a/ 'share' (M 1925); /san.yang/ 'hunting' (PA; SH 1929 has /san.yeng/); /al.ey/ 'below' (PA 1924 and M 1925, but PA 1926 /a.lay/); /macnasta/ 'met', /hɨnh.i/ 'often', /han.a/ 'one', /ciph.eyngi/ 'cane', /nem.u/ 'too much', /puth.e/ 'from, since', /halhɨ/ 'one day', /myech.hɨl/ 'a few days', /pich.oy-/ 'to shine', /mactang ha-/ 'is appropriate', /pilos.o/ 'for the first time', /mac.u o-/ 'come out to meet, come toward', /ecekk.ey/ 'day before yesterday' (PA 1927); /alh.pɨm, alh.pɨci anhkey, alph.ɨki/ 'pain, hurt' (PA 1927; SH 1930); /ket.u-/ 'take care of, look after' (SS /ke.twu-/), /nacpɨn/ 'bad', /mun.eci-/ 'fall down, collapse' (versus SS /mu.neci-/) (PA 1927); /tol.o/ 'back (adv.)' (SS /tolo/), /cickeli-/ 'chatter' (SS /ci.kkeli-/), /chac.i ha-/ 'take charge of' (SS /cha.ci ha-/), /eps.say-/ 'get rid of' (PA 1927b); /sikh.i-, sikh.ye/ 'make do', /cikh.i-/ 'guard, keep', /nanh.o-/ 'divide', /tal.ɨ-/ 'different', /pul.ɨ-/ 'call' (PC 1926); /hɨl.ɨ-/ 'flow' (KI 1929); /puch.i-/ 'affix' (PC 1926), /kac.iko/ 'carry', /salph.i-/ 'to examine' (Pro 1929); /kil.u-/ 'raise, bring up', /pay kkɨlh.pɨm/ 'seething anger in stomach' (NB 1929); /pay ka kolhpɨ-/ 'hungry' (SH 1929; SH 1930); /silh.kkɨth mek-/ 'eat to one's heart's content' (SH 1929); /himkkɨth/ 'with all one's strength' (SH 1930); /ttakttak.ul.i/ 'woodpecker' (SS /ttaktakwuli/) (SH 1929); and so on.

7. nonmorphemic spellings:
/mu.te tan.iesta/ 'attached itself and went around', /soli chesta/ 'yelled, screamed', /tɨ.lye wasta/ 'carried it inside', /ttelecesta/ 'fell down', /cal.asta/ 'grew', /kace oko/ 'bring and...', /nɨl.ecesnɨntey/ 'was extended' (PA 1927); /cci.ce se/ 'tears and...', /muk.kie/ 'gets bound' (SS /mukk.i-/) (PA 1927b); /mok.si/ 'one's share, lot' (SS /moks/) (M 1925); /man.hɨn/ 'many' (/manh.an/ in KI29), /ol.hɨn/ 'correct, right', /ile.thɨ.si/ 'in this manner' (NT 1925); /i.ce pali-/ 'forget', /cowa ha-/ 'to like', /phece se/ 'spread and...', /ku.cɨn mul/ 'dirty water', /ssa.he se/ 'build up', /ssɨ.se/ 'wash and...' (PC 1926); /ka.cɨn/ 'all sorts of', /ep.sɨl, ep.sɨm/ 'not exist', /ne.hesta/ 'placed', /kul.me cuk-/ 'starve to death', /ka.thi/ 'like', /sco.cha kasta/ 'chased after', /no.hɨn/ 'placed', /hɨ.the ceisnɨn/ 'scattered', /stɨ.keun/ 'hot', /skɨ.le/ 'recruit', /pɨ.the/ 'starting from', /pu.thɨl/ 'attach', /nop.hɨn/ 'high', /tɨlici an.kho/ 'not accept', /pa.tɨmye/ 'accept', /man.hɨn/ 'many', /e.tɨl su ista/ 'can accept', /cha.ca/ 'seek', /hayes.sɨna/ 'did, but...' (SH 1927). NB 1929 writes: "When writing, you must write knowing the roots of the words. If you write something the way it sounds, this is a mistake" (p. 34).

8. "make; build" (SS /cis-/ < MK /:ciz-/):
/cihko, ciɨl, pap cihnɨn, cih.e cun kes, kɨl ɨl cih.e, cih.ko poni/ and so on. These are odd, as MK /cih-/ meant only "attach (a name)."

9. PA 1927 has an example of a floating /h/: /kho.h.kil.i/ 'elephant'.

10. I have found one or two examples in PA 1927 of what appear to be Chinese characters meant to be read in their pure Korean /saykim/ glosses: /CHUN kwa HA ey...CHU ey...TONG ey/ 'in spring and summer...in autumn...in winter', SIPSI CEN imyen/ 'if it be before ten o'clock', /WUNG ɨn.../ 'as for bears...', /CHI/ (PA 1927, heading for a section on "teeth").

11. /poki ey koɨpki to/ '(is) indeed beautiful to look at' (PA 1927):
This seems to be an attempt to capture the long vowel of SS /kōp-/ 'beautiful'.

12. "remain" (= SS /nām-/ < MK /:nam-/):
/nalm.ɨn, nalm.a issnɨn, nalmko/ (PA 1927). Cf. also /nalm.aci/ 'remainder' (PA 1927, but also /namaci/. KI 1929 has /nalm.eci/). (PC 1926 also has /nalm.eci/).

13. TOPIC + hyphen (rarely):
/ca.yen ɨn -.../ (PA 1927). This is a Russian usage.

14. "build a nest": /ki.ttɨli-/ (PA 1927) versus SS /kis-tulita/.

15. /ey/ for genitive /ɨy/:
/twi ey salam...aph ey salam/ 'people in back...people in front" (PC 1926), and so on.

Much of the variation in Soviet Korean orthography ends in 1930 with the publication of O Ch'anghwan's *Koryŏ munjŏn* (Korean Grammar). O Ch'anghwan's name begins to appear as coauthor on Korean language textbooks from 1929, including the *New Primer for Adults* (NB 1929), from which we have seen many attempts at policy statements above. Little is known yet about O Ch'anghwan's background, but it would appear that he was born in the Russian Far East and was in one of the first classes to graduate from the Korean Pedagogical Institute in Xabarovsk. He was clearly a bright man and seems to have been influenced by Kim Tubong (1922).

The publication of his *Koryŏ munjŏn* prompted a debate with his rival, Ke Pongu,[27] on the pages of the Soviet Korean newspaper *Sŏnbong* in 1930. In a series of eight short articles called "*Koryŏ munjŏn* and My Research," Ke Pongu took issue with many of the positions adopted in O Ch'anghwan's grammar. In issue 501, he criticizes O Ch'anghwan's use of the word *chaŭm* 'consonant' rather than the traditional *chongsŏng* and *ch'osŏng* 'final' and 'initial'. In issue 502, he comes out against writing /p/ in the "*p*-irregular verbs" and wants to write /wu/ rather than /p/ in the lenited forms. He also criticizes O Ch'anghwan's treatment of *l*-extending bases like /nō-l-/ 'play', and wants to distinguish zero and /ng/ in writing by resurrecting the sign ㆁ. Then, he writes, we could write 소아지 'calf' rather than 송아지, 리어 'carp' rather than 링어, and so forth. Ke Pongu blames Ch'oe Sejin and the *Ŏnmun panjŏl* system of arranging Korean syllables for the current state of confusion!

In issue 503, Ke Pongu continues his critique of O Ch'anghwan's treatment of the irregular verbs. Thus, in the *Koryŏ munjŏn*, "*t*-irregular" verbs are treated as changing final /-l/- to /-s/ (i.e., phonetic [-t]) before consonant-initial endings: /tul-/ 'listen' > /tus-ca, tus-ko/. "Why does he regard ㅂ as so important, ㄹ so lightly?" asks

Ke Pongu. Ke Pongu wants to write /tul-kko/ for 듣고, /kel-tta/ for 걷다, and so on. In this piece, Ke Pongu also comes out in favor of writing the freestanding *sai-siot* in compounds like /may.s.tol/. As precedent, he cites Kim Senam's *Yŏgŏ yuhae* [*Yek.e* ˡ*yuhay*] and Pak Sŏngwŏn's *Chŏn'gŭm t'ongsŏk*, and even the Japanese *tu*.

In issue 504, Ke Pongu wants to change the "-lu- [-rŭ-]" of *l*-doubling verbs to "-nŭ-", and claims forms like /hulle/ 'flows' are actually pronounced *hŭlnŏ*! Likewise, /pullanse/ 'France' should be *pulnansŏ*, /sewul lo/ 'to Seoul' should be *sŏul no*, and so on.[28]

Ke Pongu's piece in issue 506 is titled "Vowel Length Is Useless." Claiming that the "four tones" of the *Hunmin chŏng'ŭm* are the result of "Chinese poisoning," he complains that "there are no strict rules for when words have short or long vowels." If the "four tones" were pernicious influence from Chinese, the length distinction is "poisoning" from Kim Tubong (1922), in this case slavishly imitating Western languages. "So," challenges Ke Pongu, "how shall we distinguish /mal/ 'words', /mal/ 'horse', /mal/ 'unit of measure', and /mal/ 'duckwood' by vowel length? If there is no way to distinguish each one of these separately, then vowel length has no use."

In issue 507, Ke Pongu continues his discussion of vowel length. Here, he attacks O Ch'anghwan's decision to abbreviate words like /cheum/ 'first' and /maum/ 'mind' to /chem/ and /mam/ on the grounds that the abbreviation obscures the etymology of the words in question.

In issue 508, he returns to the problem of /l/ and /n/: "/l/ and /n/ are different; why claim they 'change into each other'?" Again, he claims the /n/ is pronounced as such in /ppalnay/ 'laundry' and so forth. Ke Pongu complains that O Ch'anghwan's assimilation rules are wrong: "If the rule is /k/ > /ng/ before ㅇ, then 백어 /payk.e/ should become 뱅어 /paynge/, 오직어 /ocik.e/ should become 오징어 /ocinge/, and so on." O Ch'anghwan writes that /l, m, p, k/ become /n/ before /l/ (/toklip/ 'independence', /kanglyeng/ '(party) platform'), but for Ke Pongu these are just *sŭpkwanŭm*, "sounds formed by habit."[29] Ke Pongu just cannot seem to get this.

In issue 510, Ke Pongu attacks O Ch'anghwan's use of the terms /cepmi myengsa/ 'suffix noun' and /cenchi hyengyongsa/ 'prefix adjective', preferring /ceptwue/ 'suffix word' and /cepmie/ 'prefix word', respectively. In his defense, he claims that "first there were verbs, then adjectives, then the noun," betraying an exposure to the "Stadial theory" of N. Marr.[30] Ke Pongu continues this theme of etymological derivation in issues 511 and 512, giving a number of ridiculous etymologies and criticizing some of O Ch'anghwan's spellings on supposedly etymological grounds. Thus, /ta.li/ 'leg' should be /tal.i/, because etymologically this is connected with /tal-/ 'to run' and because there is no such suffix as /-li/! The words /salam, cwukem, mutem, palam/ 'person, corpse, grave, wind' should be written /sal.um, cwuk.um, mut.um, pal.um/, so O Ch'anghwan is incapable of distinguishing /e.kun/ 'word roots' from /cepmi/ 'suffixes'.

With respect to words like /kalwu, namu/ 'powder, tree', which O Ch'anghwan has becoming /kalki, namki/ in the nominative,[31] Ke Pongu takes issue not with the dialect nature of the nominative forms, but with the spelling: these should be /kal.wu, nam.wu, phulm.wu, twum.wu, kul.wu, sil.wu, pul.wu, mal.wu, cal.wu, nol.wu, mel.wu, nal.wu/, because "/-wu/ is a noun suffix," and the rest are roots.

In two lengthy replies in issues 515 and 516 under the title "After Reading '*Koryŏ munjŏn* and My Research,' " O Ch'anghwan reveals the process by which his own manuscript was selected over Ke Pongu's by the Department of Education and accuses Ke Pongu of sour grapes.

O Ch'anghwan's manuscript was subjected to criticisms and corrections at two different conferences, one in May 1929, the other in January 1930. As can be seen from the following excerpts from the foreword, the *Koryŏ munjŏn* was published as a normative grammar, establishing a new orthography and a system for teaching Korean grammar in the approximately three hundred Korean schools in the Soviet Far East:

> The goal of the Ministry of Education in publishing this book is that in the near future all will take this book as the standard in the course of unifying the Korean grammar of Maritime Koreans in all aspects of education, publishing and culture....
>
> The People's Ministry of Education, Maritime Region, Far East, while affirming that this book is the only grammar to be considered standard in Korean orthography and composition by all individuals and organs engaged in Korean education, publishing, culture, and so on, in the Maritime Region, also acknowledges that...there are bound to be many defects in the book.

> ...Before any official revisions of the contents of this book, every organ and individual engaged in Korean education, publishing, or culture in the Maritime Region must observe strictly the regulations on Korean orthography and usage in this book.

(For more on O Ch'anghwan's important grammar and his official orthography, see King 1991c.)

Thus, the Soviet Koreans had established an official, standardized orthography for Korean fully three years before the Chosŏnŏ hakhoe's Unified Orthography (1933).

Han'gŭl Orthography in the Soviet Far East: Summary

The han'gŭl materials published in the Soviet Far East from 1923 until O Ch'anghwan's grammar appeared in 1930 show a wide array of interesting and experimental features, some of which echo the experiments with on-line han'gŭl writing some dozen years earlier in Siberia. Many of the features survived as part of the official Soviet Korean orthography until the deportation of the Soviet Koreans in 1937.

The Soviet materials strove for a largely morphophonemic orthography, so much so that they often kept the infinitive vowel separate from the verb base at the expense of creating new and bizarre *patch'im* like double /ll/ (*l*-doubling bases) and /ln/ (*l*-extending bases, as in the on-line materials). Like the on-line materials, these materials show dialect influence in their treatment of /ni, ny-/, "*t*-irregular" and "*p*-irregular" verbs, and other details, and shun both the *arae a* and use of *s*-clusters for the tense, unaspirated consonants. Unlike the on-line materials, these texts wrestle with the problem of Sino-Korean vocabulary and when to use Chinese characters. Finally, these materials show an innovative use of the old "light *p*" to write Russian *v*, but with the little circle to the left of, rather than beneath, the sign for *p*.[32]

CONCLUSIONS

We have examined two different, but related, experiments with Korean writing from Russia and the USSR. Seen together, and especially in conjunction with the experiments with latinized Korean writing in the Soviet Far East in the 1930s, they comprise a new chapter in the history of the Korean language and Korean writing.

Koreans today are, with full justification, proud of their writing system. And yet, like any writing system, han'gŭl is not perfect. This was even more true at the turn of the century and continuing into the 1930s. The experiments of the editors of the *Taehanin chyŏnggy-obo* and Chu Sigyŏng with on-line writing and the efforts of Soviet Korean grammarians like O Ch'anghwan and Ke Pongu to systematize and standardize Korean writing are an integral part of attempts in this period to wrestle with traditional han'gŭl orthography's imperfections and to modernize native Korean language and writing. Many of the problems encountered by these early grammarians have continued to hound subsequent Korean language planners, and some of the solutions they tried have found echoes in the orthographies of the postwar Koreas, most particularly those of North Korea.

Much work remains to be done in uncovering the history of Korean in Russia and the USSR. What happened to the individuals behind the "on-line" proposals in Chita? Do materials survive in Russian Orthodox Church (or other) archives? The personal archives of repressed Korean intellectuals like O Ch'anghwan may reside in KGB archives. It is up to our colleagues in the former USSR to track down these materials now, for what I have presented here is only the tip of the iceberg.

NOTES

I am grateful to the International Research Exchanges Board (IREX), the Fulbright Commission, Harvard University's Korea Institute, and the Social Science Research Council for supporting research trips to the former USSR in the period 1989–1992. Thanks also to S. E. Martin, S. R. Ramsey, G. Ledyard, and Jae-hoon Yeon for helpful comments on an earlier draft of this chapter.

1. I transliterate Seoul Standard Korean (SS) forms in the main text according to McCune-Reischauer romanization, but sometimes include the Yale romanization in square brackets or slashes. For the han'gŭl of the Russian online materials, Soviet Korean data, and Middle Korean (MK), I use the Yale system, but with the following modifications: the "*arae a*" is /ʌ/ (for my modified McCune-Reischauer, too), the sign represented in Seoul Standard Korean by /u/ is /ɨ/, SS /o/ = /o/, SS /wu/ = /u/, one dot to the left (/·/) = high tone, two dots to the left (/:/) = rising tone, and low tone is unmarked. I sometimes use the period to make explicit otherwise potentially ambiguous syllable boundaries. Korean words written in capital letters represent words written in Chinese characters in the cited texts. For the Yale system, see Martin 1992.

2. Kim Chŏngsu (1989) writes that Sorae Kim Chunggŏn (1889–1933), Korean patriot and founder of a religious off-shoot from Ch'ŏndogyo, devised and advocated a separate on-line scheme for writing Korean at this time, independently of Chu Sigyŏng. For more on this and other details of the history of on-line writing in Korea, see Kim Chŏngsu 1989.

3. Cited in Kim Minsu 1973: 255.

4. Cited in Kim Minsu 1973: 256.

5. See Kim Minsu 1973 and Kim Chŏngsu 1989 for details and bibliography.

6. Except, that is, for the brief report in Kho Songmoo 1980, cited also in Kim Chŏngsu 1989, which treats mainly the cursive "on-line" sample presented in *Taehanin chyŏnggyobo*, issue no. 10.

7. The Russian experiments with "on-line" writing found interesting echoes in the Soviet attempts to latinize Korean in the 1930s. See King ms.

8. Yi Kang (1878–?) was an independence fighter born in Yonggang, P'yŏng'an province. He emigrated to the United States in 1902. It is not known when he returned to the Russian Far East, but he helped found the newspapers *Haejo sinmun* and *Taedong kongbo* in Vladivostok before working on the *Taehanin chyŏnggyobo* in Chita. See *Tonga wŏnsaek segye taebaekkwa sajŏn* (Donga's encyclopedia), 1982/1986 (5th ed.), v. 23, p. 70.

9. /hulim/ here is SS /huli-/ 'muddy'. Hence, this is a nativized Korean version of the Sino-Korean term /thak.um/ 'the muddy [voiced aspirated] sounds of Ancient Chinese'. The *Taehanin chyŏnggyobo* authors seem to equate "muddiness" with aspiration.

10. Standard Korean sources say that two of this man's *sijo* survive, but this poem does not match either of his two *sijo* reprinted in Chŏng Pyŏnguk 1980.

11. Could this be an abbreviation of /e[nmun-]i/ (*ŏnmun*, i.e., 'vernacular script'), with the incorporation of nominative /-i/ characteristic of Hamgyŏng and Soviet Korean dialects?

12. Martin, Lee, and Chang (1968) gloss this as "a brisk and lively folktune (with six words to the line)."

13. A dialect form of SS /kim/ "weeds" < MK /ki zɨm/.

14. Yi Kap (?–?) was an independence fighter born in P'yŏngwŏn, P'yŏng'an province. He joined the anti-Japanese movement after the 1905 Ŭlsa Treaty and was active in educational matters and anti-Japanese underground activities before fleeing to Siberia after a jail stint in 1907. He was a close friend and associate of Yi Kang, editor of the *Taehanin chyŏnggyobo*. See Yi Hŭisŭng et al. 1967: 587.

15. "New," that is, except for the few fifteenth- and sixteenth-century texts that followed the morphophonemic principle in their orthography: *Wŏr.in Ch'ŏn'gang chi kok* (1459) and *Sohak ŏnhae* (1586).

16. Especially if one considers the attempts to latinize Korean writing for the Soviet Koreans in the 1930s as part of the Union-wide latinization movement. See King ms.

17. For a list of the Korean-language sources cited in this section and the

abbreviations used, see the references. I am grateful to Sasha Vovin, formerly of the Institute of Oriental Studies, Leningrad Branch, and Igor' Bol'shakov, formerly of the Korea Section, Leningrad Public Library, for their help in locating these rare materials.

18. The /ɨy/ here is not etymological. /sɨy/ in the next words is Sino-Korean.

19. This may be due to influence from Hamgyŏng dialects. Ramsey reports that these verbs end in /-lq-/ in Pukch'ŏng (South Hamgyŏng) (1978: 201–205).

20. The latter is probably a spelling archaism, but note that North Hamgyŏng Yukchin dialect actually keeps these distinctions.

21. As pointed out in King 1994, this is probably due to influence from Hamgyŏng dialects, but it may also derive from a hardline morphophonemicist approach to writing verb bases consistently in one shape.

22. But note that /:toW-/ 'help' is idiosyncratically irregular in Middle Korean too. See the remarks in Martin 1992.

23. But PA 1927b has /mulɨp ɨl/, so it could be a dialect form with underlying final /-p/.

24. PC 1926 and PA 1926 also have /pas.key/ and /pask.key/. Otherwise the texts have /patk.ey/ (PA 1926; PA 1927), /patk.key, patk.ɨlu/ (PA 1927).

25. That is, they wrote a syllable-final double /ll/. See also "fell down" just below, where they wrote a syllable-final double /pp/, introducing, in effect, two new *patch'im*.

26. Presumably, they meant in syllable-initial position. See the note above.

27. Key Pongwu in the Yale system, for what SS now writes Kyey.

28. S. E. Martin (personal communication) points out that, in artificially slow, junctured pronunciation /ll/ (of just about any source) will be pronounced /...l # n.../, which probably accounts for the traditional spellings advocated by Ke Pongu.

29. Martin (personal communication) points out that *sŭpkwanŭm* is a technical term used in Japan, Korea, and perhaps also China to mean "a popular pronunciation (that is different from the historically expected or prescribed version)," often to be translated "(but) commonly pronounced...".

30. For information on Nikolaj Marr and his linguistic theories, see Alpatov 1991 and Yaguello 1991, chapter 7.

31. This mirrors the treatment of these nouns in Hamgyŏng/Soviet Korean dialects.

32. Slightly later materials also show a "light /ph/," with the little circle to the left of the aspirated /ph/ used to represent Russian *f*.

REFERENCES

Alpatov, V. M. 1991. Istorija odnogo mifa (The history of a certain myth). Moscow: Nauka.

Baskakov, N. A., ed. 1972. Voprosy sovershenstvovanija alfavitov Tjurkskix jazykov SSSR (Questions of the perfection of the alphabets of the Turkic languages of the USSR). Moscow: Nauka.

Chŏng, Pyŏnguk, ed. 1980. Sijo munhak sajŏn (Dictionary of *sijo* literature). Seoul: Sin'gu munhwa-sa.

Crisp, Simon. 1989. Soviet language planning since 1917–53 [*sic*]. In *Language planning in the Soviet Union*, ed. Michael Kirkwood, 23–45. Houndsmill: The Macmillan Press, Ltd.

Chu, Sigyŏng. 1976. Kungmun yŏn'gu (Research on Korean writing). In *Chu Sigyŏng chŏnjip* (Collected writings of Chu Sigyŏng), ed. Yi Kimun, vol. 1, 253–454. Originally published 1909. Seoul: Asea Munhwa-sa.

Kho, Song-moo (Ko Songmu). 1980. *Taehanin chyŏnggyobo* e sillin han'gŭl p'urŏ ssŭgi hŭllimch'e (The cursive on-line han'gŭl in the *Taehanin chyŏnggyobo*). *Han'gŭl sae sosik* 89, January: 8–9. Seoul: Han'gŭl hakhoe.

Kim, Chŏngsu. 1989. Han'gŭl p'urŏ ssŭgi undong (The movement to write Korean on-line). *Kugŏ saenghwal* 18: 30–50.

Kim, Minsu. 1973/1984. Kugŏ chŏngch'aengnon (A study of Korean language policy). Seoul: Tower Press.

Kim, Syn Xva (Kim Sŭnghwa). 1965. Ocherki po istorii sovetskix korejtsev (Essays on the history of the Soviet Koreans). Alma-Ata: Nauka.

Kim, Tubong. 1922/1934. Kiptŏ Chosŏn malbon (Revised and expanded Korean grammar). Seoul: Hoedong sŏgwan.

King, J. R. P. 1987. An introduction to Soviet Korean. *Language Research* (Seoul), 23:2: 233–274.

———. 1991a. Russian sources on Korean dialects. Ph.D. dissertation, Harvard University.

———. 1991b. Korean language studies in the USSR: past, present and future. *Ijungŏnŏ hakhoeji* (Seoul), vol. 8.

———. 1991c. A Soviet Korean grammar from 1930. *Han'gungmal kyoyuk* (Seoul), vol. 3.

———. 1993. Archaisms and innovations in Soviet Korean dialects. *Language Research* (Seoul), 28:2: 201–223.

———. 1994. Dialect elements in Soviet Korean publications from the 1920s. In *NSL 7: Linguistic studies in the non-Slavic languages of the Commonwealth of Independent States and the Baltic Republics*, ed. Howard I. Aronson, 151–183. Chicago: Chicago Linguistic Society.

———. (1997). A failed revolution in Korean writing: The attempts to latinize Korean in the Soviet Far East, 1930–1934. Ms.

Kirkwood, Michael, ed. 1989. Language planning in the Soviet Union. Houndsmill: The Macmillan Press, Ltd.

Martin, S. E. 1992. A reference grammar of Korean. Tokyo: Tuttle and Co.

Martin, S. E., Yang Ha Lee, and Sung-un Chang. 1968/1980. New Korean-English dictionary. Seoul: Minjungsŏrim.

Ramsey, S. R. 1978. Accent and morphology in Korean dialects. Seoul: Tower Press.

Yaguello, Marina. 1991. Lunatic lovers of language: Imaginary languages and their inventors. Translated from the original French Les fous du langage: Des langues imaginaires et de leurs inventeurs (Paris: Editions du Seuil, 1984), by Catherine Slater. Cranbury, N.J.: Associated University Presses.

Yi, Hŭisŭng, et al. 1967. Han'guk inmyŏng taesajŏn (Dictionary of Korean biography). Seoul: Sin'gu Munhwa-sa.

Yi, Kimun. 1961/1972/1983. Kugŏsa kaesŏl (Outline history of the Korean language). Seoul: Tower Press.

———. 1970. Kaehwagi ŭi kungmun yŏn'gu (Research on Korean in the Enlightenment Period). Seoul: Ilchogak Publishers.

———, ed. 1976. Chu Sigyŏng chŏnjip (Collected writings of Chu Sigyŏng). Seoul: Asea Munhwasa.

Yi, P'ilsu (Li Philswu). 1923. Chŏng'ŭm munjŏn (Grammar of "Correct Sounds"). Seoul: Chosŏn Chŏng'ŭm Puhwal-hoe.

Yu, Ch'angdon (Changton). 1979. Ijoŏ sajŏn (Dictionary of Yi dynasty Korean). Seoul: Yonsei University Press.

Soviet Korean Publications, 1923–1929

The titles below are rendered in a modified form of Yale romanization.

I Ph.Ph., O Sang.il, and O Changhwan. 1929. Say tokpon (calani ɨy), tyey 2 kwen (New textbook [for adults], vol. 2). Xabarovsk.

KI. 1929. Kolye imin cinam. Hapalopsɨkhɨ Sincinsɨkhɨ Kuyek kwa Kkulɨttalɨkinsɨkhɨ Kuyek ɨy Hyengphyen kwa isa hanɨn Pangpep ey tay haye. = Chto nuzhno znat' Korejtsu pereselentsu. Opisanie Kur-darginskogo i Sindinskogo rajonov v Xabarovskom Okruge i Pravila Pereselenija (Korean immigration guide...). Izdanie Xabarovskoj Pereselencheskoj Partij. 59 pp. Tirazh: 3000.

PC. 1926. Kongchyeng-hoy Haysam-hyen Kanpu wa Wentong Kanpu Palhayng. Ppioneylɨ citoca: Tokpon (Pioneer leader: A reader). 70 pp. Tirazh: 500.

NB. 1929. Ni, P., Osanir, and Ochanxvan. 1929. Novyj bukvar' dlja vzroslyx (New primer for adults). Part 1, 2nd ed. Xabarovsk: Knizhnoe Delo. = Pp. Ph. Ni, O Sang il, and O Changhwan. *Say tokpon (calani ɨy)*. 40 pp. Tirazh: 28000. Part 2, 99 pp., Tirazh: 28000.

Met. 1929. Osanir and Ochanxvan. 1929. Metodicheskaja zapiska k bukvarju *Novaja Shkola* (na Korejsk. jaz.). = Tokpon "sayhakkyo" kyosuse (Teacher's notes for the primer *New School*). Kyosa-yong. Xabarovsk: Knizhnoe Delo.

SH. 1929a. P. Ni, T. Ogaj, N. Ochanxvan, I. Oseled'ko, S. Txaj, Ja. Tsoj, and S. Jugaj. Novaja shkola: Pervaja kniga Korejskogo shkol'nika = Li Pyengkuk, O Sangil, O Changhwan, O.ssey.llyeyti.kko I., Yukai Ss. A., Ccoi Ya., Thay Insu. *Say hakkyo: Tokpon, tyey-ilkwen, tyey-ilphyen* (New school: A reader, volume 1, part 1). 80 pp. Xabarovsk.

SH. 1929b. *Say hakkyo: Tokpon, Tyey-sa.kwen* (New school, volume 4). = Novaja shkola. Rabochaja Kniga dlja 4-go Goda Obuchenija. 216 pp. Tirazh: 4000. Wentong kyoyuk-pu kwahak pangpep hoyɨy inka. Xabarovsk: Knizhnoe delo.

NT. 1925. Lossiya Kongsan-tang Yenhay-to Kanpu Nyeca-pu, ed. *Nyeca tay-phyo (caylyo sucip)* (Woman representative [a collection of materials]). 279 pp. Vladivostok.

AP. 1926. Nam Manchun (Li Congil, trans.). Appak patnɨn Kolye (Ilpon chimlyakcuɨy kɨypanha ey issnɨn Kolye) (Oppressed Korea [Korea under the shackles of Japanese aggression]). = Ugnetënnaja Koreja. 35 pp. Tirazh: 10000. Vladivostok.

PA. 1924. *Pulkɨn Ai*: Lo.lyek hakkyo-yong Ko.lye say tokpon (Red child: New Korean reader for use in workers' schools). Yenhay-to Kyoyuk-pu Phyenchan. 51 pp. Tirazh: 5000.

———. 1924. *Pulkɨn Ai*: Lo.lyek hakkyo-yong say tokpon. Tyey-1 kwen, tyey-2 phyen (Red child, volume 1, part 2). = Pervaja kniga dlja chtenija. 133 pp. Tirazh: 5000.

———. 1926a. *Pulkɨn Ai*: Say tokpon. Tyey-il-kwen tyey-il-phyen (Red child, volume 1, part 1). Krasnoe ditja: Korejskij bukvar'. Xabarovsk-Vladivostok: Tose cusik hoysa. 64 pp. Tirazh: 5000.

———. 1926b. *Pulkɨn Ai*: Say tokpon. Tyey-il-kwen tyey-il-phyen (Red child, volume 1, part 1 [2nd ed.]). Krasnoe ditja: Korejskij bukvar'. Izd. 2–e. Xabarovsk-Vladivostok: Tose cusik hoysa. 64 pp.

———. 1927? *Pulkɨn Ai*: Lo.lyek hakkyo-yong say tokpon (Red child). Yenhay-to Kyoyuk-pu Phyenchan. 138 pp. Haysamwi (Vladivostok).

———. 1927. *Pulkɨn Ai*: Say tokpon. Tyey-samkwen (Red child, volume 3). 276 pp. Tirazh: 5000. Xabarovsk-Vladivostok.

———. 1927. *Pulkɨn Ai*: Say tokpon. Tyey-sa.kwen (Red child, volume 4). = Krasnoe ditja: Kniga dlja chtenija na Korejskom jazyke. God. IV. 272 pp. Tirazh: 3000.

Sipwel hyekmyeng sipcu-nyen wentong kɨynyem cunpi wiwen-hoy, ed. 1927. Sipwel hyekmyeng sipcu-nyen kwa ssopeythɨ Kolye mincok (The tenth anniversary of the October Revolution and the Soviet Koreans). = Desjatiletie Oktjabr'skoj Revoljutsij i Sovetskoe Korejskoe naselenie. 109 pp. Tirazh: 3000.

Pro. 1929. Wentong Pyenkang Kyoyuk-pu Penyek-kuk Yeksul. 1929. Sengin Munmayng Thoychiso Kanglyeng (Program for the eradication of adult illiteracy) = Programma dlja zanjatij so vzroslymi v shkolax gramoty. 16 pp. Tirazh: 1000.

M. 1925. Yenhay-to hakmu.kukto cyengchi munhwa-pu phyenchan. 1925. Musik ɨl epsi hanɨn calani ɨy tokpon (An adult reader to do away with ignorance). 49 pp. Tirazh: 15000. Haysamwi = Vladivostok.

12

COMMENTARY

Samuel E. Martin

The symposium on the Korean writing system out of which this volume evolved produced a rich bounty of distinguished essays that give us new and important information not only about the creation of that remarkable script but also about the Korean language itself, as revealed in the orthography that grew out of the letter symbols when they were put to use. I will limit my comments to a few words on each of the chapters and offer extended discussion only on certain matters that particularly interest me with respect to the structure and history of the language.

Gari Ledyard describes the historical background that points to the existence of a prior need for a practical way to write the Korean language, and he finds an awareness of that at least a century and a half before the invention of han'gŭl. Sejong [Seycong] himself was an expert on Chinese theories of phonology, and some of the scholars around him were even more sophisticated, particularly Sin Sukchu [Sin Swukcwu].[1] The explanations in the work *Hunmin chŏng'ŭm haerye* [*Hwunmin cengum haylyey*] (1446) clearly state that, like the symbols for the other initials, the letters for *ng*, *l*, and *z* depict the articulatory organs but alter the form, rather than follow the principle of adding strokes to make symbols for sounds related to the basic set of initials. It might be wondered whether *ph* should not belong here, but apparently the king thought of that graph as "adding a stroke" to *p* by elongating the vertical sides so that the shape would have to be written in four strokes instead of the three that are customary for the Chinese character "mouth," which serves as a model for the *m*. Or, perhaps he put a stroke on top of the *p* and then tidied up the resulting shape by removing the horizontal stroke in the middle, afterwards lengthening the top and bottom lines so that the symbol would not be confused with that for *m*.

Chinese phonologists had failed to split the vowel from the final consonant (though the rime table authors were aware of that, as I mention below) and to identify final consonants with initial consonants. Ledyard thinks the achievement of that analysis was the result of a familiarity with the ‘Phags-pa alphabet, which recognized both phenomena.

Ledyard is perhaps hasty in concluding that Sejong [Seycong] regarded the prescriptive readings of *Tongguk chŏng'un* [*Tongkwuk cengwun*] (1448) as a failure. The king was not seeking so much to supplant the popular pronunciations given by Koreans to the Chinese words that were in common use as to inform them of the richer system of distinctions that were appropriate to the characters used in Chinese texts: in effect, a reconstruction of Middle Chinese phonology in terms of the Korean sound system as represented by the hankul symbols, and quite pronounceable by Koreans of his day. (It was three centuries later that Bernhard Karlgren did something similar in terms of the phonetic symbols of the Swedish Alphabet Society.)

I am impressed by the *Tongguk* [*Tongkwuk*] codification of character readings and agree with Sinhang Kang's remarks that they have been unduly belittled. I admire the ability of the small group of hankul writers, including the creator of the script, to master the system so thoroughly that there are very few inconsistencies in the considerable body of texts that include the readings. Surely the writers and printers did not search the dictionary every time they needed a pronunciation. Instead, they must have internalized the readings as a kind of elite standard, and they very likely tried to use that standard in saying aloud uncommon Chinese terms. That they were not entirely successful can be found in the occasional spelling slip, as when the popular reading MWUN is written (or implied) instead of the prescribed MWON ‘gate’ (see Martin 1992: 495b), and where we see in-text correction of a Chinese reading, as when LWO ‘work’ is corrected to LWOW in the margin of one text (1447 Sek 6:30b, 31a, 31b [correction smudged], 32b, and perhaps a few later pages). If you have ever heard a group of American literary academics discussing “genres,” each with his or her uncertain version of that originally French word, you can appreciate the desire of the Korean scholars for an authoritative way to nativize the classical Chinese phonetic distinctions.

Sin Sukchu [Sin Swukcwu] made use of a Yuan dynasty rime

book with prescriptive readings for the characters, which were meticulously transcribed into the innovative Mongolian script devised by the lama 'Phags-pa in 1269 to replace the earlier (and later) Uighur letters. The writing of the Chinese final labial glide -w as a "light *m*" (the *m* symbol with a little circle underneath) is taken from the Mongol usage to write the semivowel of the 'Phags-pa symbol for an initial m- that had become w-. In the Korean case, the glide was never pronounced and the appearance of the initial nasal symbol would seem odd, since it did not undergo the denasalization that marked the sound the Mongol letter was representing. The writing of the postvocalic glide was abandoned in [*Pen.yek*] *Sohak* (1518) which has relatively natural readings and writes ¨*TWO* for earlier ¨*TTWOW* 'the Way'. In adapting the Yale transliteration in order to transcribe the *Tongguk* [*Tongkwuk*] readings with the labial glide, at first I used the same symbol as for the lenited *p* in native Korean forms, a capital *W*, based on the assumption that the "light *m*" symbol was a just a variant of the "light *p*" symbol and was built on the simpler shape of "*m*" because that is the starting point for the labial series. In doing so I obscured the fact that a few phrases in *Hunmin chŏng'ŭm ŏnhae* [*Hwunmin cengum enhay*] (1451) have the string ···*W W*··· in which the small-capital *w* transcribes "light *m*" and the capital *w* transcribes an isolated "light *p*," the bilabial voiced fricative, here an allomorph of the genitive marker *s*, quite likely suppressed in pronunciation. Like the final semivowel, the isolated light *p* was probably an artifact of the phonologists, for it does not turn up in any other texts. In any event, when I decided to write the *Tongguk* [Tongkwuk] readings in small capitals, the postvocalic glide was romanized just like the prevocalic glide, simply as a "*w*" that we might refer to as the "silent *w*," taking a cue from Ledyard's apt use of "silent *h*" to describe the zero initial represented by a circle. Sejong [Seycong] seems to have used the circle to represent a feature something like "muted" in two flavors: slightly muted, that is, lenited to a (voiced) fricative; and totally muted, that is, elided. Why did he create the triangle as a "changed-shape" *s* rather than put a circle under the *s*? Probably because he recognized the sound as the Middle Chinese initial Z(Y)··· and was aware, as well, of a few non-Chinese words that begin with the voiced spirant, such as *z(y)wus* < **zywuch* 'four-stick game'. Ledyard offers the original notion that the creator of the script was tacitly operating with a process of graphic "reduction" as well as the "addition" of strokes that is explicitly mentioned, and that idea will account for several anomalies that are hard to explain otherwise as well as strengthen the case for ‘Phags-pa influence on some of the shapes of the consonant symbols. In addition to the “light *p*” and the “light *m*,” later sources include light versions of *ph* and *pp*, similarly made by subscripting a little circle. But these were intended only to show the Middle Chinese pronunciation as Chinese and were not used in the *Tongguk* [*Tongkwuk*] system to show the readings prescribed for Korean pronunciation of Chinese characters.

In addition to the four “light” initials, *Saseng thonghay* (1517, se: 5a, 6a) includes the two (left/right) extended versions of the symbols for *c cc ch s ss* among the thirty-six initials of *Guangyun* (1008) and *Yunhui* (1202), where they represent the dental and retroflex distinctions that disappeared in later Chinese and were not brought into Korea.[2] The light initials were distinguished by the Chinese phonologists to account for the north Chinese weakening of palatalized labials, such that p(y)··· > f··· and m(y)··· > w···, a change too late to influence Sino-Korean. The pre-hankul weakenings (in the central area) of native Korean ···*p*··· to ···W··· (bilabial voiced fricative) and eventually ···*w*··· (labial glide), while unrelated, were similar enough to the Chinese weakenings to lead to the writing of both with the “light *p*” symbol, while the “light *m*” symbol was reserved for writing the “silent ···W” recognized as the prescribed spelling for the theoretical labial glide at the end of certain syllables. The symbols for the light versions of *ph* and *pp* are used only in explaining the Chinese rime charts and (later) in showing the pronunciation of alien tongues, and that is largely true also of the symbols for the dental and palatal fricatives and affricates. It is interesting that neither the king nor anyone at the time noticed the parallel between the lenited version of *p*, represented by the letter *W*, and the lenition of *k* to a fricative, represented in the Yale romanization by ···G··· and in hankul by a spelling device making use of the initial null symbol.[3] If ever considered, the notion of creating a symbol such as *k* with a subscript circle may have been rejected in recognition of the fact that certain lexical cases of ···*G*··· go back to a labial rather than a velar, that is, to an earlier ···*p*··· that failed to emerge as the ···*W*··· we expect. But it seems likely that in this matter Sejong [Seycong] was concerned purely with a phonemic analysis that forced him to represent the labial frication as distinctive, since it was not predictable in any obvious or simple way. Similar and more compelling reasons led to recognition of the lenited ···*s*··· as the temporarily emergent phoneme ···*z*···, though no need was felt for a symbol to show the parallel weakening of ···*t*··· to a flap, for that did not present a new phonemic distinction and could be written with ···*l*···.

Ki-Moon Lee ['Yi Kimun] presents strong and convincing evidence that the wise king himself created the shapes of the letters and the basic concepts of the script. Not only was Sejong [Seycong] well versed in Chinese historical phonology, he also had an excellent feel for the complex structure of Korean as a spoken language and showed unusual skill in the morphophonemic analysis that underlies the admirable spelling conventions of *Wŏrin-ch'ŏn'gang-ji-gok* [*Wel.in chenkang ci kok*] (1449), a system unequaled before the decidedly morpheme-conscious *Sohak ŏnhae* [*Sohak enhay*] (1586) and later the modern system that began developing, Lee tells us, out of the research of Chu Sigyŏng [Cwu Sikyeng] around the turn of the twentieth century.

Sinhang Kang [Kang Sinhang] shows clearly that the *Tongguk* [*Tongkwuk*] vowel system closely reflects the Sino-Korean readings of Chinese characters and, like the consonant system, only suffers from an excess of ambition: it attempts to include a few Middle Chinese distinctions not maintained in Sino-Korean. The remarks quoted by Kang from texts of 1455 and 1512 indicate that the vowel articulations at that time were closer to the later vowel system than to that hypothesized by those who claim that a Great Vowel Shift took place after the creation of the script, rather than before—if, indeed, it took place at all.

Pyong-Hi Ahn [An Pyenghuy] adopts a view from Sinhang Kang [Kang Sinhang] to the effect that the symbols created for the hankul characters were shaped according to the principles of the traditional explanation of the shapes of Chinese characters that are known as *liù shū* 'six graphic types'. He thinks the type *xiàngxíng* 'pictogram' lies behind the creation of the shapes of the initials, and by more complicated reasoning deduces that the simplex and complex vowels can be similarly accounted for in terms of other types. Some of the explanations strike me as contrived to fit the hypothesis, and I am very doubtful that Sejong [Seycong] actually took into account these Chinese graphemic theories. While it is true that a weighty philosophical argument was presented for the choice of the concepts of Man, Earth, and Heaven for the basic three vowels, I suspect the argument may have been elaborated to lend a scholarly air of legitimacy to a system already devised. The important nature of these three vowels can be seen in the use of $^{u}/_{o}$ as the epenthetic vowel and ···˙*i*- as the stem of the copula (= noun predicator). As long as we are speculating on what lies behind the letter shapes, let me offer the far-fetched conjecture that the king may have had in the back of his mind the quasi-free noun ··· ˙*i* 'person' (to say nothing of the Sino-Korean ZIN), the noun *tu˙luh* 'moor, flatland', and the noun *ha˙nol(h)* 'heaven', which offer examples of the vowels in question. For the secondary set of symbols his facing of the added dot(s) toward or away from the center may reflect the rime concept of *nèi zhuǎn* 'inner series' versus *wài zhuǎn* 'outer series', a vaguely understood way of dichotomizing rimes on the basis of vowel quality.

Chin W. Kim [Kim Cin.wu] calls attention to the featural characteristic of the script, though the reference to Jakobsonian distinctive features is unfortunate, and somewhat inaccurate, as is the modernist fallacy of ascribing to King Sejong notions set forth as the latest fads of linguistic theory. What Kim leaves unmentioned is that the king had an excellent ear for phonetic similarities, and that is why he treated both postvocalic *y* and prevocalic *y* as subsyllabic versions of *i*, yet identified the prevocalic *w* as a subsyllabic kind of *wo* before *a* (writing *wa* as *wo* + *a*), but recognizing it as a kind of *wu* before *e* (writing *wu* + *e* for *we*). The phonetic difference between the two kinds of labial glide can be heard today, and the glide is markedly different from the equivalent in other languages, as you tell from listening to the English word "quiet" after hearing the Korean word **kwā.yen** 'as expected'—or "quack" after **kkwayk** 'with a quack'. (Compare "won" and **wen.**)

Young-Key Kim-Renaud [Kim Yengki] finds that the writing system reflects phonological features that are psychologically salient for Korean speakers and draws attention to the fact that complex groupings of letters into syllable blocks can facilitate the recognition of words by the reader. With respect to the soon-abandoned use of the final zero in syllables without a coda, it should be noted that the initial zero represented distinctive smooth vowel onset in Middle Chinese. The Chinese system of arranging the finals had a corresponding category for the noncoda syllables, so that it was natural for the inventor of hankul to write the zero for vowel-ending syllables, despite its redundancy given the syllable boundary. In certain romanized forms the zero is resurrected as a distinctive hyphen or dot to keep the syllable boundaries distinct or to keep morpheme shapes intact. And the doubling of the initial zero in certain Middle Korean words serves a similar function, in keeping distinct from such syllable boundaries as ···*y-yV*··· (showing the automatic spread of the stem-final palatal semivowel) those of the type ···*y-V*··· (explicitly disallowing the spread), which I interpret as ···**y–G**··· with the *G* representing a lenition of the velar *k* or the labial *p* (Martin 1992: 53–57). This is a delicate area of the phonology that is hard to navigate if the orthographic devices are confused with the phonemic and morphophonemic structures they represent.

Sang-Oak Lee ['Yi Sangek] brings out certain graphic peculiarities of the syllable blocks. I particularly like his description of the density of the blocks: some are horizontally dense, some vertically, a few are extremely dense, while others are quite sparse. The sparse ones are easier to identify and to distinguish from other blocks. Some of the vertically dense forms are hard to read in small-size type or in certain kinds of printing, as I think we have all noticed. The differences between the blocks for **nul**, **tul**, **lul**, and **thul** can be a headache for the reader, and that is primarily because of the density factor. The very simplicity of the basic symbols can lead to confusion, and it is not always easy to see an added dot (or its orientation) in syllables with the vowels **u**, **wu**, or [w]**o**, especially when these are sandwiched between initial and final consonants in the denser blocks; even less dense blocks such as **kun**, **kon**, and **kwun** are easy to misread and to misprint, and in earlier texts the difference between the syllables *tot* and *twon* is sometimes elusive. It is often hard to spot words when scanning for information, and that is one reason readers sometimes prefer text with Chinese characters, for those catch the eye immediately. I make these remarks not as criticism of the script, which is admirable in so many ways, but as an encouragement for typographers to create crisper versions of the blocks. Not all typographical innovations, however, help the reader. There is a tendency in TV captions to flatten the blocks, squashing the syllables that are vertically dense. A single final consonant is often spread beneath the vowel, and that helps, but not much in the case of pairs like **kang** versus **kam**, for the flattening of the circle representing ···**ng** makes it resemble the slightly rounded version of the ···**m** rectangle made by a good calligrapher. Problems of this sort go back a good many years, and some of the type castings or carvings found in Middle Korean texts cause similar problems, especially with respect to dense characters and with both the initial and the final *m* as contrasted with the zero and *ng*. In the earlier texts, the problems are compounded by the not uncommon obscuring of boundaries between the syllable blocks as well as the joining of separate strokes within a block (so that ···*uyk*, ···*uy*, ···*ik* can look alike). Fortunately the redundant nature of human language helps us resolve puzzles that at first baffle the eye. There is no word *'e'la*, so what looks like that in the midst of otherwise crisp type in *Wel.in chenkang ci kok* (1459 Wel 1:22b) must be ··· *'i'la* 'it is,' and that fits the context. In earlier texts we notice occasional miswriting of resemblant letters, as when *p* is written for *m* in *coGwol'Gey ho'nipyen* (1447→1562 Sek 3:25b) for ···*ho'nimyen* (= *ho'n i 'm ye n*') 'when (the gods) would make them drowsy'.[4] There are also surprising graphical oddities such as the top half of *an* printed as a mirror image in *"kel-an'ca* (1463 Pep 2:118a)[5] and the inversion of the order of the two consonants in the double-consonant final of *kolp* written as *kopl* (1617 Sin-Sok chwung 1:88), as if the scribe was momentarily indulging in the boustrophedon practice of ancient Greece, lazily avoiding a sweep back to the left side of the block before starting the lower layer.[6] How does the Korean script impress the foreign eye? One visitor described the writing he saw on the signs in Seoul as a set of "interlocking nuts and bolts," and indeed the geometric simplicity of some of the squarish versions of the blocks leads to the look of Tinkertoy structures, though that impression is softened in the more rounded versions usually favored.

Korean spelling prescriptions have been controversial from the beginning, when Sejong [Seycong] obviously favored morphophonemically oriented conventions, while others preferred not to delve too deep below the phonetic surface. The unified system put forth in 1933 is close to optimal in its treatment of morphophonemic problems, and as a result spelling practices have been largely standardized with only minor adjustments to those rules. After the political division into two Koreas, however, divergence took place in the adjustments made, and today there are a number of troublesome points of difference. The latest adjustments by the authorities in South Korea, that of writing certain forms of the copula without the automatically intercalated palatal glide and abolishing the spelling **-up.nita** in favor of **-sup.nita**, are simplifications that were earlier standardized in North Korea, so we seem to be moving toward a convergence between the two spelling standards. An excellent collection of the original papers, documents, government decrees, on the standardization of spelling, pronunciation, Chinese characters, pedagogy, and other matters in South Korea up to 1973 was published by Minsu Kim [Kim Minswu]. See also Hyon Bai Choi [Choy Hyenpay] 1954 for documents relating to the abortive attempt by Syngman Rhee [^{l}Yi Sungman] to "simplify" the orthography by reverting to the pre-1933 practices of his youth.

Ho-min Sohn [Son Homin] describes in admirable detail the differences between the orthographies of North and South Korea today. A minor point: Sohn suggests that the North Koreans base their spellings of initial **l-** and **n-** on the Phyengyang (P'yŏngyang) dialect. While that is to a certain extent true, the pronunciation of initial **l-** as a flap is an innovation promoted by the educators, for the original *l-* had merged with *n-* in that area (as elsewhere) many years ago. The surname ^{l}**No** was normally said the same way in both Seoul and Phyengyang, with the nasal, and the surname ^{l}**Yi** differed only in that the pronunciation /ni/ became /i/ in Seoul, where initial /n/ dropped before /i/ (and /y/) whether it came from a Chinese /l/ or a Chinese /n/. The name acquired its current flap in Phyengyang as a deliberate affectation, a reading pronunciation, in place of the traditional /n···/, which was retained at the expense of the /y/ in words like /neca/ for earlier /nyeca/ = ^{n}**yeca** 'woman' < **nye** + **ca**, with only a spelling contrast of the first syllable with that of /nehayng/ for /nyehayng/ = ^{l}**yehayng** 'trip, travel' < **lye** + **hayng**. Sohn also has interesting remarks on the differing results in the two Koreas of efforts to replace foreign expressions (especially those based on Japanese) with authentically Korean words.

Ross King offers a fascinating account of the various experiments in writing Korean in Russia and the USSR, and the grammatical analyses worked out by Koreans living there. He has found a rich and rewarding treasurehouse of language history that has been little known, much less explored. Of particular interest are the innovative attempts to promote linearized ("on-line") use of hankul symbols and the treatment of "*t*-irregular stems" as having a basic **···l-** (as much later, and independently, I treated them in Martin 1954),[7] and the failure to show lenition for the "*p*-irregular stems" (which I treated as **···w-**). That may have been because some of the Korean dialects found in Russia had not undergone the lenition that produced the irregularity. The occasional deviations that King points out, such as **towum** and **toa talna** from **tow-** 'help', seem to be in stems that show idiosyncratic behavior in Middle Korean, too, notably the verb for 'help' (Martin 1992: 234). It is also interesting that some of the Soviet spellings suggest the analysis **an ita** instead of **ani 'ta** for the negative copula. That view of the structure independently attracted various scholars in the twentieth century, but it is historically mistaken, since the contraction of **an** from **ani** is not seen before the late 1800s, and most Korean grammarians have preferred to leave **ani-** as an unanalyzed stem.

S. Robert Ramsey, too, is impressed with the accomplishment of the inventor of the script in perceiving that the syllable can be divided into an initial onset, a medial nucleus, and a final coda, noting that the Chinese phonologists were satisfied with a grosser analysis of the syllable into initial and rime (that is, everything else). But it should not be forgotten that the rime tables effectively, if indirectly, indicated the codas by the way they grouped syllables with the final nasals and (as "entering tone") stops. The concept of the coda was in the theoretical background available to the king. His originality lay, as Ramsey says, in recognizing the phonemic identity of the coda consonants with their corresponding initial versions. The concept of a zero initial may have been taken from Chinese phonology, but Sejong [Seycong] was quick to see the structural need for such an initial in representing morphophonemic forms. He extended the notion to a zero coda, a nice balancing touch to the graphs but of little structural use. From the beginning its use was limited to spelling out readings for Chinese characters, and it fell out of use for that purpose by the 1490s, freeing the circle so that eventually it came to represent the final ···*ng* as well as the initial zero.[8] Ramsey's elegant presentation of the phonetic values we assume for certain clustered consonant symbols is to be commended for his insights into the nature of the emphatic prefix that lies behind the *ss*··· spellings of Middle Korean, in particular the evidence cited from Ki-Moon Lee on the use of phonograms representing *hu-su*··· for the stem 'write'. Ramsey's justifiable worry that the emphatic variant of *kuzu-* (< **kusuk-*) 'lead; pull' is *skuzu-* and not ˣ*khuzu-* calls into question the assumption that the original initial of the prefix (for which the value of the twelfth-century phonogram is clearly velar) was *hu-* and that the development was just a kind of develarization or apicalization *hu-* > *s(u)-*. This appears to be a matter of timing. Forms made from **s(u)-kusuk-* must have been created after the loss of the velar quality in the fricative. There could have been an early dissimilation of the initial when it appeared before a velar, but that possibility must be rejected if we accept that the view that the prefix was present in the ancestor of *˙khu-* 'big', reconstructed as **hu-˙ku-*, following Ki-Moon Lee ['Yi Kimun] (1991: 18), rather than **ku˙hu-* (following Ramsey's well-motivated earlier hypothesis).

Just how real was the distinction of *kh-* from *hh-*? The remnants of an intensive prefix was recognized in *(h)hye-* 'pull; kindle; (etc.)' but not in **(h)hu-* = *˙khu-* 'big', perhaps because there was little remaining of a feel for the association with *ha-* 'great; much, many', which I believe was the source of *˙khu-*, despite the difference in vowel quality. That difference of quality, like the presence or absence of the earlier intensive prefix, may well have signaled a connotation of subjective ("much much!") versus objective ("not little"), as may have been true of the difference of the antonymous stem *¨cyak-* 'little, small, lacking in size/importance' (subjective) and *¨cyek-* 'little, few, lacking in quantity/number' (objective). The modern language preserves the pair meaning 'little' but it replaced the objective 'much/many' with **mānh-** < *¨manh-* < *¨man °ho-* 'much/many' < *¨man* (1586 Sohak secey: 3a) < ˙MEN 'ten thousand = myriad (a huge number)'. (It is unclear what etymological relationship, if any, can be shown between the set of stems *¨cyek-* / *¨cyak-* / *¨cywok-(wo)* 'little' and the synonymous set *hyek-* / *hyak-* / *hywok-* 'little'. Notice also *˙hyen* 'how much/many; some'.) Only one of the *Tongguk* [*Tongkwuk*] syllables beginning KH··· survived as such in the spoken language (the morpheme **khway** 'fast'); the others must have had the popular pronunciation *k*···. *Tongguk* [Tongkwuk] has many characters beginning HH···, but that owes to the artificial nature of the double-consonant prescriptions, and the popular pronunciation was with *h*... as it is today. The stem *hhye-* survives as *khye-* > *khi-* (no longer used in the meaning "pull," but "kindle; saw; etc."); and a few examples are found of *khye-* as a variant of *(h)hye-* in sixteenth-century texts. King (1988) noticed a form equivalent to **kakhun** for **khun** 'big' in Matveev's 1900 book on Vladivostok, and that may be a relic of the prefixed version of 'big' that I think must have existed, though the Matveev form seems terribly late for that.

Ramsey also comes up with an original and, I believe, correct view of the structure of the words beginning with *pst-* and *psk-*, to which I would only add the suggestion that *pst* 'time' originated as a variant of *psk* with an apicalizing assimilation of *k* to the articulatory locus of the preceding sibilant. These two quasi-free nouns, which contain no basic vowel, both meant "time". Only *pst* survives as modern **···ttay** < ˙*pst ay* 'at the time', though *psk* is etymologically present in **kki (ni)** 'mealtime' ?< ˙*psk i·n i* 'it is the time' (see Martin 1992: 759). Ramsey's final remarks on language change are more controversial. He advocates "a more punctuated model of language change," as against the traditional view of gradual and rather monolithic change. He is right if we think of the abrupt changes as being part of an unconscious decision on a particular structure to be the social norm after a period of competition among different contenders. Language is never stable, but always in flux. The individual relationships in a society are constantly being adjusted in all sorts of ways, and language is no exception. At a larger level that can be called "dialect variation." For a given moment, we try to see a stable picture of what the evidence indicates is intrinsically unstable, tidying up a fuzzy image so that it looks crisper than it is. (The universal tendency of languages to change through time can be explained as the biological result of ecological and evolutionary imperatives. See Mattingly 1972; Hill 1974.) As Ramsey wisely concludes, the Middle Korean system that is represented in the written documents characterized a relatively short stage of Korean phonological history. My only caveat is that he presumes that stage to be "atypical," a characterization that perhaps relies too heavily on what is found in contemporary Korean and overlooks some of the tantalizing hints that lie behind the evidence of earlier centuries and can be discerned when the words written in phonograms are examined with internal reconstruction in mind.

In conclusion let me express my gratitude for the effort, patience, and wisdom of Young-Key Kim-Renaud [Kim Yengki] in organizing a memorable symposium and bringing together this fine array of stimulating essays, from which I have learned much. I feel sure that my appreciation of the results of this symposium will be shared by all readers.

NOTES

1. In this commentary, Yale romanization is used for most purposes except for rendering certain proper names, which are given in the form preferred by the person named when that is known to me or in the McCune-Reischauer system when the preference is unknown to me. The Yale form is then written in brackets, and that can be readily converted to the hankul [han'gŭl] spelling. It

should be noted that modern Korean forms, given in boldface, use the letter **o** to represent the mid back rounded vowel that is written *wo* for earlier Korean (here printed in italics), and the symbol *o* represents the lost vowel **alay a** (= *a·lay o*), the under-dot, which has mostly merged with /a/ or /u/ in standard Korean. The raised dot and double-dot (dieresis or umlaut) represent Middle Korean accent in terms of high and low rising, respectively; low pitch is unmarked. The dots are placed before the syllable in close emulation of the positioning of the dots in the Middle Korean texts and do not always correspond to the morphophonemic locus because of the phonetic liaisons that go unrepresented in the syllable division. Chinese names and titles are cited in Pinyin romanization. Forms cited from Chinese and other languages of East Asia are underlined. Other conventions, such as the use of small capitals for the Middle Korean readings prescribed for Chinese characters, follow those of my reference grammar (Martin 1992). I use the word hankul (McCune-Reischauer han'gŭl) to refer to the Korean script, but it was not so called until 1910, when Chu Sigyŏng [Cwu Sikyeng] invented the term, with the imputed etymology *han kul*, "the great script" or "the main script," rather than the more obvious *Han* (< HHAN) *kul* 'the Korea(n) script'. Earlier the system was called **ēnmun** < ¨EN-MWUN 'vernacular writing'.

2. The left-and-right extended symbols are explained as symbols in *Hwunen* 14–15 but not exemplified. They are used to write the dental/palatal sibilant and affricate initials of readings for Chinese characters in 1459 Kok 10:33–34, 92–93. Are there other pages in the texts that use these letters? Unusual syllable blocks such as *WWoW-·Wwoq-tti, ppi-WWa*, and *·WWaq-·cye-·laW-·chum-·ppwu* (1459 Wel 21:70b) occur in mumbo-jumbo incantations, which (in Wel 10) also contain examples of the extended sibilant symbols. The peculiar phonology of the incantations is explicitly mentioned in 1459 Wel 10:72b.

3. The miswriting of *moyk·wo* for *moy·Gwo* (1459 Wel 8:99a) may be another spelling device to capture the phoneme *G* that represents the lenition of *k*, if not just a mistake.

4. And in *¨nwol·m ye* (?1517–¹No 2:13b), miswritten ··· *·pye*. The opposite is found in *·em·susi·kwo* (1459 Wel 23:76b), a scribal mistake for *¨ep·susi·kwo*, and *emswu·m i* (1459 Kok 7:69b) for *¨ep·swu·m i*. Also *a·hwom* (1459 Wel 7:29b) miswritten for *a·hwop*, and *·michi·la* (1459 Kok 8:18b) miswritten for *·pi.ch i·la*. Other miswritten syllables I have noticed: *¨sano·m i* for *¨salo·m i* (1459 Wel 21:169b), *·mip-two.ng olan* for *·tip-two.ng olan* (1459 Wel 8:99a), *kis·pwu·p ul* for *kis·pwu·m ul* (1463 Pep 1:169b).

5. In 1463 Pep 2:18b the syllable *mwun* is printed with a mirrored *n* on the bottom, in 7:14b the initial *k* is mirror-imaged in *·kwot*, with the downstroke on the left rather than the right.

6. But we find a simple letter reversal in the onset of the syllable *·spe* miswritten for *·pse* in 1447 Sek 13:38a. An inverted mirror image of *la* appears 1489 Kup-kan 1:24b, line 2.

7. The "*t*-irregular stems" are treated by the Hamkyeng dialects as ···**lq-** (Ramsey 1978: 205–207), and that may account for this analysis by the Soviet Koreans.

8. The final zero of the Chinese readings is omitted in various examples from 1459 Wel 21, such as ˙*NGWUY*[#]-˙*HWO*[#] (164b) and ˙*SWO*[#]-˙*HHWAY*[#] (160–161)—cf. ˙*SWO*#-˙*HHWAY*# (162b, 163a). In some cases the failure of zero to appear may be due to broken type or blanking in the reproduction, for example, ˙*KWU*[*W*]- ˙*TTYWO*[#] (165a). The extant printing of Wel 21 is a century later (1559) than the composition of the text, and that perhaps explains the discrepancies.

REFERENCES

Choi, Hyon Bai [Choy Hyenpay]. 1954. Hankul uy thwucayng [The battle over Korean spelling].

Hill, J. A. 1974. Possible continuity theories of language. *Language* 50: 134–150.

King, J. R. P. 1988. The Korean dialect materials in Matveev's *1900 Reference Book to the city of Vladivostok*. *Language Research* 29: 281–329.

Kim, Minsu [Kim Minswu]. 1973. Kwuk.e cengchayk-lon. Seoul: Kolye tayhak.kyo chwulphan-pu.

Lee, Ki-Moon [ˈYi Kimun]. 1991. Kwuk.e ehwi-sa yenkwu. Seoul: Tonga chwulphan-sa.

Martin, S. E. 1954. Korean morphophonemics. Baltimore: Linguistic Society of America.

———. 1992. A reference grammar of Korean. Rutland and Tokyo: C. E. Tuttle Co.

Mattingly, I. G. 1972. Speech cues and sign stimuli. *American Scientist* 60: 134–150.

Ramsey, S. R. 1978. Accent and morphophology in Korean dialects. Seoul: Thap chwulphan-sa.

Texts

1008 *Guangyun*
1202 *Yunhui*
1446 Hwun = *Hwunmin cengum haylyey*
1447→1562 Sek 3 = *Sekpo sangcel*, 2nd edition, volume 3
1448 Tongkwuk = *Tongkwuk cengwun*
1449 Kok = *Wel.in chenkang ci kok*
1451 Hwun-en = *Hwunmin cengum enhay*
1459 Wel = *Wel.in sekpo*
1463 Pep = *Myopep ˈyenhwa-kyeng enhay*
1489 Kup-kan = *Kwukup kan.i-pang*

? 1517- 'No = [*Pen.yek*] '*Nokeltay*
1517 *Saseng thonghay*
1518 [*Pen.yek*] *Sohak*
1586 Sohak = *Sohak enhay*
1617 Sin-Sok = *Tongkwuk Sin-Sok Samkang hayngsil-to*

APPENDIX 1: A BRIEF DESCRIPTION OF THE KOREAN ALPHABET

According to *Hunmin chŏng'ŭm haerye* (Explanations and Examples of The Correct Sounds for the Instruction of the People, 1446), the lines of consonantal letters are said to reflect schematically the shapes of the organ of speech articulating the consonant in question, as illustrated below.[1]

THE LETTERFORMS OF HAN'GŬL CONSONANTS

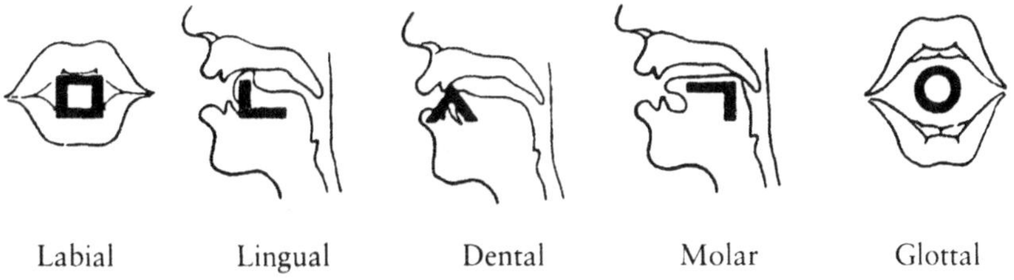

Labial Lingual Dental Molar Glottal

Labial (Bilabial)	ㅁ	ㅂ	ㅍ	ㅃ	
Lingual (Apical)	ㄴ	ㄷ	ㅌ	ㄸ	
Dental (Sibilant)	ㅅ	ㅈ	ㅊ	ㅆ	ㅉ
Molar (Dorsal/Velar)	ㆁ	ㄱ	ㅋ	ㄲ	
Glottal (Laryngeal)	ㅇ	ㆆ	ㅎ	ㆅ	

It is said that the vowel letters were formed from three symbols representing three basic elements in Chinese cosmology. The roundness of < · > stood for Heaven, the flatness of < — > for Earth, and the uprightness of < ㅣ > for Man. These schematic signs were combined to produce a variety of symbols, as shown below.[2]

THE LETTERFORMS OF HAN'GŬL VOWELS

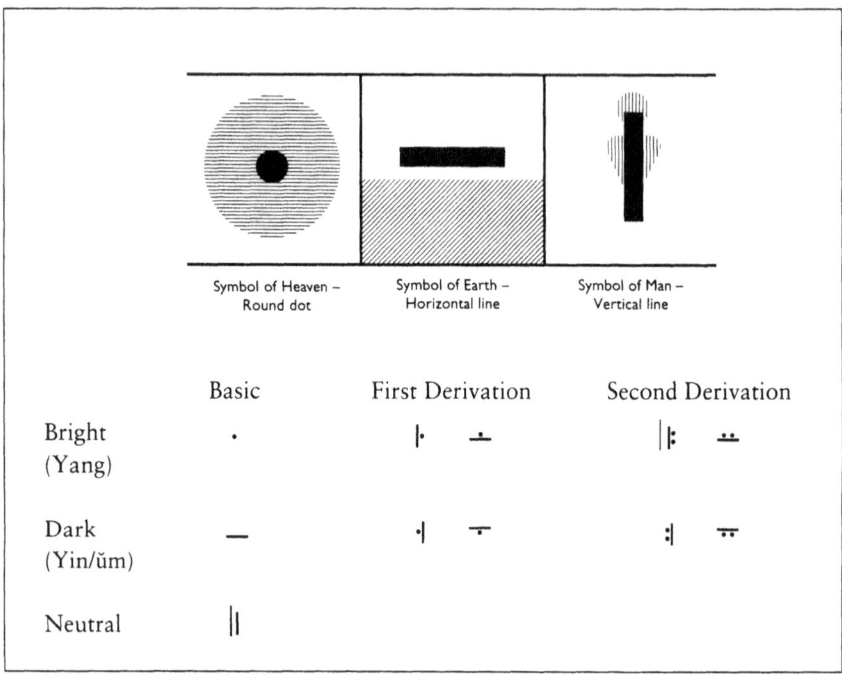

The consonantal and vowel symbols at the time of invention (1446) are shown in the following chart.

HUNMIN CHŎNG'ŬM LETTER SHAPES

Consonants

Some phonemic symbols made of complex shapes, and not on the original list, are listed in parentheses. Letters that are no longer in use are given in double parentheses.[3]

	Labial	Dental/Sibilant	Apical	Dorsal	Laryngeal
(Tense)	(ㅃ)/p'/	(ㅉ)/c'/ (ㅆ)/s'/	(ㄸ)/t'/	(ㄲ)/k'/	((ㆅ))/x'/
Aspirated	ㅍ/p^h/	ㅊ/c^h/	ㅌ/t^h/	ㅋ/k^h/	ㅎ/h/[4]
Obstruent	ㅂ/p/	ㅈ/c/ ㅅ/s/	ㄷ/t/	ㄱ/k/	((ㆆ))/ʔ/
Voiced	ㅁ/m/ ((ㅸ))/β/	((ㅿ))/z/	ㄴ/n/ ㄹ/l/	ㆁ/ŋ/ ㅇ/ɦ/	

Vowels

Vowel symbols are shown with zero initials. Again the double parentheses enclose the vowel letter that is no longer in use today.

Nonback	Back: Unrounded	Back	Back: Rounded
이/i/	으/ɨ/		우/u/
	어/ə/		오/o/
		((ᄋᆞ))/ʌ/	
	아/a/		

A *y*-onglide is expressed by an additional dot next to the dot attached to the main long stroke of the nucleus: for example, ㅑ [ya], ㅛ [yo], ㅕ [yə], ㅠ [yu]. A *w*-glide is expressed by a small ㅜ [u] or ㅗ [o] symbol attached to the left of the main vowel: for example, ㅘ [wa], ㅝ [wə], ㅙ [wai], and ㅞ [wəi]. An offglide is expressed by adding the [i] symbol to the right of the first vowel of the nucleus: ㅐ [ai], ㅔ [əi], ㅟ [ui], ㅚ [oi], and ㅢ [ɨi].

Not surprisingly, the Korean sound system has undergone a change during the five and a half centuries following the invention of the alphabet. Some sounds were lost, some were gained, and still some others have changed in their phonetic values, so that the current system is as follows.

HAN'GŬL SYMBOLS CURRENTLY IN USE

Consonants

Affricates are now palatal. Dentals and apico-alveolars are all coronal.

	Labial	Coronal	Palatal	Velar	Laryngeal
Tense obst.	ㅃ /p'/	ㄸ /t'/ ㅆ /s'/	ㅉ /c'/	ㄲ /k'/	
Asp. obst.	ㅍ /pʰ/	ㅌ /tʰ/	ㅊ /cʰ/	ㅋ /kʰ/	ㅎ /h/
Obstruent	ㅂ /p/	ㄷ /t/ ㅅ /s/	ㅈ /c/	ㄱ /k/	
Nasal	ㅁ /m/	ㄴ /n/		ㅇ /-ŋ/(/∅-/)	
Liquid		ㄹ /l/			

Vowels

Nonback		Back	
Unrounded	Rounded	Unrounded	Rounded
이 /i/ 에 /e/ 애 /ɛ/	위 /ü/ 외 /ö/	으 /ɨ/ 어 /ə/ 아 /a/	우 /u/ 오 /o/

The round dot has developed into a short line. A *y*-onglide is expressed by an additional short line. No offglide exists in present-day Korean except in the *ŭi* (/ɨi/) sequence, written as ㅢ. Four new front vowels, ㅔ /e/, ㅐ /ɛ/, ㅚ /ö/, and ㅟ /ü/, were acquired through a monophthongization process, that is, /əi/ → /e/, /ai/ → /ɛ/, /oi/ → /ö/, and /ui/ → /ü/.[5]

Han'gŭl is written in syllable blocks of approximately equal sizes, and depending on the number of alphabetic letters contained in each syllable, the size and shape of each symbol varies: the more letters within the syllable, the smaller the letter, and so forth. To form a syllable, the principle of ordering described below is used.

KOREAN SYLLABLE SHAPES

The Korean syllable consists of Consonant + Vowel Nucleus + Consonant(s). However these letters are not written on one line but in clusters of letters, where consonants envelop a vowel nucleus. The stroke order is like the one used in writing Chinese characters, from top to bottom, and from left to right. In order to achieve the optimal aesthetic effect, the size and shape of each letter are slightly modified depending on their relation with other components within a syllable, and certain spelling conventions are observed. Some examples follow.

Consonant Position

Final consonants are always written below the vowel nucleus, but initial consonants have a different relative position vis-à-vis the vowel nucleus.

1. If the vowel has a long vertical stroke (ㅏ, ㅑ, ㅓ, ㅕ, ㅐ, ㅒ, ㅔ, ㅖ, or ㅣ), write it to the right of the initial consonant. For example, the word for "Korea" (and "great"), /han/, is written as follows:

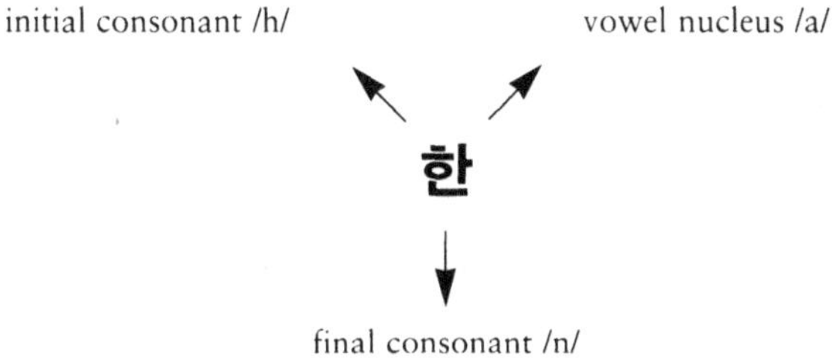

2. If the vowel has a long horizontal stroke (ㅗ, ㅛ, ㅜ, ㅠ, or ㅡ), write it below the initial consonant. For example, the word for "writing," /kɨl/ (<kŭl>), is written as follows:

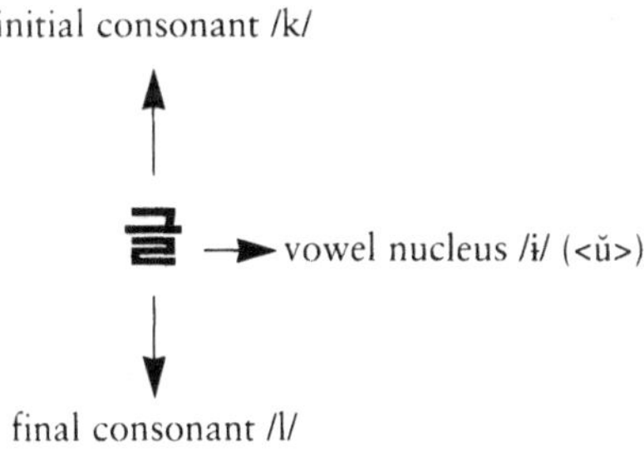

3. If a complex vowel nucleus begins with a vowel with a long horizontal stroke, that is, ㅗ, ㅜ, ㅡ, followed by a long verticle stroke, then place the initial consonant above the horizontal stroke. For example, the word for "ear," /kwi/ or /kü/, is written as follows:

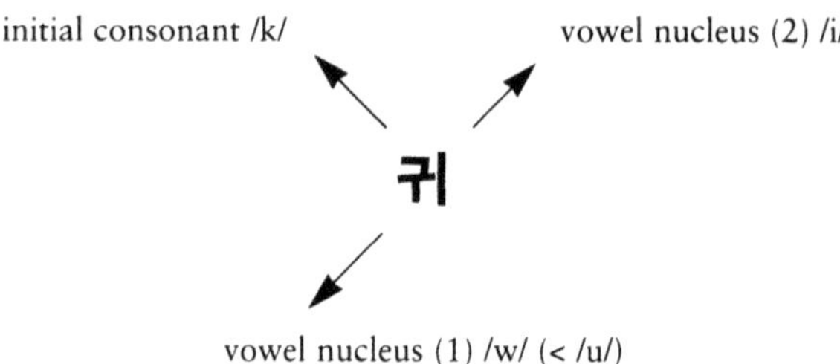

4. When there are two consonants at the end of a syllable, write them side by side, the first consonant on the left and the second one on the right. The word for "chicken," /talk/, is written as follows:

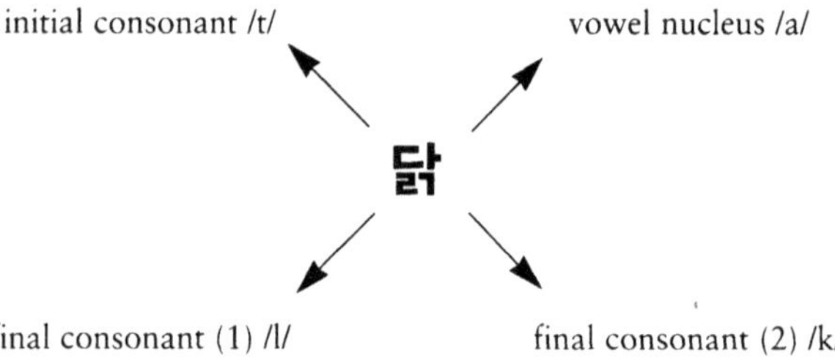

Filler Letter <Zero>

1. When a syllable lacks an initial consonant, a "zero" (o) is written in the place for the initial consonant, mainly for aesthetic reasons—to form a balanced shape for the syllable. For example, the word for "jade," /ok/, is written as follows:

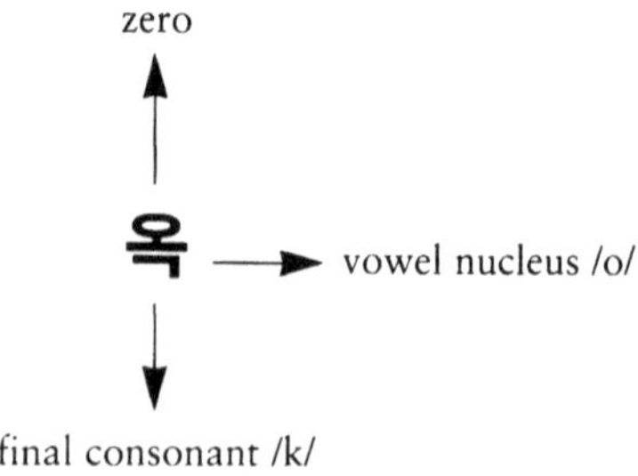

2. In present-day Korean, the zero symbol is like the one used to represent the [ŋ] sound, but since there is no syllable beginning with an [ŋ] sound, there is no confusion. The symbol (ㅇ) in syllable-initial position is a null element, but it represents the [ŋ] sound in syllable-final position. The word for "lamb," /yaŋ/ (<yang>), is written as follows:

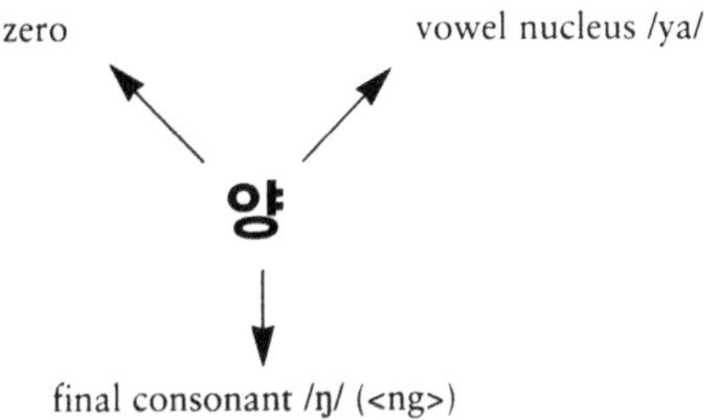

SPACING

Syllables within the same phonological phrase are written without any space between them. A phonological phrase roughly consists of a major class morpheme, such as a noun or verb stem, followed by any number of suffixes.

그의	입에서	말이	술술	쏟아져	나왔다.
he-Gen.	mouth-from	word-Subj.	flowingly	pouring	come out-Pst.-Dec.

'Words poured out of his mouth easily / He had no trouble speaking.'

MIXED SCRIPT

Chinese and other scripts can be mixed with Korean writing. The loanwords usually occupy a noun position, regardless of their original grammatical category.

『國語研究 가	어디까지	왔나? —
Korean-language-research-Subj	where-up-to	come-Pst.-Q.:

主題別 로	본	國語學 의	研究史』
subject-by	seen	Korean linguistics-Gen.	research history

'How Far Has Korean Language Research Come Around?: A History of Korean Linguistic Research by Subject' (a book title)

우리는	letter 와	graph 를	구별하지	않고
us-Top.	letter-and	graph-Obj.	distinguish	not-and

쓰는	것이다.
use-Mod.	Comp.-Cop.-Dec.

'It's just that we do not distinguish between the words "letter" and "graph."'

분위기가	참	romantic 하군요!
atomosphere-Subj.	really	being romantic-Denom.-Interj.-Dec.

'The atmosphere is really romantic [to my surprise]!'

우리	APT에는	PC 있는
us	apartment building-in-Top.	PC-Exist.-Mod.
집이	많습니다.	
home-Subj.	abound-Hon.-Dec.	

'There are many homes with personal computers in our apartment building.'

PUNCTUATION MARKS

At the time of invention, there were suprasegmental signs and pause markers (see Kim-Renaud's chapter for details). Tone/pitch-accent marks have fallen into disuse, as they have become unnecessary through language change. Modern Korean writing uses both Korean-specific (e.g., quotation marks 『 and 』) and Western-style punctuation marks with minor variations (e.g., the long dash rather than a colon for a subtitle, as shown in the examples above).

NOTES

1. Adapted with modification from Kim Jin-p'yŏng 1983: 82–83.

2. Chin W. Kim and others believe that Sejong attached this interpretation primarily in order to appease those who opposed the new script, by arguing that the script shapes are after all based on Chinese philosophy. The figure is from Kim Jin-p'yŏng 1983: 84. The vowel ㅣ is neutral in noninitial syllables but dark in a word-initial syllable (cf. Kim-Renaud 1976).

3. Doubled letters and the letter ㅸ [β] were not included in the basic list of *Hunmin chŏng'ŭm* but occupy a solid place in *Yongcharye* (Examples of the Use of the Letters) of *Haerye* as possible initials. The symbol ㆁ later became a circle and indistinguishable from the zero initial.

4. The letter ㆆ might have had a phonetic value somewhere between [h] and [xh] but phonologically can be analyzed as an /h/.

5. The new front vowels are very unstable and are undergoing further changes. For example, the two nonhigh, unrounded vowels are merging as /e/ for younger speakers, and rounded front vowels are being split into two segments, the first one turning into a [w]-onset glide, that is, /ü/ as /wi/ and /ö/ as /we/. Not only has han'gŭl been able to accommodate these changes, but the graphic shapes have been able to capture certain historical changes like monophthongization.

REFERENCES

Kim, Jin-p'yŏng. 1983. The letterforms of Han'gŭl: Its origin and process of transformation. In *The Korean language*, ed. The Korean National Commission for UNESCO, Seoul: The Si-sa-yong-o-sa and Arch Cape, 80–102.

Kim-Renaud, Young-Key. 1976. Semantic features in phonology: Evidence from vowel harmony in Korean. In *Papers from the twelfth regional meeting of the Chicago Linguistic Society*, ed. Salikoko A. Mufwene, Carol A. Walker, and Sanford B. Steever, Chicago: The Chicago Linguistic Society. 397–412.

APPENDIX 2: PHOTOGRAPHS OF THE *HUNMIN CHŎNG'ŬM* AND *HUNMIN CHŎNG'ŬM HAERYE*

Sample pages of *Hunmin chŏng'ŭm* 訓民正音 (Correct Sounds for the Instruction of the People) and *Hunmin chŏng'ŭm haerye* 訓民正音解例 (Explanations and Examples of the Correct Sounds for the Instruction of the People), 1446, Woodblock printing, 16.6 cm x 23.3 cm, Kansong Art Museum collection. Photographed on 25 June 1996 by Young-Key Kim-Renaud. (Courtesy of Kansong Art Museum, Seoul, Korea)

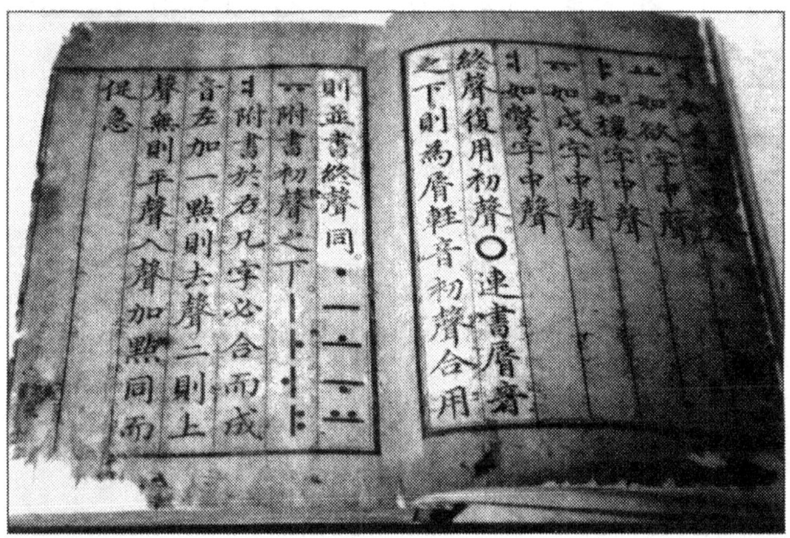
ㅑ如穰字中聲
ㅠ如戌字中聲
ㅕ如彆字中聲
終聲復用初聲ㅇ連書脣音
之下則爲脣輕音初聲合用
則並書終聲同・ㅡㅗㅜㅛㅠ
附書初聲之下ㅣㅏㅓㅑㅕ
附書於右凡字必合而成
音左加一點則去聲二則上
聲無則平聲入聲加點同而
促急

HUNMIN CHŎNG'ŬM

[The Correct Sounds for the Instruction of the People] 1446
Kansong Museum, last two pages of the main text

Translation: "For the [syllable] final sounds [consonants], one uses the letters for the initial sounds [consonants] again. The symbol ㅇ written immediately below a labial sounds makes a light labial sound. If initial sounds are used in combination, they are written side by side. It is the same for the final sounds."

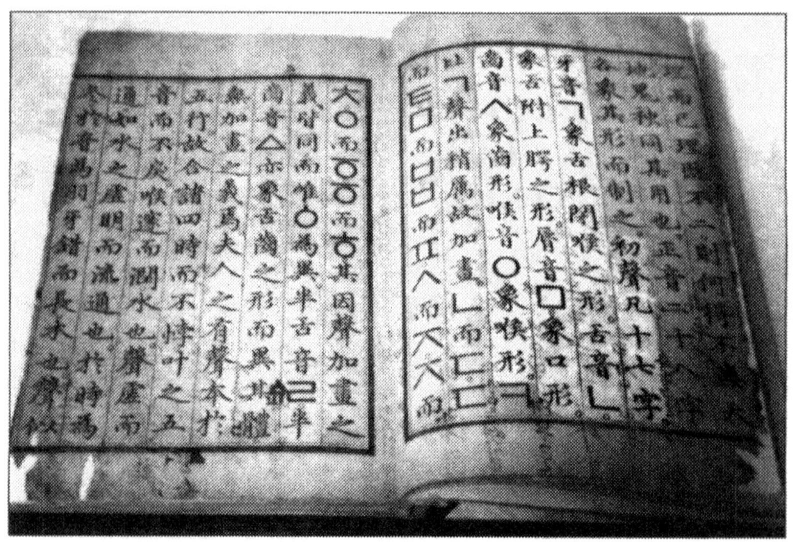

HUNMIN CHŎNG'ŬM HAERYE, CHEJAHAE

[Explanations and Examples of the Correct Sounds for the Instruction of the People, Explanation of the Design of the Letters] 1446

Translation: "There are seventeen letters for the initial sounds. The molar sound ㄱ [k] depicts the outline of the root of the tongue blocking the throat. The lingual sound ㄴ [n] depicts the outline of the tongue touching the upper palate. The labial sound ㅁ [m] depicts the outline of the mouth. The dental sound ㅅ [s] depicts the outline of the incisor. The laryngeal sound ㅇ [ɦ] depicts the outline of the throat."

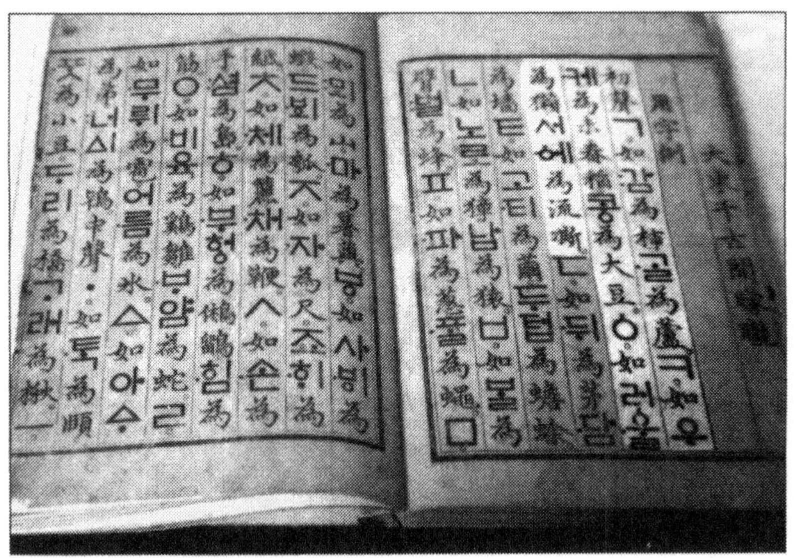

HUNMIN CHŎNG'ŬM HAERYE, YONG CHA RYE

[Explanations and Examples of the Correct Sounds for the Instruction of the People, Examples of the Use of the Letters] 1446

Translation: "Initial sounds ㄱ [k] as in: :감 [:kam] 'persimmon' and ·ᄀᆞᆯ [·kʌl] 'reed' ㅋ [kʰ] as in 우·케 [ɦu·kʰei] 'unhusked rice' and 콩 [kʰoŋ] 'soybean.' ᅌ [ŋ] as in 러·ᅌᅮᆯ [leŋ·ul] 'otter' and 서·ᅌᅦ [se·ŋei] 'floating ice'."

APPENDIX 3: PHOTOGRAPHS OF A PAGE OF A NORTH KOREAN NEWSPAPER AND A PAGE OF A SOUTH KOREAN NEWSPAPER

전세계로동자들은 단결하라!

위대한 수령 김일성동지의 주체사상으로 튼튼히 무장하자!

사상에서 주체, 정치에서 자주, 경제에서 자립, 국방에서 자위의 원칙을 계속확고히 구현해나가자!

조선로동당 중앙위원회기관지

위대한 수령 김일성동지께서

벤르빈쎈트 그레너딘즈 수상에게 축전을 보내시였다

친애하는 지도자 김정일동지께

여러 나라에서 선물을 드리였다

사회주의위업을 끝바른 승리의 길로 전진시켜나갈수 있게 하는 불멸의 기치

《민족의 영웅 김정일장군님을 모시여 마음이 든든하다》

남녘인민들이 끝없는 흠모

네팔전국주체사상토론회

까뜨만두에서 진행

A newspaper published in North Korea. It is written horizontally without Chinese characters. Its title is 로동신문 (*Rodong Newspaper*).

위성중계 서울→워싱톤 同時 인쇄 DAILY The Korea Times PART 2

한국일보

政改法案 통과
「정치改革」시동

국회 本會議, 관련3개법안 모두 처리

議員선거비용 5千7百

사무장등 징역刑땐 當選

刑받은 선거사범 10년公職

4개선거 내년 5월중 同時선거

美、슈퍼301

보류土超稅 올해 課稅

洪재무 회견 10大재벌 不動産규제도 계속

誠金유용 문책

京畿지사 면직

安賢帝「삼위일체長壽法」연

除毒·자연식·운동으로
어릴때부터 病苦 극복
이젠 百50세天壽 도전

A newspaper published in South Korea. It is written vertically and contains Chinese characters. Its title is 한국일보 (*Korea Daily*).

APPENDIX 4: COMPARISON OF ROMANIZATION SYSTEMS

There are a number of romanization systems for Korean. The two most important ones are McCune-Reischauer (see George McCune's presentation in *Transactions of the Korea Branch of the Royal Asiatic Society*, vol. 29, 1939: 1–55 and also fold-out tables) and Yale (see "Principles of the Yale Romanization" in *A Korean-English Dictionary* by Samuel E. Martin, Yang Ha Lee, and Sung-Un Chang, Yale University Press, New Haven, 1967: v).

The goals and principles of the two systems are different. The Yale system, which is preferred by linguists, is designed to reflect a one-to-one correspondence with the han'gŭl spellings. However, there are some exceptions. For example, the vowel *wu* is abbreviated to *u* after labials and after the semivowel *y* in Modern Korean, because the two sounds do not contrast in those environments. (In Middle Korean, the two are distinctive before labials but normally not after *y*.) Yale romanization also represents certain phonemic distinctions not reflected in the (South Korean) han'gŭl spellings: for example, a *q* is inserted to show that a following consonant is distinctively "reinforced." It also follows the han'gŭl spelling in showing the morphological divisions. Another advantage is that it requires no special diacritics, employing only the symbols found on the keyboard of an ordinary typewriter.

The McCune-Reischauer system seems to appeal intuitively to most other Korea scholars and has become the *de facto* official mode of romanization, adopted by libraries (including the Library of Congress), journals, and other academic and governmental publications. This popularity is due in part to the fact that the McCune-Reischauer system intends to represent the han'gŭl forms in roman letters in such a way that a reader, especially in the English-speaking world, who does not know Korean may approximate a pronunciation that would be recognizable to a Korean. In the process, even the nondistinctive allophonic variations are sometimes specified. For example, lax stops, normally voiceless, are represented by voiced stops in voiced environment and by nasals before a nasal. The coronal obstruents, *t, t', ch, ch'*, and *s*, which are unreleased and neutralized as a *t* sound in syllable-final position, are represented by a <t>, which may undergo further changes such as nasalization.

The following is a table with the han'gŭl letter forms, their names, and their basic equivalents in each of the two systems of romanization. Common variant forms are included in parentheses. However, for obvious reasons, it is not easy to compare these two systems in a simple table, and the readers are referred to the above two citations for details.

Letter-by-Letter Comparison of Romanization Systems

The Consonant Letters

	NAMES OF LETTERS	MCCUNE-REISCHAUER	YALE
ㄱ	kiyŏk/kiyek	k (g, ng)	k
ㄴ	niŭn/niun	n (l)	n
ㄷ	tigŭt/tikut	t (d, n)	t
ㄹ	riŭl/liul	l (r, n)	l
ㅁ	miŭm/mium	m	m
ㅂ	piŭp/piup	p (b)	p
ㅅ	siot/sios	s (t)	s
ㅇ	iŭng/iung	ng/null	ng/null
ㅈ	chiŭt/ciuc	ch (j, t, n)	c
ㅊ	chiŭt/chiuch	ch' (t, n)	ch
ㅋ	k'iŭk/khiukh	k' (k, ng)	kh
ㅌ	t'iŭt/thiuth	t' (t, n)	th
ㅍ	p'iŭp/phiuph	p' (p, m)	ph
ㅎ	hiŭt/hiuh	h (t, n)	h

The Complex Consonant Letters

NAMES OF LETTERS		MCCUNE-REISCHAUER	YALE
[ssang 'double, twin']			
ㄲ	ssang-giyŏk/ssang-kiyek	kk (k, ng)	kk
ㄸ	ssang-digŭt/ssang-tikut	tt	tt
ㅃ	ssang-biŭp/ssang-piup	pp	pp
ㅆ	ssang-siot/ssang-sios	ss (t, n)	ss
ㅉ	ssang-jiŭt/ssang-ciuc	tch	cc

The Vowel Letters [Names of vowel letters are the same as the sound of the letters]

The Basic Vowel Letters

		MCCUNE-REISCHAUER	YALE
ㅏ		a	a
ㅑ		ya	ya
ㅓ		ŏ	e
ㅕ		yŏ	ye
ㅗ		o	o [wo in Middle Korean]
ㅛ		yo	yo
ㅜ		u	wu
ㅠ		yu	yu
ㅡ		ŭ	u
ㅣ		i	i
.	arae a/alay a	ă	o

The Complex Vowel Letters

	McCune-Reischauer	Yale
ㅐ	ae	ay
ㅒ	yae	yay
ㅔ	e	ey
ㅖ	ye	yey
ㅘ	wa	wa
ㅙ	wae	way
ㅚ	oe	woy
ㅝ	wŏ	we
ㅞ	we	wey
ㅟ	wi	wi
ㅢ	ŭi	uy

CONTRIBUTORS

Pyong-Hi Ahn is professor of Korean language at Seoul National University and director general of the National Academy of Korean Language. Recent publications are *Kugŏsa yŏn'gu* (A study on the history of the Korean language) and *Kugŏsa charyo yŏn'gu* (A study on the historical materials of the Korean language).

Sinhang Kang, who holds a Ph.D. in Korean linguistics from Seoul National University, has been teaching at Sŏnggyun'gwan (Seng Kyun Kwan) University since 1964. His publications include *Hunmin chŏng'ŭm yŏn'gu* (A study of *Hunmin chŏng'ŭm*) and *Kugŏhaksa* (History of Korean linguistics).

Chin W. Kim is professor of linguistics and East Asian languages at the University of Illinois at Urbana-Champaign. He was chair of the Linguistics Department at Illinois and president of the International Circle of Korean Linguistics. He works in the field of phonetics, phonology, and Korean linguistics. Among his publications are *Papers in Korean Linguistics*, *Language* (in Korean), and *Sojourns in Language.*

Young-Key Kim-Renaud is professor of Korean language and culture and international affairs at George Washington University. Formerly assistant program director for linguistics at the U.S. National Science Foundation and president of the International Circle of Korean Linguistics, she has authored or edited several volumes, including *Studies in Korean Linguistics* and *Theoretical Issues in Korean Linguistics.*

Ross King received his Ph.D. in linguistics from Harvard University in 1991. Formerly chair of the Centre for Korean Studies at the School of Oriental and African Studies, University of London, he is currently assistant professor of Korean at the University of British Columbia. He is author of the two-volume work *Russian Sources on Korean Dialects.*

Gari Ledyard is King Sejong Professor of Korean Studies and director of the Center for Korean Research at Columbia University. Author of *The*

Korean Language Reform of 1446, he recently contributed the essay "Cartography in Korea" in David Woodward and J. B. Harley, eds., *History of Cartography*.

Ki-Moon Lee is professor of Korean at Seoul National University. His publications include *Kugŏsa kaesŏl* (Introduction to the history of Korean language) and *Kugŏ ŭmunsa yŏn'gu* (A study of Korean historical phonology).

Sang-Oak Lee received his doctorate in Linguistics from the University of Illinois at Urbana. Professor of Korean at Seoul National University, he is currently at the University of Sydney, where he is promoting Korean studies. He is coauthor of *Korean Phonology* and *Modern Morphology*.

Samuel E. Martin is professor emeritus at Yale University. In 1967 he published, with Yang Ha Lee and Sung-Un Chang, *A Korean-English Dictionary*. He is also the author of *A Reference Grammar of Japanese* and, most recently, *A Reference Grammar of Korean*.

S. Robert Ramsey holds a Ph.D. from Yale University. He is currently professor of East Asian linguistics at the University of Maryland and author of *Accent and Morphology in Korean Dialects*, *The Languages of China*, and "Proto-Korean and the origin of Korean accent" in Shapiro and Boltz, eds., *Asian Historical Linguistics*.

Ho-min Sohn, professor of Korean and chair of the Department of East Asian Languages and Literatures at the University of Hawai'i, is president of the American Association of Teachers of Korean. Among his publications are *Linguistic Expeditions* and *Korean*.

INDEX

Alternate forms, including those in Yale or McCune-Reischauer romanization, are enclosed in square brackets. Translations are in parentheses.

www.ingramcontent.com/pod-product-compliance
Lightning Source LLC
Chambersburg PA
CBHW061427300426
44114CB00014B/1574